Natural Histories of Discourse

Edited by *Michael Silverstein and Greg Urban*

THE UNIVERSITY OF CHICAGO PRESS
Chicago and London

MICHAEL SILVERSTEIN is the Samuel N. Harper Professor of Anthropology, Linguistics, and Psychology at the University of Chicago.
GREG URBAN is professor of anthropology at the University of Pennsylvania.

The University of Chicago Press, Chicago 60637
The University of Chicago Press, Ltd., London

05 04 03 02 01 00 99 98 97 96   5 4 3 2 1

ISBN 0-226-75769-2 (cloth)
ISBN 0-226-75770-6 (paper)

Chapter 4 was previously published in the *Yale Journal of Criticism,* 5, no. 3 (1992): 61–79 in substantially the same form. Permission to reprint is gratefully acknowledged. Chapter 9 was previously published in Seth Chaiklin and Jean Lave, eds., *Understanding Practice* (New York: Cambridge University Press, 1993), pp. 241–68. Permission to reprint is gratefully acknowledged.

Library of Congress Cataloging-in-Publication Data

Natural histories of discourse / edited by Michael Silverstein and
    Greg Urban.
        p.   cm.
    Includes bibliographical references and index.
    Contents: The natural history of discourse / Michael Silverstein
and Greg Urban / Entextualization, replication, and power / Greg
Urban—Text from talk in Tzotzil / John Haviland — The secret
life of texts / Michael Silverstein — "Self"-centering narratives /
Vincent Crapanzano—Shadow conversations / Judith T. Irvine —
Exorcisim and the description of participant roles / William F. Hanks
— Socialization to texts / James Collins — Recontextualization as
socialization : text and pragmatics in the law school classroom /
Elizabeth Mertz — The construction of an LD student / Hugh Mehan —
National spirit or the breath of nature? : the expropriation of folk
positivism in the discourse of Greek nationalism / Michael Herzfeld
— Transformations of the world in the production of Mexican
festival drama / Richard Bauman — Codafication [sic] / Greg Urban
and Michael Silverstein.
    1. Language and culture.   2. Discourse analysis.   3. Meta language.
I. Silverstein, Michael, 1945–   . II. Urban, Greg, 1949–   .
P35.N38   1996
401'.41—dc20   95-49852
                                                                              CIP

For Barney and Ben

Contents

Acknowledgments

The "text" before you is a genuine collective product. It is the result of pro-longed deliberations among its contributors, in conjunction with Don Brenneis, Ben Lee, John Lucy, Richard Parmentier, and other actual and imagined interlocutors. Richard Parmentier, in particular, undertook the organization of a session presenting our collective work, "De-Centering Discourse," at the eighty-sixth annual meeting of the American Anthropological Association in Chicago in November 1987.

How rare are those opportunities in academia for sustained meeting and intensive collaboration of scholars from institutions widely scattered across the country! Yet such is precisely what produced this "text." We owe this precious opportunity to the Center for Psychosocial Studies (now Center for Transcul-tural Studies) in Chicago, and especially to Benjamin Lee (Director of Re-search) and Bernard Weissbourd (Chairman of the Board). In the spirit of the West African *xaxaar*, in which a sponsor commissions a poem that is actually composed and performed by others, they sponsored our work. What you have before you is the result.

The Center's Administrator, Elvia Alvarez, insured the flawlessness of multiplex arrangements over several years to bring the group together at many, many meetings, and helped in a great many other ways. Editorial assistance, in the final phases, was furnished by Kristin Smith, Matthew Tomlinson, and Patricia Kent. Webb Keane, having read the manuscript, graciously pointed us to the perfect jacket illustrations. We take this opportunity to thank all of you, and, indeed, all of the "I's" whose historical unfolding have made possible our collective editorial "we."

The Natural History of Discourse

Michael Silverstein and Greg Urban

For many social scientists and humanists, the model, from Ricoeur (1981 [1971]), of culture as text that can be read—or of *a* culture as a Geertzian (1973:452) ensemble of texts—has held considerable allure. The text idea allows the analyst of culture to extract a portion of ongoing social action—discourse or some nondiscursive but nevertheless semiotic action—from its infinitely rich, exquisitely detailed context, and draw a boundary around it, inquiring into its structure and meaning. This textual fragment of culture can then be re-embedded by asking how it relates to its "context," where context is understood as nonreadable surround or background (or if the context is regarded as readable, by asking how the text relates to its "co-text").

The problem with this procedure is that it is not only the cultural analysts who find utility in this kind of idea. The processes that result in phenomenal textuality—what we have come to call the simultaneous processes of "entextualization" and "co(n)textualization"—are the central and ongoing practices within cultural orders. To equate culture with its resultant texts is to miss the fact that texts (as we see them, the precipitates of continuous cultural processes) represent one, "thing-y" phase in a broader conceptualization of cultural process. Moreover, to turn something into a text is to seem to give it a decontextualized structure and meaning, that is, a form and meaning that are imaginable apart from the spatiotemporal and other frames in which they can be said to occur. Such an autonomously meaningful object, indeed, becomes a trope for culture, understood in the sense of an ensemble of shared symbols and meanings, so that we should not be surprised at its appeal for students of culture. For if a text has a despatialized and detemporalized meaning—in short, a deprocessualized one—then that meaning can be clearly transmitted across social boundaries such as generations, without regard for the kinds of recontextualizations it might undergo. Texts can thus be seen as building blocks or atoms of shared culture. We should observe here how congenial this simplistic construction is to notions that confuse an anthropological concept of culture with those folk-derived concepts in our various learned traditions of shared or common possession of texts, whether as quasi-physical or quasi-mental objects, as the attribute of "being cultured" or "having culture." Such congeniality should, perhaps, make these concepts all the more epistemologically suspect for us, of course, in a comparative and cross-cultural enterprise.[1]

But this utility of texts is precisely what "the natives" (including us) see as well. They engage in processes of entextualization to create a seemingly shareable, transmittable culture. They can, for example, take some fragment of discourse and quote it anew, making it seem to carry a meaning independent of its situation within two now distinct co(n)texts. Or they can transcribe a fragment of oral discourse, converting it into a seemingly durable and decontextualizable form that suggests to interpreters a decontextualizable meaning as well. Or they can take such a durable text and reanimate it through a performance that, being *a* (mere) performance of *the* text, suggests various dimensions of contextualized "interpretive meaning" added on to those seemingly inherent in the text.

From this point of view, then, text is a metadiscursive notion, useful to participants in a culture as a way of creating an image of a durable, shared culture immanent in or even undifferentiated from its ensemble of realized or even potential texts. It is a metadiscursive construct—"this stretch of discourse is a text whose meaning is . . ."—that grows out of and refers to actual cultural practices, which themselves are presumably to be studied ethnographically, in addition to constituting the essence of ethnographic method itself. The present volume is a set of ethnographic explorations; however, its brand of ethnography focuses squarely upon entextualization practices rather than or in addition to texts.

We have chosen the title *Natural Histories of Discourse* to focus attention on contextually contingent semiotic processes involved in achieving text—and culture. These are recoverable in some measure only by analyti-

1. We might, in fact, speculate on this trajectory of conflation, licensed apparently by Ricoeur (1981 [1971]), of "text" with "text-artifact," the latter a more or less permanent physical object like an "inscription." Such a text-artifact stimulates an entextualization in an appropriate context; it is the mediating instrumentality of a communicative process for its perceiver, for example, a reader of an alphanumeric printed page such as the one before you. To confuse the mediating artifact and its mode of production ("inscription") for a text and the sociosemiotic processes that produce it perpetuates a particular fetishized substitution. This is perhaps not unexpected in the particular cultural condition in which "anthropology" and "cultural studies" are labels for disciplinary forms of communication. Nevertheless, it is not ultimately productive as an approach to textuality in culture.

cally engaging with textual sedimentations. Each chapter in our collective natural history thus focuses on certain analytic moments in the entextualizing/co(n)textualizing process; we arrange them in an overall (entextualizable!) attempt to highlight these moments in an orderly way. In some chapters, we focus upon the iterations of textuality, that is, upon life cycles of discourse, as in Irvine's work on a poetic genre found among Wolof speakers of Senegal: here we see performances of texts that have been commissioned, designed, produced, and reproduced in an elaborate temporalized process. We see this also in the study of textual reanimation by Richard Bauman, dealing with Mexican nativity plays.

WHAT'S IN A TEXT?

The opening papers by John Haviland and Greg Urban attempt to explore what a text is by focusing on the transcription of oral discourse, that is, on the production of a visual-channel text-artifact with a certain concreteness and manipulability. (Perhaps these text-artifactual properties are suggestive—and surely have been suggestive—of museum specimens that can be transported back from the field and evaluated for their authenticity and cultural-aesthetic authoritativeness. Such suggestiveness, in any event, in promoting the confusion of the text-artifact with the text, literalizes a metaphor of our own ethnophilological tradition that is dangerous when carried over into other traditions.) In both cases, we are dealing with the processes whereby actual written texts are produced—texts that the ethnographer wants to study as the basic building blocks of culture, the written text-artifact potentially mapping one-to-one onto the cultural text out there. But in both cases we are dealing not with how anthropologists write down what they hear, or not only with that problem, but also with how natives, trained in the practice of writing or, in one case, orally reproducing and then translating, render spoken discourse that has been lifted from one co(n)text via the then extrinsic technology of tape-recording.

In such cases, it is possible for the anthropologist to compare the transcribed (or repeated) version with the original oral communicative form. We can therefore have a native transcription and an observer transcription and compare the two artifacts in various respects, for example, for the denotational form—the account of "what was said"—apparent in the artifacts. Do we make the assumption that the observer transcription accurately represents the oral form whereas the native transcription distorts it? We are arguing that, in these cases, anthropologists have the benefit of comparison in that particular species of triangulation that is the trademark of the interpretative social sciences. Such triangulation has long been their chief tool. Studying the processes of entextualization from as many different angles as possible produces the beginnings of an understanding of culture. Hence, the *differences* between the text-artifacts allow us greater insight into the entextualization processes, which are, after all, the data of interest in the study of culture.

Now text is one kind of metadiscursive interpretation of a phase of discourse, one outcome of a process in which discourse metamorphoses and precipitates as form. In this limiting case, text is seen through text-artifact and comes to be opposed to discourse, as decontextualized is opposed to contextualized. Haviland's work plays up this opposition especially, since it focuses on how the originally tape-recorded dialogical discursive interaction is refashioned into a textual account from what Bakhtin would call a monological, or singly voiced, perspective, all the while preserving the fact of multiple speaking turns and parts. There seems to be an archetype of the text that involves a single narrative voice from which have been expunged conflicts and inconsistencies of the sort that Bakhtin located in heteroglossic, multivoiced narrative records of discourse.

But the context of the entextualization affects one's orientation to the source discourse and also the shape of the text produced. Urban's chapter suggests, in particular, that the metadiscursive understanding of the discourse process of entextualization involves assessments of participants' power and authority, such that entextualization both reflects and constitutes asymmetrical social relations, a theme that recurs in subsequent chapters. Different interpreters, understanding themselves to be—or potentially to be—in different relations to the original source discourse, produce different texts. In effect, the new text has been reconfigured to reflect the new co(n)text.

SHOULD AULD CO(N)TEXTS BE FORGOT?

The image of texts, and also of culture, deriving from this latter insight is one of a labile and mercurial insubstantiality, in which the text is figured by its always new and present co(n)text. It seems to lose touch with its past, the past, indeed, becoming a projection from the present. But is text entirely an illusion, like a three-dimensional projection from a two-dimensional image? Does textuality completely efface the traces of its antecedent co(n)texts of figuration?

This is the question posed by Michael Silverstein and by Vincent Crapanzano, both of whom begin with written text-artifacts. They try to recover the co(n)texts from which the text-artifacts were produced in transduction-inscription. To be sure, the decontextualized text, understood as a meaningful building block of culture, may have a narrative time line when evaluated purely for its literal denotational content, that is, when it is viewed simply as cohering denotational text. But does such a denotational text preserve in any sense the durational contingency, the interactional "real time," of its originary entextualization? Does it preserve, for example, the temporality of emergence of intersubjective entextualization—moments of presupposed mutual (mis)understanding of what was happening—during the event of inscribing its artifact?

The text artifact is the physical medium that seems, on the face of it, to carry an organization of information, sometimes narrative information, that we decontextualize as the denotational text we are reading. The text-artifact does indeed have a physical-temporal structure, precisely because it was originally laid down, or sedimented, in the course of a social process, unfolding in real time; on reading, it is perceived and understood in real time. We seek the durational event of the laying-down process, insofar as traces of the original co(n)text in which a discourse fragment was configured are available to us. So what we are looking for is not the denotational text directly or simply, but rather indications of more originary interactional text(s) of inscription. We seek the residue of past social interaction carried along with the sign vehicle encoding the semantic, or denotational, meaning in denotational text. (Note here our seemingly deconstructive turn, with a rather more precise differentiation of semiotic phenomena than is generally invoked, as is required by this type of recuperative reading of text-artifact.)

Silverstein looks for such interactional residue in his study of Kiksht (Wasco-Wishram Chinookan) texts originally transcribed by Edward Sapir in 1905. In his example, the traces of an emergently entextualized social interaction between a Wishram man (in English, named Peter McGuff) and a then young Edward Sapir are inscribed in such phenomena as the architecture of shifts in tense and aspect that one sequentially encounters as one moves through the text-artifact as Sapir has laid it down. But Sapir's entextualization is only one that has left traces in its artifactualized notebook form and thence its published version. McGuff seems also to have come to at least one level of entextualization of a distinctively Wasco-Wishram kind, as a contrasting organization of clues in the text artifact seems to reveal. With comparative perspective on interactional genres in this cultural tradition, these clues allow us to recapture or recreate something of the original social interaction in which Sapir's—and McGuff's very different—interactional entextualizations must have taken place.

Vincent Crapanzano takes up the nineteenth-century memoirs of someone ([Adelaide] Herculine Barbin, b. 1838–d.1868) who underwent a change in sexual identity. In his example, we have at issue not only the text-artifact from which something of the context of entextualization can be recovered, but parallel and coeval text-artifacts concerning the same events or facts that can be read with it as a kind of composite co-text or "intertext." In particular, we have not only Herculine Barbin's own memoirs but other medical and legal texts assembled by Auguste Tardieu in 1872. Among those is an e/amended birth certificate, which includes the stipulation "that the Christian name Abel be substituted for those of Adelaide Herculine." In Crapanzano's example, we are not only recovering something about the historical figure of Herculine Barbin through the traces left in a text s/he produced; we are also learning through a comparison with the composite co-text how sexual identity was produced and precipitated out of discursive practices in the mid-nineteenth century.

WHERE DOES I COME FROM?

The idea that social identities may be durable projections from texts read in terms of their entextualization processes raises further questions about the idea we started from of culture as text inserted into a social context. For that latter view, which all of the papers in the present volume criticize, presupposes a differentiated social world, existing prior to the entextualization processes. Our investigations into the natural histories of particular discourses, however, suggest that the distinction between the social and the cultural cannot be so easily made, and that social categories, if readable from entextualization processes, are just as much products of them.

The problem is addressed explicitly in the papers by Judith Irvine and William Hanks. Irvine, in particular, focuses on the personal pronouns, which we now understand in their double functional capacity. Not only do they point to role-categories that exist, in some sense, independently of entextualization process (so, categories like "I" and "you" denote individuals inhabiting roles of speaker and addressee, respectively, from this point of view), but they also serve as metadiscursive labels (that is, denotationally explicit metapragmatic expressions) that denote the achievement of such role-category inhabitance as a result of entextualizing processes themselves.

Irvine's work began as a dialogue with Stephen Levinson (1988), who had argued that the basic pronominal categories needed to be further broken down to accommodate finer distinctions in the role-underpinnings of their use, distinctions, for example, between an "author" and a "ghostor" to accommodate ghost writing. Hence, in this line of theorizing, the seemingly simple role-category of speaker corresponding to the "I" of discourse can denote any such role-combination of one or both of "author" and "ghostor," that is an authorial-ghostor, a nonghostly author, and so on. Irvine articulates the insight here that the proposal for similar further decomposition of the simplex roles is, in principle, an endless and unconstrained process, since new situations are always emerging in discursive practice in which new meanings for the personal pronouns are produced. Over the course of a connected discursive history, there are infinitely iterable laminations of newly combined roles projected by the production, reproduction, and, in effect, trans-situational *renvoi* of expressions in discourse. In short, we face an infinitely variable ventriloquation of the "I," and so forth, of discourse over time, as Bakhtin—to touch an important source once more—would have put it. This suggested, first, that there was a gap between the personal pronouns as metadiscursive forms and the discursive processes in which they were employed—in other words, that there is no one thing in the world we could call a "speaker," but infinitely many different things that elude clear decontextualized denotational circumscription in absolute and essential sociologistic terms. Secondly, we infer that the actual entextualization processes involving the equivalent of "I's" and "you's," and so forth could be constituted differently in ethnographically distinct contexts, with no limits in principle.

Irvine's main example, *xaxaar* insult poems performed at wedding ceremonies by Wolof *griottes* (women of the bardic *griot* caste), is striking in this regard. When we inquire into their essential category of speaker, we quickly see that "speaker" is a complex category indeed. The persons who perform the insult are (generally) distinct from those who actually composed or formulated it, and both are (generally) distinct from the sponsor, who pays for the event and creates the possibility for the insult session in the first place. Each role-category of person forms part of the unitary but pluri-situational discursive practice of entextualization of the genre *xaxaar* in Wolof society, and we can appreciate that the entextualization process is culturally variable and yet ethnographically describable in these terms. At the same time, such practices suggest to analysts (and, perhaps, also to participants themselves) metadiscursive interpretations. Such interpretations of operative social categories in the entextualization process can then be projected from these instances onto ones with different role configurations.

Hanks's paper takes up a distinct, but perhaps more anthropologically recognizable, set of roles, namely, those involved in Mayan shamanic curing.

While anthropologists are used to regarding a category such as that of shaman as independent of discourse and entextualization processes, and, hence, as part of the social organization to which texts can later be linked, Hanks shows that the category of shaman can in fact only be understood in relationship to role inhabitance in a set of discursive practices, namely, those of the expert in performing curing ceremonies. Being thus always inherently partly "ascribed" and partly "achieved," the status of shaman is defined by special entextualizations, since the shaman acquires prayers from other shamans, but also reworks them, based upon his or her own experience. The ascriptively authorial and agentive shaman is thus one who possesses and must possess unique texts, which yet simultaneously bear the recoverable traces of dialogism and ventriloquations by virtue of interactions with other shamans. And the shaman is one who enacts these unique texts in the elaborately ritualized discourse contexts of curing. The status of shaman is thus at least in part metadiscursively read from an ethnographically describable role in discourse practices, and is thus, properly, at least in part a metadiscursive category.

We do not yet know all that is involved in the essentialization process whereby such a metadiscursive category—a category of contingently achieved role inhabitance—is projected onto the world. Nor, in particular, do we have a specific sense of how the inhabitable category might be recoverable from the prayer texts in an analytic approach. But Hanks draws our attention, in this regard, to the important notion of genre. The prayer texts must be of a recognizable genre—that of *reésar*, or the more specific *pa??ik'* ("banish, chase away, or smash wind")—and that genre goes along with a set of prescribed speech roles and a specially organized physical space of speaking. Indeed, the genre, as a metadiscursive label for a class of recurrent entextualizations—each with its own interactional and denotative facets—is what appears to give substance and continuity to the social interactions in which the texts are produced, and, therefore, to the broader social order.

However, there is in fact a continual back-and-forth interplay between the metadiscursive category and the actual instances of discourse that it is used to categorize and interpret. On the one side, the metadiscursive category (whether that of shaman or genre) seems to freeze or fix the social-interactional text, projecting from specific entextualizations to all past or future ones, in effect providing a potential template, or model, or "canonical" textual exemplar, under proper conditions. On the other side, every discourse instance is emergent and creative and hence capable of recalibrating the metadiscursive category for future projections. The dialectical process in which metadiscursive categories engage with social-interactional entextualization/contextualization, all the while being central to local cultural concepts of status and textual genre, is highlighted in these two papers.

PASS THE TEXT, PLEASE?

If there is, in fact, a looseness of fit between metadiscursive encoding (in genre or status/role) and actual discourse practices, in every culture we find some kinds of institutions in which attempts are made to tighten the fit, to fix the relationship. We are referring, of course, to institutions of socialization, whose goal, from our present perspective, is to inculcate in effect a metadiscourse about texts and the entextualization process, rather than or in addition to securing the transmission of texts, which the culture-as-text model views as primary or even unmediated by metadiscourse or a metadiscursive consciousness.

This theme is central in the chapters by James Collins and Elizabeth Mertz, who focus on educational institutions in modern America, the grade school and law school classroom, respectively. In both cases, we confront the central theme that entextualization and texts are meaningful not just for the cultural analyst, but also for the natives, and that the institutionalized activity of projecting texts is a process deployed for strategic purposes.

Collins, in particular, focuses on the ideology of texts, reflected in metadiscourse about them and the discourse practices surrounding them in a Chicago grade school with predominantly working-class African American students. He shows that, at the metadiscursive level, written texts are regarded as linguistically transparent, with fixed, primarily denotational meanings, making them equally available to all; consequently, they are viewed as a universal means for assessing students' educational progress. In "Learning to Read," students' differential mastery of the process of finding such texts in the text-artifacts they encounter is seen by educators to correspond to differential educational progress and hence learning; ultimately, it is related to broader judgments of students' intelligence.

In actual classroom discursive practices, text-artifacts become a focus for correcting students' pronunciation in the highly ideological task of "reading aloud." Text-artifacts thus play a central role in the indexical phenomenon of discrimination of identity with respect to uses of standard reading pronunciation (as studies by Labov and many others have shown). Through pronunciation exercises with explicit correction, speakers of nonstandard English have their identities both foregrounded and devalued, with emphasis placed on the interactional work as against interpretation of any denotational text from reading the artifact (i.e., any denotational meaning the text-artifact carries). Standard speakers do not have their identities foregrounded, but appear instead to be proficient in accessing denotational textual form—the standard words and expressions—and hence, it is assumed, "transparent" semantic meanings. In the exercise, their identities are neutral. At the same time, under an ideology or metadiscourse of equal accessibility to the semantic meanings, nonstandard speakers are graded down. Hence, in this case, the educational institution not only attempts to fix a relationship between metadiscourse and textual practice, it also asserts a social hierarchy based on the differential fit between discourse practices focused on getting from text-artifact to its audible oral transduction, and the metadiscourse about the goal of reading for (denotational) meaning which is projected onto this practice actualized in the classroom.

The law school classes studied by Mertz reveal a distinct pattern. Whereas the ideological metadiscourse of textualism in the grade school class-room stresses the denotational text—the "content" in the primary sense of reference-and-predication—law school practices attempt to break down this referentialist orientation to texts, substituting for it an emphasis on the text as both part of and a reflection of social interaction. What is important in the classroom interactions Mertz studies is the focus on how texts emerge from and fit into a hierarchy of courts and procedures, and, hence, how text-artifacts can be read from the point of view of legal procedures "in" them that they "talk about" in this way. Law students have presumably spent the previous sixteen years of their educational lives regimenting their discourse around an ideology of semantic meaning and reference—through which they were differ-entiated, to be sure, from those who never made it past (standard) pronuncia-tion. They must now have their ideologies of "reading" systematically de-constructed and replaced by new ones, which will henceforth regulate their attitudes towards legal text-artifacts in particular. Legal texts must be under-stood now not as (or not only as) semantically meaningful, but additionally and, for the successful, primarily, as meaningful in this double, procedure-invoking sense.

Interestingly, therefore—as all of the studies in this volume might be read as (in)directly showing—textuality and entextualization practices turn out to be about "identity." In Collins's and Mertz's chapters crucially, texts are located in the institutionalized transformation of identity over discourse time. For in the course of coursework, individuals acquire, and have inculcated in them, not only specific entextualization practices, but also metadiscourses or ideologies about texts through which they assess their own practices in both interpretive and strategic stances. In the grade school case, it is a question of instilling a primary orientation to texts, despite identity-focused entextualizing practices, which become the "content," as it were, of entextualization. In the law school case, the issue is one of substituting one metadiscourse or ideology for another, and reorganizing attitudes towards texts for those who aspire to professional identity.

Who Says (What) "Uncle" (Is)?

That texts receive different interpretations in the grade school and law school cases highlights the strategic political importance of asserting one metadiscursive interpretation over another. Politics can be seen, from this perspective, as the struggle to entextualize authoritatively, and hence, in one relevant move, to fix certain metadiscursive perspectives on texts and discourse practices. The theme of strategic metadiscursive entextualization is the focus of chapters by Hugh Mehan and Michael Herzfeld.

Mehan tackles this problem from a microsociological perspective, studying the discursive interactions surrounding the labeling of a child as "learning disabled" (or "LD"). The LD label is metadiscursive, as we see from Mehan's examples, because it is in fact used with reference to discursive interactional patterns, over which it generalizes in certain ways. However, Mehan argues that the LD label can be seen to lie in three discernible such metadiscursive registers in the institutional process he studies: psychological, (micro-)sociological, and biographical (or "historical"). But "LD" is not simply a description detachable from its context, even in the psychological metadiscursive register where it denotes a perduring or decontextualized condition presumed to be internal to the student of whom it is predicated. Rather, even in this register, the label's inherently contextualized nature is seen in the interactional struggle of registers, where it has practical effects in structuring future discursive interactions in the very realm out of which it seems to emerge: educational practice with reference to the student at issue, the named child. Consequently, institutional practice is constituted out of a step-by-step maneuvering among embodied interests, with a kind of culminating ritual encounter that gives rise to the (meta)discursive entextualization: "Your/My child is LD."

Herzfeld's example is similar, but played out at the plane of Greek cultural nationalism during the nineteenth and early twentieth centuries. He takes up the 1929 criticisms by Yanis Apostolakis of the folksong scholarship of earlier researchers, Nikolaos Politis and Spyridon Zambelios. The argument unfolds around specific folksong text-artifacts and their texts, and hence is metadiscursive, centering on whether certain entextualizations were authentic to Greek folk culture or were Hellenic-rationalist superimpositions. In arguing the authenticity of folksong text-artifacts, the authors are doing something of broader social significance. They are attempting to define Greek folk culture and hence Greek identity through metadiscourses about specific folksongs. As Herzfeld describes the situation, the essentializing turn in finding or disputing authenticity involves a set of tropic understandings about literariness and a folk-mind highly revealing about the Herderian Romanticism in which folklor-istics grew to be a political metadiscourse of nationalism.

We are, of course, not prepared to assert that all politics takes place at the metadiscursive plane, involving struggles over the description and regula-tion of discursive practices. At the same time, acceptance of a metadiscourse by a community is always potentially politically significant. As the authors of this volume are at pains to show, metadiscursive struggle is important not only at the contested margins of a community's discursive practices, but obviously as well at the very center of a community's organizing social categories and their relationships, including political hierarchies. As their studies cumula-tively reveal, entextualization processes involve the role-bound and genre-bound creation of identities, frequently projected across interactional sites, all the while projected from some culminating moment(s). But such projective reading is, of course, itself metadiscursive, and it is guided by (or contested by) other metadiscourses which have been previously accepted (or which are potentially constitutable) through the social action of extextualization/co(n)textualization.

PLAY IT AGAIN, SAM

If so much of understanding culture involves focusing on entextualization in context, rather than (or in addition to) texts and their text-artifactual transduc-tions, whether at the discursive or metadiscursive planes, it is a curious fact that peoples everywhere seem to attempt to reperform or reanimate certain key cul-tural texts. This alerts us to the fact that not all texts are created equal. Some occupy special positions within a culture and become the focus of multiple re-realizations, each one taking them from seemingly fixed, decontextualized forms—especially where artifactualized—into living, contextually specific, momentary phenomena; others fade away.

Why should this be the case? The answer is to be found in the very idea of culture as text, which, as we argue continuously, is important not only to analysts but also to natives. Texts and text-artifacts have the ability to instan-tiate the timeless, context-free character of culture, which can be uniformly shared within a community and passed down across the generations, whether conceptually—for example, the text that is the "original intent" behind a set of artifactual or performed instances—or physically—for example, the origi-nary or restored or emended text-artifactual copy of a text. The entextualized discourse, however, whether we are focused on the interactional or denotational plane, or both, can maintain its status as emblematic of the culture only if there are periodic reperformances or re-embeddings in actual discourse contexts that count as projectively "the same."

An alternative to periodic re-embedding of selected texts would be the creation of new and distinctive texts on each successive occasion, thereby effectively obviating the need for a "canon." [2] The latter strategy is possible because each text, as we argue, by virtue of having been entextualized, has the ability to freeze-frame past and future, eliminating the dynamic and contingent social properties from which it was assembled.

But the difference between the two, we should be clear, is a matter of degree and, indeed, may depend entirely on the metadiscursive frame. For each re-embedding of a text can result in a new entextualization, so that the fixity seemingly achieved by this process is at least in part illusory. The text is made to seem more solid, however, under an ideology or metadiscourse of fixity, so that the metadiscursive perspective of there being a finite number of texts standing for or exemplifying or even being the culture suggests the existence of a shared culture. Under an ideology of textual newness, in contrast, the idea is created of a continuously moving or evolving culture, even though the "new" text—as recognized by the metadiscourse—may be no more new than the reentextualization of what a different metadiscourse recognizes as an "old" text. Certainly, some social scientific ideologies, namely, those that cast off textuality *in toto* in favor of a notion of context-specific, never-to-be-duplicated discursive practice alone, have such a view—one that announces the end of social science, among other things.

In any case, it is clear that the problematic of reanimation or reperformance is a crucial one for students of culture, and it is taken up in this volume by Richard Bauman. Bauman studies the textual re-embedding that is involved in the cyclical re-presentation of a nativity play in a Mexican town. The artifacts in which the denotational and interactional texts are stored, in this case, are written scripts, and Bauman studies the relationship between these scripts and the tape-recorded performances in a reverse mirroring of the studies by Haviland and Urban of entextualization through transcription.

We see here not only how the text as authoritative (and representative of tradition and shared culture) is faithfully reenacted, but also how the perform-

2. We put "canon" in quotation marks because a true canon requires not simply a set of texts, but also an explicit ideology or metadiscourse that those texts and no others form the core of culture. The boundary issue (canonical versus noncanonical) is crucial here, but not in the case we are describing.

ers mock and fight against the text, creating in part a Bakhtinian carnivalesque spirit of irreverence, even as they celebrate textual fixity, authority, and the continuity of culture. We see also the elaborate social process of discourse production—in analogy to the diachronic unfolding of discourse described by Irvine—in which the social order of the town is invoked and instantiated, particularly through the struggle over rights to contestation. This leads us to an entirely new understanding of why the metadiscursive ideology of mere performance engages with the ritualized carnivalesque: a literal denotational text, in a sense, continues to exist here for the townspeople only as it is in fact engaged with through the performed figurement of ritualized denotational contestation. Indeed, it may be that a denotational text—as distinct from the artifact by which it is carried—achieves wider acceptance in proportion to its ability to accommodate differing interpretations.

In any case, this is only one of the fruitful areas of investigation opened up by the study of culture not just as text, but as entextualizing processes in which the text is but one moment, and, indeed, in which the text is sometimes only implicit in an aesthetic of transposition, transduction, and translation. Entextualization reveals an architecture of social relations, and becomes the basis for numerous metadiscursive projections, as the interactional backdrop of a given text is projected onto others, producing a generic image of fixed identities and social categories. We believe that this volume raises questions about traditional social scientific and humanistic methodology, such as text gathering, as well as about key concepts, such as the separation of society or social organization from culture, which many such fields need to rethink.

THE NATURAL HISTORY OF THIS DISCOURSE

If every text has its natural history, the one before you is no different. Indeed, the various chapters are the culmination of a long interactional and redactional process, which began in 1986 when the editors organized a working group at the Center for Psychosocial Studies (now Center for Transcultural Studies) in Chicago around the theme of "Text and Social Action." In its first phase, the group met over a two-year period, at first on a monthly basis and later quarterly. Many of the participants, though not all, have contributed to this volume,[3] and while we consider the chapters to be individually authored, with final responsibility resting on the individuals in question, the ideas were shaped, and in many cases were born, in the course of intensive group discussion. In fact, the

---

3. We recall here the invaluable collegial contributions of Don Brenneis, Benjamin Lee, John Lucy, and Richard Parmentier, who were members of the original discussion group.

degree of mutual interaction reflected in this volume might suggest collective authorship of the entire work.

We say "might suggest," because it would be wrong to think of this work as one in which complete agreement has been achieved. It would be better to think of it as dialogically constructed, with the dialogue as often agonistic as cooperative. We began with a common problematic framed by the editors having to do with different views of "text," as a structure of discourse nevertheless embedded in richly contingent social action versus something formal, along the lines of text grammar, in which a text is seen as a larger-than-sentence-level output conformable to something like a grammar. We moved from there to focus upon a set of common readings, which we intensively discussed, usually in the course of an afternoon followed by a dinner, then resumed in a three- or four-hour morning session the next day followed by lunch. It was hard at points to distinguish when the formal discussions left off and the informal ones began.

An important first breakthrough on our way to this volume was the realization that the two views of text were not incompatible alternatives, but linked to distinct phases in the "entextualization" process, as we came to call it, the (at best) intersubjective and sufficient determination of a "text"—though divergent actor-perspective entextualizations also inhabit interactional realtime. We began also to draw out the dialectical relationship of entextualization to its complementary phase, "contextualization," the ever-changing "appropriate-to/effective-in" relationships that concurrently develop between text and nontext.

We began by exploring the ways in which social actors seem to lift texts from contexts, the transformations that even "the same" discourse undergoes in the process, and the social conditions making possible such entextualization in the first place. This is the observed or patent "natural history" of textuality. We first more neutrally called it a "decentering"[4] of a discourse so as to yield a sufficiently autonomous "text," and a "recentering" of such a text in another discursive "context." Of course, all discourse is always already centered in some fashion, that is, dependent on indexical ties to context. So analyzing the apparent decentering/recentering image became our collective project. To contribute to it, we produced and discussed an initial set of papers, many of which matured into contributions to this volume.

A second major breakthrough occurred with the realization that even per-

---

4. We call attention to the distinctness of this concept—a bit of a pun on the sense of "centered" as "indexically grounded" and the name of our sponsoring "Center for Psychosocial Studies"—from the similarly translated term of Jacques Derrida (1986).

sonal deictics, such as English *I* and *you*, and so on, which seemed to have fixed, understandable meanings as elementary shifters, in fact do so only through an intertextual projection at the metadiscursive plane. Recall that personal deictics present their referents as the individual(s) presupposed to be inhabiting a particular interactional role, like "speaker" or "addressee(s)." They describe their referent(s) as the role inhabitant(s) they index, and therefore have metapragmatic denotational backing; they are, in short, explicitly metadiscursive. But in what culturally specific ways does an individual come to inhabit such an interactional role? Are such interactional roles always the same? We realized in our discussions that the simple pronominal forms are, in fact, complex in semiosis. Because the pronouns are found across distinct texts, the absolutely unique, contingent specificity of the history by which individuals come to inhabit relevant roles in each instance seems to give way to an abstract essentialization, which can then be read into any given text. The attempt to fathom the meaning of that projected essence results in the realization that there are many (perhaps infinitely many) distinctions that can be regarded as features of the essentialized categories denoted as "first" and "second person." These tend to cumulate in discursive historical processes which we read as tropes such as *renvoi*, reference, reanimation, re-presentation, and so on. With these insights, we began to explore how such projections or essentializations took place in actual empirical cases, and we looked beyond the realm of elementary personal deixis.

A first attempt at public presentation was a panel at the annual meeting of the American Anthropological Association held in Chicago in autumn of 1987, when Hugh Mehan and Michael Herzfeld joined us. The papers from the panel were further discussed at subsequent meetings of the group, which included new participants as well as new papers. These old and new papers were revised, presented, discussed, and debated at subsequent meetings through the fall of 1988, when the group formally disbanded, although it met in different guises and at different times for two more years. It was agreed that the editors should assemble the papers into the present volume.

This volume, then, instantiates beyond design the very processes it describes. While the published product is explicitly entextualized and sedimented in a text-artifact, each chapter has a unique natural history, a series of prior entextualizations/texts which lie discursively behind it, and a complex diachrony of social interactions out of which it was produced and continues to be reanimated (here the gentle readership figuring centrally). We are encouraged in thinking that there will be a textual future for some of our collective conceptual approach, inasmuch as a summarizing report—a kind of promissory note—has been well received and widely cited.[5]

5. The paper is entitled "Poetics and Performance as Critical Perspectives on Language and Social Life" (Bauman and Briggs 1990); its authors generously acknowledge the inspiration for some of their ideas, such as the concept of entextualization. There have been collateral publications as well. Although Charles Briggs participated in the Center discussions only *in absentia*, Richard Bauman was an original member of and active participant in the group.

REFERENCES

Bauman, Richard, and Charles L. Briggs
   1990   Poetics and performance as critical perspectives on language and social life. *Annual Review of Anthropology* 19: 59–88.

Derrida, Jacques
   1986   Structure, sign and play in the discourse of the human sciences. In *Critical Theory since 1965*, H. Adams and L. Searle (eds.), 83–94. Tallahassee: University Presses of Florida.

Geertz, Clifford
   1973   *The Interpretation of Cultures*. New York: Basic Books.

Levinson, Stephen C.
   1988   Putting linguistics on a proper footing: Explorations in Goffman's concepts of participation. In *Erving Goffman*, P. Drew and A. Wootton (eds.), 161–227. Oxford: Polity Press.

Ricoeur, Paul
   1981 [1971]   The model of the text: Meaningful action considered as a text. In *Hermeneutics and the Human Sciences: Essays on Language, Action, and Interpretation*, J. B. Thompson (ed. and trans.), 197–221. New York: Cambridge University Press.

Recovering/Constituting Texts from Discourse

1 Entextualization, Replication, and Power

Greg Urban

One aspect of the natural history of discourse is the process of replication, with which this and the following chapter by John Haviland are concerned. If a given instance of discourse is unique by virtue of its formal properties, as well as the infinitely rich specificity of the context in which it is embedded, by definition it cannot be reproduced. Replication, however, is an attempt at reproduction, at relocating the original instance of discourse to a new context—carrying over something from the earlier to the later one. Such carrying over, or "transduction," is essential to culture understood as shareable or transmittable across the generations.

Simultaneously, replication is an empirical phenomenon or set of phenomena through which entextualization can be studied. If entextualization is understood as the process of rendering a given instance of discourse a text, detachable from its local context, replication is one way, seemingly, of implementing detachment. It tries to portray the textual as opposed to contextual aspects of the original discourse, and to capture, thereby, the decontextualized or polycontextual meanings associated with it.

At the same time, entextualization is not synonymous with replication, since the former is primarily a matter of seeming, as subsequent chapters make apparent. The broader question of entextualization involves not only how or in what measure something is culture, in the sense of being shareable or transmittable, but also how it seems to be culture with or without evidence of actual sharing or transmission or even transduction.

While the study of replication is only one way of approaching entextualization, it is a particularly revealing way, for it involves an examination not only of the original and copied discourse, but also of the social relationships obtaining between originator and copier.[1] Here I hope to lead you to explore

I especially thank Joel Kuipers for detailed comments on an earlier draft.

1. Elinor Ochs (1979), in a ground-breaking article, discusses the theory-laden character of transcription, the production of research transcripts in artifactualized writing/printing. She

what a social relationship is. Is it something that exists apart from and prior to discourse, characterizable independently? Is it, alternatively, an accumulation of instances of discourse that form a recognizable pattern? Or is it a characterization contained in the meaningful aspects of discourse?

The present chapter examines the mutual constitution of discourse and power, agency and external determination, insofar as these can be discerned in the phenomenon of replication. Together with the following chapter by Haviland, it focuses on a highly marked form of replication—transcription of tape-recorded instances of oral discourse by native speakers of the language who are members of the same speech community as the producer of the original instance. The present work differs from Haviland's, however, which begins with discourse that is originally dialogical and traces its monological regimentation through the course of its transcription. Here the investigation begins instead with monological discourse, although, as I hope to convince you, dialogicality reinserts itself in interesting ways.

In what follows, I develop a set of propositions regarding certain regularities in replication processes. Historical contingency being by definition crucial to one side of the life-cyclic processes of texts, it may seem paradoxical to search for regularities. As a stretch of discourse metamorphoses, being entextualized or recontextualized, innumerable factors intervene, making the outcome hardly a determinate one, let alone a transparent reflection of universal principles. But, at the same time, a natural historical approach does not simply celebrate contingency, while denigrating regularity. It asks us to attend to the typical as well as the unique. This chapter, and in some measure the next one by Haviland, focus on regularities in replication processes that are formulable in propositions—albeit ones in need of further empirical confirmation.

HOW ARE ORIGINAL AND COPY RELATED?

Replication is only one among the possible interrelationships between discourse instances; another, of special interest from the point of view of dialogicality, is response (cf. Goffman 1981). In response, the original discourse is not

---

argues that transcription typically excludes visual cues and even some sound cues, and, furthermore, that it conventionalizes discourse representations with respect to space: left-to-right and top-to-bottom linearity. I thus loosely follow her, in this chapter, in focusing on differences between original (or performance) and copy (or re(-)presentation). However, here I differ with her insofar as I deal not with transcriptions made by researchers and used directly as "data," but with transcriptions made by "natives," and, hence, studiable alongside and in comparison with transcriptions made by me as the researcher. It is the comparisons of my own copies with those made by Nānmla and Wāñpō that provide me with evidence regarding replication.

copied, as in replication, but reacted to. A simple example will make this clear. Suppose the original discourse instance is "Do you want to eat?" (As you will see below, this is taken from an actual example; it is not as cardboard as it at first appears.) In the case of replication, you would see a copy of that original: "Do you want to eat?" In the case of response, however, you would find a new instance, such as, "No, I don't want to eat," which is related to the original but formulated as a reaction to it.

The discourse interrelationships of replication and response can be posited by an outside observer, but they can also form part of the discourse surrounding the instance in question. That is, they can form part of the meta-discourse subscribed to by the participants. In considering the problem of replication, and especially how the original and copy are related, one needs to inquire into how that relationship is encoded in the circulating metadiscourse. The latter, indeed, may in turn be affecting the replication process.

Metadiscourse provides as well a crucial link between discourse and the so-called social, that is, relations characterizable independently of discursive interaction. In the case of replication, the original discourse must have been produced by some individual or group—the *originator*. Correspondingly, the copy is also produced by an individual or group—the *copier*. In talking about the social relationship between originator and copier, characterizations of the social are dependent on characterizations of the discourse. Hence, they are dependent upon metadiscourse. This is true whether one talks directly about the asymmetrical power relationships obtaining between originator and copier as such, or about the social relationships between the individuals (for example, grandfather-grandson) who just happen to be related to one another in the instance as originator to copier. Linkage of the social to the discursive can only be made through the metadiscursive, and metadiscourse forms part of the circulating discourse as well as being something superimposed by an analyst.

One task of the present paper is to examine the relationship between the original and copied discourse in cases of replication, and to ask whether the social relations between originator and copier affect the copying process. From the point of view of metadiscourse, however, the issue is as well how the situation and task are construed. I hope to show that there is a correlation between the social relationships and discursive relationships that is simultaneously a correlation between discourse relationships and metadiscursive characterizations.

The metadiscursive problematic immediately leads to another question. There are metadiscursive characterizations not just of the relationship between original instance and copied instance, and of the social relationship between originator and copier, but also of the relationship between originator and original instance and copier and copied instance. Is the originator seen as a true originator, that is, as someone who produced the original instance *sui generis*? Alternatively, is the originator seen as a copier of other instances themselves more authentic? This is the problematic of authoritative discourse as raised by Voloshinov (1973).

From here it is a short step to questions about whether some kinds of discourse are intrinsically more shareable than others. I will try to show from a study of the transcription process that discourse carries markers—metadiscursive markers—of the relationship between originator and original instance, and that, furthermore, some kinds of discourse are more copiable and hence more shareable than others because of those markers. That is, some kinds of discourse make for better culture, in its classic sense of sharing and transmission across the generations.

THE SITUATION AT HAND

The specific propositions I wish to develop derive from observations made among an indigenous group living at P.I. Ibirama[2] in southern Brazil. The primary data are transcriptions of tape-recorded discourse done by (1) a young man, Nãnmla, whom I trained how to write phonemically, and (2) an elder man, Wãñpõ, who would repeat for me syllable-by-syllable what was on tape for me to transcribe. In addition, I have some general observations about what is transcribable by native informants and what is not, together with broader ethnographic observations about social relationships.

The bulk of the data are Nãnmla's several hundred pages of transcription, mostly of mythological and historical narratives, done in late 1981 and through 1982. The material transcribed was tape-recorded by me in 1974–1976 and in 1981–1982. I also independently transcribed and translated much of it.

Virtually all of the tape-recorded discourse has as its originator a male elder of the group. All of the several hundred remaining native residents of the P.I. Ibirama community are related genealogically in one way or another, and each of these originating men was a kinsman of Nãnmla. In one case, it was Nãnmla's own grandfather (MF). There is no question that the originator-copier relationship here is an asymmetrical one, with the originator an authority figure for the copier. Nãnmla was constantly at pains to produce an exact

2. "P.I." refers to *Posto Indígena* ("Indigenous Post") and is used to designate one of the government-run indigenous reservations in Brazil. The group living there is referred to in the literature by various terms: for example, Shokleng, Xokleng, Aweikoma, Botocudo, Kaingang of Santa Catarina.

replica of the "authoritative" discourse he heard on the tape. Moreover, the relationship was such that he would never challenge the validity of that discourse.

I chose Nānmla for transcription work in the first place because he excelled in school. At the time he began working with me, he was eighteen years old and was in the equivalent of junior high school in a town near the reserve. He was the only member of the community at that level. Children at the time were receiving four years of elementary education in government-run schools on the reserve. Nānmla was thoroughly fluent both in the native language, having grown up in a largely monolingual environment, and in Portuguese, which he acquired primarily in elementary school.

The originators of the discourse were either monolinguals or bilinguals in varying degrees. Almost all of them had been born before the first peaceful contacts between the indigenous group and Brazilian national society. None of them had had any schooling. They were rightly regarded by Nānmla as bearers of the ancient cultural tradition, and it is safe to say that he conceived of the originator-copier relationship, if not in terms of true origination, then at least in terms of a privileged access to the authentic discourse that he did not share. Although I do not have tape-recorded examples, Nānmla's explicit discourse about his relationship to the elders—and, hence, his metadiscourse about the original-copy and originator-copier relationships—acknowledged this asymmetry. He would consistently downplay his own ability to understand and produce the kinds of discourse he listened to on tape, and affirm the elders' privileged position.

The copier-copy relationship was defined in part by me. I spent several months training Nānmla how to transcribe phonemically, and we worked with actual tape recordings after he had become relatively proficient. I taught him how to (1) represent each phoneme of the native language, (2) provide graphic spaces between words, (3) give an interlinear translation, where possible, below the word, and (4) give a free translation into Portuguese below that. I did not teach him to represent lines or to punctuate, leaving this entirely up to him. In general, he created numbered line breaks based upon chunks of discourse he could keep in his head at one time for transcription purposes. He would relisten to portions when in doubt, and he would go over the entire text for accuracy upon completion.

Nānmla understood his task to be one of accurately replicating the oral form. He saw the texts he produced as something he did for me, and it was clear that my relationship to him was analogous to that of teacher to student. In addition, I paid him for his transcription work, in order to subsidize his schooling. This is something I did not do with the elder men with whom I also worked. We developed instead a system of generalized reciprocity, wherein I would give gifts to them and they would help me. Much of the oral discourse I recorded may have been influenced by this spirit of generalized reciprocity, even when it was collected in "natural" contexts.

As a counterinstance to the evidence from Nānmla, I also examined transcription work I did in 1975 with a reasonably bilingual elder, named Wãñpõ. Wãñpõ did not consider himself to be among the most knowledgeable of the elders, but he did regard himself as having been brought up in the traditional culture. He helped me to transcribe an hour-long stretch of mythological discourse, which had been narrated by Nil, who very definitely regarded himself as the leading ritual specialist. Nil was entirely monolingual, and the eldest living man in the community. Moreover, he had been the son of the great chief Gakrã, who made the first contacts with the white man. There is no question in this case that Nil regarded his own discourse as absolutely authoritative and traditional. Wãñpõ and Nil were cousins, and it is clear that Wãñpõ recognized Nil's claim as a ritual specialist, but he thought of him in this area as more of a *primus inter pares* than as a truly authoritative other, contrary to the relationship Nānmla had with all of the elders. Wãñpõ tended to regard Nil as someone who had had access to the authentic originals, but he also regarded himself in this way. Nil's originals, which were really copies of earlier discourse instances, were not that much better than the originals Wãñpõ himself might produce. So the discursive relationship between Wãñpõ and Nil was more egalitarian than that between Nānmla and Wãñpõ. This is something Wãñpõ would indicate verbally by saying that he knew the story in question as well. For this reason, the contrast between Wãñpõ's and Nānmla's transcriptions makes a good test case for the influence of the originator-copier relationship on the discourse-replication process.

The actual transcription process involved my playing back a portion of the tape. Wãñpõ would listen to it, then say it back slowly to me, syllable by syllable. I would repeat the syllable orally and write it down. I was not yet fluent in the native language, and the process helped me to learn it. It is important to observe that the syllable-by-syllable repetition is the traditional method of teaching the origin myth (Urban 1991). In contrast with my relationship to Nānmla, where I was regarded as the teacher, Wãñpõ was a mentor to me and tended to socialize me into indigenous ways of doing things. This mentor relationship was openly acknowledged by both of us. The copier-copy relationship was thus formulated metadiscursively as in part didactic, a way of helping me to learn the traditional culture and language from someone who knew them.

It is also clear that Wãñpõ, because he recognized the originator-copier relationship as involving only relative authoritativeness, placed less emphasis on the originator-original relationship. The discourse he was helping me to transcribe he regarded as "traditional," and thus not the exclusive property of Nil. He had repeatedly heard, and himself told, the same stories on numerous occasions. Correspondingly, he did not hang on Nil's every word.

It should be noted in regard to Nil in particular, but also to all of the elders in general, that there was a great deal of criticism of the traditional discourse, which may be thought of in terms of the original-copy relationship. One other individual, for example, who considered himself a ritual specialist on a par with Nil, repeatedly questioned Nil's competence with respect to the origin myth. When in fact their two versions were compared (Urban 1991), it turned out that they were nearly identical, very often word-for-word. The important point here is that the originator-copier relationship between elders is very different from that between elder and youngster.

How Does a Copy Differ from Its Original?

For the replication of culture as embodied in discourse, one central issue is the similarity of the copy to the original as regards the segmentable linguistic form. The discovery made during the present research on native transcription is that the copy is very often distinct from the original. The copy may (1) contain features which are apparently lacking in the original, but also (2) lack features that are characteristic of the original, and even (3) transform elements of the original into new elements. The constant differences are similar to those described for the Mayan case by Haviland in the following chapter.

I do not wish to underplay the methodological problems involved in comparing the copy with the original. In the case of Nãnmla's transcriptions, the copy is the actual representation of the discourse on paper, a sample of which can be seen in Figure 1.1. In the case of Wãñpõ's work, the copy is a graphic rendition by me of the syllable-by-syllable explication of the original as it appears on tape. My own comparison of the original with the copy in each case has been done by listening to the tape recording of the original while reading the transcribed text. In addition, I have myself transcribed the original, and have used that transcription as a reflection of the original, always going to the tape when discrepancies were found. The important point is that the discrepancies of interest here are phonemically renderable discrepancies; indeed, they involve grammatical particles, whole words, and even sentence-long stretches of discourse.

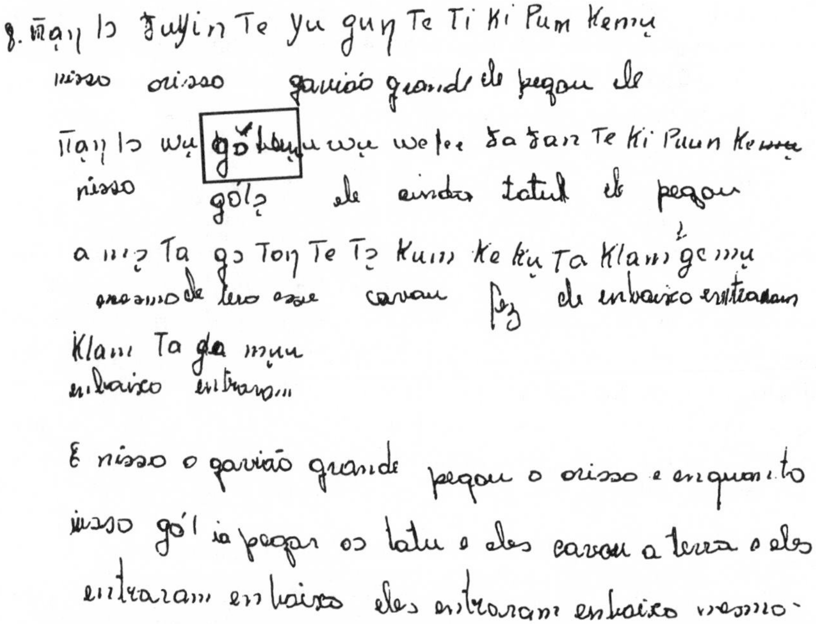
E nisso o gavião grande pegou o orisso e enquanto nisso gól ia pegar os tatu e eles cavou a terra e eles entraram enbaixo eles entraram enbaixo mesmo.

FIGURE 1.1 Reproduction of section of Nãnmla's transcription. From the second line, this reproduction corresponds to example (5b). Box has been drawn over segment where text has been repaired by writing *gòlõ* over *how*.

As may be expected from the previous discussion, Nãnmla's transcriptions are generally closer to phoneme-by-phoneme accuracy than are Wãnpõ's. His pattern of insertion is largely a "grammaticalizing" one. He regularly adds syllables and words, especially at the ends of utterances, to make the tape-recorded text conform to a grammatical ideal of completion. Most often these insertions are of sentence-final aspectual particles, as in Example 1, where the italicized material has no phonetic trace in the tape recording:

Example 1

kũ	mẽg	ti	tõ	uyol	ti	tañ	yè	ti	to	nẽ	*wã*
conj.	jaguar	def.	erg.	tapir	def.	kill	purpose	he	beside	sit	*stative*

The jaguar had sat next to the tapir in order to kill him.

Such insertions were found in 17 of the 112 lines (i.e., 15%) in this text. Most of them were of a single syllable-length particle, as in the above example. However, in two cases, Nãnmla inserted two syllables of a trisyllabic word, only the first of which was reflected phonetically on the tape. As in Example 2, both involved the word *kànãtẽ:*

Example 2

    uyol ti   ti yè   hãlike kàn*ãtẽ*
    tapir def. he sing like   *go about*

The tapir went about singing like him.

There are occasional insertions of other words, such as the quotative particle, but the sentence-final aspectual particle is the most commonly added one. In most cases, the particles tend to occur at intonational and stress troughs in the stretch of oral discourse.

In elicited sentences, these predicating particles are invariably present. They evidently form part of what linguists call an intuited grammar of the language. In actual discourse, they are frequently absent. The intriguing fact is that they get reinserted in the course of unreflective transcription. In other words, transcription, as intersemiotic conversion, tends to reshape the spoken image into something resembling the spoken form produced in the relatively more formal, self-conscious context of elicitation.

The insertion of these forms adds to the explicitly coded semantic meaning of the text. However, in each of the cases investigated so far, the correct choice of particle can be inferred from other grammatical and discourse features, for example, the ergative case marking of noun phrases in Example 1, which is associated with the resultative stative particle *wã* (Urban 1985). In Example 3, the choice of the deleted *mũ* particle (active, complete) could be inferred from two facts: a grammatical one, namely, accusative case marking, and a discourse one, the relative position of this line within the overall narrative—we are expecting a summary statement about how things came to be as they are:

Example 3

    ug   ti   wü . . . "mlal" kè tã tẽ *mũ*
    wild pig def. nom.   "mlal" do he go *completive*

The wild pig went away going "mlal;"

    ñãglò   kòñãl   ti   "ñugñugug" kò ti   mẽ tẽ *mũ*
    however monkey def. "ñugñugug" tree def. dist. go *completive*

however, the monkey went through the trees going "ñugñugug."

This is reinforced by the change of topic from "wild pig" to "monkey" in the following line, which is semantically parallel.

The general inference to be drawn from these data is that the intersemiotic conversion involved in transcription tends to make *semantically explicit* (by means of segmentable forms) what is *pragmatically inferrable* from the spoken form. In this, the transcribed form resembles what is produced orally in the formal situation of elicitation. The data from Wãñpõ, who was recounting orally what he heard on the tape syllable by syllable, show precisely the same pattern. The replication of oral discourse in these situations—where maximum attention is being paid to the discourse and there is minimal time lag between hearing and replicating—regularly involves a transformation in the direction of semantic explicitness. I encourage you to compare these results with those presented by Haviland in the following chapter.

The divergence between original and replica may be due to the specific situation of replication, namely, one in which the copier is at pains to produce deliberate and elaborated discourse. The tentative correlation is formulated in the following proposition:

Proposition 1: When replication occurs in relatively deliberate contexts (such as that of transcription), the copy may differ from the original by including segmentable forms not found in the original that explicitly encode meanings that are only pragmatically inferrable from the original.

This is an example of what was referred to earlier as "transduction"—the carrying over of something from one context to the next, in this case, in a new form. In the native transcription example, the new context of copying differs from the original context of narration. It involves a more deliberate orientation to discourse, with an attenuated ability to communicate through intonation, stress, and other paralinguistic devices, and downplays the flow of the narrative in favor of clause-level meanings. Meanings that were carried by the pragmatic forms in the earlier context are recreated in the new one, but this time through segmentable semantic forms.

There is another way in which both Nãnmla's and Wãñpõ's replicas diverge from the original. They both delete some portions from the original that are metadiscursive in character, especially those that indicate that the discourse contains "errors" which need to be corrected to mend the intended "text." Rather than transcribe the metadiscursive instructions, both Wãñpõ and Nãnmla instead dutifully repair the text. Such instructions draw boundaries around portions of the discourse, constituting those portions as part of a text and excluding other portions, and it is the constituted text that is replicated. These metadiscursive instructions are thus entextualizing, telling hearers how to make a text out of the discursive materials with which they have been presented, suggesting what should be replicated and what should not.

In some cases, the metadiscursive instruction to delete is indicated by a pragmatic feature itself, such as intonation contour, pause, or voice quality. In Example 4, for instance, the bracketed material is present in the spoken original, and is clearly audible, but does not appear in the transcription produced by Nãnmla:

Example 4

kũ   zuyin   lã   ti   wũ   [mẽ mẽ]   ki yànke   tũ tẽ
conj. porcupine quill def. nom. [dist. dist.] in penetrate not incomplete

"And the porcupine's quills were [all about, all about] not penetrating."

Here intonation contour (rising on *ki* as a continuation of *wũ*, with the two *mẽ*'s being set apart) and the abrupt checking of the vowel articulation of the two "extraneous" distributive particles (*mẽ*) signal to the listener that the narrator considers himself to have made a mistake. What is of interest is that Nãnmla, in his capacity as transcriber, responds to the narrator's metatextual cue and eliminates the distributive particles from the transcription.

In other cases, which are perhaps even more striking, the metadiscursive instruction is encoded in the semantics of the discourse itself, as in Example 5a, which is my own transcription and is, consequently, as close an approximation in graphically represented segmentable form as I can make to the original:

Example 5a

ñãglò   wũ   how   ũ   wũ   wel zazan   tẽ   ki punke
however nom. wildcat one nom. still armadillo def. in set upon

hãmõ tã gò   tògti tõ   kumke
thus   he ground this   with dig

kũ tã klãm ge   mũ
and he under enter compl.

klãm tã la   mũ
under he there compl.

tatà gòlõ how   ũ   wã gòlõ ẽñ cõ   kàgnãg wã
there gòlõ wildcat one stat. gòlõ I   erg. err   stat.

gòlõ wũ   ti ki punke   kũ gò   ti   klãm
gòlõ nom. he in set upon and ground def. under

Meanwhile, a *how* (a type of wild cat) was about to set upon the armadillo. Right there he dug a hole and he entered below. He was there below. There the *gòlõ*, a type of *how*, the *gòlõ*, I made a mistake, the *gòlõ* set upon him and (he was) below the ground.

Nãnmla's replica is given in Example 5b:

Example 5b

```
ñãglò    wũ    gòlõ    ũ    wũ    wel zazan        tẽ    ki punke
however nom.  wildcat one  nom.  still armadillo def.  in  set upon
```

```
hãmõ tã   gò     tògti tõ    kumke
thus   he ground this   with dig
```

```
kũ   tã   klãm   ge      mũ
and  he  under  enter  compl.
```

```
klãm   tã   la      mũ
under  he  there  compl.
```

Meanwhile, a *gòlõ* was about to set upon the armadillo. Right there he dug a hole and he entered below. He was there below.

Such differences appear in the transcription work of both Nãnmla and Wãñpõ, and hence seem to be relatively independent of the relationship between originator and copier, or even of the broader network of social relations in which the anthropologist is included. There are several examples in the data of Nãnmla and Wãñpõ transcribing the same passage in the same way, in each case deleting the materials they were told (metadiscursively) to delete by the originator in the original discourse itself. Example 6 will suffice:

Example 6
Original:

```
kũ   a     yïyï   tẽ      hãlike tẽ        ke          mũ
and  your  name  def.  like    incompl.  quotative  compl.
```

```
ẽñ   yïyï   hã   wũ    zàgpope          [voicelessly released glottal stop]
my   name  focus nom.  proper name  [ahem]
```

```
ẽñ   yïyï   hã   wũ    zẽzẽ             ke    tẽ
my   name  focus nom.  proper name  fut.  incompl.
```

" 'And what would your name be?' (he) said.
'My name would be zàgpope [ahem]
My name would be zẽzẽ.' "

Nãnmla's Copy:

```
kũ   a     yïyï   tẽ      hãlike tẽ        ke          mũ
and  your  name  def.  like    incompl.  quotative  compl.
```

```
ẽñ   yïyï   hã   wũ    zẽzẽ             ke    tẽ
my   name  focus nom.  proper name  fut.  incompl.
```

" 'And what would your name be?' (he) said.
'My name would be zẽzẽ.' "

Wãñpõ's Copy:

```
a     yïyï   tẽ      hãlike tẽ
your  name  def.  like    incompl.
```

ēñ yïyï hā   wū   zēzē   ke tē
my name focus nom. proper name fut. incompl.

" 'What would your name be?'
'My name would be zēzē.' "

Here the initiator of the discourse signaled pragmatically—through a glottal stop with explosive voiceless release—that the material that came before it was an error. In each case, the replicators acknowledged this, deleting the "error" in the course of replicating the original.

The various examples of this phenomenon can be summarized in a second proposition concerning the constant differences between original and copy:

Proposition 2: A copy may differ from its original by lacking portions of the original that are metadiscursive instructions, especially indications of mistakes or deviations from an intended "text," and by "correcting" the mistakes so indicated.

The important point for present purposes about these differences is that they are relatively independent of the social relationships that obtain between the originator and copier and, in this case, anthropologist. The research to date suggests two types of factors that may be responsible for these differences. One is the context in which the replication takes place (Proposition 1). The context studied in this paper is a specialized one, but if the general proposition put forth here is correct, it should be possible to detect such constant shifts in other contexts of replication, for example, between the "same" myth told in a formalized ritual context versus in the relatively informal domestic situation.

The second factor is the metadiscursive components of the initial discourse itself. In the present examples, the differences between originator and copier have to do with the deletion of metadiscursive instructions about how the original is to be copied, and the performance of the suggested corrections. The key point is that portions of a given discourse instance may signal themselves as being not a part of the "text," but rather instructions about how that discourse is to be approached as a text, through replication or with some form of response. These portions of the discourse provide a blueprint for the entextualization, regardless of whether that entextualization actually occurs in the course of replication. It is as if the metadiscursive portions of the discourse were invisible (or inaudible) and yet capable of exercising an effect on the listener. They do not carry over when the replication occurs. Transduction here involves deleting the metadiscursive portion and performing the transformation indicated by it in the course of replication.

These special portions of the discourse are metasignals. The listener is aware of what they mean, and the meaning is disjunctive with respect to the broader stretch of discourse in which they are embedded; in fact, their meaning concerns how the broader discourse is to be understood or interpreted or entextualized—that is, removed from its present context and fashioned into a decontextualized or polycontextual text. For this reason, the metasignals become an important resource for manipulation and the exercise of power.

How Does Power Affect Replication?

In addition to differences between the original and the copy that can be traced to context or to the metadiscursive instructions contained within the original discourse itself, there are differences that have to do with the social relationships between the originator and copier. In the present research, these are differing patterns of divergence between original and copy that showed up in the transcription work of Wãñpõ and Nãnmla. The differences can be summed up by saying that Wãñpõ's copies were less faithful reproductions of the originals than were Nãnmla's. Wãñpõ was an elder, more or less on a par with the originators, and he considered himself to be my mentor. Nãnmla, by contrast, was a young man, who regarded the elders as bearers of the ancient traditions and who saw me as his mentor.

A study of Wãnpõ's copies reveals two general kinds of divergence from the original discourse that are not present in Nãnmla's copies. First, there is substitution of material that is semantically equivalent but of different segmentable form, although semantic transformations can in fact be introduced. Such substitutions are generally either lexical or phrasal, but go up to clause-level ones. Second, there are deletions of materials, typically whole clauses, that are regarded as either redundant, irrelevant, or not part of what Wãñpõ understands to be the canonical myth—based upon the originals he himself had access to. Example 7 is a reasonably typical, if complex, example of the kinds of changes that are involved:

Example 7
Original:

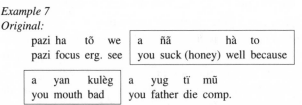

pazi	ha	tõ	we	a	ñã		hà	to
pazi	focus	erg.	see	you	suck (honey)		well	because

a	yan	kulèg	a	yug	tï	mũ
you	mouth	bad	you	father	die	comp.

"Pazi, it can be seen that you suck honey a lot and for that reason are toothless (have a bad mouth), and because of this your father died." [Or, "Pazi, it can be seen that your sucking honey a lot and for that reason your being toothless (having a bad mouth) is why your father died."]

Wãñpõ's Copy:

pazi	a	ñã	cul	ha	to
pazi	you	suck (honey)	like	<u>focus</u>	because

	a	yug	tẽ	tï	mũ
	you	father	<u>def.</u>	die	comp.

"Pazi, it is your liking to suck honey that has caused your father to die."

The segmentable materials are displayed in their analogous positions, a space in Wãñpõ's copy indicating where he has deleted material from the original. His insertions are indicated by a single underscore. The reader will notice that he has deleted one clause ("it can be seen that") and inserted two particles, the focus marker and a definite article.

The material shown in boxes in the original is transformed in Wãñpõ's copy into that shown inside the box there. His statement—"your liking to suck honey"—replaces the grammatically more complex formulation in the original, where there are two clauses that are barely intelligible to one not versed in the origin-myth style. Wãñpõ's version, however, is more or less equivalent in meaning to the original: "your sucking honey a lot and your being toothless (having a bad mouth) for that reason." Without going into the whole story from which this fragment is excerpted, I note that this passage has to do with how Pazi's voracious appetite led to his father's death as the latter sought to procure food for him.

The original itself seems less than fully grammatical, from the point of view of a native speaker's intuitions about the well-formedness of decontextualized clauses. This can be seen in Nãnmla's copy, which, as I have suggested, is much closer to the original. His principal addition is a conjunction, which gives the original a grammatical completeness that it seems otherwise to lack. The asterisks indicate what were apparently transcription errors on Nãnmla's part. In one instance, he transcribed the word *ñã* ("to suck when eating," used especially in connection with honey) as *ya* ("tooth"), which makes no sense, although his free translation includes the phrase "to suck (honey)," as if he had grasped the overall meaning even though he did not accurately represent this word. When the phrase appeared earlier in the narration, he heard it as *ñã*, as did Wãñpõ. The meaning of the phrase was evidently not patent to him, and he was struggling to comprehend the grammatical complexities of the discourse more generally. In the other instance (Example 8), it appears that he inadvertently wrote down the wrong vowel.

Example 8
Nānmla's Copy:

pazi	ha	tõ	we	a	ya*	hà	to
pazi	focus	erg.	see	you	tooth?	well	because

õ*	yan	kulèg	kū	a	yug	tï	mū
yes?	mouth	bad	conj.	you	father	die	comp.

"Pazi, it can be seen that you suck honey a lot and for that reason are toothless (have a bad mouth), and therefore your father died." [Or, "Pazi, it can be seen that your sucking honey a lot and for that reason being toothless (having a bad mouth) is the reason your father died."]

From the point of view of his own explicit metadiscourse, Wãñpõ does not regard the relationship between originator and original discourse as privileged, although he did acknowledge Nil's mastery of the traditional culture and grant that it was superior to his own. Unlike Nānmla, who hung on the authoritativeness of Nil's words, Wãñpõ saw the original as itself another copy. As such, it was not necessarily more definitive than other copies. Since Wãñpõ had heard and himself told this myth on numerous occasions, he had a sense that the discourse produced by Nil was a copy of other originals to which he had had equal access.

What is especially intriguing about the liberties Wãñpõ took with Nil's discourse is that there is a community-wide ideology or metadiscourse about the myth studied here. It is said that the myth should be told syllable by syllable, word by word, as mentioned earlier. This pertains to the actual ritualized style of telling it, which involves two speakers: one says the syllable, and the other repeats. But it is also true of the overall stretch of discourse, which should be handed down across the generations. Hence, the fact that Wãñpõ modified Nil's text so significantly is testimony to the importance for the replication process of the social relations between originator and copier and also anthropologist.

When Wãñpõ transforms the discourse through deletion and substitution, he is in effect responding to it, albeit not explicitly. He is not only copying it; he is using the original as a kind of cue or stimulus for telling his own story, producing his own original discourse. So the relationship between the copier and the copy (between Wãñpõ and his version) is different from that obtaining in Nānmla's case. Wãñpõ sees Nil's original instance as another copy not much better—if at all better—than his own. For elders, the various copies compete with one another for recognition as more true or faithful or authentic. In contrast, for a young man like Nānmla, the elder's original instance is an embodiment of tradition, in relationship to which his own copy must be an accurate replica.

The tendency for elders to respond to tellings of myths by other elders is relatively attenuated in Wãñpõ's case, since he did regard Nil as more knowledgeable. When other elders listened to the Nil tape, especially if they were from a different faction, they responded to it directly and often critically, claiming that certain parts were not "correct," and giving the "proper" version. In these situations they were not placed in the role of copier, since I had not asked them to repeat what Nil had said, nor had I asked them to comment on the tape or to criticize it. Their criticism is therefore evidence that in elder-to-elder relations a tendency exists for the discourse of another—in this case, traditional mythological discourse—to be responded to rather than replicated. This is summed up in the following proposition:

> *Proposition 3:* The more symmetrical and egalitarian the relationship between originator and copier (or the more authoritative the copier with respect to the person for whom the copy is being made), the greater will be the divergence between copy and original, and the more likely will it be for the copier to respond to the originator.

DOES SOME DISCOURSE MAKE FOR BETTER CULTURE?

It is a seeming paradox that asymmetrical social relations are conducive to discourse transmission and replication more readily than egalitarian or symmetrical ones, and yet many small-scale societies such as the P.I. Ibirama community, which are egalitarian at least insofar as the group of elders is concerned, are built upon a shared culture model. One might rather anticipate that an exchange model would dominate in such cases, which does seem to be true for the northern and western regions of Amerindian South America, but not for Central Brazil. One key to this seeming paradox is the type of discourse in question. Here I want to reformulate an old problem by means of the question, Why are myths good to share?

The framework I propose focuses attention on the original discourse and its relationship to the originator. In egalitarian relations between originator and copier, the copier tends to respond to the originator rather than simply to copy. That is what conduces towards a dialogical, exchange configuration within the egalitarian group. But a further variable is the nature of the original discourse itself. How does the original discourse, through its built-in metadiscursive signals, represent the relationship between originator and copier? I propose that the tendency to respond rather than replicate correlates with the degree to which the original discourse is viewed as a personal expression of the originator. Replication is more likely to occur where the original represents itself as detached from the originator, for example, as traditional knowledge or as a group rather than an individual product.

The data to support this are still meager, so you should take this proposition as especially tentative, but I am trying to point to an overall pattern, of which this seems to be a part. The data consist of observations about the conditions under which tape-recording was metadiscursively favored or frowned upon during the course of field research, and about the problems of elicitation. Regarding the former, I was always encouraged to record what were regarded as traditional discourse productions, including myth tellings, historical narrations, singing, ceremonial dialogues, and certain kinds of ritual wailing. I was not discouraged from recording everyday conversation, except that pertaining to politically sensitive issues. However, there was a general reluctance to transcribe the everyday, especially by those who participated in it. Interestingly, roundtable discussions involving several participants were easier to record and to transcribe. It seems, therefore, that the more an extended stretch of discourse was an individual product, and especially the more the individual had an emotional involvement in it, the less permissible it was for me to tape-record and transcribe it. Permissibility in this case can be seen as an index of replicability.

This might not prove true in other field situations, for example, where the relationship between anthropologist and community is problematized metadiscursively in terms of exploitation. In such instances, traditional discursive expressions are viewed as quasi-personal expressions—the patrimony of the group, which is to be kept from outsiders, not to be replicated and passed on beyond the boundaries of the group. Members of the P.I. Ibirama community, however, viewed my efforts at recording their traditional culture as generally positive. The recording was seen as a way to preserve and pass on the culture.

The key characteristic of the kinds of discourse that are regarded as recordable and also replicable is that the metadiscourse understands them to be traditional or group expressions, not intimately linked to the individual expresser. The nonrecordable/nonreplicable discourse, in contrast, is coded metadiscursively as an individual expression, a unique product or property of the producer.

Some evidence regarding the formal devices that indicate attachment can be gleaned from informant work on elicitation. Most of this, regrettably, is impressionistic, since careful records were not kept of the phenomenon under consideration. The data here come from the margins of research. Nevertheless, it is of interest that, while endeavoring to elicit sentences in the native language by means of Portuguese, some problems emerged with respect to deictics, especially those involving questions, as in Example 9:

Example 9
> GU: Como é que se diz: "Você quer comer?"
> How do you say: "Do you want to eat?"
>
> CONSULTANT: i   ẽñ ko ke tũ   tẽ
>   no I   eat fut. neg. imperf.
>   "No, I don't want to eat."

The consultant continued with the elicitation frame involving translation, but rather than translate the Portuguese question into a question in the native language, he responded to the question in the native language. I would not have regarded this as evidence of anything but confusion had it not occurred across consultants. Moreover, the problem never arose when elicited sentences were in the third person and declarative. It seems that sentences anchored in the present, especially those involving first- and second-person deictics and interrogative marking, call up the desire to respond more than do sentences involving third-person declarative constructions.

From this point of view, it is interesting that myths and historical narratives are so pervasively third person, declarative, and past. Where the first person appears, it is typically in the form a disclaimer (e.g., "my father told me this," "I don't know what this means, but . . . ," etc.). This is true as well for other recordable/replicable types of discourse, except ritual wailing. Where the "I" does appear elsewhere outside of quotation, it is a theatrical "I," not pointing to the speaker of the utterance as an individual, but rather marking a stereotypical individual or discursively invoked character.

In ritual wailing or lament, the true "I" is used, although there are no true "you's" pointing to actual interlocutors. Here it is important to note, however, that I was not encouraged to tape-record all instances of ritual wailing. The closer the instance was to actual grief, the less I was urged to record and transcribe it. Conversely, the more stereotyped the instance was, the more recordable and transcribable it became. Correspondingly, individual members of the P.I. Ibirama community did not regard it as appropriate to overtly copy the ritual lamentations of another. The similarities between instances were unacknowledged, resulting from implicit rather than metadiscursively explicit borrowing or copying. This is just the opposite of the case in myth telling, where the metadiscursively explicit purpose is to reproduce accurately the discourse of the elders. Laments were supposed to be, instead, individual creations and expressions, stereotyped and conventionalized as they may have been. These general observations are summarized in propositions 4a and 4b:

> *Proposition 4a*: The more the discourse is overtly coded as a unique instance, produced by its originator, and linked to a present context and circumstances, the less likely will the copier be to (want to) replicate it or metadiscursively to acknowledge the copy as a replication, and the more likely will the copier be to respond to it.

> *Proposition 4b*: The more discourse is overtly coded as nonpersonal,[3] that is, not as something generated by the originator but as transmitted by him or her, and the less it is linked to a present context and circumstances, the more likely will the copier be to replicate it; hence, the more shareable it is.

There is another technique that can be used to detach the original discourse from the originator, and consequently to make it more sharable. This involves making the production a group rather than an individual effort. The effect can be seen in many central Brazilian Amerindian societies in the myth-telling process itself. Among the Kalapalo (Basso 1985), myth-telling necessarily involves a "what-sayer," who continuously prompts the primary teller, and without whom the telling could not take place. As mentioned earlier, at P.I. Ibirama there is a ritualized telling of the origin myth that involves two speakers, one of whom utters a syllable and the second of whom echoes it. The telling is a cooperative venture, although here cooperation involves precise replication.

Similar processes can be seen as well in the political discussions of the Shavante as described by Graham (1993). There the relationship between individuals and their words is downplayed in group discussions, during which many individuals talk simultaneously. The words enter a kind of cauldron, where they mix and boil and fuse into a collective product, whose specific

---

3. The notion of nonpersonal coding is akin to Bauman's (1977, 1986) concept of "performance"—"a way of speaking, the essence of which resides in the assumption of responsibility to an audience for a display of communicative skill, highlighting the way in which communication is carried out, above and beyond its referential content" (1986:3). However, performance encompasses emergent, creative expressions, as well as traditional ones, leading us away from the problematic of entextualization and replication. The two converge in the area of traditional performance or reperformance.

authors have been forgotten. Having been stripped of their individual characteristics, they can be shared and circulated throughout the community.[4]

Discourse that is directly attached to an individual producer can be replicated—or so we would predict from the discussion so far—but this is more
likely to be the case in asymmetrical social relations than in symmetrical ones.
In the P.I. Ibirama and other egalitarian Amerindian societies of central Brazil,
such asymmetry is lodged principally in age-graded relations.

WHERE IS THE POWER IN REPLICATION?

At first blush, the power in replication seems to reside with the copier. After
all, once originators have produced their initial discourse instances, there
seems to be nothing they can do to control the replication process. Furthermore, we know from the earlier examples that copiers do indeed change the
original in replicating it—from Nãnmla's modest grammaticalizing additions
to Wãñpõ's major deletions and transformations. Because of temporal anteced-
ence—the original preceding the copy—the actual work of replication is done
by the copier, who apparently controls the replication process.

It is not quite that simple, however, for others have a stake in the replication as well. In general we are dealing with a copy made for public inspec-
tion, appreciation, or approval. In the native transcription investigated here, the
other is, minimally, the anthropologist, who must approve of the replication if
the process is to continue. Even in the case of naturally occurring replication,
we find evidence of external control over the replication. In the ceremonial
origin myth-telling style at P.I. Ibirama described earlier, where each syllable
uttered by the originator must be precisely echoed by the copier, any "errors"
in the replication process can be detected by the originator or members of the
audience. These latter can cause the replication to cease. Similarly, in narrations of individual myths, audiences can criticize and alter and even stop the
narration, which is, of course, itself a replica of some earlier narration, if they
feel that it is not taking place as it should. Replication, in other words, while
open to manipulation by copiers, is also subject to control by others, including
the originator. The question concerns how far the copier can go in effecting
changes. When will the editorial work draw criticism for its modifications?

Control over the replication by persons other than the copier is based on
metadiscourse about the copying process. Anyone who contributes metadis-

4. It is unclear how these kinds of collective productions fit into the classification of cooperative illocutionary acts provided by Hancher (1979), building on Searle (1969, 1976).

course about an instance of replication participates in control over the replication process. That metadiscourse is a kind of response to the copy as discourse, and, similarly, the metadiscourse is also itself public, susceptible to criticism as it circulates (by means of replication) in the community. The important point here, however, is that insofar as replication evokes a metadiscursive response, it involves dialogicality. In other words, replication depends on response. It becomes monological only when and insofar as the metadiscourse pertaining to it is also monological, that is, when that metadiscourse is replicated throughout the community that oversees the replication of the object discourse. The processes of replication of object discourses thus depend on the processes of replication of metadiscourses.

It is not only the copier and those overseeing the copying process who have control over replication, however. As I have tried to show, the originator can build entextualizing cues into the original—metadiscursive instructions about how the replication is to take place, about what counts as "text." These are powerful tools because they allow originators editorial control over future replications. The beauty of them is that copiers seem to follow the instructions regardless of the power differentials between them and the originators. While, in general, replication proceeds most perfectly when the relationship between originator and copier is asymmetrical, the originator can control the copying process through entextualization cues even when the copier is equal in status to the originator. The built-in metadiscourse apparently is not seen as part of the discourse and hence not as something that needs responding to. It slips by at face value.

I have argued that at the micro-level, originator, copier, and others exert influence over the replication process, although the scope of that influence remains to be established. However, it is important to recognize that control is also lodged in the form of the discourse itself. Some kinds of discourse make for better culture than others. Discourse presenting itself through deictics and other devices as closely bound to the originator and to the local context of origination tends to be responded to rather than replicated. Hence, it serves less well as culture in the classical sense. In contrast, discourse marking itself as detached from the local is correspondingly more replicable and is therefore better culture. This may help to explain why in so many societies myths are essential culture, a distilled type that presents itself as decontextualized or polycontextual, not serving the local interests of any of the participants in the replication process and hence being more readily replicated by all. Myths facilitate transduction by reducing the number of changes in form that must be made to relocate the discourse from one context to another.

What would it take to nudge relatively egalitarian relations in the direction of asymmetrical power? Judging from the preceding, we would have to see a transformation in the metadiscursive understanding of the replication process. The accepted, circulating understanding would have to construe some individuals as originators—for example, bearers of the ancient traditions—and others as copiers, with replication becoming essentially unidirectional. This would be an incremental change, to be sure, given that some elders, such as Nil, already assume the role of *primus inter pares,* but it would be an ultimately radical one, redefining the sociopolitical structure. We could imagine such a radical transformation occurring gradually through micromanipulations on the scale described here. Similar incremental changes could take place in the metadiscursive coding of the original-originator relationship, the original being construed as more closely bound up with its originator. Presumably, however, for the latter to occur, a metadiscursive conception of asymmetrical replication would already have to be in place.

In any case, these are the kinds of questions raised by a microdiscursive approach to replication, as one manifestation of entextualization. The problematic of power from this point of view is squarely centered on the metadiscourse-discourse relationship. The following chapter by Haviland raises additional questions, especially regarding the transcription of originally dialogical discourse. It asks in effect, Is dialogical discourse monologically replicable?

REFERENCES

Basso, Ellen
    1985   *A Musical View of the Universe: Kalapalo Myth and Ritual Performances.* Philadelphia: University of Pennsylvania Press.

Bauman, Richard
    1977   *Verbal Art as Performance.* Rowley, MA: Newbury House Publishers.
    1986   *Story, Performance, and Event: Contextual Studies of Oral Narrative.* Cambridge: Cambridge University Press.

Goffman, Erving
    1981   *Forms of Talk.* Philadelphia: University of Pennsylvania Press.

Graham, Laura
    1993   A public sphere in Amazonia? The de-personalized collaborative construction of discourse in Xavante. *American Ethnologist* 20(4): 717–741.

Hancher, Michael
    1979   The classification of cooperative illocutionary acts. *Language in Society* 8: 1–14.

Ochs, Elinor
    1979   Transcription as theory. In *Developmental Pragmatics*, E. Ochs and B. B. Schieffelin (eds.), 43–72. New York: Academic Press.

Searle, John R.
  1969 *Speech Acts: An Essay in the Philosophy of Language.* Cambridge: Cambridge University Press.
  1976 A classification of illocutionary acts. *Language in Society* 5: 1–23.
Urban, Greg
  1985 Ergativity and accusativity in Shokleng. *International Journal of American Linguistics* 51(2): 164–187.
  1991 *A Discourse-Centered Approach to Culture: Native South American Myths and Rituals.* Austin: University of Texas Press.
Voloshinov, V. N.
  1973 *Marxism and the Philosophy of Language.* L. Matejka and I. R. Titunik (trans.). New York: Seminar Press.

2   Text from Talk in Tzotzil

John B. Haviland

Tzotzil Literacy

There is a growing literature on the nature of written language and its relation to spoken forms.[1] Part of the interest of this relationship derives from the conviction of many authors that the canons of writing and written style exert a powerful influence at least on people's conceptions of language, if not on their overt linguistic practices. The relation of spoken to written language is thus of compelling linguistic interest. More widely, for scholars such as Goody (1977), writing as an institution—as a "technology of the intellect"—transforms the cognitive possibilities of social beings, with profound effects on the resulting social forms. More locally, the habits and standards of literacy are often taken to be the measure against which people's intellectual achievements or capacities are measured: here the canons of writing, instilled through education, become normative instruments of power—the power to define what counts not merely as "correct," but also as "sensible," "logical," "coherent," or even, simply, "tellable." In this sense, a theory of written language becomes a potent instrument of social policy and political maneuver.

If we are to assess the theories that underlie such instruments, we need to understand what the canons of writing are, and where they come from. Here one ought to go beyond the literary traditions of the West, although little work has so far been done with naive or spontaneous writers, whose written productions emerge free from imposed standards, free from preexisting literary institutions.[2]

For their comments on earlier drafts, I would like to thank Don Brenneis, Shirley Heath, Charles Ferguson, Judith Langer, Lourdes de León, and John Rickford in addition to the editors of this volume. An early version of this chapter was presented at the Stanford University School of Education, Feb. 12, 1986.

1. See Goody and Watt (1963), Chafe (1982), and Chafe and Danielewicz (1985).

2. Marianne Mithun (1985) examines Mohawk speakers' written narratives, showing how important features—syntactic, lexical, and pragmatic—of spoken Mohawk are first reversed when

When naive writers, newly literate and familiar with few canons of textual form or content, produce written versions of originally spoken material, how do they go about it? In recent years, a few Tzotzil speakers from the highlands of Chiapas, Mexico, have begun to write. Some of these writers began their careers as bilingual teachers, *promotores culturales* (cultural promoters) for government agencies, or as "informants" for anthropologists or linguists; their incentive was, in the first instance, the standard *pesos*-per-page salary that they could thereby command. Many Tzotzil writers have begun to produce stories, books, or pamphlets, modeled on similar products familiar elsewhere in Mexican society.[3] Recently there have appeared Tzotzil plays, organized around written scripts; and intrepid Tzotzil travelers have begun to compose letters, telegrams, and even faxes in their native tongue.[4]

A few Tzotziles have also tried explicitly to render into written form material which starts its life as *speech*: texts from talk. Writing dramatic dialogue, transcribing a curer's prayer in an ethnography, or inscribing a customary spoken greeting on a facsimile note all require just such a rendering. A dual process is involved: first detaching the speech from its indexical surround, its natural home; and second repackaging the written words in an appropriate textual form.

I will discuss two special sorts of such entextualized speech, one produced by a Tzotzil writer from a tape-recorded multiparty gossip session, and the other the conjoint product of a group of Indian literacy trainees who transcribed a staged conversation as part of a literacy workshop. In neither case were external

writers literate in English begin to produce texts in Mohawk. Later, as writers polish their styles and mature in the craft of writing, such features begin to reappear although in a new form appropriate to the virtues of a written medium. Robert M. Laughlin (in press) considers the relations of style and voicing that obtain between a spoken Tzotzil autobiographical narrative and its written rendition by a trained Tzotzil writer. He discovers many of the same register changes I mention here and characterizes the style of the written text as "less personal" than that of the original spoken narrative.

3. See, for example, Arias (1990), or Pérez López (1990); also, the growing production of *Sna Jtz'ibajom*, a Tzotzil/Tzeltal writers cooperative, founded by Robert M. Laughlin. In his bilingual Tzotzil/Spanish monograph about the history and customs of the municipality of San Pedro Chenalhó, Arias makes a single concession to marked oral forms: his conclusion is framed in the eloquent poetic parallelism of traditional ritual speech (see Haviland 1987b).

4. Although fuller study would take us well beyond the bounds of this paper, it is worth observing how the normal etiquette of spoken greeting is both preserved and transformed in, for example, a fax sent to his family at home by a twenty-two-year-old Zinacantec visiting in the United States in September 1993. The literal question syntax of standard greetings—*mi li'ote* 'Are you here?'; *mi ja' to yechoxuk* 'Are you still well?'—survives unscathed in this medium which traverses from "here" to "there" and which allows only an oblique and delayed reply.

standards for the written renditions explicitly applied, nor were the writers familiar with a preestablished literary tradition, Spanish or otherwise.

From these texts there emerge the following apparent native criteria for written renditions of speech:

1. Normalizing—imposing a standard or normal form on—pragmatic features of the original speech context, especially the organization of its participants and relations between author and audience
2. Smoothing the turn structure and other interactional features in the newly fabricated textual context
3. Eliminating processing difficulties: production, reception, and grammatical hitches in the original speech
4. Searching for a register appropriate to the text
5. Perhaps least surprising, adjusting the referential focus of the emerging narrative.

I present exhibits based on this material to display the process by which speakers "reduce" their spoken words to writing: the natural history of entextualization. Parallel, and potentially embarrassing, morals about our own anthropological practices of entextualization or "decentering," faintly disguised by my own naive talk of "transcription," [5] should be easy to draw.

FROM THE SPOKEN WORD TO THE WRITTEN TEXT: TWO EXAMPLES

In 1970 and 1971 I amassed a corpus of multiparty conversation from tape-recorded sessions in which groups of Zinacantec men gathered together with explicit instructions to gossip about their fellows. In some cases the gossipers were hamlet neighbors of the gossipees (who were always absent, at least from the sessions in which they were being talked about). In other cases they were from other hamlets and might have been acquainted with the gossip targets only by reputation if at all. The resulting sessions were lively, ribald, and highly entertaining for all of us who participated.[6]

I used several methods for transcribing the tapes. Some I did myself, inventing as I went along *ad hoc* standards for representing multiple participants, back-channels (Yngve 1970), and so forth. Others I wrote down with the aid of one of the Zinacantec gossipers, who helped me puzzle out difficult bits of Tzotzil. Transcripts were also produced by a third method. Another of the gossipers was Little Romin, a trained Harvard Chiapas Project informant who was

---

5. See Ochs (1979).
6. See Haviland (1977) for some results of this exercise.

comfortable writing Tzotzil. After showing him a few of the sample transcripts I had produced, I gave him his own tape recorder and some of the tapes and asked him to write down selected parts by himself. As I had done in my own transcripts, Little Romin kept track of individual participants. I further badgered him into writing down what at first seemed to him inessential repetition. Little Romin had to construct for himself some notion of (more or less) faithful or accurate rendering into writing of what he heard on tape, although he evidently also felt the pull of narrative coherence as he wrote.

Armed with a different standard of the detail appropriate to conversational transcripts,[7] I have recently retranscribed some of the passages that Little Romin wrote on his own. The present study analyzes fragments from one of these gossip sessions, matched pairs of the two written renditions: my transcription of what I hear on the tape, and the version Little Romin decided to write down. The excerpt in question comes from one of the most hilarious sessions of all, which crippled the original participants with riotous, convulsive laughter long into a rainy Chiapas afternoon.

The original impetus for this study, though, came from a subsequent experience in Chiapas. As part of a Tzotzil literacy workshop, conducted together with Lourdes de León,[8] I recorded a short conversation between two Tzotzil speakers from different *municipios* (townships) in Highland Chiapas. Both were *alfabetizadores*, adult literacy teacher-trainees, with basic but minimal Spanish literacy skills, who were learning for the first time to read and write in their native language. For the most part these Indians had never seen a written text in Tzotzil, nor had they considered the possibility of such an object.

I transcribed the recorded conversation according to my own standards and presented a written version of the transcript to the group for their comments, reactions, and revisions. Somewhat to my surprise, they evinced spontaneous criteria both for correcting, and subsequently for altering my original transcript. That is, they quickly understood that I had tried to get down on paper exactly what had been said, and by whom. Yet they showed no hesitation in pronouncing some parts of the resulting transcript inappropriate for a written text, prompting them to edit it in various ways.

The main empirical moral I should like to extract from these serendipitous materials is this: These speakers, whose experience with reading and writing in any language (let alone their own) is next to nil, nonetheless by their

---

7. See Atkinson and Heritage (1984: ix–xvi) for a recent incarnation of the standard; such a tradition did not exist in 1970 in the public domain.

8. The workshop, in San Cristóbal de las Casas in October, 1985, was sponsored by the Instituto Nacional de Educación para los Adultos (see Haviland and de León 1985).

practice are able implicitly to indicate *what a text should be like*. Of what does their textual *canon* consist? Where does it come from?

ABOUT THE TRANSCRIPTS

First let me explain the Tzotzil materials, excerpted in what follows. There are two "complete texts" involved. The first is based on the staged workshop conversation about the day when the volcano *El Chichonal* erupted, at Easter 1982, snuffing out the sun and blanketing the entire Tzotzil area with a thick layer of volcanic ash. The emerging tale is one of fear and confusion, thoughts of the end of the world and mythological disaster, and frantic attempts by Indians to return to their villages to die in their own land.

The second text is extracted from a gossip free-for-all about the exploits of a licentious old woman and one Proylan, her former lover, with whom she had carried on a celebrated affair involving cornfield trysts and mischievous spying schoolchildren with slingshots.

Fragments from both conversations appear with my glossed transcription in one version and, in corresponding lines, the edited (native) rendition—resulting either from a collaborative editing session on the part of the literacy trainees, or from a single naive Tzotzil writer's understanding of the task of transcription—in the other. Forms in **boldface** have been altered or eliminated in the native rendition. The text from which cited lines are drawn can be identified by the names "Volcano" for the Chichonal story, "Lovers" for the gossip session, and when necessary by a suffixed number: 1 denotes my detailed transcript, and 2 denotes the edited written version. Thus, for example, Lovers2 refers to the anthropological informant Little Romin's rendition of the Proylan gossip session, while Volcano1 is my putative transcript of the literacy workshop conversation.

NAIVE WRITERS' WRITTEN RENDERINGS OF SPOKEN TZOTZIL

It seems clear that the surgery performed on the original conversational materials in order to produce a native written text falls into discrete categories. Let me consider several varieties.

PRAGMATIC NORMALIZATION

The most obvious difference between the conversation and the resulting textual sediment is the nature of the context in which each exists: the world, both social and material, within which it lives its pragmatic life. In the conversational world, there are participants whose very faces, let alone voices, are present and salient. There are purposes, personalities, and power. There is also a breathless, almost competitive, creativity about the conversational moment: speakers vie with each other for the floor, the word, and the moral, pushing topics in edge-wise and interlocutors aside. In the written text, all of these features are pecu-liarly bleached, or, as I have put it, *normalized*.

Consider such pragmatically active words as nonreferential indices. The quotative particle *la*, for example, accompanies declarative sentences in Tzotzil to mark them as hearsay: not directly attested by the speaker.[9] The particle is, for example, particularly appropriate to myths.[10] The indexicality of such a word is particularly obvious when it appears in an interrogative sentence, as in line 4 of the volcano conversation:[11]

Volcano1
4 a;   mi li'-oxuk   'ox **la**   k'alal i-yal   tan-e
       Q here-2Apl CL LA when CP-descend ash-CL

Were you here when the ashes fell *la*?

The quotative effect here must be understood to fall on the illocutionary force of the utterance, rather than on its propositional content. The quotative

9. Michael Silverstein, in conversation, suggests the following formulation: the particle *la* and its functional relatives in other languages, which mark a proposition (appropriately modalized) as originating with or vouched for by someone other than the speaker, create a new *frame*, "a perspective that projects the illocutionary relation between some [implicated] *other(s)* and the addressee of the actual message." See also Irvine (this volume), Hanks (this volume), and Havi-land (1987a, 1991). Since the actual speaker may or may not be included in the purview of this implicated other, *la* can also have a softening force (in commands, for instance).

10. See Laughlin (1977:94), who describes a venerable Zinacantec storyteller as follows: "Quite deliberately he neglected to add the particle *la* which indicates that the story was only hearsay, for he wants you to know that he was there at the time of the creation."

11. Tzotzil is written here in a Spanish-based practical orthography, in which C' represents a glottalized consonant, and ' represents a glottal stop. Letters have by and large the pronunciation of the corresponding letter in Mexican Spanish; most notably, *x* stands for a voiceless palatal fricative, *j* for a voiceless glottal fricative, *ch* for a voiceless palatal affricate. In morpheme-by-morpheme glosses, the following abbreviations appear: ! = assertive predicate; 1 = numeral one, or first person; 1PL = first-person plural suffix; 1PX = first person plural exclusive; 2 = second person; 3 = third person; A = absolutive; E = ergative; ART = article; ASP = neutral aspect marker; ASP+3E = aspect marker plus third ergative portmanteau; BEN = benefactive or ditran-sitive suffix; CL = clitic; CONJ = conjunction; CP = completive aspect; DESID = desiderative clitic; ICP = incomplete aspect; ICP+3E = incomplete plus third-person ergative portmanteau; IRREAL = irrealis suffix; NEG = negative particle; P = Proylan (a name); PF = perfect aspect suffix; PL = plural suffix; PREP = preposition; Q = interrogative particle; REL = relational clitic; SC = San Cristóbal (place name).

particle must be understood, that is, to point implicitly to a questioner other than the speaker himself.

> Were you here when the ashes fell? (X [that is, someone else] wants to know; or X asked me to ask you.)

The actual speaker is, as it were, merely quoting or relaying another's question.

Notably, the first change that the Tzotzil writers wanted to make in my literacy workshop transcript was to eliminate this *la* from their written text. Said the speaker himself: "It doesn't *do* anything." Yet all were agreed that the *la* was on the tape, and that it was not *chopol* (bad, or ungrammatical). What is wrong with the particle in the written text is that it points inexorably to another shadowy conversational presence who, in the rest of the text, is to remain invisible: to the person who asked the original question about the day the ashes fell, namely, to me myself, trying to launch the conversation. The micropolitics of the conversational moment, in which the anthropologist-teacher *directs* Tzotzil literacy students to converse, do not emerge in the orthogonal textual representation of the conversation,[12] which is thus normalized to a different, idealized, dialogic format in which only the speaking interlocutors are directly represented.

Generally, in transcribing the gossip session, the Tzotzil writer leaves the quotative *la* intact, preserving the depicted speakers' evidential integrity. Interestingly, Little Romin rewrites the remarks of one of the gossipers, at line 219 of the Proylan story. My transcription has CA saying,

Lovers1

219 ca; y-ich'   **la** uli'   li s-bek' y-a-te   xi-ik i-k-a'i
    3E-receive LA slingshot ART 3E-seed 3E-penis-CL say-PL CP-1E-hear

He got shot *la* in the balls with a slingshot, they say, I have heard.

The native writer introduces a further evidential remove in his more colorful rephrasing:

12. Notice that the particle *la* does survive at other points in the volcano text, for example at Volcano: 99. Here X is talking about his mother and her companions, from whom he was separated at the moment of the eruption.

    Volcano2:
        toj   i-xi'-ik   **la**   ta   j-'ech'el
        much COM-be_afraid-PL **QUOT** PREP 1-time
        they got terribly frightened right away (la = so they say).
    The report (presumably theirs) of their fright falls within the ambit of both participants and emplotted protagonists who survive as characters in the textual narrative of Volcano2.

Lovers2
219 ca; kabron pero k'u   t-s-sa'   ti   buy   x-jipjon   s-bek'
          damn   but   what ICP-3E-seek CONJ where ASP-swinging 3E-seed
          y-at-e   xi-ik **la** un
          3E-penis-CL say-PL LA CL

> Damn, but what is he up to flinging his balls about like that, they said *la*.

In the original line, the *la* records the fact, also represented explicitly by
the framing verbs *xiik* 'they said' and *ika'i* 'I have heard', that the speaker is
reporting what someone else has said about what happened: that the miscreant
lover was shot in the testicles with a slingshot. In the embellished text, the
speaker puts alleged words directly into the mouths of the little children who
watched the lovers in the cornfield, and the *la* now suggests, "This is what they
are *said* to have said (as they watched)."

At Lovers: 190, another *la* is lost in the native writer's normalization of
the conversation. Judging from my own transcript of the sequence, the particle
was interactionally the prelude to a joking invitation to another interlocutor to
elaborate on the tale. R is telling about the mischievous students who went out
to recess—*la*, 'it is said'—and later discovered the lovers in the cornfield. R
goes on to suggest that M, another man present in the gossip session, was himself one of those schoolchildren.

Lovers1
190 r; k'alal ta   x-lok'-ik   ta   rekreo li   jchanvun-etik **la**   une
          when ICP ASP-exit-PL PREP recess ART student-PL   LA CL

> when the school kids went out for recess *la*. . .
> . . .

192   x-chan-oj   nan   vun j-chi'il-tik   li'   une je je
          3E-study-PF perhaps paper 1E-companion-1PL   here CL

> Perhaps our companion here was in school then himself.

This *la* appears both to introduce a joking insinuation (that M was one of the
slingshot-wielders) and indirectly to invite M either to take up the story, or at
least to defend himself from the charge. M in fact proceeds to do just that,
starting off with a little laugh.

193 m; je
194   k'u   cha'al jchanvun-on
            what way   student-1A

> How could I have been a student?

By contrast, in the Tzotzil transcriber's version of the sequence, this little interactive scuffle, signaled by the evidential, is represented as an orderly exchange of narrative turns. M is no longer represented as defending himself but simply as continuing the story in a joking vein.

Lovers2

190 r; k'alal ta   x-lok'-ik   ta   rekreo li   jchanvun-etik une
        when ICP ASP-exit-PL PREP recess ART student-PL   CL

   when the school kids get out for recess.

191   ja'o nan   k'alal x-chan-oj   vun li   j-chi'il-tik   le'   une
       just perhaps when 3E-learn-PF paper ART 1E-companion-1PL there CL

   Perhaps it was when our companion there was still in school?

196 m; je   juta   yu'-me   ja' s-k'el-oj   i-y-ak'-be-ik   un
        what whore because-DESID ! 3E-watch-PF CP-3E-give-BEN-PL CL
             taj-e
             that-CL

   Damn, THAT one was the one who watched them doing it!

The textual rendition simply carries the story forward without the negotiated multiple dialogues and interactional asides that characterized the gossip itself.

Other Evidential Particles and Discursive Coherence

Tzotzil makes frequent use of further evidential particles, two of which also play important roles in sequencing turns in conversation. Both orient the propositional content of an utterance to the preceding utterances, commenting in one way or another on a presumed body of information shared between interlocutors, often called "common ground" (Clark 1992). The two particles are *yu'van* and *a'a*, both usually translated "indeed." Neither particle can easily be attached to a sentence in isolation, however, because both imply in relation to the current utterance an evidential commentary on a (real or presupposable) preceding utterance.

Thus, *yu'van*, in utterance final position, suggests, "of course, indeed, what I am now saying is true, and you should have known it (despite the fact that you appear to have forgotten it or to be ignoring it, perhaps deliberately)." [13] Since *yu'van* is tied to a prior utterance, when a written text irons out

13. A more perspicacious and motivated analysis of this and the other particles mentioned is necessary here. See Haviland (1987a) and Haviland (1989) for some alleged improvements. Silverstein (personal communication) points out the similarity to English utterance-initial unstressed "of course." Etymologically, this particle derives from *y-u'* (3E-cause, i.e., 'because') and *van* 'perhaps' (only in interrogative contexts); thus 'is it perhaps because [of that]?'

the content of an argument or position, negotiated over several conversational turns, and collapses it onto a single, unitary, synthetic turn, the particle itself has to go. This happens to CN's overlapped remarks, at lines Lovers1: 270–271, where he is arguing that the identity of the slingshot-shooting miscreant must have become public knowledge, since even he, a man from another hamlet, had heard the gossip.

Lovers1

270 cn; an   pero te   (i-vinaj)   ta   tz'akal un **yu'van**
          why but   there CP-appear PREP later   CL YU'VAN

Well, in that case it did come out later *after all.*

271   k'u ti   i-vinaj   to t-s-lo'ilta-ik   to i-k-a'i   taj un
       what CONJ CP-appear still PREP-3E-gossip-PL still CP-1E-hear that CL

since it came out later, they gossiped about her later and I heard about that.

But what starts out as an oppositional or contrastive maneuver in the gossip session becomes, in the native writer's rendition, simply a confirmatory remark, in the midst of seeming general agreement. Thus the particle *yu'van* disappears.

Lovers2

270 cn; an   pero y-u'un   i-vinaj   to un k'u ti   i-s-lo'ilta-ik   to
          why but   3E-cause CP-appear still CL what CONJ CP-3E-gossip-PL still
          i-k-a'i   taj un
          CP-1E-hear that CL

Why then it must have come out, if they gossiped about it and I heard that.

Sentence final *a'a* means "it's obvious," or "I already knew that." It suggests the speaker's knowing agreement with an immediately prior utterance; thus, where that utterance is absent in an edited text, the particle itself loses its place.

Moreover, when a conversation follows various currents at the same time, it may be necessary for a speaker to design a single utterance so as both to make his own point and to react to another's prior or current turn simultaneously, thus changing horses in conversational midstream. Such unhorsing seems to occur, for example, at Lovers1:173. M remarks that Proylan went into his cornfield in the first place on a mission to guard his young crop against marauding dogs. However, M's speech is almost totally overlapped; he adds *a'a* apparently in agreement with what has just overlapped him (that Proylan had his love trysts in the corn field):

Lovers1

169 r;   pero ta   y-ut   chobtik   une
          but   PREP 3E-inside cornfields CL

          But in the midst of the cornfields.

                        [
170 cn;   (. . . nab ti   y-al-oj   une)
                        lake CONJ 3E-say-PF CL

                        (the lake, they must have thought.)

171 r;   ta   y-ut   chobtik   la a'a
          PREP 3E-inside cornfields LA A'A

          Yes, they say right among the corn plants.

          [
172 m; k'el-tz'i'   y-ilel   ch-bat taj
        watch-dog 3E-seeing ICP-go that

        It looked as though that (guy) was going to check for dogs

173   taj mol Proylan nan   **a'a**
        that old   Proylan perhaps A'A

        old Proylan was—*yeah*—

        [   ]
174 r; li Proylan-e   che'e j-na'-tik   mi ta   x-ba   s-k'el
        ART Proylan-CL then   1E-know-1PL Q ICP ASP-go 3E-watch
              x-chob   ta   ti'   nab
              3E-cornfield PREP   mouth lake

        Who knows if P was going to look over his cornfield at the edge of the lake.

In Little Romin's written version, however, both of the first two lines are attributed to M, who now need only agree with the previous suggestion that something happened in the cornfield (hence an *a'a* is preserved in Lovers2: 169), and whose talk is no longer bothered by overlapping interlocutors in the edited written text.

Lovers2

169 m; in the cornfields **la a'a**
            he went to check for dogs, Proylan did
171 r; old Proylan went to look at his cornfield . . .

Another evidential particle, *nan* 'perhaps,' suggests propositional uncertainty and can thus be a device for conveying interactional (perhaps even moral) effect, functioning as an element in a conversational stratagem. Insofar as the textual rendering of a conversational moment may represent a rearrangement of the interactional balance between conversants, or a manipulation of their moral stances, it may be useful to adjust such a marker of doubt in a written text.

Whereas, in the rapid flow of conversation, speakers must continually monitor each other's turns, so that they know what will count—in the moment—as agreement or disagreement, the linear world of the text seems to smooth out such interactional details. Consider the complex exchange, at Lovers1: 323–331, where the gossip session is at a point of transition: having described the old lady's misadventures with young Proylan, the group moves on to consider whether she has engaged in any other improprieties. Two participants, R and CA, seem gradually, and simultaneously, to remember the same story, and their fragmentary turns each prompt the other to continue. As her new sin emerges (sleeping with the people who used to take her home, drunk, after she performed a curing ceremony), the two speakers are in an intricate dance of doubt, agreement, and confirmation, marked by evidential particles that track the state of discursive play at each moment.

Lovers1
322 ca; mi s-pas proval li   mas krem yan li   j-ch'il-tik
       Q 3E-do attempt ART more boy other ART 1E-companion-1PL

    Has she tried any more of our youngsters, our countrymen?

                              [
323 r;   an   ja' mu   j-na'
                              why ! NEG 1E-know

                              Why, I just don't know.

324   an o   **la** i-s-
       why exist LA CP-3E-

    Why, she [did] (*I've heard say*)—

R remembers having heard (see the particle *la* at 324) that the old lady had also been in trouble on another occasion. But before he manages to say where and when, CA suggests (with a hedging *nan* 'perhaps') that it involved occasions when she was being taken home:

325 ca; pero ja' nan   ta   y-ak'el-e
        but ! NAN PREP 3E-giving-CL

    But *perhaps* that was when she was being taken . . .

        [

326 r;   ch-ich'   intyeksyon k'alal
               ICP+3E-receive injections   when

               She got injections when . . .

R continues, over the interruption of CA, who suggests that the old woman's misbehavior took place *ta yak'el* 'when she was being taken (home).' R takes up CA's phrase in line 327,[14] and adds the clarification that she was being escorted home after having performed a curing ceremony. R's final *a'a* at 328 apparently signals his agreement with CA about the circumstances.

327   li   y-ak'el   k'alal x-
       ART 3E-giving when ASP-

       she was being taken [home] after . . .

328   ch-'ilolaj a'a
       ICP-cure A'A

       . . . she has cured, indeed.

       [
329 ca; ja' k-a'y-oj   **a'a**
     !   1E-hear-PF A'A

       Yes, I've heard that.

330   k'alal tz-sut   tal   ta   s-na   li   jchamel ya'el
       when ICP-return coming PREP 3E-house ART patient it_seems

       When she comes back from the house of the patient, it seems.

331   chbat   ta   ilole
       ICP-go PREP curing

       When she has gone to cure.

Simultaneously, at line 329, CA agrees with R (also using the particle *a'a*), saying that he has also heard this story and that it had to do with the old lady's misbehavior after curing ceremonies.

In the written version, this elaborate interactive exchange is smoothed out and regularized, and the surviving evidentials are adjusted to suggest a more orderly, linear, emerging story line, contributions to which are made by each participant in turn, reflecting definite states of knowledge at each point.

14. He accommodates his already enunciated but cut-off ergative prefix (*s-* at the end of line 324) to the new verb root *'ich'* with which he overlaps CA in the continuing line 326.

Lovers2

322-3m; pero o   la   x-ich'   indeksion[15] ta   yan   o   un
        but exist LA ASP+3E-receive injection   prep other REL CL

But they say she has gotten injections from others.

325 ca; ja' taj y-ak'el-e
         !   that 3E-giving-CL

That's when they take her [home].

327-8r; ja' taj y-ak'el   k'al ta   x-'ilolaj   **a'a**
         !   that 3E-giving when ICP ASP-cure   A'A

Yes, that's when they take her home after she cures.

329 ca; ja' k-a'y-oj   **a'a**
         !   1E-hear-PF   A'A

Yes, I've heard about that.

330   k'al sut(t)al   ta   s-na   li   jchamel ya'el-e
         when return-coming PREP 3E-house ART patient it_seems-CL

When she comes back from the house of the patient, it seems.

331   bu   ch-bat ta   ilol-e
         when ICP-go PREP curing-CL

When she has gone to cure.

The first suggestion about the story (and the evidential hedge represented by *la*) is now put in the mouth of another speaker, M, at lines 322–3. The rest of the story emerges in a sequence of orderly exchanges between R and CA, with each turn echoing agreement (marked by *a'a*) with its predecessor. What starts out as disorderly multiple-party conversation in Lovers1 emerges as shared or dialogically animated narrative monologue in Lovers2.

THE IMPOSITION OF A STANDARDIZED OR IDEALIZED SPEECH CONTEXT

It was clear to the Tzotzil writers that a written rendition, unlike the spoken conversation from which it derives, has been ripped from its physical setting. The immediate context of speech—the physical as well as the social environment—must recede in prominence.

For example, the writers elected to omit a deictic reference, at Volcano1: 41, since no Chiapas sun warms the written text.

---

15. Little Romin, the Tzotzil transcriber, has here rendered the Tzotzil pronunciation of the Spanish loanword *inyección* differently from my own hearing at Lovers1:326 above.

Volcano1

37 a; bweno k'u x-'elan k'al i-k'ot   une
      well   what ASP-be when CP-arrive CL

   Good, so what was it like when [the ash] began to fall?

38   mi 'ora i-'ik'ub   ta   j-mek k'u x-'elan?
      Q now CP-darken PREP 1-time what ASP-be

   Did it get dark right away, or what?

39 x; k'unk'un ik'ub
      slow   darken

   It got dark slowly.

40 s; ko'ol chk tok
      equal like cloud

   Just like fog (or clouds).

41 x; jech nox chk k'u   cha'al este .. **li'** x-k-al-tik-e
      thus just like what way   uh   here ASP-1E-say-1PL-CL

   It was just like .. uh .. *now*, as it were.

42   sak   to   'ox **a'a**
      white still then A'A

   Yes it was still light then.

This passage is simplified as follows:

Volcano2

38   mi 'ora i'ik'ub tajmek, k'u x'elan?

   Did it get dark right away, or what?

39 x; k'unk'un ik'ub.

   It got dark slowly.

40 s; ko'ol chk tok.

   Just like fog (or clouds).

42 x; sak to'ox.

   It was still light then.

Notice that just as the inappropriate—because unrecoverable?—deictic reference (*li'* 'here, now') of line 41 is eliminated, the evidential *a'a* in the next line must also be pruned, as there is nothing left in the previous turn with which it can signal agreement.

   The idealized context of speech has a social dimension as well. I have suggested that these naive writers began with no established canon of written text for Tzotzil. Of course, they were not without canons of discursive form. Indeed, a central point of interest in this (more or less natural) evolution of a written genre is its indebtedness to existing standards for speech. A prominent feature of much Tzotzil talk is its convergence on a *dialogic* format. Even when there are multiple conversationalists, speech tends towards an ideal *dyad*, with one central speaker, and one designated interlocutor, or *jtak'vanej* 'answerer'. (See Haviland 1988, 1990; Goffman 1979.) When speech departs from this ideal—as in an angry squabble before the magistrate, or a joking gossip free-for-all—social arrangements often conspire to nudge or elbow participants back into orderly line. Indeed, skilled talkers count among their talents the ability to engineer an orderly exchange of turns, to suppress their own voices when they would hinder such exchange, and to trumpet them when such an exercise of verbal power will reimpose order. Such idealized dialogicality represents a *normalization* in its own right, producing in speech a convergence of very different verbal forms and tasks, and often masking the creative, multi-vocal, social complexity of emerging discourse. It does not surprise us that these novice Tzotzil writers impose a written counterpart of spoken dialogue on their edited texts, thus reducing interactive disorder to a textured but single thread of talk.

In the literacy workshop, for example, writers routinely and consciously purged overlaps and repetitions to straighten out the dialogue. Several passages already cited illustrate the phenomenon. For another example, I transcribed Volcano: 67–70 as follows:

Volcano1

67   o   bu   l-a-bat-ik
      exist where CP-2A-go-PL

      Or did you go somewhere else?

                [
68 x;   vo'on-e este
                I-CL   uh

                Well, I , uh . . .

69   k'alal este tal   ti   tan x-k-al-tik-e
      when uh   come ART ash ASP-1E-say-1PL-CL

      When the ashes came, as we say.

70   este li'   oy-un   ta   Jobel-e
      uh   here exist-1A PREP SC-CL

      Uh, I was here in San Cristóbal.

71 a;   aa
72 x;   li'   oy-un   ta   Jobel
    here exist-1A PREP SC

    I was here in San Cristóbal.

The same passage appears in the writers' version as follows:

Volcano2
67   o   bu   l-a-bat-ik?
    exist where CP-2A-go-PL

    [Or] did you go somewhere else?

69 x;   k'alal tal   ti   tan-e,
    when come ART ash-CL

    When the ashes came

70   li'   oy-un   ta   Jobel-e.
    here exist-1A PREP SC-CL

    I was here in San Cristóbal.

More interestingly, there is also a smoothing of interactional edges. Where in the original conversations there were frequent struggles not only for the floor but for what might be called rights of authorship (for example, rights to tell a particularly juicy bit, to deliver the punchline, or to be able to finish a story line), the edited versions sometimes reorganize the emerging story so as to make things come out more neatly.[16]

The recasting of authorship, for example, occurs at Volcano:77. A is seemingly trying to preempt the narrative floor in preparation for launching his own story.

Volcano1
74 x;   tal   este k-ak'   j-nichim-kutik x-k-al-tik
    come uh 1E-give 1E-flower-1PX ASP-1E-say-1PL

    we had . uh . come to give our flowers, as we say.

75   porke jech kostumbre oy-utik x-k-al-tik
    because thus custom   exist-1P ASP-1E-say-1PL

    Because that's the custom we have, as it were.

76   komo nopol xa   este semana santa x-k-al-tik
    as   near already uh week   holy ASP-1E-say-1PL

    Because, as we say, it was getting close to Holy Week.

---

16. Textual reorganizations of this kind may, of course, be as much products of the different *interactional context of the transcription* as results of some emerging textual canon. The writers share a common goal—settling on a text—whereas as conversationalists they were in competition for the floor, for rights to tell the story.

77 a;   eso, nopol
    yes near

    Right, it was getting close.

78   mi y-olon   mi s-lajel   ech'el
    Q 3E-below Q 3E-ending away

    Was it before (Easter), or already afterwards?

79   vo'on-e ch' ay xa   x-k-a'i
    I-CL   lose already ASP-1E-hear

    I have forgotten.

80 x;   mo'oj, y-olon   to   'ox
    no   3E-below still then

    No, it was still before.

In the edited version, his turn is reduced to pure questioning, so that X is represented as continuing, unmolested, with his own narrative.

Volcano2

74 x;   tal kak' jnichimkutik,

    We had come to give (an offering of) our flowers,

75   **yu'un**[17] jech kostumbrekutik.

    Because that's our custom.

76   **yu'un** nopol xa semana santa.

    Since it was getting close to Holy Week.

78 a;   mi yolon mi slajel ech'el?

    Was it before (Easter), or already afterwards?

80 x;   mo'oj, yolon to'ox.

    No, it was still before.

A more radical sort of reorganization takes place in a fragment of the gossip session which we have already met.

Lovers1

171 r;   ta   y-ut   chobtik   la a'a
    PREP 3E-inside cornfields LA A'A

    Yes, they say right among the corn plants.

    [   ]

17. Such changes as the substitution of Tzotzil *yu'un* for Spanish *porque* reflect a conscious decision on the part of the literacy trainees, to which I return in "Form, Style, and Register Issues," to purge from their written text all Spanish loans in favor of their closest native equivalents.

172 m; k'el-tz'i'   y-ilel   ch-bat taj
        watch-dog 3E-seeing ICP-go that

        It looked as though that (guy) was going to check for dogs

173   taj   mol Proylan nan   a'a
        that old P   perhaps A'A

        old Proylan was—*yeah*—

        [   ]
174 r; li   Proylan-e che'e j-na'-tik   mi ta   x-ba   s-k'el
        ART P-CL   then   1E-know-1PL Q ICP ASP-go 3E-watch
                x-chob   ta   ti'   nab
                3E-cornfield PREP mouth lake

        Who knows if P was going to look over his cornfield at the edge of the lake.

Here a chance remark by R at line 171 in the original is misattributed
in line 169 in the edited text to M, the established narrator of the moment.
M's subsequent rejoinder is in turn attributed to R, creating a more orderly
(dia)logic in the emerging story. (The question is when, why, and where the
lovers made their way into the cornfields. The reason was supposedly that dogs
had been eating the young ears of corn. Proylan, the owner, had gone to inspect
the damage.)

Lovers2
169 m; ta   yut   chobtik   la   **a'a**
        PREP 3E-inside cornfields LA A'A

        Yeah they say in the cornfields.

172   a   k'el-tz'i'   la yil   ch-bat taj yil   proylan-e
        go watch-dog LA disgusting ICP-go that disgusting P-CL

        He went to watch for dogs, I hear, that disgusting Proylan.

174 r; li   **mol** proylan-e y-u'un   ch-ba s-k'el   x-chob   ta
        ART old P-CL   3E-cause ICP-go 3E-watch 3E-cornfield PREP
                ti'   nab
                mouth lake

        Old Proylan went to look over his cornfields by the lake.

Much conversational back-channel—normally required in polite Tzotzil
conversation—is purged from the written texts, as is multiple repetition, a phenomenon prominent in Tzotzil talk. Sometimes the interactive flavor and collaborative phraseology of the original talk is kept, although overt repetition is
eliminated. Certain interactional struggles, signaled in talk by explicit "paragraph markers," which serve to reclaim the audience's attention and thus the
floor (*va'i un*, literally 'so listen!'), are simply done away with in the written

versions. Conversely, some transition points in the narrative are made cleaner, disguising the fact that considerable efforts were required to achieve them in the conversational moment.

Related to such interactional smoothing is the ironing out in the edited text of irrelevant issues in the participant structure underlying the conversation, including what can be described as relations of identity, dominance, subordination, and deference. In speech, participants negotiate rights to telling the story, and the authority to tell it; they also compete as appropriate hearers or interlocutors; and they may explicitly and implicitly portray their relation and moral stance to the narrative, to its protagonists, and to the other participants in the speech event. Many such issues of "footing" (Goffman 1979) are blunted or eliminated in the naive writers' texts.

Consider, for example, the inappropriate "self-referential honorific" occurring at one point in the gossip session when a speaker refers to the old lady being discussed as *jme'tik Petu'* 'our mother Petrona.' This first-person plural inclusive possessive form is appropriate to, among others, familiar nonrelatives (where it contrasts with, e.g., *me' Petu'* 'mother P' appropriate to junior kinsmen, or *me'tik Petu'* 'mother P' [without the first-person possessive prefix *j*-] appropriate to a more distant acquaintance). Under the circumstances, such implicit claims to relationship are both inappropriate and somewhat ludicrous (since the whole point of the story is to ridicule the lewd old lady), and in the edited written version the reference is altered to *taj me'el Petu'* 'that old lady P,' implying no specific relationship with any of the speakers.

In general, facets of the relationships between interlocutors, patently available and interactionally exploitable if not necessarily exploited in the discursive event, are submerged in the decentered texts I have been presenting. They are only available to be read out *behind* the pragmatic bleaching and normalization. In the volcano conversation, for example, the fact that one of the narrators is a Zinacantec, whose Tzotzil dialect is also spoken by the workshop leader, gives his words a certain subtle prestige, a slight advantage over the variant of the other narrator, whose Chamula dialect is different. The only residue of this imbalance in the resulting text appears in potentially ambiguous phonological and morphological choices, which during editing were routinely resolved in favor of the dominant Zinacantec forms. I will return below to the evolution of a written standard from such micropolitics.

PROCESSING ISSUES

Not surprisingly, these naive Tzotzil writers discovered that speakers "make mistakes" that must not be slavishly reproduced in written texts. With neither

Saussurean nor Chomskian coaching, they came to reject parts of texts, even straightforwardly transcribable ones, as inappropriate.

HESITATIONS, FALSE STARTS, AND OTHER DYSFLUENCIES

In the Volcano transcript, most of the editing effort was devoted to eliminating hesitations, false starts, and other signs that the original conversationalists were nervous and uncertain in their talk. Pause markers of all kinds (*este, pues, bueno,* loans from Spanish, and *ali,* in Tzotzil) were routinely omitted from both texts. Similarly, certain repetitive expressions were systematically pruned, particularly *xkaltik* '(as) we say', a rough Tzotzil equivalent of the ubiquitous American English *y'know.* Speaker errors and hesitations were similarly smoothed. The writers confidently spotted—and purged—production errors, some involving mistaken intents, some involving speaker uncertainty (as, for example, at Volcano:68, in a passage we have already seen), others involving awkward expressions which resulted from mislaunching an utterance, which thus required reformulation.

On the other hand, in the written version of the gossip session, the transcriber decided to leave intact some speech twitches characteristic of several of the participants, much as a novelist will endow his characters with verbal signatures. CN, a well-known fast-talker, retains his habitual form of words—he ends his phrases with *uk une* (literally 'also then')—even in places where on the original tape he does not appear to use the words. The transcriber puts into this man's mouth words that make him *sound like himself.* Thus, for example, the following set of lines in Lovers1 is reduced to a single, stereotyped line in Lovers2.

Lovers1
287 cn; pen-
288 batz'i pentejo ali   k-itz'in   i-k-a'i   ox
     real   asshole ART 1E-brother CP-3E-hear then

     "What a real asshole my brother is!" is what I heard

289 x-chi   li   mol Prutarko
     ASP-say ART old   Plutarco

     old Man Plutarco say.

Lovers2
288 cn; pentejo **tajmek** [18] li kitz'ine xi li mol Prutarko **uk une**

     "My brother is a real asshole," says old Plutarco, too.

18. The intensifier *batz'i* 'really' is also replaced, in Lovers2, with another intensifier, *tajmek* 'very'.

It is also unsurprising that the naive writers should apparently have felt free to edit the recorded utterances according either to standards of grammaticality and "intelligibility" [19] or to judgments about register and appropriate levels of formality. They altered everything from lexical items to verbal inflections, from auxiliary verbs to particles showing interclausal linkages. The literacy trainees even sought an orthographic solution to an intonational problem, introducing commas to help clarify an otherwise ambiguous parsing.

There is obviously a special problem that ordinary writers do not face in the written rendition of what starts as a spoken conversation: what to do with unintelligible material or uncertain hearings. In the Volcano conversation, the writers and I jointly decided on a transcription of the original, resolving questions of interpretation by committee, until we had a transcript from which we could proceed. In the Lovers transcript, the transcriber was on his own, and occasionally what he wrote seems to result from embellishment and overinterpretation of material on the original tape that is difficult to hear, overlapped, or plainly unintelligible.[20] There are numerous revealing instances in the text. For example, at Lovers: 226, where CN makes a joke,

Lovers1
226 cn; ay x-chi   xa   nan   li   mol   une ja ja ja
       oh ASP-say already perhaps ART old-man CL

    "Ay" said the old fellow, probably, ha ha ha.

the transcriber interprets it as a *different* joke:

Lovers2
226 cn; muk' xa   jal   x-ixtalan   li   mol **uk**   un
        NEG already long(time) ASP+3E-play ART old also CL

    The old fellow didn't get to play around very long.

I have already mentioned such embellishment and reattribution in the case of another joke, at Lovers: 219–222.

19. The tape recordings I have of the editing sessions for the Chichonal text contain such evaluative expressions as *chopol* 'bad', *mu stak'* 'it won't serve', *mu a'ibaj lek* 'you can't understand it clearly', applied to utterances that need reformulation.

20. I have not, since beginning this investigation, taken the obvious step of listening again to the original tape recording with the original transcriber—now a distinguished ex-President and powerful political figure in the *Partido Revolucionario Institucional*—to puzzle out his interpretations. I have, however, checked my own transcription with other Zinacantecs.

CONTENT ISSUES

Clearly, the task of producing a text (which involves fixing its content, what it is "about") puts strong constraints on these naive writers. Exactly where such constraints arise is worth pursuing in more detail. Do these writers develop a "story" that schematically divides the relevant from the inconsequential? Do plots—whether of disasters with denouements or jokes with punchlines—have an internal momentum and contour which must be maintained in a written rendition? Is there a kind of referential focus here, which causes writers to stick to "the facts?"

We encounter in these empirical specimens what might be called the power of narrative to regiment its own decentering.[21] In familiar ways, the story itself produces its own kind of normalization, although the process is arguably a dialectic between the narrative "facts" and the needs of the discursive moment. Nonetheless, the reduction of conversational discourse to orthogonal text cannot simply be a result of pragmatic "bleaching," since the narrative "events," the momentum of the "story," the "denouement," and its evaluative "moral" all independently motivate the pruning of those conversational sequences which do not advance narrative ends. The urge to keep to a central story line is also, I may add, driven both by the concerns of the discursive moment—when one "story" can be arguably represented as better than another—and by a retrospective interpretive glance at the moment of writing. The tale of volcanic disaster in Tzotzil terms is *lo'il no'ox* 'just talk, conversation'. The gossip about the slatternly old lady is a possessed deverbal noun, from the same root: *slo'iltael* 'the story told *on her*'. The morphology here suggests that *certain* narratives—*lo'iltael*—being aimed and barbed, are more *tellable* than others which are 'mere talk'.

ELIMINATING IRRELEVANCIES AND SIDETRACKS

I have already mentioned that in the volcano story the writers began at an early stage to prune from the written text all extraneous characters, including me, limiting the text to two storytellers and their mutual interaction.

In the gossip text, however, the Zinacantec transcriber needed to make more complex decisions about both the internal momentum and dramatic logic of the story. A clear example comes when the written text slyly cuts any mention of the schoolchildren's slingshots until the appropriate moment, apparently

---

21. Consider the classical treatment of narrative and the strong social demands on its discursive realization in Labov (1972); see also Haviland (1977, Ch. 4).

so as not to undermine the coming comic sequence in which the lovers are attacked from behind with slingshot pellets, bringing the cornfield tryst to an abrupt and painful end. Perhaps the author does not want his readers—just as, in the original telling he did not want his audience—to see the joke coming before he is ready to deliver it; or perhaps the writer, like the teller, wants the right—and the space—to deliver the punchline himself. Compare the following transcribed fragment of a passage we have met before with the subsequent written formulation by Little Romin.

Lovers1

210 r;   s-lok'-oj   la   li   s-vex   une
         3E-remove-PF LA   ART 3E-pants CL

They say he had taken off his pants.

211   x-vinaj   li   s-bek'   y-at   ta   s-pat   une
         ASP-appear ART   3E-seed 3E-penis PREP 3E-back   CL

His balls were visible from behind.

                            [
212 m;   ja ja ja
213 r;   y-a:k'-be   ech'el
         3E-give-BEN away

He was giving it to her (facing away from them).

214 all;   ja ja jAA JAA
215 ca; i-k-a'i   ti   ji-
        CP-1E-hear CONJ

What I heard was that . . .

        [
216 all;   ((laughter))
217 ca; y-ich'   la-
        3E-receive LA

That apparently he got it . . .

        [
218 all;   ((laughter))
219 ca; y-ich'   la uli'   li   s-bek'   y-at-e   xi-ik   i-k-a'i
        3E-receive LA slingshot ART 3E-seed 3E-penis say-PL CP-1E-hear

that apparently he got hit by the slingshot right on the balls, they say, I've heard.

        [
220 all;   ((laugh))

221 j; ja' nan   ch-p'it   lok'el nan   li   povre
    !   perhaps ICP-jump exiting perhaps ART poor

The poor fellow perhaps jumped right out.

Little Romin, in his own transcription, renders the same passage as follows:

Lovers2
210 r; s-lok'-oj   la li   s-vex   une
    3E-remove-PF LA ART 3E-pants CL

They say he had taken off his pants.

211   x-vinaj   li   s-bek'   y-at   ta   s-pat   une
    ASP-appear ART 3E-seed 3E-penis PREP 3E-back CL

His balls were visible from behind.

213   i-y-ak'-be   **la** ech'el **un**
    CP-3E-give-BEN LA away   CL

He was giving it to her (facing away from them), it's said.

219 ca; kabron pero k'u   tz-sa'   ti   buy   x-jipjon   s-bek'
    damn   but what ICP+3E-seek CONJ where ASP-flinging 3E-seed
        y-at-e   xi-ik   la un
        3E-penis-CL say-PL LA CL

Damn, but what is he up to flinging his balls about like that, they said,
supposedly.

220 x; aj aj aj aj
221 d; pero batz'i x-mut'lij   xa   j-na'   un
    but really ASP-jerking/shrinking already 1E-know CL

But he must have been just about to ejaculate, I bet.

Little Romin eliminates CA's upstaging mention of the slingshot, at line 219,
and presents the story—which, incidentally, *he* was telling (he appears as R in
the transcript)—in his own way.

The Tzotzil writers seem to have invented their own version of an inherently propositional view of language, in which superficially different formulations can be reduced to a common shared referential content. The problem is
particularly pressing in the task they faced: to reduce a multiparty conversation
with considerable overlap and interaction to a coherent linear text. The process
of writing seems to allow a pragmatic restructuring, tending towards an ultimately monologic form, where propositional content takes precedence over the
indexical microcosm of the parent interaction, and where interactive richness
is pruned in favor of monologic narrative.

Some textual reformulations are offered in the guise of mere corrections. During the editing session one speaker, X, offered an improved version of "what he meant to say" at Volcano: 46.[22] The original line,

Volcano1

k-a'-uk   y-u'un   wo'-uk   nox x-tal-e
1E-think-IRREAL 3E-cause water-IRREAL only ASP-come-CL

I thought that only rain was coming.

is re-rendered as

Volcano2

ko'olaj x-chi'uk vo'   i-tal.
equals 3E-with water CP-come

It was the same as if it were about to rain.

The reformulation, according to X, captured his intended meaning better than what he actually heard himself say on the tape.

At a higher level, where, because of interruptions or generalized hilarity, episodes in the original interaction are unable to reach a satisfactory narrative conclusion, the writers occasionally introduce order from without. For example, Little Romin frames the slingshot sequence with an initial "paragraph marker" *va'i un* (where the original text has none), and he closes the scene in proper fashion with a clause-final clitic *une* at line 205.

Lovers2

200 r; v-a'i   un
        2E-hear CL

     so listen

201 li   jchanvun-etik une
     ART student-PL   CL

     the schoolchildren . . .

202 ta   x-bat-ik   un
     ICP ASP-go-PL CL

     they went

203 ta   sa'-ik   mut ta x-lok'-ik   j-likel   ta   rekreo un
     ICP 3E+seek-PL bird ICP ASP-exit-PL 1-moment PREP recess CL

     they hunted birds when they got out for a moment of recess.

22. *Mu a'ibaj k'usi xk'ot 'o* 'one can't understand what it leads to' is the criticism X launched against his own recorded utterance.

204 ta   x-bat-ik   ta   y-ut   chobtik   un
     ICP ASP-go-PL PREP 3E-inside cornfields CL

     they went into the cornfields.

205 ja' ti   bu   x-va'et-ik   une
     !   ART where ASP-standing-PL CL

     or wherever they happened to loiter about.

The written text thus imposes an episodic structure which in the original conversation can be inferred only from the interaction and not from the actual
language.

FORM, STYLE, AND REGISTER ISSUES

Finally, differences between the original conversational performances and the
written renditions reflect these Tzotzil writers' decisions about which *varieties*
of language to reproduce in the texts they are creating. Despite a reputation
(and a talent) for ridiculing their neighbors' dialects, the Tzotzil writers were
enthusiastic about representing not only their own speech but also that of others, in readable form. The literacy teachers, for example, welcomed an alphabet
in which each speaker would write as he or she spoke. The resulting dialect
tolerance was combined with apparent criteria of dialect purity, so that sometimes speakers' written words were adjusted to coincide with their own appropriate dialects, even when the spoken words were, by such a criterion, "in
error." [23]

Moreover, the literacy trainees displayed a developed consciousness
about Tzotzil as a dominated language, and unsurprisingly (though to a certain
extent, as a result of our urgings) began a campaign to purge Spanish from
their Tzotzil texts. Throughout the editing process, with increasing enthusiasm
the writers excised Spanish loans, including connectives that are a routine part
of ordinary speech, and substituted the nearest (and often infrequently used)
Tzotzil equivalents. Words like *porque* 'because', *como* 'like', and even *pero*
'but', fell away before Tzotzil paraphrases, or were simply omitted when the
writers found them redundant in the context of an overall Tzotzil construction.

Even the gossip group created its own special euphemisms. The language
of "injections" evolved during the gossip sessions, from an apparently creative
initial use to a generalized group in-joke. The expression was incorporated

23. Laughlin (in press) remarks that a Chamulan's speech as it is rendered into writing by
another Chamulan is pruned of the Zinacantecoisms that the speaker has picked up in the course
of his working life.

willy-nilly into the written text, and, duly, into the speech of at least a small group of Zinacantec hamlet-mates—including Little Romin himself, who still uses it twenty-five years later in joking conversation.[24]

THE PRAGMATIC NORMALIZATION OF THE WRITTEN TEXT

Between a conversational moment and representations of entextualized telos, the balance between what Silverstein (1976) called relatively presupposing and relatively creative (entailing) indexes in speech must necessarily shift. Partly this is a sequential spelling out of indexical givens in the texts I have presented. Participants no longer present themselves as human faces, with biographies and competing interests, but only as disembodied words. There is no longer a negotiable universe of discourse, but instead a textually established corpus of common knowledge, whose mutuality is not between interlocutors but between text-artifact and reader. The channel eliminates in obvious but occasionally profound ways the context of situation of some originary text. Any text resulting from writing eliminates the warmth of the sun that the original conversants could point to deictically. It erases the tension between tellers, the scramble for punchlines, and the secret animosities between rivals for the floor thinly masked behind mildly competitive words, that were all too obvious to us gossipers. The remnants of such micropolitics are buried behind the process of entextualization itself. Little Romin, taking authorial control of the gossip text, nudges his own words—and his narrative authority—vaguely to center stage. The literacy trainees endow the adopted Tzotzil dialect of the anthropologist leader with a passive prestige in the textual sediment, even as the anthropologist himself is rendered discursively invisible. And so on.

I have spoken about the pragmatic *normalization* involved when a text is extracted from a discursive center—say, a multiparty gossip session—and recast onto simpler, or at least transformed, indexical terrain: a linear narrative, or a semantic dialogue with simulated multiple voices presented in a monologic pragmatic medium. Perhaps writing as mere technology is responsible for much of the normalization I have described. Goody argues that the inven-

---

24. Don Brenneis has pointed out, in discussion, that the process of entextualization can lead, at a later point, to retellings: the reincorporation into speech of something once reduced to text. See also Haviland and de León (1988), and Sherzer (1983: 201 ff.). Here we see a single symptom of the more global process: the gossip group develops its own highly context-specific turns of phrase. These are in turn frozen onto a written page. At the same time, through a parallel process of decentering, the writer himself generalizes their usage by incorporating such phrases, now with echoes of their dialogic origins, into less context-bound speech.

tion of writing and its institutional spread trigger a series of transformations of mind at the level of society as a whole. Much of the effect he attributes almost mechanically to the tangible product of writing—the manipulable, examinable, physical text-artifact itself:

> When an utterance is put in writing it can be inspected in much greater detail, in its parts as well as in its whole, backwards as well as forwards, out of context as well as in its setting; in other words, it can be subjected to a quite different type of scrutiny and critique than is possible with purely verbal communication. Speech is no longer tied to an 'occasion'; it becomes timeless. Nor is it attached to a person; on paper it becomes more abstract, more depersonalized. (1977: 44)

The pragmatic reduction of spoken words in the texts produced by naive Tzotzil writers thus exemplifies minuscule preliminary steps down Goody's longer road to what is claimed to be a distinctively "modern" cognition.

In this view, literacy emancipates its beneficiaries from the contingency of the indexical surround, including personae and activities:

> Words assume a different relationship to action and to object when they are on paper than when they are spoken. They are no longer bound up directly with 'reality'; the written word becomes a separate 'thing', abstracted to some extent from the flow of speech, shedding its close entailment with action, with power over matter. (Goody 1977: 46)

However, part of the warrant for pragmatic normalization in these written texts derives from something deeper than technology. I have suggested, for example, that narrative may by its nature exhibit a strong decenterability, so strong that alternate texts and voices are drowned out in the process of creating coherence around a monologic story line. Bauman argues that

> Events are not the external raw materials out of which narratives are constructed, but rather the reverse: Events are abstractions from narrative. It is the structures of signification in narrative that give coherence to events in our understanding. (Bauman 1986: 5)

Events are thus segments of some entextualized narrative.

Pragmatic normalization in moving to text from talk (evident in the relation that a narrative conversation has to its text-artifactual representation as accomplished by writers or transcribers), thus has an analog in what we might

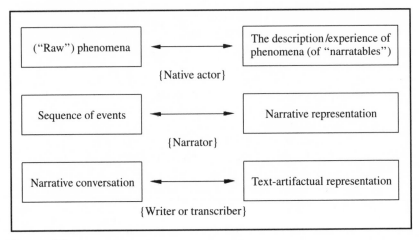

FIGURE 2.1

call *referential normalization,* the process by which a narrative core is extracted/
overlaid on a sequence of events, a feat engineered and accomplished by a
storyteller and her or his interlocutors.

There is a further analogy. The classificatory imperative of language itself means that all utterances, spoken or written, convert "raw" phenomena—
whatever these may be—into the discrete units of experience, specific "narratables" now cast into linguistic chunks whose size and shape depend on
grammatical and morpho-lexical categories of the language in question, "fashioned" in speech. The agents of this ubiquitous process are, of course, speakers
(i.e., actors) in general. There is thus (minimally) a three-step process of normalization, illustrated in Figure 2.1.

Moving from talk to text is thus a single moment in a larger, ubiquitous
process of shearing away context to permit representation, the target of our
joint metaphors of "decentering" and "entextualization." The process requires
filtering of the various indexical phenomena that defines narratables and incorporating those that survive into the text-artifact. Any narrative that results is
more completely and autonomously determined—decentered or entextualized,
or, perhaps, "(re)centered" on the text-artifact itself—than it was in the interaction from which it sprang.

There are at least two further important matters which have lurked in
the background here, and which I will simply note in closing. The first is the
ethnographic question about Tzotzil "genres": narratives, conversations, "gossip," or "jokes." How do such models together with local canons of the "interaction order" (Goffman 1983) interrelate with the sorts of phenomena I have

reported?[25] Zinacantecs are, I think, less interested in, say, the precise timing of overlap or the mechanics of repair than in what makes a good story, or how to frame events and opinions in a form that everyone can agree on. I have mentioned that talk, in Tzotzil *lo'il* 'talk, conversation', via the derived verb *-lo'ilta* 'tell stories *on* (somebody)', can be conceptualized to be aimed at a victim. Implicitly, Zinacantecs, like everyone else, know that only certain sorts of things can be told and only about certain people. Not all news is newsworthy; not all *lo'il* can be aimed. By extension, then, one presumes that only some (aspects of) tellings can be written, or in the absence of the ethnographer's promptings would be worth writing.

An important aspect of apparent Tzotzil theory about narrating becomes evident in Zinacantec legal discourse. In the courtroom before a Tzotzil magistrate, interest often centers less on the narrative sequence of a witness's account than on whether *itz'ep'uj sk'op*—whether 'his word slipped'. Did he, that is, inadvertently change his story, blurting out an inconsistency? The Tzotzil notion of "replication" (when a witness is asked to tell his story several times) is here seen to involve a referential thread together with the precise formulation of crucial details. A further look at the work of current Tzotzil writers will need to explore the connections between locally constituted genres and consciously fashioned texts.

Finally, this brings me to an issue I have left largely in the air: the matter of power, authorship, and authority. On the one hand, social power is mediated through the texts it produces (allows). An American court insists on "the whole truth," while a Zinacantec magistrate searches for a "ratifiable account," replete not only with (self-)confirmatory detail but also with opportunities for agreement or at least mutual acquiescence between antagonists. We are again balanced between coherence and accuracy.

However, the trick of producing text from discourse has a more immediate politico-economic dimension as well. After all, the Tzotzil writers whose products I have surveyed here were in various ways doing my bidding. How did they understand their tasks? What did they think I wanted from them? What did they want from me? Both the literacy trainees hoping for a relatively well-paid government job if they could just satisfy our criteria for accurate writing, and Little Romin transcribing my gossip tapes at a standard salary of so much per page, had clear economic stakes in the production of their texts. For Tzotziles—from anthropological consultant to bilingual schoolteacher,

---

25. A parallel question arises about the theorist's notion of "transcript," exemplified in my own texts.

from Indian writer funded by development grants to mini-bus driver hoping for a driver's license, or would-be migrant worker looking for travel papers— literacy pays. Perhaps more than pragmatics and in ways to be explored, pesos motivate the production of text from talk.

I have noted that the power of narrative itself may have compelling effects: the stories of Proylan and the old lady, or the volcanic eruption, may by their very nature warrant decentering/entextualizing, thereby producing the illusion of coherent, integrated texts that can stand clear of the circumstances of their production. We engage in this sort of sleight of hand all the time, often perhaps unwittingly, in doing ethnography. I have here recorded the sad fact that heretofore innocent Tzotziles can be induced to engage in similar conjuring tricks.

REFERENCES

Arias, Jacinto
  1990   *San Pedro Chenalhó, Algo de su Historia, Cuentos y Costumbres.* Tuxtla Gtz., Chis: Instituto Chiapaneco de Cultura.

Atkinson, J. M., and John Heritage
  1984   *Structures of Social Action.* Cambridge: Cambridge University Press.

Bauman, Richard
  1986   *Story, Performance, and Event: Contextual Studies of Oral Narrative.* New York: Cambridge University Press.

Chafe, Wallace
  1982   Integration and involvement in speaking, writing, and oral literature. In *Spoken and Written Language: Exploring Orality and Literacy*, D. Tannen (ed.), 35–53. Norwood, New Jersey: Ablex.

Chafe, Wallace, and Jane Danielewicz
  1985   Properties of spoken and written language. In *Comprehending Oral and Written Language*, R. H. and S. J. Samuels (eds.), 83–113. New York: Academic Press.

Clark, Herbert
  1992   *Arenas of Language Use.* Chicago: CSLI & University of Chicago Press.

Goffman, Erving
  1979   Footing. *Semiotica* 25: 1–29.
  1983   The interaction order. *American Sociological Review* 48: 1–17.

Goody, J.
  1977   *The Domestication of the Savage Mind.* Cambridge: Cambridge University Press.

Goody, J. and I. Watt
  1963   The consequences of literacy. *Comparative Studies in Society and History* 5: 304–45.

Haviland, John B.
1977   *Gossip, Reputation, and Knowledge in Zinacantan.* Chicago: University of Chicago Press.
1987a Fighting words: evidential particles, affect and argument. *Proceedings of the Berkeley Linguistics Society* 13: 343–354.
1987b Lenguaje ritual sin ritual. Paper presented to I Coloquio Swadesh, IIA-UNAM, Mexico City, Oct. 1987. (Forthcoming in *Tlalocan.*)
1988   A father-mother talks back: The micro-creation of context in Tzotzil. Paper presented to the conference on "Interpretive Sociolinguistics III: Contextualization" organized by Peter Auer and Aldo di Luzio at the University of Konstanz, October 2–6, 1988.
1989   Sure, sure: Evidence and affect. *Text* 9(1): 27–68.
1990   "We want to borrow your mouth": Tzotzil marital squabbles. *Anthropological Linguistics* 30(3–4): 395–447.
1991   Projections, transpositions, and relativity. Working paper no. 3, Cognitive Anthropology Research Group, Max-Planck-Institut für Psycholinguistik, Nijmegen. (To appear in *Rethinking Linguistic Relativity*, J. J. Gumperz and S. C. Levinson, (eds.). Cambridge: Cambridge University Press.)

Haviland, John B., and Lourdes de León
1985   Un modelo lingüístico para la alfabetización en Tzotzil. Mexico, D.F.: Instituto Nacional de Educación para los Adultos.
1988   *Me tengo que tragar mis broncas* [I have to swallow my problems]. Paper presented to the session on interactive narrative, organized by Charles Goodwin and Alessandro Duranti, annual meeting of the American Anthropological Association, Phoenix, November, 1988.

Labov, William
1972   The transformation of experience in narrative syntax. In *Language in the Inner City: Studies in the Black English Vernacular*, chapter 9, 354–396. Philadelphia: University of Pennsylvania Press.

Laughlin, Robert M.
1977   Of cabbages and kings: Tales from Zinacantán. Smithsonian Contributions to Anthropology, no. 23. Washington, DC: Smithsonian Institution Press.
(in press)   In the Book of Matthew Thus Spake John. In *Discourse in Mayan Languages*, J. M. Brody (ed.).

Mithun, Marianne
1985   When speakers write. *Proceedings of the Berkeley Linguistics Society* 11: 259–272.

Ochs, Elinor
1979   Transcription as theory. In *Developmental Pragmatics*, E. Ochs and B. Schieffelin (eds.), 43–72. New York: Academic Press.

Pérez López, Enrique
1990   *Chamula, un Pueblo Indígena Tzotzil.* Tuxtla Gtz., Chis: Instituto Chiapaneco de Cultura.

Sherzer, Joel
    1983   *Kuna Ways of Speaking*. Austin: University of Texas Press.

Silverstein, Michael
    1976   Shifters, linguistic categories, and cultural description. In *Meaning in Anthropology*, K. H. Basso and H. A. Selby (eds.), 11–55. Albuquerque: University of New Mexico Press.

Yngve, V. H.
    1970   On getting a word in edgewise. *Papers from the Sixth Regional Meeting, Chicago Linguistic Society*, M. A. Campbell (ed.), 567–578. Chicago: Department of Linguistics, University of Chicago.

Discovering Discourse in Text

3   The Secret Life of Texts

Michael Silverstein

A text-artifact, such as a graphic array on the printed page, demands an entextualizing uptake so as to determine, on encounter, at least one text-in-context. This is commonly called "reading a text," or, worse, "reading the text." Reading is, of course, a socioculturally contextualized practice of entextualization, which demands its own ethnographic account (see, for example, Boyarin [ed.] 1993). Here, however, we are interested in another aspect of the graphically (or otherwise) based achievement of textuality: texts are interdiscursive with respect to other text occasions, especially to relatively more originary or precedential ones with respect to which a "reading," for example, is achieved.[1] We thus might ask about those text processes presupposed in a reading by interrogating their traces in the artifactual form of interest. We can engage in reading a text, as it were, to shed ethnographic light on an earlier, otherwise secret discursive life of the text(s) therein.

In particular, we are here interested in the recovery of apparently multiple entextualizations-in-context by the two participants in an ethnographic

---

1. There is a parallel here, it seems, to the "causal theory" of reference emerging from Kripke (1972) and Putnam (1975). In that view of how one achieves extensional reference, in addition to such contextual factors as the contextual conditions of the instance of referring at issue, we must in effect reconstruct a socioculturally specific chain of referring occasions licensed or warranted by the continuity of referring events from some originary, "baptismal" one, in which an authoritative extending of some object with a word or expression creates a "prototype" referent. Note how the causal theory problematizes (1) the sociocultural authoritativeness of performative baptism as the originary foundation (even if only an ideologically presumed one), and (2) the nature of the historical—"causal"—connectivity across referring-events from originary link to last link in a chain of such events. There are many interesting social anthropological and cognitive issues involved in both of these factors, beyond what Kripke or Putnam seem to have imagined.

Here, too, we problematize how an entextualization based in "reading" a text-artifact can be connected to (1′) originary contextualization(s) when a prototype artifact was created, and (2′) to traces of continuity that allow an informed "reading" at a sociohistorically distinct era of entextualizing practice.

and linguistic encounter of long ago, seeking the "dialogicality" (Bakhtin 1981: 279 ff.) preserved in the artifact. And we are interested in the light this situation sheds on the activity of text gathering as part of a museological encounter with culture and language, the encounter that produces text-artifacts in various semiotic modalities, among them articulate language.

CIRCUMSTANCES OF ENCOUNTER; PHILOLOGY OF ARTIFACT

There is a short text-artifact, published in 1909 by Edward Sapir in his volume of *Wishram Texts* (Sapir 1909: 188–91) in facing-page original Kiksht (Wasco-Wishram Chinookan) and translated English. Sapir entitled it "Winter Bathing." It is the tenth of twelve short texts on "Customs" included in the standard-issue Boasian collection of myths, tales, ethnologic narratives, and so on. One of the twelve pieces on "Customs" is the Shaker Table Grace in Kiksht, a set piece still recited from memory, I can attest, seventy years later. Of the rest, interestingly, "Winter Bathing" is the only one told in what seems to be a narrative first person.

That is, there seems to be something of the "reminiscence" about the text in this text-artifact. It is distinct in this way from the generalized—indeed, generic—third-person usitative (habitual) modality in which nine of the others are cast ("If a young man should die, the people mourn." [Death]). It is also distinct from the first-person hypothetical that occurs in one other piece, deictically anchoring its otherwise logically relational third-person discourse on kinship, by fixing the ego of egocentric reckoning literally on the deictic ego ("Now my son is ready to marry the girl; she is to become his wife." [Marriage]). "Winter Bathing," it would appear, is a text-artifact set off from the others in this section in this, as in other ways.

Such distinctive characteristics as the "voicings" of the text (Bakhtin 1981: 275–366) revealed in the metapragmatic function of "calibration" of deictics (Silverstein 1993) help us to constitute our reading(s). They allow us to reconstruct something of its circumstances of "originary" entextualization (insofar as this concept makes sense) as this has resulted in the inscription of the text-artifact we encounter with a specific form and contextual surround. In this case, we map out how the artifactual traces project at least two originary metapragmatic calibrations that in turn constitute a revealing index of the interaction between the then-young Edward Sapir (1884–1939) and the two generationally distinct types of Kiksht speakers he consulted and worked with on the Yakima Reservation in the summer of 1905, undertaking his first fieldwork after a post-baccalaureate year of study under Boas.

In the introduction to the published volume (Sapir 1909: ix–xiii) we are given to understand that Sapir worked principally with a then elderly Louis Simpson, Kiksht name Mánait (born ca. 1835), who dictated "[t]he bulk of the linguistic material obtained in the field . . . , Pete McGuff serving as interpreter" (Sapir 1909: x). Sapir claims that "Pete McGuff himself was the narrator of most of the remainder"—one "Myth" (Sapir 1909: 120–31), four "Customs" (Sapir 1909: 182–91), including, interestingly, the text at issue on "Winter Bathing," and Kiksht translations made from some English-language letters (Sapir 1909: 194–99)—though we are told further that there are "texts . . . taken down by Pete himself[, which] were dictated by various elderly Indians,—Yaryarone, Sophia Klickitat, Jane Meacham, and A'newikus" (Sapir 1909: x–xi),[2] after Sapir had returned to New York. These McGuff sent to him in phonetically transcribed, interlinearly glossed form for (minor) editing and arrangement into the published scheme of four distinct text types.

Indeed, though Sapir tells us that "[t]he arrangement of the texts into the heads of Myths, Customs, Letters, Non-Mythical Narratives[3] . . . is self-explanatory, and need not be commented upon" (1909: xii), indicating its routine or settled nature within the Boasian purview, we might dwell on this somewhat as an aid to reading. As noted, "Winter Bathing" stands out among the texts grouped by Sapir as descriptions of Indian custom, that is, exposition or exemplification of the traditional Wishram ways of life. It has a distinct voicing, to be sure, as noted above, but this is true also of the longest text (Sapir

2. We can identify with reasonable certainty three of the named individuals from interview-based genealogical and related data in my collection of field materials, produced in fieldwork during 1966–1974. [For financial support of these field trips, I thank the National Science Foundation, the Phillips Fund (American Philosophical Society), the Society of Fellows (Harvard University), and the Adolph Lichtstern Research Fund (Department of Anthropology, University of Chicago).] The first was Yáyaun or Yayáwun (pronunciations vary), a then (1905) older Wishram man who lived in White Swan, Washington, as recalled in 1971 by Louis Simpson's niece (brother's daughter), who remembered Sapir as a houseguest and other information about the 1905 fieldwork. The second was most likely Pete McGuff's mother, also known as Sophie Williams, "Indian" name Cha'íyawa. The third was Jane Meacham, Louis and Tom Simpson's aunt (father's sister), whose Kiksht name was Sxʷíai. The fourth name does not appear in my records. Note that Sapir was following Boasian principles of seeking to train a local speaker in phonetic—really, something like Sweet's "broad" or later "phonemic"—transcription, maintaining by correspondence a flow of text-artifacts produced in this way. McGuff corresponded with Sapir on matters of grammar and translation during the preparation of the volume, and in many respects is, in fact, its coeditor.

3. Sapir includes an appendix (1909:232–5) of "Supplementary Upper Chinookan Texts," one Wasco, one Clackamas, "collected by Dr. Franz Boas in 1892 at Grand Ronde Reservation in northwestern Oregon, and . . . kindly put at my disposal by him" (Sapir 1909:232, n.1). The Clackamas piece has been discussed by Hymes (1984).

1909: 204–27), which is classified as one of the nonmythical narratives. So wherein lies the apparent principle of classification?

It would appear that, first, the nonmythical narratives (two from Mr. Simpson via Sapir transcription, two from Mrs. Klickitat via McGuff transcription) are construed as a kind of oral historiography, in the sense of constituting reports of presumptive large-scale happenings or events in the contingent real-time of the societal order. Sapir even provides footnotes to each with corroborative and other factual considerations, evidentiary parallels, dates, and so on. So in content Mr. Simpson's account of the Paiute War must have constituted for Sapir "eyewitness first-person reportage/recollection," I-was-there historiography, complete with many asides to interpret specific episodes in terms of what can only be called custom. The historical consciousness of a then-young Sapir could in this way distinguish Mr. Simpson's war stories from Mr. McGuff's story of his "Winter Bathing."

Second, there is a Kiksht lexical distinction between two kinds of special narrative genre, (i-)qánuchk,[4] translatable as 'myth', and (it-)qíxhikalhx '(human era) recounting; story'. Many of the latter category are stories—even with named protagonists—that would count more as our "tales," because their plots concern fantastic doings, that is, doings that cannot be experienced in the ordinary reality of here-and-now human conditions. Sapir clearly recognized this latter kind of qíxhikalhx, as shown in his editing of the 1885 collection (in English) of Jeremiah Curtin's "Wasco Tales and Myths" that he published together with his *Wishram Texts*. He divides the twenty-five Curtin pieces into five groupings, termed "Tales, Guardian-Spirit Stories, Coyote Stories, [At'at'álhia] Stories, and Miscellaneous Myths" (Sapir [ed.] 1909: 239). The first two of Sapir's head captions would fall within qíxhikalhx, though we should note that he may have recognized the special relationship between the various encountered "guardian spirits" (about which more below) and the expectable animal characters of mythology by calling these "stories," along with

---

4. The transcription is fairly standard for this language within the Americanist tradition, save for the use of the digraph-series *ch, sh,* and so on for the usual single characters bearing superposed wedge for the initial segments of English *chin, shirt,* and so on. Also, the digraph with *h* (thus: *xh*) will be used for the uvular (back) series of sounds, as in the last segment of German *Buch,* phonologically always distinct from the corresponding velar (front), here written simply *x*; this same device will distinguish the voiceless correspondent of *l*. The initial, parenthesized morphological element in common nouns is the 'number-gender' prefix, generally obligatory even in the simple citation form of such words (see Silverstein 1977; 1984). Categorial coding of 'singular' : 'dual' : '(individuable) plural' crosses that of 'masculine' : 'feminine' : 'neuter-collective/aggregate' in these elements, which number five in all.

those of Coyote and Basket-Ogress. Yet, guardian-spiritship was, in fact, a quest of ordinary Wishrams, the successful conduct of which was an important goal of a personal sense of empowering physical and emotional well-being and social worth; Mr. McGuff's reminiscence, dealing with these matters, sits oddly in the rubric of mere "Custom," then, unless as an indication that Sapir was unable to place it either as a nonmythical narrative, like Mr. Simpson's reminiscence of the Paiute War, or as a *qíxhikalhx* of a clear [wonder]tale variety. So he retreated to "Custom" out of a perhaps relativistic politeness to an interlocutor who claimed, to Sapir's vicarious embarrassment, to have sought the fantastic in personal epistemological realtime.

This points, thirdly, and one might argue most decisively, to Sapir's expressed views about the two principals with whom he worked during that first field summer, Louis Simpson and Peter McGuff. These views (Sapir 1909: xi–xii) should be quoted verbatim:

> A few words in reference to Louis Simpson and Pete McGuff may not be out of place. Louis Simpson is a fair example of the older type of Wishram Indian, now passing away. Of short and stocky build, bow-legged from constant riding on horseback, he is about seventy or seventy five years of age, of an impatient and somewhat selfwilled temperament, dramatically talkative, with a good deal of the love of gain and bargain-driving proclivities with which many of the early Western travellers charged the Indians about The Dalles; yet, despite this, he proved to be a lovable personality, owing chiefly to his keen sense of humor. He has a command of Wishram, Klickitat, and the Chinook jargon; but his English is extremely broken, hardly intelligible at times. Superficially, Louis is a convert to the ways of the whites; in other words, he is a "civilized" Indian,—lives in a frame house, raises and sells wheat and hay, is dressed in white man's clothes, is theoretically a Methodist. Judging by the contents of his mind, however, he is to all intents and purposes an unadulterated Indian. He implicitly believes in the truth of all the myths he narrated, no matter how puerile or ribald they might seem. Coyote he considers as worthy of the highest respect, despite the ridiculous and lascivious sides of his character; and with him he is strongly inclined to identify the Christ of the whites, for both he and Coyote lived many generations ago, and appeared in this world in order to better the lot of mankind. On one point Louis always insisted with great emphasis,—the myths as he told them were not invented by himself, but have been handed down from time immemorial, and hence have good claims to being

considered truth. Pete McGuff, on the other hand, may serve as a type of the younger generation of Indian, though only a half-blood (his father was a negro, his mother is a full-blood Indian). Having lived much of his life with the Wishrams, he speaks their language fluently, though long contact in early life with the Cascades Indians on the Columbia is responsible for a number of un-Wishram phonetic peculiarities that the linguistic material obtained from him exhibits. He has not of course that feeling for the old Indian life, and faith in the truth of the myths, that a man like Louis Simpson has; nevertheless, in spite of his white man's rationalism, he is not at all disposed to dismiss as idle the ideas of the Indians in regard to medicine-men and guardian spirits. He has been trained in the Agency school, reads and writes English well, and in general displayed throughout remarkable intelligence; he has been of the greatest help to me, both in the field and in correspondence, and I take this opportunity of thanking him.

These characterizing remarks are unmistakable in contrasting the two men along isomorphic distinctions of generation as well as cultural, psychosocial (attitudinal), racial, and linguistic purity in Wishram (Indian)-vs.-other terms.

There is a real sense, then, in which McGuff was, for Sapir, an interlocutor "closer" to himself than Simpson. By virtue of schooling, and so forth, McGuff crosses the line of the fieldwork encounter so as to become, indeed, a projectively collaborative voice whose reminiscences, even, are taken to have been offered in the perspectival spirit of exemplificatory ethnographic material and/or objective description, that is, essentially salvage-ethnographic reportage, as is Sapir's apparent intention in publishing such passages on "customs" as this one, or in other anthropological writings.[5] Thus it is particularly note-

5. Thus note that Sapir recommended Peter McGuff as an interpreter to Melville Jacobs in the latter's own first fieldwork, on Klikitat ([Northern] Sahaptin), when Jacobs went out to Washington in the summer of 1926 to begin doctoral research, also from Boas's Columbia University department. Jacobs (1929: 242) reported as follows about Mr. McGuff, who worked with him that year as an interpreter for Klikitat text dictation by Joe Hunt:

> The stories told in July and August, 1926, were read off by me [from transcription—MS] and translated by Peter McGuff, Wishram by native speech, aged about 50, a rather sophisticated native who learned Klikitat fairly well because of constant intimacy with Sahaptins in the Yakima-Columbia region. McGuff . . . was a student at Chemawa [Indian Training School near Salem, Oregon] and in addition, could read and write in the phonetic script used. He had been taught to do so by Dr. Edward Sapir in 1905. In spite of remarkable aptitude for linguistic work, McGuff's Klikitat

worthy to Sapir that "in spite of [McGuff's] white man's rationalism, he is not at all disposed to dismiss as idle the ideas of the Indians in regard to medicine-men and guardian spirits"; the text artifact in question, "Winter Bathing," is in fact about the latter. In it, we might say, we can find evidence that something else was being entextualized from Mr. McGuff's perspective. Determining exactly what this text was, and what its genre characteristics are, requires an examination of the artifactual inscription.

Denotational Text Architectonics and Linear Structure

As I noted above, the artifact is printed on facing pages (Sapir 1909: 188–91) of Kiksht and English, the first verso and second recto, starting in the middle of one opening of pages, and continuing to the middle of the next. In Figure 3.1, I reproduce Sapir's original published arrangement, uniting the material into a single left-right pair of Kiksht and English versions, preserving Sapir's printed paragraphing, while adding subscripts $_a$ and $_b$ to Sapir's line numbers to keep the reference indexes of the two original Kiksht pages distinct. I have also added some annotations that call attention to the overall architecture of the "literal" denotational text I believe we can recover here, upon which the following considerations can be brought to bear.[6]

---

translations were not as well given as [another interpreter's—MS], because of his lesser familiarity with the dialect and mythology.

Observe that this would put Mr. McGuff's birthdate at around 1870 to 1875, making him about 30–35 years of age when he worked with Sapir in 1905. Note also that despite McGuff's ability to "read and write in the phonetic script used," Jacobs read the dictated Hunt material back to him to have him translate, preserving more explicitly the distance between lettered researcher and mediating "native" in the presence of Mr. and Mrs. Hunt. (Of Mr. Hunt, by the way, Jacobs gives a characterization nicely paralleling the one Sapir gave of Mr. Simpson, quoted above, using such phrasings as: "He is thoroughly a Klikitat; . . . Mentally he lives in a closed Klikitat Indian world. . . . Few Christian notions have really touched him. . . . He is classed by officialdom as one of the old irreconcilables.")

6. In 1990, through the kindness—here gratefully acknowledged—of Martin L. Levitt, then Assistant Manuscripts Librarian, now Associate Librarian for Administration, I had the opportunity to examine Sapir's Wishram field notebooks now deposited in the Manuscripts Department of the Library of the American Philosophical Society. They had been for some decades in the possession of Sapir's Chicago and Yale student Walter Dyk (see Eggan and Silverstein 1974) and then of Dell Hymes.

The group of texts on "Customs" attributed to McGuff by Sapir in the published edition do, indeed, all occur together, in Sapir's hand, in notebook 2, on numbered pages 135–141 (the numeration scheme proceeding from right to left in the instance). That is, they do indeed appear

Mr. McGuff's text has two major divisions, formally distinguished at line 7_b by the switch from consistent use of the future/conditional/usitative verbal inflection, marked by circumfix a- . . . -a on finite narrative forms, to consistent use of remote, nonmythic past verbal inflection, marked by initial prefix ga- and sixth-position proximad directional deictic -t-, as in 11_b ga_1-n_2-i_4-ghi_5-t_6-$\sqrt{kl_7}$ 'I$_2$ saw$_{5+7}$ him$_4$ long-ago$_{1+6}$'.[7] At this point in the serial flow of talk, there is a shift from speaking of the habitual occurrences of childhood, when hapless falling asleep during wintertime late-evening myth performances led inexorably to the "punishment" of having to bathe ritually in the Columbia River (or equivalent). Mr. McGuff shifts at line 7_b to a commentary on what this "custom" was then understood to be all about, and then to the remark—with the irony of "his white man's rationalism," perhaps?—that it seems to have only partially worked for him, if at all.

But up to this point of division, what Mr. McGuff has dictated is organized around four quotations, outlined in Figure 3.1 with solid lines. Each quotation,

---

to have been dictations to Sapir. (There is even a piece on facing pages 138a–b in English, indicating it could not have been from Mr. Simpson, whose English was "hardly intelligible at times.") "Winter Bathing" occurs on pages 139–141. Sapir supplies interlinear gloss to the Kiksht text, as well as superscript keyings of clarifying paradigmatic material for words and constructions that appears to have been part of the translation and explication process.

When we compare the notebook version with the printed version, we find that there are numerous minor changes in transcription: (1) fixing up errors in catching the notoriously difficult velar-uvular distinction (k:q; x:xh; etc.) that is not always clearly articulated in some contexts, which Sapir obviously later normalized according to his post-field emerging lexical knowledge; (2) treatment of vowel truncations in phrasal juncture ($k'aya^+mxhghwadama$ in the notebook becomes $k'ay^+amxhghwadama$ in the printed version [line 11_a] 'you will not go and bathe', etc.), where Sapir formulates an editorial rule for printed versions that truncates vowels of clitics and non-heads of phrases, restoring the morphological vowels of head words, or otherwise truncates the first of two vowels in sandhi; (3) only one actual reordering, of the verb $amxtachgwa$ 'you will come (up with your head) out of the water', occurs, in printed lines 22_a–23_a, where Sapir has put it into its appropriate place according to the logic of serial order of denoted ritual actions being described at that point with highly parallelistic text segments.

7. The subscript numbers in the morphological analysis of the Kiksht form, to which I have keyed pieces of the English translation, represent the order-class arrangement of complex words. While it is not necessary that a member of every order-class occur in every word, the general rule is that at a given plane of derivation from any word-root and its inflection, the subscript integers must increase monotonically from left to right. For further details on tense and aspect formations, and the use of directional deictics -u_6- 'distad' and -t_6- 'proximad', see Silverstein 1974: S95; and especially Hymes 1975. For an outline of the Kiksht inflectional and derivational systems, see Silverstein 1976: 129–49; 1984.

of varying length, is attributed simply to that "impersonal" or generic speaker among the old people of olden times. Such people ascriptively were the repositories of knowledge, the centers of authority and authoritativeness, and the upholders of traditional custom, including telling myths in wintertime, seeing to it that children trained for physical, emotional, and spiritual strength, and so forth, as the roles are described in this reminiscence. Each quotation is introduced in parallel form with a finite framing verb (metapragmatic descriptor) in the generic third-person agent, first-person patient usitative, a_1-q_2-n_3-u_6-$\sqrt{lxam_7}$-a_{12} 'they$_2$ would$_{1+12}$ say-to$_7$ me$_3$; I$_3$ would$_{1+12}$ be-told$_{7+2}$'. Each quotation, as so framed, is the culminative segment within its segment, all of what precedes it serving to set up the situation in which such words would have been spoken to the then-young Mr. McGuff. This narrative style is quite familiar from both *qánuchk* and *qíxhikalhx*.

Further, if we think of each quotation and its preceding material as forming a bipartite unit of introductory frame plus character's utterance, the first three of such units all seem to be parallel in developing the theme of bathing in particular, and thus form an obvious denotational unity, while the fourth quotation seems to concern looking at/away from the household hearth and its fire, with no lexical or semantic material about bathing.

Note that the first quotation (lines 10_a–11_a) is in the form of a double protasis-apodosis, the first positive, the second negative ("if *P*, then *Q*; if not *P*, then not *Q*"). Here, in the conditional with circumfix *a*- . . . -*a*, the relationship is established between the circumstance of falling asleep (a_1-m_3-u_6-$\sqrt{ghupt_7}$-$íd_{10}$-a_{12} 'you$_3$ will$_{1+12}$ fall-asleep$_{7+10}$') and the somnolent child's having to be waked up in the night in order to go to bathe (a_1-m_4+xh-$\sqrt{ghwád_7}$-am_{10}-a_{12} 'you$_4$ will$_{1+12}$ go-and$_{10}$ bathe$_7$ ([your]self)').

The second quotation is simply the single imperative form, "Go and bathe yourself!" uttered on occasion by one of the old people (*ilh-q'íyuqt*)[8] when the then young McGuff, as he recalls in narration, had in fact fallen asleep before the myth performance was concluded and had been awakened for his "punishment."

The third quotation gives elaborate, specific instructions on exactly how to "bathe" in the icy and ice-covered water of the river. Again here, all of the finite verb forms are inflected with circumfix *a*- . . . -*a* and second-person sin-

---

8. Observe that the framing verb -$\sqrt{lxam_7}$ here agrees in number and gender with its subject, *ilh-q'íyuqt*, (third-person) neuter-collective, and hence has inflectional prefix -lhg_2- 'third-person neuter-coll. ergative'.

A'ngadix· nk!a'ckacbɛt itq!ē'yôqtikc qxa'nutck atgiu'xwa
tcagɛ'lqłix·.   Aga kwô'ba nxugui'tcatkt.   Aqnôlxa'ma :

"I"   10 ⌐ "Cma'n' amugopti'da a'-itsxɛp nā'wit amxqwô'dama;⌐
cma'nix k!ā'y' amugopti'da k!ā'y' amxgwa'dama." ⌐ Yax'
itck!a'xc iqxa'nutck nk!a'ckacbɛt ag' adnɛnk!na'mxida
da'xka da'ud aqxnulxa'm' ag' anxuguwi'tcatkɛma. Cma'ni
ā'-itsxɛb anugopti'da sa'qᵘ ałixu'łgw' aqxɛnugo'tcgɛma.

"II"   15 Ałgɛnu'łxam' iłq!ē'yôqt: ⌐ "Mxgwa'tam." ⌐ Kĭ'nua q!ɛ'm
anxu'xw' aga dnu qxa'daga hā'-ai 'nu'ya.   Da'kdag aq-
nu'xwa ngaqᵘda'tx qa'xb' iłɛlɛqła't łiabla'd ika'ba ô'watci
da'ukwa daq!a'b ixi'gat.

Ałgĭ'nɛluda iq!ĭ'stɛn bama capca'p qiuxu'nnił ika'ba.
20 Ałgɛnulxa'ma : ⌐ "Sāqᵘ lxô'b amiu'xwa-axdix·a ; lɛ'b amxu'xwa, amxkta'tcgw', amxɛlga'gw', asɛmxɛlu'tka a'tpxiamd
aga'lax, wā' 'mxu'xw' amglu'maya ; lɛ'b amxu'xw', amx-
ta'tcgw' asɛmxɛlu'tka tc!ē'q!kɛmt giga'd, wā' nā'wid wi't!'
"III"   amxu'xwa ; lɛ'b amxu'xw', amxda'tcgwa, wi't!a daukw' am-
25 glu'maya, iwa'd asɛmxɛlu'tka tc!ē'q!kɛmt ; lɛ'b amxu'xw',
amxda'tcgw', asɛmxɛlu'tk' u'lpqdiamd aga'lax, wā' 'mxu'-
xwa ; lɛ'b amxu'xwa łagwɛ'nɛmix·, mxda'tcgw', aminxa'-
nauɛnx' igu'cax, wā' 'mxu'xw', aga kô'pt, amxatk!wa'ya."

'Ga ya'xdau andi'mamabɛt aga a'ngadix· ugwi'łx·ix·
watu'ł, iłgna'łxat qxɛmx·i'udɛmax itanłĭ'qłĭq iłxk!wa'iulkł.
5 Qxnulxa'ma : ⌐ "Nā'qxi qsakli'dɛlk wa'tuł ; iwa'd ɛmxɛl-
ga'gwa, imipu'tc ya'lud wa'tuł ; pᵘ' agɛmu'xwa kᵛᵛɛ'ldix·,
"IV"   agɛmu'xwa k'u'ldix· amū'mda." ⌐ Ya'xtau qxē'dau ga-
qxɛ'ntx bama k!ā'y' iła'mqt kwô'dau iłałxē'wulx, a'watci
da'ukwa iyu'łmax giłgɛlxu'lal.   Aga ga'nuit nk!a'ckac bama'
10 k!ā'ya qxa'ntcix itctcgɛ'mɛm ; da'minua tkłxē'wulx ; k!ma
k!ā'ya ganigi'tkɛl dan ia'xleu iyu'łmax,[1] qɛ'nɛgi łkâ'n
iälgwi'lit. ⌐ Cma'ni k!ā'y' ika'ba wi'małba ix·tma'xix· aknĭ'm

footnote   a'watci abu'd iē'luxt ; łaka'xt' iłtcqoa' 'łɛnxɛlgwô'da. Abu'd
a'watci 'knĭ'm łcta'cq tcagɛ'lqłix· tcłɛlbô'nił da'minua a'-ic
15 qxi ma'nk tslu'nus a-itsā's. ⌐ Qxł'dau.

FIGURE 3.1 Sapir's text-artifact with structural annotations

gular subject -*m*-. After the first clause telling the addressee (young McGuff)
to chop through the ice, the rest is organized into segments with a high degree
of parallelism, each one describing how he is to immerse himself, come up out
of the water facing in a particular cardinal direction, and shout "Wah!" The
series of actions, plunging in and emerging with a particular orientation, moves
through five points that determine a hemisphere around the axial vertical of the
child's body, in the order Down–East–North–South–West–Up. Down/Up is
the axial dimension that frames the entire series; East/West is the next inner-
most frame, the upriver/downriver axis of the Columbia River at the culturally
ascribed location; North/South is the direction across the river, perpendicular

A long while ago, when I was a boy, the old men would tell myths in winter. Now there I was listening to them. I would be told: "If you fall asleep before it is finished, straightway you will have to go and bathe. If you do not fall asleep, you will not go and bathe." Now I was fond of myths when I was a boy, so I would be satisfied with the things that I was told and would listen to them. If I fell asleep too early, (when) it was all finished, they would wake me up. An old man would say to me: "Go in bathing!" I would try to refuse, but in vain, so I just had to go. I was undressed entirely naked where he knew there was lots of ice or also where it was pressed together tight.

He would give me an ax for chopping up the ice. He would say to me: "You will chop right through it, you will dive under water, you will stick your head out, you will turn around, you will look to the rising sun, you will cry out 'wā!', you will shout. You will duck down under water, you will stick your head out, you will look across this way (i.e., north), straightway you will again shout 'wā!' You will duck down under water, you will stick your head out, again you will shout as before, you will look across yonder (i.e., south). You will duck down under water, you will stick your head out, you will look to the setting sun, you will shout 'wā!' You will duck down under water for the fifth time, you will stick your head out, you will look up to the sky. Then enough; you will return home."

Now when I came home, a fire was already burning. On the ends of my head-hair icicles were dangling. I would be told: "Don't be looking at the fire; turn away from it, present your buttocks to the fire. It will quickly blow at you and make you grow quickly." That is how I was done to in order not to be sick and in order to be strong, or, just so, in order to prepare one for a guardian spirit. And indeed ever since I was a child I have never been sick; I have always been strong. But not at all have I seen anything that they call a guardian spirit,[1] I do not know what it is like. Sometimes, although there is no ice in the river, it is present in a canoe or a boat; in that same water I would bathe myself. In winter the water of a boat or canoe always freezes, which is just a little bit cool. Thus.

to the East/West in the plane of the hemisphere's cross-section. Note how the series of actions constructs the three axes and their projective cosmos through the deictic origin of the performer's-body-in-river. This can be seen in Figure 3.2a.

Thus the three quotational units bring us to Mr. McGuff's habitual experience of the ritual of "punishment" bathing in wintertime. Clearly this is something of an obligatory punishment, since children would, of course, always have fallen asleep in the course of storytelling that went on far, far into the night. Once we see that there is a cosmically grounded self-placement involved in ritual bathing, it is not hard to understand that the "punishment" was an obliga-

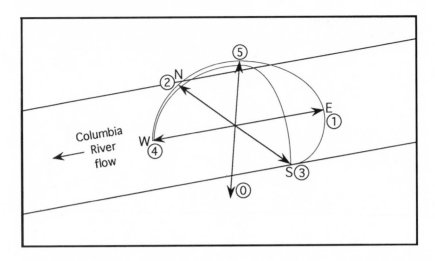

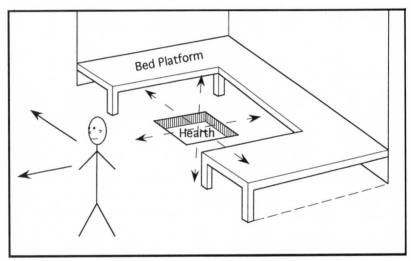

FIGURE 3.2 [a] Ritualized riverine bathing; [b] ritualized self-positioning at home hearth

tory part of growing up for anyone for whom there were aspirations of achievement.

The narrative unit made up of the fourth quotation and its introductory material, by contrast, describes a scene characteristic after the ritual bathing. Remarkably, the introductory material here in lines 3_b to 5_b is syntactically formed in striking parallelism to the introductory material of the first quotation, in lines 8_a to 9_a. That is, the very syntactic form of parallelism in the framing material makes of this an episode introduced to parallel the entire preceding series of quotation units, an episode located once more in the house, after the culminative, solitary experience of riverine ritual enjoined in quotation-segment three.

Mr. McGuff's young self is once more the perspectival center of deixis-within-the-narrative here. And we, as addressees of the 1905 McGuff's voicing of reminiscence, are once more transposed to this center, just as in the initial quotation segment earlier in line 9_a, which uses what we might term the "historical simultaneous" form n_3-xh-u_4-g $^wi_5$-[$w\hat{\imath}$]cha+$\sqrt{t}k_7$-t_{10} 'I$_3$ am$_{10}$ "giving-ear"$_7$-to$_5$ them$_4$'. Linguistically, we have parallel 'when'-clauses marked by enclitic #bt, followed by a descriptor involving something the old people characteristically did from the young McGuff's perspective, followed by a 'simultaneous/present-continuative' clause describing young McGuff in that scene as the deictic origin (located 'here' and 'now' for purposes of tense, evidentiality, and other presupposing indexical categories), followed by the framing verb *aqnulxama* and its framed quotation.[9]

This fourth quotation, however, seems at first to be completely unrelated to the sequence of three in the first part. It is an injunction to the lad to turn his buttocks to the fire, looking out-and-away from it, so that the fire, quickly blowing on him, will make him grow quickly. As shown in Figure 3.2b, within the house the arrangement of the boy's dripping-wet body with respect to the central hearth forms, in microcosm, an icon (diagram) of positioning in the axially centered space of the macrocosm already established in-and-by the riverine bathing ritual. So the ritual efficacy of the "blowing" (shouting out "Wah!") by the "punished" child in the riverine-centered macrocosm is reciprocated by "blowing" by the nurturant fire in the domestic, hearth-centered

---

9. There is the exceedingly revealing use of an evidential passive form [a_3-]u_6-$\sqrt{g}w\hat{\imath}lhx_7$-$ix_{12}$ $w\acute{a}_3$-$tulh$ 'it$_3$ must-have-been-kindled$_7$ the-fire$_3$' in line 3_b as a parallel ascription to the one in line 8_a about the old people, 'they would tell (lit., 'make') myths in winter'. While the overt subject is $w\acute{a}tulh$ 'fire', notwithstanding, a transitive q_2- or tg_2- or lhg_2- predication for some nonspecific but definite agency ('they must have [already] kindled it') is pragmatically entailed by the use of the evidential passive (see Silverstein 1978; 1981: 10–14 for details). Such an evidential passive is here an unmistakable form of indirect free style, for which the availability of the deictically anchoring consciousness required for its use is permitted to the reminiscing narrator. It makes an entirely new genre of voicing available. Note that the evidential passive is found only in Wishram-Wasco localism among all the dialects of Kiksht, and it presumably emerged as a grammatical category in Mr. McGuff's generation, not in Mr. Simpson's. My own language consultants, some consociates and approximate coevals of Mr. McGuff, knew and used these forms; the example at hand is the unique occurrence, so far as is known, in the entire *Wishram Texts*.

microcosm. The child faces away from the domestic hearth—looking outward from it, though still in the house—in the direction he will take as he "goes out" into the world of adulthood.

The diagrammatic similarity of the two situations described in this reminiscence narrative is unmistakable, and the interpretation of their relationship is suggestive. But what clinches the argument is the existence of a pair of Chinookan-family-wide verbal roots (thus reconstructible as common inheritance), occurring in all dialects either independently or as a compounded (ninth order-class) root that goes together with another, main root (denoting motion or location) of the inflectional stem. In one sense, these roots $-\sqrt{pchk^w}$ and $-\sqrt{lhxh}$ mean '(motion/location) out-of-/away-from-water [sc., river, lake, ocean]' and '(motion/location) in(to)-/towards-water [sc., river, lake, ocean]'; they are understood to be respectively towards/away from the various culturally understood realms of human habitation and activity (land, campsite, village, etc.). In a second sense, the roots refer to the opposition of orientation away from/toward hearth or fire. Here we have, in other words, a lexicalized opposition that unites the macrocosm-microcosm trope-in-depiction contained in the denotational text the structure of which we have been theorizing.[10] Mr. McGuff's reminiscences flowing from the situation of didactic myth performances to the "punishment" of having to bathe ritually in the river and back to the nurturing hearth-fire exemplify the schematic unity the lexical pair captures in its denotational senses.

At this point, we have been brought by Mr. McGuff to the major division of the text, marked by the shift in tense noted at the outset of our analysis. Mr. McGuff reveals here, in summary, *why* these were the recurrent experiences of the "long ago wintertimes when [he] was a (preadolescent) child." While the experiences themselves were recounted in the temporally unanchored usitative/ conditional aspect, the reasons for them and Mr. McGuff's other commentary are anchored as having happened in the 'remote (nonmythic) past', deictically calibrated, in other words, to the moment and event of communication. "That is how I was done to (ga_1-q_2-n_3-t_6-$\sqrt{xh_7}$)," he tells Sapir, "so as never to be sick, to be strong, and likewise so a guardian spirit ('spirit power') prepared for [me]." And though from childhood he has never been ill and has in fact been

10. This is an interesting area for comparative and areal research on schematizations of spatial and phenomenal realms in Northwest Coast cultures. See for example Enrico 1985 on a parallel among the Masset (Haida), where the hearth-fire is clearly a point of cross-realm axiality (hence, transfer-point across) temporal and supernatural realms, a microcosm of the village-point on the vast ocean-cosmos in macrocosm.

always vigorous, he has never encountered "a guardian spirit of any kind (*dan iaxhliu*), whatever that might look like."

There follows a passage which I have labeled a footnote in Figure 3.1. It explains that even when there was no ice in the Columbia River, ice would form in the bottoms of (traditional) canoes or (modern) boats, and Mr. McGuff would bathe himself in the ritual of "punishment" in these, rather than directly in the river.

It has been suggested[11] that this passage may, in fact, not be an after-thought to the first part, especially to the second and third quotation-units, which make reference to the ice-covered water central perhaps to the full ritual efficacy of winter "bathing"—and to the vividness of the account being told in hot Yakima Valley summertime of 1905 (ice, icicles, and freezing water are mentioned in lines 17_a–18_a, 19_a, and 4_b, as well as here in lines 12_b and 14_b). Rather, one might see this as an explicit excuse or explanation/rumination that makes plausible why, come to think of it, Mr. McGuff does not, in fact, have a guardian spirit: maybe it was that seemingly nonoptimal bathing in canoe- and boat-bottoms during the not-so-cold wintertimes, or perhaps early winter mornings when young McGuff's trainers did not take him all the way into the river itself.

Whatever the exact status, if resolvable, of the textual passage from lines 12_b to 15_b—and both possibilities make perfect sense—we see that as deno-tational text, the organization into a hierarchical architecture of segments emerges over the course of 1905 dictation-time in a way that makes the last ga_1- . . . -t_6- section (line 7_b to the end) function as the denotational frame that retrospectively puts the first part (to line 7_b) into very personal, very "present-ist" historical perspective as a custom experienced by the narrating self. In Mr. McGuff's case, it is a custom the practice of which has been, to him, only partially successful, and certainly not in the way most valued for the Wishram and other indigenous peoples of the region: facilitating the acquisition of a guardian spirit.

Locating the Genre(s) of Interactional Text(s) Here

It seems clear that Sapir thought himself to be taking down from McGuff an unproblematically expository "ethnologic" text, in the same manner as he had that summer been doing, along with McGuff's help, from the older Mr. Simp-

11. By several students in my course, "Language in Culture," at The University of Chicago in Winter Quarter, 1990, principally Adam Rose, whom I thank here for the suggestion.

son, and as McGuff would himself do in turn on Sapir's behalf when Sapir went back to New York. Indeed, from its beginning down through line 7_b, the denoted world, the universe within the narrative, is the habitual "customary" experience of an already bygone era with its seemingly more "Indian" way of life, a universe that Mr. McGuff experienced when he was a youngster, notwithstanding his only half-Wishram "blood."

In the denotational text we have theorized, the deictic center (or "pragmatic calibration"; Silverstein 1993: 48–53) shifts from the denotationally displaced one[12] of the narrated character's perspective in the first part to the frankly retrospective consciousness, in the second part, of the 1905-McGuff-in-the-apple-orchard-in-White-Swan, sitting with his somewhat younger interlocutor. For his part Sapir, presumably, could assimilate these latter comments as framing-from-afar (recall the *ga- . . . -t-* tense forms here), afterthoughts about the "customs" described in the first part, bringing the ethnographic detail, as it were, up to date from its earlier timeless realm of repeatable and repeated "custom" to document what had become of the practices of his youth, especially in any aftereffects.

But recall Sapir's slight (seeming) puzzlement at the limits of Mr. McGuff's non-Wishram and modern rationalism, especially on the subject of precisely such practices as these, where humans make contact as they can with the much-desired and prestigious other epistemic realm of the cosmic and supernatural. In this context, it would appear that Mr. McGuff, though perhaps intending at the outset to be giving a gloss to some "custom" alluded to in the summer's work with the nonanglophone Mr. Simpson, has ultimately entextualized a determinately distinct type of text.

The type is one that Sapir probably could not have recognized, but which later workers can immediately recall in many examples from Kiksht-speaking interlocutors and others sixty and even seventy years later. After hearing several such accounts, I formulated for myself the mnemonic handle of "How/

12. Note that this displacement is achieved by a cumulative, text-realtime chaining of deictics, denotational characterizations, and further deictics that presuppose the latter. First, Mr. McGuff uses the inherently deictic adverbial *ánghadix* 'long ago' as the first word of the piece in line 8_a, giving temporal anchoring as "reportively" calibrated events. Then he describes the interval "when I [= PMcG] was a child," within which were the recurrent interval-events "in wintertime" within which again "the old people would perform myths." *Agha kᵂába* 'now there' (i.e., where-when the myths were being told) n_3-*xh*-u_4-*g*ᵂ*i̯₅*-[*wi̯*]*cha*-√*tk₇*-t_{10} 'I₃ am listening to them₄', framing everything that follows in this section of narrative as now deictically centered on the character/consciousness of young McGuff attending to myths there-and-then. This becomes, in the narrative, the secondary perspectival (indexically presupposable) origin, and hence the secondary deictic origin within the whole first part of the denotational text.

Why I (or some other named individual) do(es)n't have a spirit power." Obviously still a cause of some anxiety and wonderment to Mr. McGuff's consociates whom I knew in their later years, it is not hard to imagine that this would be a projective focus of self-conceptualization for any traditionally influenced Wishram (or other regional group member) in 1905.[13] This would be particularly true for Mr. McGuff, whom people in later years specifically remembered as a "breed" (i.e., half-breed) in sometimes pointed racial terms, and whose Wishram identity would, no doubt, have been at issue in a number of ways.

Such is the text that seems to be clearly emerging or in play by the interactional point at which *a-* . . . *-a* inflectional forms of the denotational narrative give way to *ga-* . . . *t-* forms; and perhaps it had been in play for Mr. McGuff even from the beginning. This *interactional text*, this structured doing-things-with-words in the sphere of meaningful, genred social action, has, remarkably enough, a complex set of tropic relationships of meta-level diagrammaticity, converseness, complementarity, and logical negation to the phenomena it both presupposes and thematizes, which are all, as we have seen, *textual* phenomena, both discursive and otherwise.

One such relationship is with "traditional" myth-performance itself, the very activity of which is the hypothesis underlying the emplotment in the first

13. In their *Wishram Ethnography* of 1930, Leslie Spier and Edward Sapir combined their information from the summers of 1924–25 and 1905, respectively, and give a treatment of these matters in "traditional" Wishram society as the ethnographic timeline in sections captioned "Acquiring Power" and "Childhood" (Spier and Sapir 1930: 238–40, 256–58). The relationship between training to receive a guardian spirit and actually receiving one is reported, and they even quote in English the text of "Winter Bathing" at p. 257, but without any comment or explication. "It does not seem possible," Spier and Sapir observe (1930: 238), "that anyone would maintain failure in his quest for power," since as they understand the matter "the measure of success [in life] was held to be directly dependent on the extent of power, and this was held to vary from one individual to another." Guardian-spirit power was always revealed minimally (consistent with indexes of validity and authenticity), retrodictively (with the exception of shamans, most floridly only when the bearer was near death), and indirectly (through stereotyped indexical hints of differential specificity). (See Hymes 1966: 137–41, 149–56 on the Wishram ethnosociology of knowledge involved.) Yet here we seem to have the emergence-text in our records of a genre that appears on the face of it to admit to just that very traditionally inconceivable failure—notwithstanding the fact that, as of 1930 (when information would have been coming back to Spier and Sapir from Walter Dyk's [cf. n. 5] then-ongoing fieldwork), "[t]he belief in these spirit powers is still very strong and many Indians who seem to be thoroughly civilized and sophisticated have spirits secretly" (1930: 239). Recall Sapir's (1909: xi–xii) remarks quoted above. Perhaps we may see it differently with our gaze directed to the coeval rather than the retrospected ethnographic horizon: It is just *because of* the anxieties of identity that such a text-genre emerges as a recurring projective representation of disappearing "Indianness," as I am, in effect, suggesting.

part. As can be gathered from the denotational text, myth-telling was a characteristic event of winter nights, in which a very senior mythteller would recount/enact these as didactic pieces at least nominally for the youngsters gathered in a household (though of course the youngsters would unfortunately have the temerity to fall asleep before everything was told, and thus needed "punishment," that is, riverine "training" as a consequence). Consistent with the didactic nature of this genre of performance, at the conclusion of a canonical myth narrative (told in 'remote past' or 'past usitatives' in ga_1- . . . . -u_6- . . . (-$(a)xh_{11}$), by the way) comes a section in which the happenings and characterizations of the myth era are made relevant to the era-narratively-to-come, that is, the era in which the narrator and audience members live and are experiencing the ordained effects of the myth era. There is a Kiksht metapragmatic term for this section of the text, translated into local English as "X spoiled Y," for example, "Coyote spoiled Weasel"; it is the inflectable verb theme $[]_2$-$[]_4$-xh_5-$\sqrt{g^w á_7}$-$m(a)_{8.1}$- -it_{10} '$[]_2$ transform $[]_4$', which describes the event of announcement, by a myth-era protagonist or by the narrative voice, of how the characters and scenes of action will emerge phenomenally to the people of the coming (= present) era. When we consider that the guardian spirits that youngsters sought present themselves in the form of such species and "natural" phenomena as are the myth-to-present-era characters, the vivid relationship becomes clear to us between two performative events: the transformation-into-the-present narratively effected in the myth performance so as to prepare the world in renewal for (us) humans and, revealed as necessary through myth-performance (where children ascriptively lack audience endurance) the ritual "punishment" of a child's riverine bathing so as to get strength enough to be favored by the appearance of a spirit power.

The fact is, Mr. McGuff's "reminiscence" has, *mutatis mutandis*, all the structure of a myth performance. It characterizes a bygone era, *ánghadix*, in which the myth-narrating tradition was vigorous. It describes his younger self as a character in this bygone era, along with nameless old people, and it does so in a usitative-conditional inflectional form that indicates a repetitive timelessness. At printed line 7_b, the "transformation" is announced, albeit a negative transformation or an only partially effected one, in which, though he gained health and hardiness, he has never had the much-longed-for encounter with the life-transforming guardian spirit, despite the fact that he indeed appreciated the wisdom of the elders and paid careful attention to them (lines 11_a–13_a), and even carefully followed the directions about the bathing and other, related domestic ritual. (Could his fate have perhaps been due to bathing in canoes and boats [lines 12_b-15_b]?)

To be sure, the bygone era may well have had only a mythic reality for the 35-year-old Mr. McGuff. Removed in time by the intervention of U.S. Government schooling at Chemawa, removed in place from the villages of the Columbia River to White Swan, Washington, here he is in the rapidly developing agricultural economy of the Yakima Valley, which was then undergoing transformation by irrigation. And here he is, in the blazing heat of the summer of 1905, telling this personal "myth" to the schoolteacherish Edward Sapir, aged twenty-one, who, no matter how sympathetic as an individual, certainly embodied the very techniques of learning and wisdom of the enveloping society that had made the old people's "Indian" knowledge ineffective for Mr. McGuff's generation. Yet McGuff, mediating between the obviously more "genuine" and "traditional" Wishram Indian, Louis Simpson, and the friendly and inquiring New Yorker, Sapir,[14] was of course a person doubly peripheralized in the identity schemata of both cultures.

So in a sense McGuff and Sapir are in the curious position of ersatz Indian elder and quondam youngster, the former supplying "traditional" wisdom to the inquiring latter, who wants to write it down and disseminate it in the very society that has called it into question and even condemned it. With scholarly Euro-Americans wanting to have myth dictations (if not performances) on their terms, organized by academic calendars—thus, in summertime in broad daylight, not caring for the taboo this breaks by inverting the proper seasonality and diurnality—no wonder the knowledge and skill thereby displayed and deployed, even by a half-Indian, can only be partially—if at all—effective.

And the point is, the ironic voice of Peter McGuff that entextualizes this interactional text (as Edward Sapir was, no doubt, entextualizing one very different!) has come to realize both that in the Wishram universe it has not, in fact, gotten a spirit power, and that in the interlocutory universe of the larger society it will probably not obtain the equivalent.

APPENDIX

The following is a representation in transcript form of the complete text of "Winter Bathing," which visually incorporates—through physical arrangement—all of the observed parallelisms, hierarchical segmentations, and so forth on which the present analysis of entextualization depends. It is keyed to the original line numbers of Sapir's 1909 printed version as well, though its interlinear English translation departs from the printed translation at numerous points where further research has yielded greater accu-

---

14. To the extent meaningful to the locals, Sapir must have seemed to drop in on them from another planet, let alone era of modernity, in coming from the fabled New York.

racy. The transcript was prepared by Robert E. Moore in collaboration with Michael Silverstein; I thank Mr. Moore for permission to reproduce it here.

[Peter McGuff, "Winter Bathing" (Sapir 1909:188–191)]

ES/MS

8a/1	ángadix· n-k'áškaš#bət |	[a]A
	Long ago when I was a boy	
/9a/2	it-q'íuqt-ikš qánučk a-tg-i-ú-x̣ʷa /čagə́lqɫix·.|	[b]
	the old people would tell myths in winter.	
9a/3	aga kʷába n-x̣-u-gʷí-[wi]ča-tk-t. ‖	[c]
	Now there I am listening to them.	
9a/4	a-q-n-u-lxám-a:	
	I would be told:	
10a/5	"šmán[ix] a-m-u-g̣uptíd-a áicxəp |	[d]B
	"If you fall asleep too early,	
10a/6	"náwit a-m-x̣-qʷə́d-am-a; ‖	[e]
	"straightway you will have to go and bathe.	
11a/7	"šmánix k'áy⁺ a-m-u-g̣uptíd-a |	[d']
	"If you do not fall asleep,	
11a/8	"k'áy⁺ a-m-x̣-gʷád-am-a." ‖	[e']
	"you will not go and bathe."	
/12a/9	yax⁺ /i-č-k'áx̣š i-qánučk n-k'áškaš#bət |	[a']A'
	Now I was fond of myths when I was a boy,	
/13a/10	ag⁺ a-d-n-n-k'nám-xid-a /dáxka dáud⁺ a-q-n-u-lxám⁺	[b']
	so I would be satisfied with the things that I was told	
13a/11	ag⁺ a-n-x̣-u-g̣u-wíča-tk-ma. ‖	[c']
	and I would listen to them.	
/14a/12	šmáni /áicxəb a-n-u-g̣uptíd-a |	[d″]C
	If I fell asleep too early,	
14a/13	sáqʷ a-ɫ-i-x-ú-ɫkʷ⁺ |	
	[when] he would be all finished,	
14a/14	a-q-n-u-g̣účg-ma. ‖	
	[then] I would be awakened.	
15a/15	a-ɫg-n-ú-lxam⁺ iɫ-q'íuqt,	
	An old man would tell me,	

15a/16   "m-x̣-gʷát-am." ‖   [eʺ]
                "Go in bathing!"

/16a/17   kínwa q'ə́m /a-n-x̣-ú-x̣ʷ⁺ | aga dnu qádaga há?ai [a-]n-ú-ya.‖
          Vainly would I feign slothfulness, for indeed I simply had to go.

/17a/18   dákdag a-q-/n-ú-x̣ʷa n-gaqᵘdátx | D
                I would be stripped naked

/18a/19   qáx̣b⁺ i-ł-l-qłá-t ł-ia-blád i-kába,| áwači /dáukʷa daq'áb
          i-xí-ga-t.‖*
          where he knew there was lots of ice, or likewise where it was densely
          packed.*

19a/20   a-łg-í-n-l-u-d-a i-q'ístn | bama šapšáp q-i-u-x̣ú-nił i-kába.‖
          He would give an axe to me, for breaking up the ice.

20a/21   a-łg-n-u-lxám-a,
          He would tell me,

20a/22   "saqʷ λ̣x̣ə́b a-m-i-ú-x̣ʷa:x-d-ix·-a ‖
                "You will chop right through it,

21a/23   "lə́b a-m-x̣-ú-x̣ʷ-a, |
                "you will dive under,

21a/24   "a-m-x-k-tá-čgʷ⁺, ‖
                "you will stick your head out,

21a/25   "a-m-x̣⁺l-gá-gʷ⁺, |
                "you will turn yourself around,

/22a/26   "a-s-m-xl-ú-tg-a á-t-p-x#yamt /a-gáλax̣, ‖
                "you will look toward the rising sun,

22a/27   " 'wá!' [a-]m-x̣-ú-x̣ʷ⁺ a-m-g-lúma-ya; ‖
                " 'wá!' you will 'go', you will shout;

22a/28   "lə́b a-m-x̣-ú-x̣ʷ⁺ |
                "you will dive under,

/23a/29   "a-m-x-/tá-čgʷ⁺ |
                "you will stick your head out,

23a/30   "a-s-m-xl-ú-tk-a#č'ɛ́qłk-mt gigád ‖
                "you will look across this way [i.e., north],

/24a/31   " 'wá!' náwid wít'⁺ /a-m-x̣-ú-x̣ʷa; ‖
                " 'wá!' right away again you'll 'go'.

24a/32   "lə́b a-m-x̣-ú-x̣ʷ⁺ |
                "You will dive under,

24a/33   "a-m-x-dá-čgʷ⁺ ‖
                "you will stick your head out,

/25a/34   "wít'a daukʷ⁺ a-m-/g-lúma-ya, ‖
                "again as before you will shout,

            χ
25a/35   "iwád a-s-m-xl-ú-tk-a č'ɛ́qɫk-mt; ‖
                "you will look across yonder [i.e., south].

25a/36   "lə́b a-m-x̣-ú-x̣ʷ⁺ |
                "You will dive under,

26a/37   "a-m-x-dá-čgʷ⁺ |
                "you will stick your head out,

26a/38   "a-s-m-xl-ú-tk⁺ [a-]ú-l-pq-d#iamt ag̣áƛax, ‖
                "you will look toward the setting sun

/27a/39   " 'wá!' ⁺m-x̣-ú-/x̣ʷa; ‖
                " 'wá!' you'll 'go'.

27a/40   "lə́b a-m-x̣-ú-x̣ʷa |
                "You will dive under

27a/41   "ɫa-gʷə́nm-ix·, |
                "for the fifth time,

27a/42   "[a-]m-x-dá-čgʷ⁺ |
                "you will stick your head out,

28a/44   "a-m-i-n-x̣ána-wənx i-gúšax̣, ‖
                "you will look up to the sky,

28a/45   " 'wa!' ⁺m-x̣-ú-x̣ʷ⁺ ‖
                " 'wá!' you'll 'go'.

28a/46   "aga kə́pt; | a-m-xa-t-k'ʷá-ya." ‖
                "Then enough; you will return home."

3b/47   [a]ga yáx̣dau a-n-d-í-mam[-a]#bət |
                Now when I would arrive home,

/4b/48   aga ángadix· [a-]u-gʷíɫx·-ix· /wa-túɫ, |
                now a fire is already burning [for some time].

4b/49   iɫ-g-náɫx̣at qəmx·íud-max̣ i-tanɫíqɫiq i-ɫ-x-k'ʷá-iu-l-k-ɫ. ‖
                On the ends of my head-hair icicles are dangling.

5b/50	[a-]q-n-u-lxám-a,
	I would be told,
5b/51	"náqi q-s-a-k'í-[t-]d+l+k wá-tuł; ‖
	"One doesn't look at the fire;
/6b/52	"iwád a-m-x̱+l-/gá-gʷa,	
	"turn around that way,
6b/53	"i-mi-púč yá-l-u-d wá-tuł; ‖
	"give your buttocks to the fire.
6b/54	"p'ú a-g-m-ú-x̱ʷa k'ʷə́ldix·,	
	"Quickly it will blow on you,
7b/55	"a-g-m-ú-x̱ʷa k'úldix· a-m-ú-md-a." ‖
	"it will make you grow quickly."

/8b/56	yáx̱tau qídau ga-/q-ń-t-x̱ bama
	That is how I was done to so that
8b/57	k'áy⁺ i-łá-mqt
	one might not be sickly
8b/58	kʷádau it-ła-łx̱íwulx,
	and that one might be strong,
/9b/59	áwači /dáukʷa i-yúłmax̱ k#i-ł-gl-x̱ú-lal.
	or, just so, that a guardian spirit would ready itself for one.
9b/60	aga gánuit n-k'áškaš#bamá
	And indeed ever since I was a child
10b/61	k'áya qánčix i-č-čgə́məm;
	I have never been sick,
10b/62	dáminwa t-k-łx̱íwulx;
	I have always been strong.
/11b/63	k'ma /k'áya ga-n-i-gí-t-kəl dan i-iá-x̱liu i-yúłmax̱, qə́ngi łkə́n i-iæ-lgʷílit.
	But never have I seen what is called a guardian spirit, whatever it might look like.

["Footnote" (ES 12b-15b):]

*(šmáni k'áy[a] i-kába wí-mał-ba ix·tmáxix, a-kním áwači a-búd

*(Although (there is) no ice in the river from time to time, it will be present

i-ɛ́-l-u-x̣-t; łakáxt[au] ił-čqʷá [a-]ł-n-x̣+l-g ʷɔ́d-a.
in a canoe or a boat; in that same water would I bathe myself.

a-búd áwači [a-]kním [i]ł-štá-šq čagɔ́lqłix· č-ł-l-bú-nił dáminwa.
The water of a boat or a canoe in winter always freezes.

áiš qi mánk c'únus ai-cás.)
It's just a little bit cooler.)

15b   qidau.
            Thus.

REFERENCES

Bakhtin, Mikhail M.
    1981   *The Dialogic Imagination: Four Essays.* Michael Holquist (ed.), Caryl Em-
            erson and Michael Holquist (trans.). Austin: University of Texas Press.

Boyarin, Jonathan (ed.)
    1993   *The Ethnography of Reading.* Berkeley and Los Angeles: University of Cali-
            fornia Press.

Eggan, Fred, and Michael Silverstein
    1974   Walter Dyk, 1899–1972. *American Anthropologist* 76: 86–87.

Enrico, John
    1985   The fire as conduit to the other world: A note on Haida deixis and Haida
            belief. *International Journal of American Linguistics* 51: 400–402.

Hymes, Dell
    1966   Two types of linguistic relativity (with examples from Amerindian ethnogra-
            phy). In *Sociolinguistics*, W. Bright (ed.), 114–67. The Hague: Mouton.
    1975   From space to time in tenses in Kiksht. *International Journal of American
            Linguistics* 41: 313–29.
    1984   The earliest Clackamas text. *International Journal of American Linguistics*
            50: 358–83.

Jacobs, Melville
    1929   Northwest Sahaptin texts, 1. *University of Washington Publications in An-
            thropology*, vol. 2, no. 6. Seattle: University of Washington Press.

Kripke, Saul A.
    1972   Naming and necessity. In *Semantics*, D. Davidson and G. Harman (eds.),
            253–355. Dordrecht: D. Reidel Publishing Co.

Putnam, Hilary
    1975   The meaning of 'meaning'. In *Philosophical Papers*, vol. 2, *Mind, Language,
            and Reality*, 215–71. Cambridge: Cambridge University Press.

Sapir, Edward
    1909   Wishram texts. *Publications of the American Ethnological Society*, vol. 2.
            Leyden: E. J. Brill.

1909   (ed.). Wasco tales and myths, collected by Jeremiah Curtin. In Sapir 1909, 237–314.

Silverstein, Michael
1974   Dialectal developments in Chinookan tense-aspect systems: An areal-historical analysis. *Publications in Anthropology and Linguistics, Memoirs*, no. 29. Chicago: University of Chicago Press.
1976   Hierarchy of features and ergativity. In *Grammatical Categories in Australian Languages*, R. M. W. Dixon (ed.), 112–71. Canberra, A.C.T.: Australian Institute of Aboriginal Studies.
1977   Person, number, gender in Chinook: Syntactic rule and morphological analogy. *Proceedings of the Berkeley Linguistics Society* 3: 143–56.
1978   Deixis and deducibility in a Wasco-Wishram passive of evidence. *Proceedings of the Berkeley Linguistics Society* 4: 238–53.
1981   The limits of awareness. *Sociolinguistic Working Papers*, no. 84. Austin: Southwest Educational Development Laboratory.
1984   Wasco-Wishram lexical derivational processes *vs.* word-internal syntax. In *Papers from the Parasession on Lexical Semantics*, Chicago, 27–28 April 1984, D. Testen et al. (ed.), 270–88. Chicago: Chicago Linguistic Society.
1993   Metapragmatic discourse and metapragmatic function. In *Reflexive Language: Reported Speech and Metapragmatics*, J. A. Lucy (ed.), 33–58. Cambridge: Cambridge University Press.

Spier, Leslie, and Edward Sapir
1930   Wishram ethnography. *University of Washington Publications in Anthropology*, vol. 3, no. 3. Seattle: University of Washington Press.

4 "Self"-Centering Narratives

Vincent Crapanzano

I

On June 22, 1860, in the village of Saint Jean d'Angely, near La Rochelle, the following marginal note was made on the birth certificate of Adelaïde Herculine Barbin, who had been born twenty-one years earlier on November 8, 1838.

> In its decision of June 21, 1860 the civil court of Saint Jean d'Angely ordered that the attached certificate be corrected in the following way: 1.) that the concerned child be designated as of the male sex; and 2.) that the Christian name Abel be substituted for those of Adelaïde Herculine. (Barbin 1978: 160)[1]

The decreed change of sex was based on the conclusions of an extensive medical examination: "Alexina [Adelaïde Barbin's nickname] is a man, without doubt a hermaphrodite, but with an evident predominance of the male sex" (Barbin 1978: 137–140). The awkward conclusion—based on Barbin's life history, anatomy, physiology ("At night, voluptuous sensations are followed by a spermatic flow, with which her linen is spotted and starched" [Barbin 1978: 140]), and her attraction to women—raises questions about social, particularly gender, classifications and their power over both the lives people live and the way they tell them.

In this essay I will focus on the *telling* of Barbin's life history, specifically on a fragment that purports to be an autobiography or an autobiographical novel. My concern is neither psychological nor anthropological but textual. The dramatic dislocation that followed Barbin's reclassification (and perhaps anticipated it, less dramatically) determined his/her life historical narrative in terms both of content and interlocutory, or dialogical, structure, but it did not do so completely. No doubt gender relations prevalent in nineteenth-century France, no doubt attitudes toward the body, sexuality, identity, aberration, so-

1. This book contains the autobiographical fragment, *Mes Souvenirs*, which will hereafter be cited in the text as *MS*. All translations from the French are my own.

cial classification, medicine, and the State, indeed language, text, and narrative, affected—and effected—this dislocation and its story. It would be a mistake, though, to understand the dislocation and its story particularistically, in terms only of the psychology or physiology of Barbin's hermaphroditism. Such reductive understanding, characteristic of many popular and less than popular psychologies—psychologies that do not acknowledge, or bracket off too easily, narrative conventions—is essentialist, ultimately tautological. It precludes consideration of narrative constraints, of the tension between the "lived" and the narrative, of the possibility of succumbing to, of being submerged in, a "prescribed" narrative or losing that narrative possibility.

Barbin's life can be understood in terms of the loss of a genre—the loss of those conventionalized discursive strategies by which a man (or woman) of Barbin's provincial, bourgeois background could "meaningfully" articulate his (her) life—or past, giving seemingly full expression to his (her) self. It has also to be understood in terms of a desperate clinging to this genre, when it was no longer, if it ever had been, adequate to the experiences it sought to organize. This genre, these discursive strategies, could not give Barbin a vantage point, an identity, in the engendered discourse they assumed. They presume a continuity and (conventionalized) breaks with that continuity (e.g., the changes that occur with maturity, *Bildung*, or even conversion) that were irrelevant to Barbin's life trajectory. Barbin was quite literally trajectile—thrown across an uncrossable border—and this tra-jectory, this being thrown across, not only questioned the system of classification that created that border but its very assumption. While others, those who reclassified him, for example, were able to rationalize or ignore the implications of Barbin's reclassification, he himself could not, for he had no distance, no position, from which to rationalize it. He could not ignore it.

In any communication, including the literary, a speaker (or, equivalently, an author) assumes through complicated indexical (anaphoric and cataphoric) processes a (fixed) vantage point, or the illusion of such a vantage point, over what he or she wishes to communicate. "Any truly creative voice can only be the *second* voice in discourse," Bakhtin (1986: 110) observes. Though the speaker may think his or her words spontaneous, free, entirely his or her own, subject only to the demands of his or her presumed interlocutors, they are in fact always constrained by the community's linguistic and cultural—its *sprachliche*—tradition. The utterances reflect, Bakhtin notes, the conditions and goals of specific human activities "not only through their content (thematic) and linguistic style, that is the selection of the lexical, phraseological, and grammatical resources of the language, but above all through compositional structure" (Bakhtin 1986: 60). These utterances relate to "relatively stable types" of responses—Bakhtin's speech genres—that have developed with respect to different spheres of activity within the speech community and with which, I would stress, they are in a potentially creative tension. An utterance always situates itself pragmatically with respect to prevailing discursive conventions, succumbing slavishly, for example, to them (as in the cliché, stereotypic talk, Heidegger's *Gerede*), assuming an ironic or parodic distance, a disengagement, from them, or, more radically, transgressing them iconoclastically (as in Dada). There can of course never be a complete break with convention for then there would be no interlocution—no communication other than the communication (if that is assumed) of no communication.

The issue here is one, I suppose, of creativity. To what extent does an individual simply comply with convention and succumb to constraint? To what extent is he or she afforded the possibility of creative play within—and with—these conventions and constraints? To what extent does the individual resist such conventions and constraints without somehow falling out of communication, out of society, into madness and mortal isolation? In the case of Barbin, as we shall see, the change of civil status marked a break so radical that he fell out of (narrative) time, not only with his past but with the genres and conventions he had for creatively articulating that past. His life as a schoolgirl could only be articulated in a genre so frozen that there was no real interlocutory possibility and consequently no possibility for that play that leads to a "successful" search for the self (Winnicott 1971). Barbin's life as a young man could not be articulated in any continuous fashion. He was compelled to write, indeed to live, to die, in a world so idiomatically engendered that he could take no creative position toward his own life, his own identity. He could have no real second voice, though, as we shall see, he approximates one at times.

In this essay, I will try to resist essentialization and reduction—to preserve the tension between the lived, the contingent, the immediate, and narrative formulation. Narratives of the self are more than a story, a chronology, a history of the self (however defined); they are taken to be a means of knowing the self.[2] As such, at least in our medicalized era, they have, among others, a therapeutic intention (however masked) that has replaced or, more accurately, come to dominate other intentions—the confessional, the pedagogical, indeed

---

2. *Narrative* is derived through the Latin *gnārus* ('knowing') from the Indo-European root *gnō* ('to know'). *Narrative* is related to *gnosis* and other words in English, ranging from *cunning* to *notation*, from *quaint* to *recognition*, from *diagnosis* to *connoisseur*, and perhaps from *norm* to *enormous*.

the exorcistic—that prevailed in other ages. For us they describe self-discovery and facilitate "personal growth."

Rather than viewing the Barbin manuscript as a symptom of hermaphroditism (though it may well be), I will view it as a symptom of a radical break in the (expected) life course of its author, as a failed attempt to discover therapeutically, as it were, a narrative that could account for that break. This dramatic discontinuity highlights the interlocutory structure—the dialogical play—that is present, I suggest, though less salient, in more conventional life stories. It is certainly present in conversion stories, accounts of therapeutic and pedagogic change, and those of historically contingent change, but it is also present, structurally, in any life-historical narrative insofar as it demands the taking on of an external, a transcendent, vantage point on one's life. In at least the Western autobiographical tradition, there is, I would argue, an inevitable split between the narrating I(s) and the narrated I(s) that is conventionally ignored where there is a presumption of continuity, but the split cannot be ignored where that presumption is questioned, as it is in Barbin's case. The split creates the space in which the two I(s) engage with each other dialogically.

The Barbin collection, called *Herculine Barbin dite Alexina B*, consists of official documents, a few press reports, a chronology, and, of primary interest to us, the autobiographical fragment, *Mes Souvenirs*, which was published posthumously by Auguste Tardieu in his *Questions médico-légales de l'identité* in 1872. Tardieu justifies the publication of Barbin's memoirs on the basis of what they tell us about the influence of genital malformation on affective faculties and moral dispositions and about the social and individual consequences of an erroneous determination of the sexual identity of a child. Tardieu's publication is an example of what Foucault calls the literature of medical libertinage—a genre popular in the nineteenth century and not unknown today.

Foucault's own collection is, ironically, an example of the genre of medico-structural libertinage.[3] He published it in a series called *Les vies par-*

---

3. Foucault does not interpret the Barbin papers in the French edition; he promises to do so in his *History of Sexuality*. In his short introduction to the English edition of *Herculine Barbin* (Barbin 1980), Foucault discusses the text in terms of sexual classification, insisting curiously that *Mes Souvenirs* "baffles every possible attempt to make an identification":

> It seems that nobody in Alexina's feminine milieu consented to play that difficult game of truth which the doctors later imposed on his indeterminate anatomy, until a discovery that everybody delayed for as long as possible was finally precipitated by two men, a priest and a doctor. It seems that nobody who looked at it was aware of his somewhat awkward, graceless body, which became more and more abnormal in the company of those girls among whom he grew up. Yet it exercised over every-

allèles—a play on the parallel lives written by Plutarch and others in ancient and medieval times. Foucault's parallel lives are those, however, that because of their divergence can never meet—even in infinity. They are part of a genre that is perhaps more popular in continental Europe than in England and the United States: a collection of primary texts or documents relating to the "same" person, theme, or event with editorial comment and sometimes interpretation. These collections raise intriguing epistemological, historiographical, and hermeneutical problems, including those of evidence, contextualization, intertextuality, construction, and exposition. Although the documents in such collections refer to the "same" person, theme or event, they do not form a coherent, seamless text. They are, as Foucault observes for his Pierre Rivière dossier, in "a strange contest," caught, as it were, in a battle for ultimate authority—for an ultimate reading (Foucault 1975: 10).

Insofar as the documents are differentially legitimated by various organs of the state, the outcome of the battle of discourses (when it occurs) is historically predetermined. The reader of such collections is, however, granted an interpretative freedom that is limited less by the authority of the documents themselves than by the editor's intervention. Indeed, the documentary pretense of such collections masks the role of the editor (in the case in point the several

---

body, or rather over every female, a certain power of fascination that misted their eyes and stopped every question on their lips. The warmth that this strange presence gave to the contacts, the caresses, the kisses that ran through the play of those adolescent girls was welcomed by everybody with a tenderness that was all the greater because no curiosity mingled with it. Falsely naive girls, old teachers who thought they were shrewd—they were all alike as blind as characters in a Greek fable when, uncomprehendingly, they saw this puny Achilles hidden in their boarding school. (Foucault, 1980: xii)

Even a superficial reading of *Mes Souvenirs* suggests the inadequacy of Foucault's observation. Certainly Barbin was aware of her difference and masked it when and where she could; she also suggests, implicitly, why it was of advantage for some of those around her, particularly the owner of the school where she taught, to ignore her differences. Foucault's further observation that she described her world as though everything took place in a world of feelings "where the identity of the partners and above all the enigmatic character around whom everything centered has no importance" can hardly be taken as an accurate portrayal of that world. It is Barbin's symptomatic portrayal! Finally, Foucault's suggestion that what the author of *Mes Souvenirs* evokes is "the happy limbo of a non-identity" in an all-female world offers an incredibly oversimplified reading of the text, indeed of its motivation, for Barbin's text is, as we shall see, centered on her difference—a difference which can only emerge perceptually through an awareness of normative criteria of sex and gender attributions. Barbin certainly knew she was in a girls' school, that she was considered a girl, and that she was both like and unlike the other girls in her school.

editors) in constituting the several texts as a unitary one and in determining *its* possible interpretations.

II

Richard Bauman (1986: 5) writes, "Current literary interest in narrated events and their relationship to narrative centers around two principal issues: the formal relationship between narratives and the events they recount, and the ontological and epistemological status of the narrated events themselves." He notes that in the study of folklore the relationship between narrative and the narrated is understood in terms of iconicity: narratives are seen as verbal icons of the events, or "action structures," they recount. Emphasis is placed on the isomorphism between icon and event and on the formal means by which this "isomorphic" (should we read "mimetic?") relationship is maintained. Traditionally, the event is seen as somehow antecedent to its iconic expression, but, as Bauman observes, some theorists are now reversing the precedence. Events are abstractions from narrative. It is the structures of signification in narrative that give coherence to events in our understanding, that enable us to construct in the interdependent process of narration and interpretation a coherent set of interrelationships that we call an "event" (Bauman 1986: 5).

The argument is of course not as new as Bauman would have it. Sartre was saying the same thing in the forties, and we should not forget the medieval nominalists. But Bauman's own position is more interesting: A focus on narration and interpretation conjointly permits the integration of narration and narrated within a single frame of reference. Whatever its "real" status, the narrated event is emergent in the narrative performance.

What has to be clarified is exactly how this emergence occurs. I would argue—but cannot develop the argument fully here—that an adequate theory of emergence has to be based upon a multifunctional, dialogical approach to discourse. By a multifunctional approach to discourse, I mean one that takes into account not only language's semantico-referential capacity, stressed in our Western understanding of language, but also its context-calling capacities (see Silverstein 1979 and Crapanzano 1992). These would include such pragmatic functions as the indexical and performative as well as metapragmatic functions that govern the pragmatically relevant contexts, foci of interest (say, on language itself, Jakobson's poetic *Einstellung*), permissible hermeneutic ("read me as") strategies (including those of textual construction itself) and, most important for our purposes, the constitution of extra- and intratextual selves ("authors" and "narrator," "readers," and those internal interlocutors whom

Gerard Genette calls *narrataires*) and the (dialogical) relations that obtain or do not obtain among them. (In collections like the Barbin dossier, we would ideally have to include the several editors and their relations.) Any dynamic theory of narration would also have to consider the presumptive, the inclusive and preclusive, and the anticipated (I would argue, dialogical) relations between levels of narration (i.e., the narrational, the narrative, and the narrated) and the personae, or selves, constituted at each of these levels.[4] Though analytically separable, they are in fact always in some sort of (vulnerably creative) tension.

I stress here the continuous, emergent process of self-constitution through the mediation of the other, itself continuously emergent. Characterizations of the other, which are subject to the constraints of cultural convention, (self's) desire, and the resistance of the other (alter's desire), give the illusion at least of arresting the continuous dialectical movement of self-constitution by proclaiming a fixed alterity and, thereby, a fixed self. The movement is circular—and no temporal (only an expository) priority should be given to characterizing the other. These characterizations of the other and, consequently, of the self are embedded in a dialectical movement that is expressed in "real" or "internal" dialogues and that is denied in the typificatory process itself, at least in those cultures that decontextualize their characterizations and understand them in essentialist terms. In other words, the interactional or dialogical—the political—situation of self- and other-characterization is denied significance when such characterizations are understood as an "essential" attribute of the characterized self or other (Crapanzano 1992: 91–112).

How are we to understand these parties to self-constituting (here, literary) interlocution? Are we referring to the author, the narrator, or the narrator's narrated subject? Are we referring to an editor, or editors, whose self-constitutive act is, at least in Western literature, usually ignored—masked ideologically by his or her "objective stance" and stylistically by, among other devices, a display of consistent voices?[5] Are we referring to the reader as interlocutor, the

---

4. I follow Genette, who distinguishes three levels of narration (*récit*): narration (*l'acte narratif producteur*, a signifying performance), narrative (*le récit*, that which is performed, the utterance, discourse, the narrative text—the signifier), and the narrated (*l'histoire*, the subject of that which is performed, the narrative content, diegesis—the signified). See Genette (1972: 72) and Benveniste (1966). I will use *narrative* to refer to all three levels of narration and for the way the narration and the narrated as well as narrative marks interpretation, distributes functional priorities, and relates to other texts and performances.

5. I cannot enter into a detailed analysis of the role of the editor as a privileged and empowered reader who has some, though by no means all, of the power and privilege of the author. Certainly the editor—even the internal editor, that is, the author's editorial voice—mediates the dialogues that constitute any textual production.

narrataire, that is, a diegetic interlocutor, or to some even more complex "internal" interlocutor? I suggest they have to be understood not just in terms of ordinary social and psychological typifications, as role players or characters, but in all their (often contradictory) symbolic complexity. Further, are the separations we make between levels of narrative participation, between authors, editors, and readers *and* narrators and *narrataires* as impermeable as some critics would have it? I would argue that we have to sacrifice analytic purity if we are to come to any understanding of how narratives of the self "self"-constitute. We have, I believe, to recognize that it is precisely the dialogical play—the interlocution—between textual levels and between what René Spitzer called the *erzählendes Ich*, the narrating *I*, and the *erzähltes Ich*, the narrated *I* (and, I would add, the *erzählendes Du* and the *erzähltes Du*) that has to be examined case by case if we are to achieve any understanding of these narratives of the self (Bakhtin 1986: 103–131). Insofar as an author is sensitive to the stylistic nuances of his characters, including the narrator and the *narrataire*, the characters take on an "independence" not only from the author, whose textual control is always illusory, but from one another (see Crapanzano 1992 and Mecke 1990). They are in their own way each embedded in a history that extends beyond the text—the specific narrative occasion. The social, the communicational space of narration is richly responsive. The author engages dialogically with his narrator and the narrator's *narrataires* as well as with the characters the narrator "creates"; and the narrator engages in a similar fashion with his *narrataires*—and, more interestingly, with his characters.[6] The reader as ultimate interlocutor is drawn inevitably into the arena of dialogical engagement. The allure a text holds for a reader stems in part from the delight of the control he has had in its production through the anticipation of his response. This assertive delight is of course coupled with the delight in being rhetorically seduced into having the "appropriate"—*the desired*—response.

III

Mes Souvenirs is a novelistic, autobiographical account of 128 pages of which the first 111 pages form a continuous narrative of the author/narrator's life until, declared a man, he leaves for Paris. The author uses the standard literary tenses, the aorist and the imperfect, which give the story—the *histoire*—a cer-

---

6. In his last works, Bakhtin seems to recognize this dialogical possibility between author and character, but he insists rather more strongly than I would on the author's ultimate control. See Bakhtin (1986: 103–31).

tain autonomy, a distance from the author/narrator.[7] The last 17 pages are fragments concerning her life as a man in Paris, which, despite their having been
found on separate scraps of paper, are integrated into the text without any indication of how they have been ordered. Their ordering reflects Tardieu's—the
editor's—literary sensibility (e.g., his sense of an ending) and his psychological culture (e.g., his understanding of alienation and marginalization). Some
of the fragments are written in the present tense; others in the perfect (*passé
composé*) and imperfect; and still others in the aorist and imperfect. In Emile
Benveniste's terms, some verge on the autonomous *histoire*, like the coherent
sections, and others are manifestly interlocutory, that is, *discours*.[8] The entire
text comes to resemble one of those nineteenth-century romantic novels which
ends abruptly, in fragments, with the death of the protagonist.

Mes Souvenirs is written in the first person, and, though we learn through
the title that its author is Herculine Barbin *dite* Alexina B., the narrator is called
Camille. We do not know whether Camille was Barbin's invention or Tardieu's.
Although it is possible that Tardieu changed the name in order to protect the
author's identity, Foucault thinks it likely (but why, he does not say) that the
name Camille was the author's invention and that its usage indicates an intention to publish the *Souvenirs*. One can think of many other reasons for using a
pseudonym, including the desire to disengage oneself, in bad faith perhaps,
from one's past, or to obtain "distance" and "perspective." *Camille* can of
course be a man's name or a woman's name.

7. In the *histoire*, which he distinguishes from the *discours*, Benveniste notes that there is
no longer really a narrator:

> Les événements sont posés comme ils se sont produits à mesure qu'ils apparaissent
> à l'horizon de l'histoire. Personne ne parle ici: les événements semblent se raconter
> eux-mêmes. (Benveniste 1966: 241)

The autonomous quality of the *histoire* depends, according to Benveniste (1966: 239), on the use
of the aorist coupled with the absence of first- and second-person pronouns: "L'histoire ne dira
jamais *je* ni *tu*, ni *ici*, ni *maintenant*, parce qu'il n'empruntera jamais l'appareil formel du discours
qui consiste d'abord dans la relation de personne *je:tu*." In the first-person autobiographical narrative, like Barbin's, the "autonomous dimension" depends solely on the aorist. The narrated self
tends toward a passivity that is subverted by the "active" narrator with whom the self is identified.
The split between tense and pronominal usage produces a tension—the possibility of a dialogical,
a responsive relationship—between the narrated self and the narrator's self.

8. See Benveniste (1966). The juxtaposition of *histoire*-like texts with *discours* produces
a "noisy"—a frenetic—intratextuality in the fragmentary section. Not only are the fragments
separate from the coherent section with which they, particularly the *discours*-like, engage poorly,
but they are separated from one another. Both the narrator's self and the narrated self, both Herculine and Abel (see below) are themselves fragment-specific, and yet the fragments are not without thematic and rhetorical cohesion.

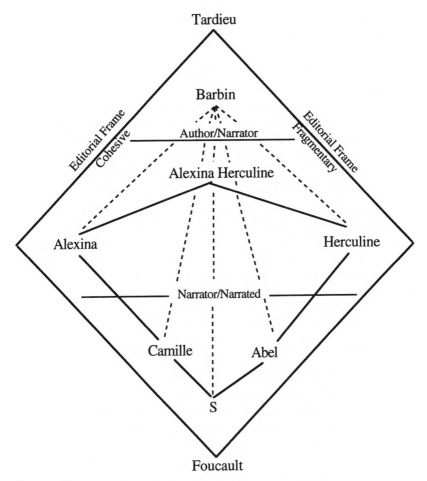

Figure 4.1

I will adopt the following conventions, as best I can, to describe the several personae, or selves, in *Mes Souvenirs*, recognizing that my usage is mechanical and denies precisely the dialogical interdependence I want to stress. It is necessary, though, if we are to appreciate the complex dialogical structure of the text (see Figure 4.1). I will refer to Barbin as the author of the text; Alexina as the narrator of the first, coherent part and Camille as her subject or narrated self; Herculine as the narrator of the fragments and Abel as his subject or narrated self. Given the totalizing presumption of *Mes Souvenirs* (note the *Mes*!), Alexina and Herculine are collapsed into a single narrator, and I will refer to this narrator as Alexina Herculine. Camille and Abel are also collapsed into an unnameable, fragmented, maimed, though perduring, subject—an object/subject of desire, Edenic longing, and hope—who is constituted both thematically (through the narrative itself) and rhetorically (through various prospective and retrospective devices). It is, however, ultimately the editor Tardieu (and by extension Foucault) who produces this identity by conjoining the coherent and fragmentary texts (as well as arranging the fragmentary texts themselves). Put another way, by uniting the several texts, the editor implicates the reader in the unification of their narrated subjects. Had the author (before, indeed through, his death) anticipated the editorial conjunction? The reader's construction?[9]

We have no external evidence from which to determine when and where the text was written and whether it was written continuously or at different times. From internal evidence, we can assume that it was written in Paris after the author/narrator was reclassified as a male. Barbin adheres here to ordinary Western novelistic and autobiographical conventions by not spelling out when and where the act of narration occurred. Everything occurs as though the act of narration has no duration or as if its duration has no relevance. As Genette observes,

> One of the fictions of literary narration, perhaps the most powerful, because it occurs, as it were, unperceived, is that it has to do with an instantaneous act, without temporal dimension. Sometimes one dates it, but one never measures it. (Genette 1972: 234)

Time—growth, development, change—are diegetic in this tradition, but as Genette observes, in autobiographical and autobiographical-like narratives, "the story leads the hero to the point where one awaits the narrator in order that these two hypostases join one another and are at last merged" (Genette 1972: 236). The distance that separates them tends toward zero, but it is never obliterated. It is this "distance" that affords dialogical play, facilitates a narrator's ironic posture, permits his or her struggle for textual control, perpetuates even the illusion of his total control.

The penultimate paragraph of Barbin's coherent text specifies the time of its writing, that is, the writing of that paragraph, as two years after the death of Camille's (Barbin's?) benefactor, M. de Saint-M., who died after Camille left for Paris. The reference to the death of Camille's benefactor is important less because of the actual role he is described as playing in Camille's life than as

---

9. We should note an inevitable movement toward death in *Mes Souvenirs*—one that is announced in the very first sentence of the text: "I approach, without doubt, the fatal term of my existence" (*MS* 9). Through Barbin's extratextual suicide, the story swings back full circle on itself!

symbolizing the separation of Abel from his past as Camille and as indicating the present emotional state of Herculine, who now merges with Abel.

> Ah, since then, in the midst of the disgust, the bitterness that over-whelms me, I am able to glimpse the frightening emptiness that his absence has made. (*MS* 111)

Alexina/Herculine [10] goes on to describe her/his loneliness and then summa-rizes her/his life-story—the one we have read.

> A new phase of my double and strange existence dates from my arrival in Paris. Raised for twenty years among girls, I was first and for two years a lady's maid. At sixteen and a half I entered the teaching school of . . . as a student-teacher. At nineteen I received my teaching certificate; several months later I was directing a well-known girls boarding school in the district of . . . I left it at twenty-one. It was the month of April. At the end of the same year I was in Paris [working for] the railroad . . . (*MS* 111; ellipses are Barbin's).
>
> De mon arrivée à Paris, date une nouvelle phase de mon double et bizarre existence. Elevé pendant vingt ans au milieu de jeunes filles, je fus d'abord et pendent deux années, au plus, femme de chambre. A seize ans et demi j'entrais en qualité d'élève-maîtresse à l'école normale de . . . A dix-neuf ans j'obtins mon brevet d'in-stitutrice; quelques mois après je dirigeais un pensionnat assez renommé dans l'arrondissement de . . . ; j'en sortais à vingt et un ans. C'étais au mois d'avril. A la fin de la même année j'étais à Paris, au chemin de fer . . .

This summary, itself interrupted, arrested, a fragment, marks the end of the coherent narrative and the beginning of the fragmented one, if indeed we can call the fragments with which *Mes Souvenirs* ends a narrative. The sum-mary is a mechanical, lifeless repetition of what had been elaborated, at times imaginatively, with verve, at times, with literary romantic clichés, in the pre-ceding 111 pages. Its ellipses ("the teaching school of . . .", "the district of . . .") are more than literary conventions; they mark a forced anonymity—a past that must always be disguised if not effaced. Although I cannot enter into a detailed analysis of the use of tense in the passage, I should point out that it confuses the narrator's (the narrational) present ("Je suis seul") with the nar-rative—reflective and controlling—present ("De mon arrivée à Paris, date une

---

10. In this transitional paragraph, the two narrators and the two narrated selves cannot be distinguished.

nouvelle phase . . .") through a curious use of the imperfect tense that brings historical time, that of the preterite ("Je fus d'abord . . .", "J'obtins") up to the time of narration: "J'en sortais à vingt et un ans . . ." [11] We are here at that asymptotic moment of autobiography when the difference between narrative time—diegetic time—and the time of narration approaches zero, but they remain always separate by a hair's breadth; when the narrating *I* and the narrated *I* are about to merge but remain infinitely apart. The narrative cannot proceed as such.

The passage reflects formally the inevitable failure of self-narrative possibility (at least as it has developed in the West)—of the possibility of the full emergence of the self as at once narrated and narrating. For, if I may speak figuratively, who would then hear Herculine's cry, "I am alone?" The submerged, self-constituting dialogical relationship between the narrating self and the narrated self would collapse, and self-constitution would have to depend fully on another, more resistant, more independent, and paradoxically never specified interlocutor, the *narrataire*—the reader, ultimately—in his or her full symbolic array.

The passage marks the death of Camille and the birth of Abel(s) as well as a never fully articulated change in the narrator. Alexina becomes Herculine(s) just as Camille gives way to Abel(s). Neither Alexina nor Camille loses her anaphoric, indeed her cataphoric, possibility, for then there would be no "intrigue," only two distinct texts (Halliday and Hasan 1976: 17). They are collapsed, as it were, into the desired though nameless subject, as in my schema in Figure 4.1. The continuity between the coherent text and the fragments is facilitated by the coupling in the summary paragraph of thematic retrospection with an aposiopesis—the interruption—that announces the fragments to come. The frequent use in the coherent text of prolepsis (e.g., "Later, in the middle of storm and errors of my life . . ." [*MS* 10]) also contributes to this sense of continuity. The transition is intense, knotted, paralyzing, clotted. The self-constituting or at least self-expressive dialogical possibilities are enormous, especially if we consider potential changes in the imagined readers and *narrataires*.

What is extraordinary about the summary is that it leaves out the very event that was responsible for Camille's leaving the school and coming to Paris,

---

11. The imperfect tense in French generally expresses duration, repetition, the habitual; it refers to an event in the past (relative to the time of utterance) that is not yet complete. It may, however, refer to a past event that took place at a precise time—as here or earlier in the paragraph ("j'entrais"). Though occurring in the past, events—like leaving the boarding school—or their consequences, continue into the future, here up to the moment of narration.

which is given central importance in Alexina's tale. Indeed, her whole story builds up melodramatically to the discovery of Camille's "male" hermaphroditism. Alexina describes the incident in detail. Camille has been working at the girl's school and has been having an affair with Sarah, the daughter of the school's owner. She has always been careful to avoid exposing her "male" body—she has no hips, no breasts, and a downy face that she shaves with a scissors. But she is suffering from such terrible cramps that she is forced to see a doctor.

> During the examination, I heard him sigh, as though he were not satisfied with his findings. . . . Standing near my bed, the doctor looked at me with interested attention. Muted exclamations of this sort escaped him: "My God! Is this possible!" . . . The hand of the doctor moved indecisively, trembling, to my stomach, to the locus of my pain. . . . He sat down next to me, and gently insisted that I be brave. He himself needed to be. The decomposure of his face betrayed extraordinary agitation. "I beg you," I said. "Leave me. You are killing me!"—"Mademoiselle, I only need a minute, and it will be finished." Already his hand was sliding under the sheet and stopped at the painful spot. He pressed it several times as though he were looking for a solution to a difficult problem. He did not stop there!!! He found the explanation he needed! But it was easy to see that it surpassed his expectations. (*MS* 78–79)

It is the denouement of the story, its tragic moment, Camille's, Alexina's, indeed Barbin's, *moment.* Despite all the anguish, the shame and fear, the curse, associated with the discovery of her genital deformities, we have to recognize a certain "impurity" in Alexina's description of the doctor's examination: an innocent delight in Camille's importance, in her difference. Yes, in even the melodrama of her own description. It is certainly one of the most elaborate scenes in the *Souvenirs.* But Alexina also takes delight in its titillating, its licentious, its libertine effect. On whom? we have to ask.

The first 111 pages of *Mes Souvenirs* reads, at least superficially, like a popular nineteenth-century sentimental novel with many Gothic features. It is written simply, intimately, at times melodramatically, with exaggerations of emotion and intimations of impending disaster, much as a schoolgirl of Barbin's provincial bourgeois background would have written it. (Her father died when she was little; her mother became a governess-companion in the noble Saint-M. family; she was raised first in an orphanage and then in convent school.) Barbin has succumbed to the conventions and clichés of his chosen genre. He writes with unreflected immediacy. He has no sense of history, no sense of the contingency of the society in which he finds himself, no *real* critical perspective on it. What irony he expresses is conventional and does not affect his relationship to the text. He does not seem to be so fully separated from his narrator Alexina (just as Alexina does not seem to be so very distinct from Camille) as to permit a truly ironic posture.

There are times when the narrator, Alexina, appears to be carried away by some immediate emotion, usually concerning her loneliness or her bitterness, but she is soon caught up in her narrative. She begins *Mes Souvenirs* as follows:

> I am twenty-five years old and although still young, I am approaching, without any doubt, the fatal term of my existence.

> I have suffered a lot, and I have suffered alone! alone! abandoned by all! My place was not marked in this world which has eluded me, which has cursed me. Not a living being should be associated with the immense pain that took hold of me at the end of childhood, at that age when everything is beautiful, because everything is young and glittering with the future.

> That age did not exist for me. I kept, from that age, an instinctive distance from the world, as if I had already been able to understand that I would have to live there a stranger. (*MS* 9)

Alexina's emotional outburst, a convention of the sentimental novel, is soon reduced to a banal reflection on her childhood—a reflection that portends gothic disaster. What this disaster is, we do not know. We can imagine a curse, a branding, ravishment, imprisonment. All of these, I should note, are at least metaphorically true for Alexina Herculine, and she articulates her genital malformation in these terms. She is the innocent heroine who has been cursed, branded, ravished, and imprisoned in her isolation. She has been marked in a literal, a scriptorial sense, perhaps by God, certainly by the State, which can tolerate no social classificatory ambiguity (see Herzfeld 1986). So cast, her hermaphroditism and her reclassification become at times paradigmatic equivalents of standard events in the gothic narrative, and through this figuration, they lose their immediate, their lived, their psychological effect. We—and perhaps Barbin herself—lose track of their reality and the terrible consequences they have for her as we follow the conventional, the syntagmatic, progression of her tale.

Despite the conventionally postulated, temporally and spatially removed, transcendent position of the narrator, who should be immune to the effects of his or her own narrative (for, in autobiography at least, it should lead to where he or she is), the position of the narrator (and presumably the author) does *not* in fact remain constant, certainly not in even the coherent section of *Mes Souvenirs*. The narrative proceeds chronologically and reflects Camille's growth, her *Bildung*, her gradual discovery of her sexual difference, the shame associated with it, the transformation of innocent, adolescent passion into mature sexual longing. And the narrator, who has, so to speak, the whole story before him/her, uses literary artifice, with some talent, as we have seen, to present this *Bildung* mimetically.[12] We have intimations of the future, but we do not know what that future is (though presumably the narrator does, whatever his position).

The narrator is not, however, immune to the effects of his/her own tale, as I have said, and as we read *Mes Souvenirs*, we come to recognize several different voices that emerge as the story progresses. Even though they mark different, contradictory sensibilities, they do not give way to one another but coexist in an uneasy tension that may reflect Barbin's maimed identity. The most striking of these changes in voice is from that of the innocent schoolgirl who has perhaps read too many sentimental novels to that of the budding—the somewhat masculine—libertine, whom we distinguished in Alexina's description of the doctor's examination. This second voice is evident in the following passage, where Alexina describes Camille's infatuation with Sarah.

> Once prayers were said and the pupils put to bed, we often talked for long hours, my friend and I. I would find her at her bed, and my happiness was to perform for her those little cares a mother gives her child. Gradually I got used to undressing her. Were she to remove a pin without me, I would become almost jealous. (*MS* 57)

She relishes in the "delicious têtes-à-tête" in which Sarah addresses her with a masculine pronoun (*MS* 68). In still other passages, Alexina delights in casting Camille as a seducer and is bemused at times by her crises of guilt, but most often she is carried away by the curse she bears.

> Am I guilty, criminal, because a crude error has given me a place in the world which should not have been mine? (*MS* 64)

12. I use *Bildung* with some hesitation, for taken as a whole, *Mes Souvenirs* has a strong, *gegen-Bildung* direction. There is growth into adulthood, even into manhood, but that adulthood, that manhood, is empty. Strung together, the fragments become picaresque—a series of adventures and misadventures, perceptions and misperceptions, that lead—that can lead—nowhere.

The interlocutory structure of these passages deserves consideration. Alexina is so moved by Camille's story—her own—that she calls out to a textually indeterminate interlocutor who seems to escape from the text itself. He or she is no—or at least not only—a *narrataire* but the reader cast as a witness to her plight. Insofar as she addresses an extra-diegetic interlocutor, Alexina (or, more accurately Alexina Herculine) also escapes the text and becomes, as it were, Barbin.

Reflections on the implications of what is being described, commentaries on the text itself, and ironic and other locutions that demand narrative evaluation are, however, rare in the coherent section of *Mes Souvenirs*. When they occur, their banality precludes the distance they demand. Despite Alexina's different voices, some of which, like that of the emergent libertine, appear to be more ironically postured than others, Barbin does not seem able to exploit the dialogical possibilities afforded by his "asymptotic" distance from the text to gain (ironic) control over it. His textual avatars, Alexina and Camille, replicate this incapacity. The "coherent" story appears to be so compelling that he cannot disengage himself from it; he cannot attain an independent vantage point. It becomes *the* constituted memory, a sort of personal myth, that precludes an open-ended, creative, a dialogical self-constitution. Barbin is left with only a ready-made self. In other words, Barbin's self—his identity—rests less on immediate interlocution than on submission to a literary form, a genre.

It is this submission that I refer to as *genre submergence*. The dialectics of self-constitution is so strongly determined by the genre to which the author has succumbed that spontaneous, creative, agonistic engagement with his reader(s) and at other levels with his narrative and narrated selves and their interlocutors in all their symbolic complexity is drastically reduced. They become empty functions within the genre. Secondary characters are flattened, and "life-giving" imagery, tropes like hypotyposis, and even the punctuation (the exclamation points) show their banal artifice—their impotence. There are of course moments in which Barbin's struggle with the genre gives his story unique life, but, for the most part, its particularity does not rest on discomfort with the genre but with its bizarre subject matter.

In the first part of the *Souvenirs*, there is a striking parallel between the absence of locutions that invoke the reader and the relative absence of diegetic interlocution. Direct discourse is rare and serves an emphatic rather than a dialogical function, as in Alexina's description of the doctor's examination. Characters in Camille's life are stereotypic, described in clichés: the consumptive school friend who dies, the noble nun, the generous aristocrat, the harsh confessor, and the understanding Monsignor. Occasionally, though, Alexina captures an ambivalence, a contradiction in character or sentiment. She describes, for example, one of the Ursuline nuns at the convent where she was educated. The nun's "noble features" express a "jealous sadness" which Alexina attributes to her affection for her (*MS* 13). More often, however, empty rhetorical complexity substitutes for psychological perception. Alexina writes of one of Camille's teachers,

> I challenge the most sceptical man in the world to live close to so noble, so pure, so truly Christian a being without feeling inclined to cherish a religion that is capable of giving birth to such traits. (*MS* 36)

Characters are actors in Camille's world. Only toward the end of the coherent section, after Camille's hermaphroditic condition has been discovered, does Alexina begin to take account of their subjectivity. Referring to Sarah, whom she has had to abandon, she remarks,

> I knew her enough to be perfectly convinced that she suffered, without cursing me for it, in silence and with courage. (*MS* 104)

The other's point of view is acknowledged.

Ironically, the revelation of Camille's hermaphroditism frees Alexina's interlocutory—her dialogical—imagination from the constraints of the genre in which she has submerged herself, just as she is deprived of such dialogical possibility by the state-decreed change of sex. Just as Alexina's self is about to emerge, she is ruthlessly deprived of that possibility. She becomes Herculine and her subject, her narrated self, Abel. But Herculine has neither the interlocutory possibility for constituting that new self nor an appropriate genre, however constraining, for describing Abel. He (if in fact I can use a singular and singularizing pronoun to characterize the figure—Abel—who emerges from the fragments) lives in isolation in Paris.

> Immediately, generously, I broke with all memories of my past. I buried myself alive, young, in that eternal solitude that I find everywhere, in the midst of the turmoil of the crowd, as in the most obscure retreat. (*MS* 114; see also 115) [13]

Indeed, he lives in the crowd. It provides him with a repertoire of imagined interlocutors, observers, judges even, whom he observes impersonally but with intensity. "All these young faces which breathe the joy of their age seem to

13. There are times, however, when Herculine takes consolation in his memories of his love for Sarah (*MS* 115), whom he does not name.

read in mine some frightening truth whose secret escapes them" (*MS* 118). He despises them and envies them at once. With hauteur, he condemns the debauchery of men and then adds that he too has dreamed of "delirious nights" and "burning passions," which he can only know through intuition (*MS* 113). He indulges himself in his suffering, his loneliness, the emptiness of his life, the desire for death. He takes solace in his uniqueness. "The real experience I acquired from a woman's heart places me well above some critics whose appreciations, I must say, have shocked me more than once by their falseness" (*MS* 119). Like Teiresias, whom he does not name, he has an understanding of women that no man can have (*MS* 119–120).[14]

Alexina, now Herculine, is deprived of a narrative. He can only write fragments, which, presumably, only an other, that empowered reader, the editor Tardieu, can arrange. These fragments are often self-reflective and have a depth that is lacking in the coherent narrative. It is, however, a depth that is subverted by the exaggerated artifice of Herculine's language. What is striking about the fragments is that they are almost all invocations to others. They are filled with questions. They are manifestly interlocutory, but they have, they can have, no meaningful dialogical possibility. Herculine addresses Abel in the first fragment:

> Go, cursed one, carry out your task. The world that you invoke was
> not made for you. You were not made for it. (*MS* 111)

We find no similar mode of address in the coherent section of the *Souvenirs*. Subsequent fragments are addressed to the sexually corrupt male world, from which Herculine angrily (at times puritanically) dissociates himself, to God ("Lord! Lord! Is not the chalice of my pain yet empty!" [*MS* 115]), and to the reader ("You who read me . . ." [*MS* 123]), from whom he demands understanding. As we might expect, these interlocutions are accompanied by attempts to understand how the other perceives Abel. Herculine stresses Abel's uniqueness.[15] He recognizes the effect of Abel's cold glance on those around him. It forces their respect (*MS* 118). Sight has become Abel's principal modality, though Herculine does describe several job interviews, giving quotations, suggesting dialogue. (For a time, Abel was jobless and poor.) Abel ar-

14. He does draw an unspecified parallel between his transformation and those in Ovid's *Metamorphoses*.

15. Throughout *Mes Souvenirs*, Camille's and then Abel's difference is stressed not only on physiological but also on social—class—grounds. She stresses, for example, her special position in the orphanage (*MS* 11). Difference gives thematic cohesion to the coherent and fragmentary sections of the memoir.

ranges to work as a ship's boy, to go to the United States, to escape it all, to find a new identity, but in the end he remains in Paris, working for the railroad which had laid him off and then reinstated him.

Nearly all of the fragments are concerned in one way or another with death. For Abel's pained soul it is an "ineffable softness" (*MS* 122). He walks in the cemetery of Montmartre. He indulges in morbid reflection, reminiscent of Hamlet's:

> I feel an indefinable tenderness for him whose bones are there beneath my feet. This man, who was a stranger to me, becomes a brother. I converse with his soul, freed from its earthly chains; a captive, I call devoutly for the moment when I shall be able to join him. (*MS* 122)

Death becomes his anticipation. There this "unhappy exile from the world" will finally find "his country, his brothers, his friends." He imagines morosely the discovery of his body. Doctors will examine it and cast new light on it.

> O princes of science, enlightened chemists, whose names echo through the world, analyze then, if it is possible, all the pains that have burned, that have devoured, this heart, to its last fibers; all the burning tears that have drowned it, dried it out in their savage embrace. (*MS* 116)

It is romantic agony at its most banal. But death does take possession of him. We learn from the editors that at the age of thirty Barbin killed himself. In that act Herculine and Abel are finally united—through a reader who knows more than what the text can reveal.

The Barbin collection poses many more questions than I have raised and tried to answer. We write about the dialectics of self-constitution, their interlocutory basis and their dialogical expression, without always fully appreciating the constraints that are imposed on that process by language and its oral and written conventions, its genres. Dialogue, as I have argued elsewhere (Crapanzano 1992), is never dyadic; for even when only two are conversing, they are always making reference to—struggling with—a third, that authority-giving function that governs the conventions of the dialogue (including those that permit its entextualization and proclaim its unity, its continuity or discontinuity). This third may be understood as law, grammar, or tradition; it may be embodied in a person, a god, or the state. There are moments when self and other submit, slavelike, to those conventions, denying, as it were, the possibility of the full emergence of their selves. And though we, coming from as individualistic a society as we do, condemn that conformity (among those like us at least), we must, I think, recognize the sometimes desperate desire to succumb to an already warranted narrative of the self. What we can learn from the Barbin manuscript has less to do with the terror of conformity to a genre, to an already told tale, than to the horror of being deprived of any story whatsoever.

REFERENCES

Bakhktin, M. M.
  1985   *The Dialogic Imagination: Four Essays*, Michael Holquist (ed.); Caryl Emerson and Michael Holquist (trans.). Austin: University of Texas Press.
  1986   *Speech Genres and Other Late Essays*, Caryl Emerson and Michael Holquist (ed.); Vern W. McGee (trans.). Austin: University of Texas Press.

Barbin, Herculine
  1978   *Herculine Barbin dite Alexina B*. Paris: Gallimard.
  1980   *Herculine Barbin*. New York: Pantheon.

Bauman, Richard
  1986   *Story, Performance, and Event: Contextual Studies of Oral Narrative*. Cambridge: Cambridge University Press.

Benveniste, Emile
  1966   Les relations de temps dans le verbe français. In *Problèmes de linguistique générale*, vol. 1, 237–250. Paris: Gallimard.

Crapanzano, Vincent
  1977   *Tuhami: Portrait of a Moroccan*. Chicago: University of Chicago Press.
  1992   *Hermes' Dilemma and Hamlet's Desire: On the Epistemology of Interpretation*. Cambridge, Mass.: Harvard University Press.

Genette, Gerard
  1972   *Figures III*. Paris: Editions du Seuil.

Foucault, Michel
  1975   (ed.). *I Pierre Riviere, having slaughtered my mother, my sister, and my brother . . .* New York: Pantheon.
  1980   Introduction. In *Herculine Barbin*, vii–xvii. New York: Pantheon.

Halliday, M. A. K., and R. Hasan
  1976   *Cohesion in English*. London: Longman.

Herzfeld, Michael
  1986   Of definitions and boundaries: The status of culture in the culture of the state. In *Discourse and the Social Life of Meaning*, P. P. Chock and J. R. Wyman (eds.), 75–94. Washington, DC: Smithsonian Press.

Mecke, Jochen
  1990   Dialogue in narration (the narrative principle). In *The Interpretation of Dialogue*, T. Maranhão (ed.), 195–215. Chicago: University of Chicago Press.

Silverstein, Michael
  1979   Language structure and linguistic ideology. In *The Elements: A Parasession on Linguistic Units and Levels*, P. Clyne, W. Hanks, and C. Hofbauer (eds.), 193–247. Chicago: Chicago Linguistic Society.

Winnicott, D. W.
  1971   *Play and Reality*. London: Tavistock.

Interdiscursive Foundations:
The Diachrony of Texts

5   Shadow Conversations:

The Indeterminacy of Participant Roles

Judith T. Irvine

INTRODUCTION

For some time now, those who study discourse from a contextual perspective have expressed dissatisfaction with the classic linguistic model of the communicative act: the isolated sentence tossed (like a football) by an anonymous Speaker, whose qualifications for play are specified only as "competence," to an even more anonymous Hearer who supposedly catches it. Several aspects of this model have provoked criticism: the difference between sentence, utterance, and turn at talk; the relation between the utterance and the rest of the discourse of which it is a part; and the sociological conditions of play and qualifications of the players, to name only some. What I focus on in this paper are the concepts of Speaker and Hearer, and relevant Others—the structure of participation in the game.

The classic model's participant roles were devised to account for grammatical phenomena such as person and the various kinds of deixis relating thereto. Newer versions have attempted to relate these phenomena to a greater sense of the complexity of the social occasions in which talk occurs, and to the relationship between participant role and social identity. Here I pursue some of the same themes, but with attention to the problem of intertextuality—links between an episode of talk and other episodes, real or imagined.

Intertextuality may be a poor term for these purposes, because it suggests that we focus only on "text" as a special form of discourse distinct from (say) ordinary conversation, and because it tends to obscure the discourses' social origins. Moreover, both this term and *dialogicality* carry some intellectual bag-

I am much indebted to Stephen Levinson for his stimulating paper and comments. I would also like to thank Jane Hill for conversations relating to another project (Hill and Irvine 1993) on which I draw extensively in the present paper. Wolof examples in this paper are based on fieldwork in a village in the Préfecture de Tivaouane, Senegal, in 1970–71, 1975, 1977, and 1984. Financial support for that fieldwork was provided by the National Institute of Mental Health, the National Science Foundation, and Brandeis University.

gage from their roots in literary criticism which one may not want entirely to retain, for example an implication that literary discourse is one's principal subject matter. The point, however, is that those scholars who are concerned with intertextuality and dialogic relations, and those who are concerned with the sociolinguistics of discourse, converge on some similar questions about participant roles, although posing them in different terms.

Our focus, then, is on participant roles as a special nexus of grammar, pragmatic relations, emergent stretches of talk, and context (social, cultural, and diachronic). Questions about participant roles and questions about textuality, I suggest, have a great deal to do with one another.

THE INITIAL PROBLEM: MAPPING ROLE STRUCTURES ONTO PARTICIPANTS

In recent years, several writers have questioned the utility of the classic categories of participation. As Goffman wrote (in "Footing," 1981: 129): "It is my belief that the language that students have drawn on for talking about speaking and hearing is not well adapted to its purpose. . . . It takes global folk categories (like speaker and hearer) for granted instead of decomposing them into smaller, analytically coherent elements." To this end, in *Frame Analysis* (1974: 517 ff.), Goffman had distinguished several possible realizations of a "speaker:" as Principal, as Animator, and as Figure, among others. The Principal (or Originator) is the party held committed to the position attested to by the content of an utterance, while the Animator is the party who physically transmits it. The Figure, perhaps most obviously realized in theatrical performance, is the character, persona, or entity projected into the audience's imagination by means of the performer's actions. Similarly, Dell Hymes (1972: 58–60), also questioning these categories, distinguished Speaker (or Sender) from Addressor, and Hearer (or Receiver, or Audience) from Addressee; and the distinction between Hearer and Addressee has proved analytically important in several respects (see, e.g., Levinson 1983: 72, Clark and Carlson 1982). It is now widely agreed that Addressee is often the more central and useful notion, even within the traditional model.

While Goffman's work was essential in calling attention to the complexity of participation structures constructed in the speech event and indexed in the speech signal, he did not systematize the analysis to the extent that some of his readers looked for. Recently, in a characteristically stimulating paper, Levinson (1988) has addressed himself to that task, taking up Goffman's suggestion that the concepts of Speaker and Hearer (or, Addressee) should be decomposed into a set of underlying constituent concepts. Instead of the usual concepts of Speaker and Addressee there are sets of roles, some on the production end and some on the reception end. Levinson arrives at some seventeen participant roles, hierarchically organized and systematized in a scheme of defining feature matrices. Thus, for example, in his scheme the "ordinary speaker" (termed Author) is a participant holding responsibility for several different aspects of message production simultaneously: for motivating it, for supplying its form, and for actually transmitting it. Author is therefore defined as [+MOTIVE], [+TRANSMISSION], and [+FORM]. Were these responsibilities not to coincide, the same features (MOTIVE, TRANSMISSION, and FORM) would define such roles as Relayer ([+T, −M, −F]), Sponsor ([−T, +M, −F]), Ghostor (ghost writer; [−T, −M, +F]), and so on. Several more components are required to bring the total of the roles they define up to seventeen. These roles and components are considered basic and primary—candidates for linguistic or sociolinguistic universals.

The crucial examples, for Levinson and other authors taking a decompositional approach, are those where the participant role fragments are inhabited by different persons. A global role such as Speaker must be decomposed, it is argued, because there are many forms of talk in which it would have to be mapped onto several persons, who take on different aspects of the role. Goffman points out, for example, that "When . . . John answers Mary's phone call and as a favor to her turns to Harry and says, 'Mary wants to know if you can come there tonight,' then John would seem to be no longer functioning in a dual capacity. He is the emitter of an invitation, but Mary is its responsible origin, even though, as we say, she did not convey it 'in person'" (1974: 517– 18). Note that, according to this view, these "persons" need not all be physically present. Even Mary's electronic trace on the telephone is not really required, since John might equally well relay Mary's invitation after the phone call from her is over. And Ghostor is a participant in Levinson's scheme by virtue of having formulated the talk relayed by someone else, not because of physical presence at the time of the relay.

This mapping problem has been recognized by a number of scholars. Schegloff (1987), for instance, without specifically advocating a decompositional approach, distinguishes between participants (that is, persons) and parties (roles and alignments), on the basis of examples of group conversations showing different kinds of simultaneous talk and, therefore, various forms of coparticipation.

However, the mapping problem arises not only in cases where there are too many individuals for the roles of Speaker, Addressee, and Other to accommodate; it also arises when there are too few. Consider self-talk, for example, where Speaker and Addressee coincide in the same person (though not, perhaps, in the same "self"). Similarly, consider the expression of "role distance" (Goffman 1961: 143), where a person subdivides, as it were, into the self who performs a line of talk or action and the self (or selves) who comment upon it. As Hymes has noted (1974: 54), "the common dyadic model of speaker-hearer specifies sometimes too many, sometimes too few, sometimes the wrong participants."

The distinctions these authors make are useful ones, and I do not disagree with them; indeed, I shall borrow from their terminology and their examples. But I believe that Levinson and others who would decompose Speaker and Addressee into a set of analytically primary components have got the analysis back-to-front. To focus on the role fragments, rather than the fragmentation process, reifies the fragments and, presumably, limits them to a finite number. Yet, one might well suspect that the number of such participant roles (PRs) arrived at by the decompositional approach may prove endless. Certainly I can think of some not yet provided for in Levinson's scheme, the most complex decompositional model to date. Consider, for instance, the person quoted against his or her will; the absent party named in an accusation (the "Fingeree?"); the role in a stage play, as opposed to the actor playing it; [1] the person a child is named after, who may (if living) then have certain specified responsibilities toward the child—all these possibilities seem to me unrepresented in Levinson's system. We will at least still need some way to arrive at further distinctions. Will we end up having to propose "primary" PRs that are highly culture-specific?

More important, however, is the question of context. How, if at all, is the analysis of participation in an "utterance event" [2] to consider the ways in which the many contextualizations of an utterance, including a context of other discourses, impinge upon it? The problem of participation structures is not separate from the other problems of the classic model, mentioned above—its iso-

1. As mentioned earlier, in this regard Goffman (1974) distinguished among the Figure (theatrical character or persona projected by the actor), the Animator (the actor), and the Author (composer of the play). Despite the theatrical examples, Goffman suggests that these distinctions are not limited to the stage but apply, as well, in everyday life. Levinson does not seem to take up the idea of Figure as a basic participant role, however.

2. Note Levinson's important distinction between speech event and utterance event. These two levels of organization potentially define different kinds of participant roles. Like Levinson, I focus on the utterance-event level. See discussion in a later section.

lated, decontextualized sentences. For, if a sentence's context of use includes other sentences and other discourses, it also includes their participants. If one tries to remedy the classic model's deficiencies by complicating it, taking some features from its erstwhile "context" and building them into the model, but retaining the classic model's universalism and boundedness, then the problem of context is simply pushed back a step. This, I believe, is a danger with decompositional approaches to participant roles, if the role fragments are still conceived of as primary, universal, and finite in number. The PRs in Levinson's "feature" model are as decontextualized as in the classic model, though more numerous.

It has long been a hallmark of sociolinguistic work to explore how linguistic forms relate to, presuppose, or creatively define a "context of use," or depend upon such context for their interpretations. But those explorations have inevitably raised questions about the dimensions and boundedness of context itself, indeed about the very notion of context.[3] As Goffman (1976) recognized, one cannot predict from the form of an utterance the aspects of its context that may be critical to its interpretation; nor can one expect the relevant aspects of context to be finite or bounded. The problem of participant roles is part of this larger set of issues: an utterance's conversational "reach," backward and forward; the interpretive frameworks on which participants draw; the social personae whose voices are echoed, commented upon, or responded to; whether participants acknowledge that they are engaged in a joint conversational activity at all; and so on. A communicative act has a relation to other acts, including the past, the future, the hypothetical, the conspicuously avoided, and so on, and these relations—intersecting frames, if you will—inform the participation structure of the moment.

For these reasons I think it more useful to retain a quite simple set of primary participant roles (Speaker, Addressee, and third parties present and absent), while deriving the more subtle types (Sponsor, Ghost writer, etc.) from a notion of intersecting frames and dialogic relations. Here I draw in part upon the work of Bakhtin and his circle (Bakhtin 1981, 1984; Voloshinov 1973 [1930]), whose discussions of "voice" and authorship raise issues similarly touching the problem of participant roles. Arising from literary concerns about forms of narration and the representation of speech in the novel, as well as from the linguistic analysis of reported speech, the Bakhtinian notion of multivocality focuses on the forms of discourse that cannot be attributed simply to the act of an individual Speaker or Author. The "double-voiced utterance"

3. See Duranti and Goodwin, *Rethinking Context* (1992).

is the utterance whose form and significance presuppose a second voice—another party—whose utterances are invoked by the one at hand because they are partly imitated, quoted, or argued against.

The best approach to the mapping problem, then, may be to resist the temptation to try to arrive at a single, all-purpose solution that thrusts the problem into the background as merely the rationale for a scheme of PRs. Instead, the mapping problem itself—the process by which participation structures are constructed, imagined, and socially distributed—is what should come to the fore. It is not only an analytical problem; it is also a participants' problem, to which there are creative, if often evanescent, solutions.

An Example: The Performance of Wolof Insult Poems

In illustration of some of these issues, let us consider a situation that might suggest a need to distinguish among many participant roles. In the rural community in Senegal where I have worked there is a form of insult poetry called *xaxaar*, performed at weddings after the bride moves into her husband's household.[4] The poetry session, which lasts about two hours, is sponsored by the new bride's co-wives and the other women who have married into her husband's patrilineage and household (his brother's wives, for example). But although the co-wives sponsor the insult session, if they are high-ranking they do not normally perform in it. The insults are actually performed by lower-ranking women, usually griots (i.e., women of the low-ranking bardic "caste"). However, the sponsoring women, and other local women of high rank, may take part in composing the poems. So, for a few days before the event, griot women visit their patronesses to prepare poems as well as other aspects of the wedding festivities. Although these preparatory meetings are usually private, sometimes women can be seen huddled together in a corner, in pairs or threesomes, their mumbled conversation punctuated by shrieks of laughter as they jointly put together poems for the wedding.

Still, the composition process remains sufficiently secret and collusive that at the actual wedding a particular poem cannot be definitively identified with an individual author. The griot woman uttering it can claim to be doing only that—merely acting as a transmitter, with no responsibility for substance, while the sponsoring women can claim that they sponsored the event only in general, and have no personal responsibility for the special nastiness of a particular poem. And some of these poems are truly nasty—personal, cleverly worded, and wounding.

4. For a longer description and discussion see Irvine (1993).

Thus the responsibility for an insult's occurrence is dispersed over several parties: the actual utterer (Transmitter); the Sponsor, who pays for the event and is responsible for there being a session of insults, but not for its particulars; and the (unidentifiable) Formulator/Composer, responsible for the main wording of a particular poem. Moreover, one could also distinguish several different parties on the receiving end of the insult utterance. First there is the bride, ostensibly the poem's Addressee. The performer points at her, and she is usually the referent of most of the poem's second-person pronouns. Then there are also the bride's kin, who are often the subject-matter and targets of the insults; for, following the principle that the bride may be insulted through insults to her family and friends, the poems tend to reach toward the most prominent of her relatives, persons whose doings (especially if scandalous) are of community-wide interest. Though most of these people are not present at the poetry session, word of a clever insult is sure to reach them. Finally there is the audience, consisting of the groom's family and guests, even onlookers and passers-by. The audience, in gradually widening segments, joins in and serves as chorus during the poem's performance, alternating with the soloist and repeating the initial couplet of the poem. These people are also likely eventually to repeat the insults to other audiences in later conversations.

Consider, then, the following passage from a *xaxaar* poem performed at a wedding in a noble-ranking family:

Example 1

Choral couplet:[5]

1	*M– G– né na, baalal ma Màka—*	M– G– said, "Forgive me, Màka—"
2	*sa xaj gi demul.*	your pilgrimage didn't work.

Soloist:

3	*M– G– moo jénaxi tookër, lan*	M– G–, he is a bush-rat; whatever
4	*la mu gis jàppéwaan ni ci cop.*	he saw, he grabbed, mounting it (and spoiling it).
5	*Du ko laaj—mu dajéwoon.*	He didn't ask—he just coupled.

The soloist performing here is a griot woman; the drum accompanists are griot men. The choral refrain is first taken up by an inner circle of (mainly) griot women, those who will be soloists in other poems, but after several repetitions other women in the audience join in. Eventually, then, the chorus is chanted by women of many ranks—all the authorized guests, that is, since the sponsoring hostesses, the bride's own party, and any unofficial onlookers (such

---

5. Initially introduced by the soloist, who teaches it to the drum accompanists and the chorus, this first couplet is repeated as a refrain throughout the poem.

Table 5.1: Personnel at a Wolof *Xaxaar*

Production Personnel	Location	Reception Personnel
Soloist	Foreground center	Bride
Chorus (inner); Drummers	Inner circle	
Chorus (outer)	Outer circle	Invited audience; Onlookers
Sponsoring co-wives	Background	Bride's kinswoman
	Background or absent	Groom
Formulator (unidentified)	Unidentified or absent	Bride's other relatives (absent)

as high-ranking men) do not speak. But just as the guests did not compose the insult, which they merely repeat, so the soloist herself owes (or can claim to owe) the essentials or the entirety of the poem to an earlier, joint composition process involving high-ranking women who motivate and help compose but do not perform. The noble women who sponsored the *xaxaar* session, some of whom may have helped compose poems, are present but keep well in the background. Meanwhile, although the bride herself is present, most of her kin are not—including M– G–, her classificatory mother's brother, a prominent village elder and the subject of the poem. In fact M– G–'s alleged goings-on with the wives of other men, such as a certain man named Màka (note the pun with Mecca, pronounced *màka* in Wolof), whose wife of many years was so smitten with M– G– that she divorced Màka to marry him, are favorite topics for *xaxaar* poems at weddings even of his most distant kin. (See Irvine [1993] for further discussion of this case, including the cumulative effect of insult poems on M– G–'s political career.)

A clearer picture of the involvement of these parties in the situation at hand can be seen from Table 5.1, which divides the parties into production personnel and reception personnel.

In terms of participant roles, then, for each insult utterance one might distinguish Sponsor, Formulator, Speaker (i.e., Transmitter) and Co-Speakers, Addressee, Hearers, and Target. Indeed Levinson, citing this very example from an unpublished paper of mine, further distinguishes Indirect Targets (the bride's kin if present) from Ultimate Destinations (the bride's kin if absent).

I agree that these distinctions are appropriate, but not that they are primary or that there is a fixed, finite, universal list of PRs of this sort. To begin with, the list of PRs noted so far is not complete. For example, we have not yet distinguished between personnel whose roles have an indexical relation to the utterance and personnel explicitly named in the utterance (surely an important distinction if we want to be able to relate participant roles to grammatical phenomena). That is to say, there is a difference between persons named or denoted in an utterance text and persons only situationally linked to that text by their presence or their relationship to other relevant personnel. M–G–, identified so far as a Target (or Ultimate Destination), stands in both relationships to the text, since he is named in it; the bride's mother, on the other hand, though also a Target, stands only in an indexical presuppositional relation, since the text does not refer to her. One reason I point out this difference is that the bride's mother, by virtue of her close kinship with the bride and responsibility for the bride's moral upbringing, is implicitly a Target of any insult poem addressed to the bride. M–G–, however, as a more distant kinsman, must be named if he is to be involved at all. The same is true of Màka, "addressed" by the chorus when it takes on (animates) the role of M–G–. In fact, the choral couplet of the poem presents a particularly complex PR structure because of its use of quotation and address forms.[6]

But there is another issue here that is more important, since it concerns the very reason for distinguishing among PRs in the first place. Notice that in this Wolof example the distinction between Sponsor, Formulator, Transmitter, and so on, only arises because the insult utterance can be presumed to be part of a sequence of utterance events (and of speech events). Presumably, the insult has not been composed on the spot. Instead, there has been an earlier conversation in which the present Transmitter was instructed in what to say—in which she was Addressee, not Speaker. Presumably, too, there are likely to be conversations in the future in which the insult will be repeated, its utterers on those occasions being persons who are now present only as members of the audience (Levinson's notion of Ultimate Destinations presumes this)—and so on. Whether or not those past conversations actually occurred, or whether the future ones do, is not the point. They are implicated anyway, and the significance of the insult—perhaps even the possibility of daring to insult an important person, or wording the insult sharply—depends on this complex of implicated dialogues. The insult utterance's relationship with a presupposed earlier utterance event, whose participants cannot all be firmly identified, helps the performer get away with making a seriously wounding statement. And the in-

6. In partial explication, the choral co-utterers take on the role of M-G- when they quote him as addressing Màka, but they abandon that role in the next line when referring to "your pilgrimage." Here they have switched to addressing M-G-, an El-Hajj who has made the pilgrimage to Mecca (in Wolof, Màka). Village gossip alleges that M-G- made the pilgrimage to atone for his philandering, but (it is claimed) to little avail.

sult utterance's relationship with likely future utterance events, in which the insult is to be repeated, helps make the insult hurt.

Thus an utterance has implicit links to many dialogues, not only the present one, which together inform its significance, influence its form, and contribute to its performative force. To distinguish Sponsor, Formulator, Transmitter, Addressee, Hearers, and Targets for the Wolof insult utterance is to invoke its presupposed diachronic contextualization. The relationship between the immediate utterance event and these implicated dialogues—projectively constructed by interactants as part of the pragmatic reasoning by which they interpret an utterance and understand its significance—gives rise to the fragmentation of participant roles.

Utterance Event vs. Speech Event

Although the discussion of participation frames has focused so far on the utterance event, utterances are set within larger wholes which also have a bearing on how participation is organized. An utterance, that is, occurs within a dialogue which is in turn part of a speech event—an organized stretch of discourse with some internal structure, performance conventions, and an overarching structure of participation.

As Levinson (1988) points out, it is crucial to distinguish these two levels of organization of participant roles: the PRs applicable to the utterance event, and those relating to the larger, more inclusive speech event. The roles discussed in the Wolof insult-poetry case, for example, apply at the utterance level. Only there do they have consistent incumbents. Thus someone who is Formulator for one utterance may be Transmitter for another, and so on. Meanwhile, other roles might be defined that applied only to the speech-event level. At the Wolof wedding, the chorus (the set of persons who repeat an insult couplet or refrain, between a soloist's verses) might be such a role; the prosecutor in an American trial would be another example.

In identifying utterance-level PRs, it is important not to confuse them with roles that apply at the speech-event level. The prosecutor is sometimes Speaker, sometimes Addressee, for example, as he or she interacts with witnesses, judge, and others. The Wolof *xaxaar* chorus members are sometimes (co-)Speakers, when the refrain is actually being uttered; sometimes Addressees, when the soloist teaches the refrain to them; and sometimes merely audience, when they listen to the soloist's performance between refrains. But while the speech event is not what is immediately at issue in defining utterance-level PRs, it does provide an important contextualization frame for the utterances that occur in it—for their dialogic relationships. In a sense this relationship is diachronic, involving an utterance's implicational "reach" backward and forward within the event. But it is more than that, since the speech event represents a structuring of discourse relationships, not merely a sequence.

Again, Wolof insult poems provide some illustrations. For instance, in Example 1, the chorus only joins in on the choral couplet (lines 1–2) after they have heard it uttered several times by the soloist. In such performances they become Co-Speakers only after occupying the role of Addressees the moment before (when the soloist usually gazes at them and may even direct them to "Repeat after me"). At the end of the whole performance session, however, comes a final poem which the chorus performs in unison without any such instruction by a soloist. The chorus could not do this, of course, had not some substantial subgroup colluded on what the poem was to be, during conversations in the days before the wedding. A similar discourse history has occurred, therefore, but outside the bounds of the speech event as a whole rather than within it. The effect of the final choral utterance differs from that of the other choral couplets. Not only does the final chorus signal the close of the event, but the representation of community opinion is summarized and hammered home by this final outpouring of united voices whose message has no traceable individual source.

As another example, consider what happens when a Wolof griot approaches a noble in a public place. On calling out the noble's name in greeting, the griot may then attempt to launch into a performance of praise-singing— loud, stylized recitation of the noble's family history, for which payment can be demanded on the spot. Nobles who are worried about their financial resources may try to evade the encounter, or to postpone it by engaging the griot in an immediate *tête-à-tête* (in which later performance opportunities are promised). They will fail if they do not act quickly to preclude the griot's engagement of a larger audience, before whom they would be shamed if they could not pay.[7] The moment of greeting, therefore, is a moment of creative contextualization. Which speech event does the greeting herald, a public performance of praise-oratory or a private conversation? Are other people within earshot drawn into the circle of participation as audience, or excluded from it? Two different sets of speech-event PRs, and consequent dialogues, are implicated as possibilities.

7. Nobles do not always wish to avoid praise-singing; they enjoy it and consider it important to their reputations. They merely worry about their ability to pay for it. The griot, for his (or her) part, is not necessarily being specially aggressive or demanding, only advertising the noble to others. If griots do not celebrate their nobles, the nobles eventually get quite miffed.

I shall return to the matter of diachronic contextualization in a later section, to illustrate its complexity; but it is not the only kind of intertextuality, or implicated dialogue, that needs to be considered. To identify some of these other types, let us first take up some grammatical phenomena relating to participant roles.

DEICTIC FIELDS AND CONTEXTUALIZATION FRAMES

For many linguists the classic picture of the communicative act, with Speaker tossing a sentence over to Hearer who decodes it, has served only as backdrop to an analysis in which the two participants could thereafter be ignored. Where they could not be ignored, however, is in the study of such grammatical phenomena as person. Perhaps the most seminal work on grammatical person is that of Emile Benveniste (1971 [1946], [1956], [1958]), who, in the process of examining its grammatical realizations, argued that the linguistic status of "person" is the very foundation of subjectivity, even of self-consciousness (1971 [1958]: 224). For Benveniste, the "speaking subject" exists not in nature but in culture, constructed in the deictic field created in the moment of speaking.[8]

The personal pronouns *I* and *you* are not simply tools fabricated to label a Speaker and Hearer somehow existing independently of language. Instead, it is through verbal dialogue that human beings constitute themselves as self and other, "within the condition of intersubjectivity" (1971 [1958]: 230).[9]

That the personal pronouns are so fundamental in human life is, for Benveniste, evidenced in part by their universality: "a language without the expression of person cannot be imagined" (1971 [1958]: 225). Not all the pronouns included in the usual grammatical paradigms actually have the quality of "person," however. As some earlier grammarians had also done, Benveniste distinguished between *I/you* and *he* (and other so-called third-person forms). *I/you* are pronouns "characterized by the sign of person" (1971 [1946]: 200) because, as shifters, they refer only within the particular acts of speaking in which they occur, while the "third person" is really the nonperson, that which the Arab grammarians had called the "absent." Yet, because of its impersonality, Benveniste suggests, the third-person form is well suited for special uses, "as a form of address with someone who is present when one wishes to remove

8. I owe this point to Jane Hill.
9. For further explorations of Benveniste's ideas about subjectivity, intersubjectivity, and culture, see Singer (1984) and Lee and Urban (1989).

him from the personal sphere of 'you'" (1971 [1946]: 200), either to show respect or to insult. In a similar vein Benveniste examines several kinds of what we might call "slippage" of person and/or number, such as the royal *we*. In the first and second persons, he argues, "plural" forms are not really plural at all but, instead, are "amplified" persons, enlarging the personal *I* or *you* by annexing some non-*I*, or non-*you*—some possibly impersonal Other. Number slippages are thus interpretable as harnessing the potential impersonality of the annexing form. Benveniste's examples also include concord violations such as the Franco-Provençal *nous suis* and literary expressions such as Rimbaud's *je est un autre*, as special effects derived from entangling personal with impersonal realms (1971 [1946]: 202–04).

If the personal pronouns *I* and *you* establish a deictic field at the moment of speaking, and in so doing constitute a set of basic social relationships (the speaking subject *I*, the exterior person *you*, and a realm of nonpersons),[10] then, Benveniste's analysis suggests, the deictic field admits complications, slippages, and amplifications. A useful way to look at these complications is as multiple deictic fields or participation frames superimposed, as it were, on one another. That is, slippages involve complex participant role structures arrived at by imposing alternative deictic fields on the pragmatic present, through creative blendings and mismatchings of deictic categories with their interactional context.[11] The strong sense of a divided and alienated self in Rimbaud's statement is thus accomplished by imposing, on the speaking subject *je*, an alternative deictic field that excludes it from the realm of the personal (i.e., of potential subjectivity), in *est un autre*. In this concord "violation," third-personhood is not only predicated of the grammatical subject *je* but projected back over it.

Benveniste did not examine deictic complexities in stretches of discourse beyond the sentence. Snippets of dialogue may, however, reveal properties similar to the slippages and complications in his examples. Consider, for instance, the dialogue in Example 2 (from Sacks, Schegloff, and Jefferson 1978: 29; cited in Levinson 1988):

10. Another way to think of nonpersons might be as "nonsubjectivities." Note, however, that Fillmore's (1971) analysis of the pronoun *we* may suggest the need to distinguish, within the realm of nonpersons, between entities/beings with the potential for subjectivity and those lacking such potential. As Fillmore points out, when someone comes to a door and asks, "May we come in?" the *we* would normally be taken as including some other human being, or possibly the speaker's pet dog, but not (say) fleas inhabiting the speaker's clothing.

11. For an influential discussion of shifters and creative indexicality, see Silverstein (1976).

Example 2
> SHARON: You didn' come tuh talk tuh Karen?
> MARK: No, Karen—Karen'n I're having a fight,
>   (0.4)
>   after she went out with Keith an' not with (me)
> RUTHIE: Hah hah hah hah
> KAREN: Wul, Mark, you never asked me out.

In this bit of dialogue, when Mark is answering Sharon's question, and apparently addressing her, he refers to Karen in the third person even though Karen is present. We may infer that Karen, with whom he has had some minor misunderstanding, is the Target of his utterance: she is present but she is treated as if she were absent (with linguistic third person). The structure of an as-if conversation in which Karen is absent is superimposed on the situation where she is actually present.

Notice that this inference, and the assignment of Karen to the role of Target, depends on our being able to assume that Mark intends Karen to become aware of what he said. Either he knows she is within earshot, or he assumes there is a relationship between Sharon and Karen such that Sharon will convey the message. The analysis must be different if, at the moment of Mark's utterance, Karen is hiding behind a tree and she and Sharon have never previously met. But if Karen's physical position obviously places her within the geography of Mark's view and potential addressees, Mark could hardly deny knowing she would hear what he said.[12] The visual field, and its organization through gaze, positioning, and gesture, are crucial to an interpretation of participant roles. Just as a Speaker's gaze and gesture may select an Addressee in the absence of any *you* pronouns, so does visual evidence imply a deictic field which may or may not coincide with the field constituted through linguistic means.

Visual contextualization must therefore be added to the diachronic contextualization suggested in the discussion of Wolof insult performances, as another way of constituting complex participation frames. In any situation of physical copresence, the participant roles constituted verbally will inevitably be compared with those constituted (or suggested) visually. In fact, the pragmatic effects of many (most?) types of person or number slippage depend on a disjunction of linguistic form with visual evidence. The French pronoun *vous*

---

12. Actually, other conditions would also have to be met. For example, there would have to be evidence that Karen is conscious and reason to believe she is mentally competent to understand Mark's utterance.

is only honorific if it cannot be interpreted as plural—as it might be if several potential Addressees are present and the Speaker's gaze wanders among them.[13]

Grammatical person is of course not the only aspect of linguistic form relevant to participation frames. Gumperz's work on contextualization cues (e.g., 1982) is suggestive in this regard, and points toward code-switches as an especially likely contextualization strategy. Example 3 shows how code-switches, in addition to person and gaze, implicate at least two different participant role structures that fluctuate over the same personnel during a few seconds' talk. This bit of conversation took place early in my fieldwork in a Wolof village in 1970.

In Example 3, M and S have come to visit me one evening in my workroom (located within M's compound). S, a high-caste man, has been persuaded to tell a folktale, although his high rank makes it not really appropriate for him to do so. M, another high-caste man, is S's political and economic patron, formerly also his brother-in-law. Also present is A, an American visitor who speaks French (the official language of Senegal) but not Wolof. I (JTI), who speak both Wolof and French, am present in the background, preparing coffee for the guests.

Example 3
The underlined utterances are in French.

1 M.	(laughs) *am piil*—<u>pas besoin de piles,</u>	(laughs) A battery—<u>no need for</u>
	<u>ce machin.</u>	<u>batteries in that thing.</u>
2 A.	<u>Parce que c'est très sensible.</u>	<u>Because it's very sensitive.</u>
3 S.	<u>Ah oui.</u>	<u>Ah yes.</u>
4 A.	<u>C'est très sensible.</u>	<u>It's very sensitive.</u>
5 M.	<u>Eh bien,</u> *dëfë—dëfë am*	<u>Well, because</u>—because his
6	*doole, dëram, bu mu jógé*	stammering will provide the
7	*sa gëmmiñ.*	power, when it comes out of
		your mouth.

Though focusing on loud speaking rather than upon the folktale performance *per se*, M is teasing S about behaving inappropriately for his rank. Ostensibly M addresses his remarks to A, looking at A and the machine in lines 1–5, switching into French, and (in line 6, *dëram* 'his stammering')

13. Though visual evidence of singular Addressee may be crucial, it is not sufficient, since the plurality of second-person plural forms may (nonhonorifically) refer to absent others, for example, as comembers of Addressee's social category: "You (*vous*) mailmen have new uniforms this year, don't you?"

referring to S in the third person, as if S were absent. But M's switch into Wolof in line 5, and his later switch to a second-person form for S in line 7 (*sa gëmmiñ* 'your mouth') suggest S as Addressee. Thus there is a slippage both of person and of code here, as if two dialogues—one in which M addresses A in French while S is absent, and one in which M addresses S in Wolof while A is absent—were superimposed on one another.[14]

So far, then, analysis of these examples suggests a set of basic participation relations consisting of Speaker, Addressee, and Third Parties.[15] Complex pragmatic effects then derive from signs implicating other participation frames as alternative or supplementary deictic fields. One such complexity concerns how a linguistically constituted participation frame relates to a visually suggested deictic field (visually evidenced at least by who is present/absent, but also manipulated through body position, gesture, and gaze). Special effects and combinations are also accomplished by person-switches and by code-switches, as well as by a presumptive history of discourses.

These examples suggest to me that the complex laminations of participant roles are best thought of as the result of multiple framing processes. We can use a notion of multiple contextualization frames for the analysis of participant roles, for an utterance is situated not only in the dialogic relation immediately given in grammatical person forms, but in many such relations, overt, covert, and implicit. Overt signals implicating participation frames are of many kinds; Gumperz's (1982) discussions of contextualization cues provide insight into their variety.

PARTICIPATION FRAMES IN REPORTED SPEECH

Although I have given some prominence to an analysis of grammatical person as constituting participant roles, person forms do not only refer to such parties as the pragmatic utterer and his/her Addressee. As Urban (1989: 29) has pointed out, "the 'I' of discourse is not only an actual in-the-world subject, indexically referred to by means of the first person form. The discourse 'I' can

14. The teasing strategy was quite effective. S clammed up and produced practically nothing. See Irvine (1993) for further discussion.

15. Among Third Parties it may turn out to be useful to distinguish, at a more subtle level, Alignable Parties—that is, those participants who can be aligned with Speaker or Addressee as extra first or second persons—from Excluded parties. Examples of Alignable parties might include myself (JTI) in the preceding dialogue (example 3), or the Speaker's dog in Fillmore's 1971 discussion. Fillmore's flea, or any other being having no right to participate in dialogue, would be Excluded. On the other hand, the condition of "potential subjectivity" discussed in note 10 may make this distinction unnecessary.

also be any being or entity, imaginary or not, capable of being reported as speaker. The central question here concerns the relationship between this reported 'I' and the indexical referential 'I' that points to a subject." If I utter a sentence with a direct quotation, such as that given in Example 4, the *I* of the embedded quotation is not me (the pragmatic speaker):

Example 4
   "He$_i$ said, 'I$_i$ am going.' "

Instead, the embedded *I* refers back to the subject of the main clause, *he*. All languages permit this kind of construction, in which (to use Goffman's terms) the speaker "animates" the persona of another, taking on another subjectivity for the duration of the reported speech.

   With reported speech forms, then, the speaker constructs or represents a projective relation among dialogues: a projecting one (i.e., the pragmatic present) and a projected or implicated one, whose utterance is quoted (see Rumsey 1990: 347). In Example 4 the projection reaches into the past, reporting the quoted speech as having occurred earlier, and now merely being repeated by the present speaker. Although such "historical" projections are common, projections may also reach into the future, or into a hypothetical case, as in Example 5.

Example 5
   "He$_i$ might say, 'I$_i$ am going.' "

   Notice that while constructions like Examples 4 and 5 spell out the relationship between projecting and projected dialogues by constructing the projected one referentially (in the main clause), reported speech need not always display its framing overtly. In English, if the projected dialogue is lengthy, some sentences will omit the "He said" clause of Example 4, the frame being retrievable from an earlier portion of the discourse.[16] It is also possible, however, for quotative framing to be implicated, or "understood," when no actual quotative clause or marker has appeared in the dialogue at all. Proverbs, for example, in Wolof as in many other languages, are understood to be quotations received from ancestral generations. Recognizable by genre conventions and metaphorical content, they are not marked by any quotative construction. What makes them recognizable, actually, is a stripped-down morphology and syntax

16. Languages apparently differ on this point, some insisting on overt quotative marking on each sentence—even, in Ge'ez, on each major constituent within a quoted utterance (see Bender, Fulass, and Cowley [1976]).

lacking such deictic forms as might attach to the pragmatic present, as in Example 6:

Example 6
lambi muus, jénaax du ca bàkku

'At the cats' wrestling match, the mouse does not contend' (literally, 'is not heralded' [sc., as a contestant]).

This proverb sentence has none of the markers of tense, or of spatial or discourse deixis, that would normally characterize a Wolof conversational utterance.[17] Since it is not necessary for a Wolof proverb to be familiar to its audience to be accepted as such, presumably a speaker might be able to invent one and have it be taken as ancestral wisdom. As in the invented traditions discussed by Hobsbawm (1983), a dialogue among ancestral speakers would thus be implicated by the proverb form, although it would have no actual historical basis.

The signs that implicate quotative framing need not, in all cases, even be linguistic. In Weyéwa (Indonesia) rituals described by Kuipers (1993), the timetable of a ritual sequence suffices to implicate quotative framing. In these rituals, orators represent the statements and intentions of ancestors, and by a certain point in the lengthy sequence of rituals the projection of ancestral intent should have been thoroughly achieved—so thoroughly that an orator's performance needs no quotative forms to be understood as quotation. Indeed, to include a quotative form at this time might inappropriately call attention to the pragmatic present, as if it were not completely dominated by the ancestral voice. And among Wolof again, as among several adjacent peoples, quotative framing is virtually implicit in the social identity of griot, so central is quotative 'transmission' (*jottali*) to the very definition of the griot's place in society. That is, quotative framing is implicated (at least as a possibility) simply by the social identity of a sentence's utterer, if the utterer is a griot. Projected dialogues may thus be implicated by a variety of means, nonlinguistic as well as linguistic.

Now, in this relationship between the implicated (projected) speech situation and the projecting one, how permeable are the participation frames? In reported speech, when do aspects of one frame "leak" into the other? The Wolof insult performances described earlier depend on a relative imperme-

17. A morpheme-by-morpheme analysis would look as follows:

lamb	*i*	*muus*	*jénaax*	*du*	*ca*	*bàkk*	*u*
wrestling match/	of (pl.)/	cat/	mouse/	neg/	there/	praise-drumming/	inversive

ability of frames. Performers utter scathing and obscene statements, accusing important people of sexual misconduct, crime, and witchcraft. Sometimes the allegations are taken to be quite credible. Yet neither the performers nor the people who later repeat the accusations in conversation can be held responsible for the opinion thus articulated. Quoting insulates the pragmatic speaker from personal responsibility for the quoted words.

Consider, however, Example 7, from a Mexicano (Nahuatl) speaker recorded by Jane Hill (Hill and Irvine [1993: 13]). A bilingual woman explains that one important benefit of speaking Mexicano is to understand and respond to insults Mexicano speakers address to strangers who come to their towns:

Example 7
> Porque quēmaniān āmo nicmatīz de ōme, hasta nēchtēhuīcaltīlīz in nonāntzīn, pero in āmo nictendēroa tlen nēchilia, hasta nēchilīz, "Chinga tu madre," con perdón de Diós, quēn nicmatīz tlen nēchilia?

> Because if I didn't speak two languages, someone might say something about my mother, but when I don't understand what he is saying to me, even if he says to me, "Fuck your mother," begging God's pardon, how would I know what he is saying to me?

As Hill writes, "Here, even though the obscenity is assigned to a third party, the speaker has still uttered it in her own voice; in Goffman's terms, she has 'animated' the utterance. Yet she clearly does not see herself as morally neutral in this role; she must ask God's forgiveness for the obscenity, even though it is not 'hers.' "

The danger of leakage seems, in this example, to be related to the obscenity of the quoted text; but in other cases the danger may derive from something else. A Wolof griot, for instance, telling me a story about the kings and heroes of two centuries ago, quoted a remark by the king of Kajoor in which there was a grammatical anomaly. The griot interrupted his tale to make absolutely sure I realized it was the king, and not the griot reporting his speech, who was responsible for the grammatical "error."

While these examples show speakers guarding against the danger of leakage from the quoted material (the "source" dialogue) onto the quoter, leakage may also go in the other direction. To animate another's voice gives one a marvelous opportunity to comment on it subtly—to shift its wording, exaggeratedly mimic its style, or supplement its expressive features. In Nukulaelae (Polynesia), as described by Besnier (1993), for example, speakers use reported speech as a vehicle for affective expression, culturally devalued. The speaker's own affectivity leaks into the quoted voice. By similar means, but with more positive cultural value attached, the Wolof griot supplies affective animation to the message of the noble for whom he or she acts as transmitter. Indeed this is part of the cultural rationale for the griot's role. Griots are supposed to be volatile people, excitable and exciting to others, and endowed with the rhetorical skills to move an audience. Nobles, supposedly more stolid and laconic, must engage griots to address the audience on their behalf. The arrangement in which the griot animates the noble's voice is thought to benefit both parties. Notice, however, that most of the benefit gained by the griot comes in the form of cash rather than from the act of animation itself. The benefit leaked onto Wolof griots from the sources they animate is small and slow-acting compared to that which a Pentecostalist, speaking in tongues, is thought to acquire from the Holy Ghost whose voice is thus transmitted.[18]

These examples give some idea of the complexity of relationships between participation frames—those in the pragmatic present and those implicated, intended, and imagined. Cultural frameworks and ideologies contribute to the values attaching to these relationships, and to the kinds of participants who may be implicated (such as spirits who possess their human animators). The examples also suggest that just which linguistic features leak between participation frames is, in part at least, culturally determined.

Our examples have not illustrated indirect quotation, however, where (some have argued) grammatical constraints might be more important. Indirect quotation requires deictic features—minimally, person—to be imported from the main clause into the quotation clause. Importation of person and tense in English is shown in Example 8 (compare Example 4):

Example 8
He$_i$ said that he$_i$ was going.

In the relationship between the clauses, various aspects of the language's syntactic system come into play. These have provided an important line of evidence for linguists' examining the linguistic representation of "point of view" (Chafe 1976) and the decomposability of the "speaking subject"—a problem relating to the fragmentation of the Speaker participant role.[19] Kuno (1976) and Banfield (1982), for example, maintain that point of view is syntactically constrained, so that a given syntactic domain cannot manifest more than one. Banfield further proposes, however, that there are actually several types of subjectivities: Speaker, Self, and the S (speaker) of pragmatics are different (and syntactic constraints limit their co-occurrence). The analysis thus suggests a

18. For discussion and references, see Irvine (1982).
19. For discussion of this literature, I am indebted to Jane Hill.

complex set of participation frames but certain limits on the forms of "anima-tion" that can be expressed.[20]

Banfield's work is based primarily on the analysis of literary genres, es-pecially the representation of subjectivity in novelistic discourse. Other stu-dents of novelistic discourse, however, notably Bakhtin and his circle, propose that the representation of subjectivity is the result of a far more complex com-bination of voices. Echoes of the speech of others appear in one's discourse not only in overtly marked constructions (the overt representation of their talk, whether in direct or indirect quotation, or even "free indirect style"), but in many covert forms as well—forms that imitate, stylize, or parody the stylistic features associated with other persons, genres, times, and places (Bakhtin 1981 [1934–35]). Although an author may manipulate the evocations of other speakers, it is not clear that he or she may avoid them. So pervasive is this process that it puts in doubt the very possibility that a sentence might represent but a single subjectivity. Words, forms, and styles bear the traces of those who have used them in the past. In the Bakhtinian view a multiplicity of frames is inevitable, as a consequence of language's participation in society and history.

Bakhtin's arguments are not limited to literary discourse, although that was his starting point (but see Voloshinov 1973 [1930]). The idea of inter-twined voices recognizes the complexity of the sources on which a speaker draws, and the complexity of the speaker's commentary on those sources, which are included in an utterance. The "double-voiced utterance" is one whose form and significance presuppose a second voice, another speaker, whose words are borrowed, mocked, responded to, or given provocation. The double-voiced utterance has a complex history, in this sense, and a complex future. But the notion of voice, and the emphasis on subjectivity and authorship in the novel, perhaps tend to weight the analysis more in the direction of pro-duction processes than is suitable for our present purposes. Rather than multi-vocal, we might consider a speech situation to be multiply dialogical: it is not just the speaker who is doubled (or multiplied) by other voices, but a set of

20. In a recent paper, Alan Rumsey (1990) has further argued that cultural ideologies con-tribute to the syntactic features of reported speech. Not all languages have the same kinds of constructions for reported speech as English; some languages, Rumsey argues, make no syntactic distinction between direct and indirect quotation, and in other constructions as well do not distin-guish between reporting the gist of a message and reporting its wording. That they do not, he suggests, reflects an associated ideology in which words are forms of action—as opposed to a Western ideological disjunction between language and the world. Note, however, that the presence of such an ideology may not be a sufficient condition for the grammatical phenomena Rumsey discusses. Thus one could argue that Wolof share a linguistic ideology in which words are actions, not merely labels; yet their language does provide for both direct and indirect quotation.

dialogic relations that are crucially informed by other sets—shadow conversations that surround the conversation at hand.

Unlike some of the other analyses discussed in earlier pages, this one is open-ended. There is no preconceived limit to the contextualizations, or the shadow conversations that a speaker might have in mind or an interpreter might imagine, in retrospect, to be pertinent. Consider, for example, the "secondary dialogues" with absent interlocutors, discussed by Crapanzano (1988: 3)—those "silent but forceful secondary, or shadow, dialogues that accompany any primary dialogue (e.g., the dialogue between the student of anthropology who engages silently with his mentors back home and all they symbolize as he converses with his friends in the field)." As Bakhtin's comments on stylization and parody suggest, we must also consider dialogues that are implicated by being imitated, or by serving as model (stylistically, perhaps) for the conduct of the present one—as, for instance, if one were to imitate courtroom talk or the language of international relations when negotiating a family dispute. And, finally, a dialogue may be implicated by being conspicuously avoided. Thus political antagonists, finding themselves invited to the same cocktail party, may tacitly agree to limit themselves to innocuous small talk, or to evade engagement as much as possible, in order to avoid confrontation; yet their antagonism may be obvious to everyone from the very manner of their avoiding the expression of it.[21]

WOLOF INSULT POEMS REVISITED: TEXT AND DISCOURSE

Let us return now to the Wolof *xaxaar* insults for a more complex view of diachronic contextualization and participation frames. The *xaxaar* insult poem discussed earlier and excerpted in Example 1 was recorded at the time of its performance. Yet, it was suggested, the performance of an insult poem is but

---

21. Some of Grice's examples of conversational implicature involve utterances that are conspicuously avoided. Consider, for instance, the dialogue in the following example (Grice 1975), where B avoids responding to A's remark (refusing uptake, one might say, characteristic of the role of Addressee):

A. Mrs. X is an old bag.

B. (pause) The weather has been quite delightful today, hasn't it?

Consider, too, his example (*ibid.*) of a recommendation letter whose writer says only positive things about a job candidate but conspicuously avoids mention of crucial aspects of his qualifications. This example, incidentally, illustrates the contribution of cultural frameworks and intersubjectivity to the implicature process. The person who receives this recommendation letter will interpret it as negative only if he or she can assume its author shares an understanding of what it should have contained. Only then can the omissions be taken as intentional. Anyone who has experience reading recommendation letters from abroad will be familiar with this problem.

one moment in a diachronic chain of discourses, a moment which presumes earlier moments and in which later moments are already envisioned. To illustrate the complexity of the relationships among these implicated dialogues and their participation frames, let us consider a *xaxaar* poem retrieved at a later point in such a chain. As it happens, although diachronic contextualization is obviously important in this example, some of the other forms of dialogic implication are illustrated as well.

This poem was presented to me as a written text, recorded and read aloud to me by a local griot, Majaan M–. Some days earlier I had asked Majaan to act as "journalist" and fill a notebook with local news and items of interest. One of the items in his notebook, titled simply "Xaxaar" without attribution of authorship, was the Wolof text in Example 9. The conversation in which he read it aloud to me and discussed its language and its history took place in my workroom in the village chief's compound. Just outside on the veranda, presumably within earshot, was S–G–, the chief's senior wife, president of the village women's political organization.

In Example 9, the Wolof poem is rendered in standard orthography rather than in Majaan's idiosyncratic spelling. The contextualizing part of what Majaan told me is presented in translation and derives from my written notes on the conversation. I did not tape-record this session, since Majaan considered tape recordings as "performances," and the text he read to me came from a women's genre which he, as a man, had a right to report but not to perform. Majaan reported the insult poem as follows.

Example 9
"This *xaxaar* (insult poem) was addressed to Khadi N–, the Imam's wife, when her daughter got married:

1	*Mbaa Khadi N– dikkul?*	Hasn't Khadi N– arrived?
2	*Khadi mii tàkk tubééy te du góór,*	This Khadi ties on trousers and isn't a man,
3	*te loo nas mu nocci.*	and whatever you thread your needle with, she lifts it off.[22]
4	*Moo! Khadi N– yow ba ngga dajé ak*	Well! Khadi N–, you, when you meet with
5	*Mor M–, moo loo ci jilé?*	Mor M–, well!, What do you take away?
6	*Bëqté wu rëy, rangoon yu né mbacc,*	A big load of snot,[23] tears openly flowing,

22. That is, she steals your men.
23. *Bëqté*, 'snot': possible pun with *mbëgté*, 'love.'

7	*ku ne' ber-ub kelem?*	(because) each (of you) has to have a separate plate?[24]
8	*Yaa di buur bu sol màntó—*	You are the king wearing the royal mantle—
9	*jiitali dagam.*	Lead us in pursuit of him.
10	*Ne léén ko "nyaala gaaynago"*	Tell them, "The Greatest Person" (praise-term)[25]—
11	*looloo di ag peyam.*	That will be his reward.
12	*Awu léén ko: mu riir-a-riir*	Repeat after me:[26] She goes rumble,
13	*te rijaax te tàlltàli,*	thump and clatter,
14	*ni 'g rirandol gu ànd aki sabar.*	Thus sounds the *rirandol* (earth drum) accompanying the *sabar* (dance drums).
15	*Yaai dóju dënnu.*	You[27] are thunderstones.
16	*Ku la soq njël di na yex a reer.*	Whoever pounds your daily millet will be late eating supper.
17	*Yaai dóju dënnu.*	You are thunderstones.

"This *xaxaar* was performed last year, about eight months ago, by S–N– M–, one of my sisters, who told it to me. These words are very rich. The woman was very angry and came after her, until S– N– was afraid. Now S–N– wouldn't dare perform it again. You see, Khadi N– thought she was too high to be addressed in the *xaxaar*, because she is the wife of the Imam. She said, she had no scandal in her life. Well, as for that, if she didn't want to be addressed in *xaxaar*, she shouldn't have let her daughter get married."

Majaan presents his written text as a record of a performance by his sister S– N–, collected retrospectively in a conversation with her in which she reported what had happened in the performance and afterwards. Majaan himself had not attended. From the evidence presented by Majaan, let us examine the participant role structures of the performance event. Although Majaan says the poem was "addressed to" Khadi, mother of the bride, she was not present. The second-person forms in lines 4, 5, 8, 10 (imperative), 15, 16, and 17 refer to her as if she were present, but in terms of the actual event, she is the poem's

24. That is, they can't eat together—or have sex—because they are not married, and because they are of different ranks. Khadi N– does not actually outrank Mor M–, except insofar as she and the rest of the Imam's family might be trying to lay claim to higher rank—a claim the poem accuses her of unjustly making.

25. *nyaala gaaynago:* a praise-term used in formal praise-poetry. The poem apparently has Khadi instructing her followers to praise her in terms reserved for royal heroes.

26. *Awu leen ko:* conventional phrase instructing the chorus at a wedding to repeat the following couplet as a choral refrain.

27. Singular, addressed to Khadi.

absent Target, while its immediate Addressee is her daughter the bride. Other second-person forms (lines 3, 12) refer to the chorus and audience, in passages where Khadi is referred to in third-person forms. The poem thus shifts among participant role structures involving various different Addressees, including the "as-if" Addressee Khadi. It also involves several parties as Speakers: the performer, S– N–; Khadi, implicated (fictionally) as speaker in lines 10–11; and the chorus, projected (lines 12–14) as Co-Speakers when the performer instructs them to say something and then, presumably, actually Co-Speakers if they do repeat what they are told. (Line 1 would also be a choral line, uttered twice to make a couplet.)

The gist of the poem is to accuse Khadi of getting above herself—of claiming higher rank than her alleged behavior would reveal her to have— perhaps even caste climbing. But while the poem makes its accusation only within the confines of a traditional genre of ritual insult, the conversations that repeat the poem accuse her quite baldly. It is Khadi's alleged reaction to the poem that, retrospectively, gives the poem special force and proves its point, since the angry reaction displays precisely the gossip-worthy behavior she had claimed was absent from her life. Apparently, her surprising anger, and her inappropriate blaming of the performer S– N–, also led villagers to wonder whether there might be some truth to the alleged involvement with Mor M– (a wealthy shopkeeper).

It is somewhat unusual for a conversation about a *xaxaar* poem to emphasize the identity of its performer so strongly as Majaan did. Why might he have done so? One reason may lie in his contention that it was inappropriate for Khadi to blame the performer; the fact that she did only shows what a skilful performer S– N– was. (But it does not assign responsibility to S–N– for motivating the insult—no *xaxaar* performer bears that. Recall that the genre presumes earlier conversations between sponsors and performers.) Another factor, however, is that Majaan needed to show legitimate access to the text, so that he could not be supposed to have invented any of it himself. He was merely reporting what his sister had told him. He was Transmitter, but he was not Performer (in the sense of taking responsibility for a display), Formulator, or Sponsor. In his presentation of the poem to me, reading from a written text allowed him to fine-tune his participant role particularly effectively. Whether by necessity or convenience, he read the text aloud in such a hesitant and affectless manner as to strip his utterance of the prosodic signs of a performer's involvement. Narrowing his role to that of Transmitter, he animated only the informational minimum of his sister's voice.

Majaan's conversation with me implicates a discourse history of considerable length, a history of dialogues leading up to the present and, in being implicated, allowing him to frame his own participation as but a tiny fragment of a production role. But there are even more dialogues implicated here than these retrospective ones. To begin with, although I was clearly the present Addressee, Majaan was surely aware of S– G–'s presence just outside the door. Even if she did not hear him, there was the likelihood that I would talk about the conversation with her and, perhaps, with one or two other close associates. Since S– G– was an important local figure, who had been involved in marriage negotiations with the Imam's (thus Khadi N–'s) family, I suspect that S– G– was also an intended destination for Majaan's presentation. She too was being warned of the griots' power over reputation. And finally, there is a projection into a more distant future and more distant place. When he presented his journalist notebook to me, Majaan could expect that I would take the material back to America to report the events of village life to new audiences. The notebook's destination had already been agreed upon. So Majaan, selecting texts and news for his notebook, must have envisioned a chain of discourse relations extending into the future—all the way, gentle reader, to you.

CONCLUSION

With this last example we move from the problem of participant roles to the problem of textuality. Several kinds of "texts" made their appearance: Majaan's written presentation of a *xaxaar* poem; my edited version (changing orthography, punctuation, and adding translation and explanatory footnotes), based more on his oral rendering than on his written one; the "text" of our conversation; and, by implication, Majaan's sister's report to her brother, her own public performance earlier, and so on. A chain of discourse interweaves poem and conversation at many junctures. The chain we may reconstruct here starts with a conversation in which Majaan's sister and her patroness(es) jointly initiate the composition of a poem. The poem's performance—in which the earlier composition event is assumed—transforms it into an object detached, in a way, from its ongoing pragmatic relations. Genre conventions of meter, assonance, and other features that apply within the poem but not outside it help mark the boundaries of this linguistic object and help secure the impression that it has some independent existence, transcending the present moment and the present speaker. Unmoored from the present, it is more easily transported into the future. Understood as having already occurred in other dialogues, and destined to occur in still more, it is intrinsically tied to none.

Perhaps one would want to say that the independence, or pragmatic transcendence, of this set of utterances—what makes it a transferable object—is what gives it a sense of "textuality." But if so, it is a textuality that presupposes the conversational moments it purports to transcend. As I have argued earlier, the *xaxaar* poems could not take the form they do if their utterers had to take responsibility for more than merely making public a statement constructed elsewhere. And the poems would not have the force they do if they did not presuppose the likelihood of future repetitions in subsequent dialogues. As the chain of discourse progresses, the "transcendent" text carries traces of its history along with it, as the conversations in which it is repeated provide new reportable material that add to its significance. Accompanied by an account of its discourse history, Majaan's sister's poem goes international.

There is no necessary limit to these contextualizations and discourse histories—to the sense in which a multitude of other dialogues are implicated in the one at hand. By the same token, I believe, there is no necessary limit to the participation frames that can be imposed on the pragmatic present, fragmenting its participant roles and recombining them, in a complex calculus of mapping roles onto persons present and absent (or, internally, onto aspects of selves). The intricate laminations of participant roles, the many shadow conversations they reflect, and the discourses they inform belong to the same dialogic process.

REFERENCES

Bakhtin, M. M.
    1981 [1934–35]   *The Dialogic Imagination: Four Essays*. Michael Holquist (ed.), Caryl Emerson and Michael Holquist (trans.). Austin: University of Texas Press.
    1984   *Problems of Dostoevsky's Poetics*. Caryl Emerson (ed. and trans.). Minneapolis: University of Minnesota Press.

Banfield, Anne
    1982   *Unspeakable Sentences*. London: Routledge & Kegan Paul.

Bender, M. L., H. Fulass, and R. Cowley
    1976   Two Ethio-Semitic languages. In *Language in Ethiopia*, M. L. Bender, J. D. Bowen, R. L. Cooper, and C. A. Ferguson (eds.), 99–119. London: Oxford University Press.

Benveniste, Emile
    1971 [1946]   Relationships of person in the verb. In *Problems in General Linguistics*, ch. 18, 195–204. Coral Gables: University of Miami Press.
    1971 [1956]   The nature of pronouns. In *Problems in General Linguistics*, ch. 20, 217–22. Coral Gables: University of Miami Press.
    1971 [1958]   Subjectivity in language. In *Problems in General Linguistics*, ch. 21, 223–30. Coral Gables: University of Miami Press.

Besnier, Niko
   1993   Reported speech and affect on Nukulaelae. In *Responsibility and Evidence in Oral Discourse*, J. Hill and J. Irvine (eds.), 161–81. Cambridge: Cambridge University Press.

Chafe, Wallace A.
   1976   Givenness, contrastiveness, definiteness, subjects, topics, and point of view. In *Subject and Topic*, C.N. Li (ed.), 25–56. New York: Academic Press.

Clark, H., and T. Carlson
   1982   Hearers and speech acts. *Language* 58: 332–73.

Crapanzano, Vincent
   1988   On self characterization. *Working Papers and Proceedings of the Center for Psychosocial Studies*, #24. Chicago: Center for Psychosocial Studies.

Duranti, Alessandro, and Charles Goodwin (eds.)
   1992   *Rethinking Context*. Cambridge: Cambridge University Press

Fillmore, Charles
   1971   *Santa Cruz Lectures on Deixis*. Bloomington: Indiana University Linguistics Club.

Goffman, Erving
   1961   *Encounters: Two Studies in the Sociology of Interaction*. Indianapolis: Bobbs-Merrill.
   1974   *Frame Analysis: An Essay on the Organization of Experience*. New York: Harper and Row.
   1976   Replies and responses. *Language in Society* 5(3): 257–313.
   1981   *Forms of Talk*. Philadelphia: University of Pennsylvania Press.

Grice, H. Paul
   1975   Logic and conversation. In *Syntax and Semantics*, Vol. 3, *Speech Acts*, P. Cole and J. Morgan (eds.), 41–58. New York: Academic Press.

Gumperz, John
   1982   *Discourse Strategies*. Cambridge: Cambridge University Press.

Hill, Jane, and Judith T. Irvine
   1993   Introduction. In *Responsibility and Evidence in Oral Discourse,* J. Hill and J. Irvine (eds.), 1–23. Cambridge: Cambridge University Press.

Hobsbawm, Eric
   1983   Introduction: Inventing tradition. In *The Invention of Tradition*, E. Hobsbawm and T. Ranger (eds.), 1–14. Cambridge: Cambridge University Press.

Hymes, Dell
   1972   Models of the interaction of language and social life. In *Directions in Sociolinguistics: The Ethnography of Speaking*, J. Gumperz and D. Hymes (eds.), 35–71. New York: Holt, Rinehart & Winston.
   1974   *Foundations in Sociolinguistics: An Ethnographic Approach*. Philadelphia: University of Pennsylvania Press.

Irvine, Judith T.
   1982   The creation of identity in spirit mediumship and possession. In *Semantic*

Anthropology, D. Parkin (ed.), 241–60. A.S.A. Monographs #22. London: Academic Press.

1993   Insult and responsibility: Verbal abuse in a Wolof village. In *Responsibility and Evidence in Oral Discourse*, J. Hill and J. Irvine (eds.), 105–34. Cambridge: Cambridge University Press.

Kuipers, Joel
1993   Reported speech and the reproduction of authority among the Weyewa. In *Responsibility and Evidence in Oral Discourse*, J. Hill and J. Irvine (eds.), 88–104. Cambridge: Cambridge University Press.

Kuno, Susumu
1976   Subject, theme, and the speaker's empathy: A re-examination of relativization phenomena. In *Subject and Topic*, C.N. Li (ed.), 417–44. New York: Academic Press.

Lee, Benjamin, and Greg Urban (eds.)
1989   *Semiotics, Self, and Society*. Berlin: Mouton de Gruyter.

Levinson, Stephen C.
1983   *Pragmatics*. Cambridge: Cambridge University Press.
1988   Putting linguistics on a proper footing: Explorations in Goffman's concepts of participation. In *Erving Goffman: An Interdisciplinary Appreciation*, P. Drew and A. Wootton (eds.), 161–227. Oxford: Polity Press.

Rumsey, Alan
1990   Wording, meaning, and linguistic ideology. *American Anthropologist* 92: 346–61.

Sacks, Harvey, Emanuel Schegloff, and Gail Jefferson
1978   A simplest systematics for the organization of turn taking for conversation. In *Studies in the Organization of Conversational Interaction*, J. Schenkein (ed.), 7–55. New York: Academic Press.

Schegloff, Emanuel
1987   Parties and joint talk. Paper presented at annual meetings of American Anthropological Association, Chicago.

Silverstein, Michael
1976   Shifters, linguistic categories, and cultural description. In *Meaning in Anthropology*, K. Basso and H. Selby (eds.), 11–55. Albuquerque: University of New Mexico Press.

Singer, Milton
1984   *Man's Glassy Essence: Explorations in Semiotic Anthropology*. Bloomington: Indiana University Press.

Urban, Greg
1989   The 'I' of discourse. In *Semiotics, Self, and Society*, B. Lee and G. Urban (eds.), 27–51. Berlin: Mouton de Gruyter.

Voloshinov, V. N.
1973 [1930]   *Marxism and the Philosophy of Language*. L. Matejka and I. R. Titunik (trans.). New York: Seminar Press.

6 Exorcism and the Description
of Participant Roles

William F. Hanks

INTRODUCTION

In the course of ritual performance, a Maya shaman transforms his patient's reality by creating a universal space around himself and the altar at which he performs. This practice is a major source of shamanic power, involving the use of specialized knowledge and the systematic reconstitution of lived space. It rests on a special way of combining the perspectively oriented fields of the human body (of shaman and beneficiaries), the altar with its icons, the reference space projected by the verbal discourse, and the absolute space of cardinal locations and cosmological dimensions. Producing the intervention of spirit forces of which only the shaman is aware, while transforming the bodily states of human beneficiaries, these ritual performances pose interesting problems for the analysis of participant roles in verbal events.[1] What kind of coparticipation is sustained in such events, given the fundamental asymmetries in what shamans and their patients understand about what is going on? What is the relation between the mediation of asymmetry and the effectiveness of the performance in securing the intended outcomes? What kind of approach to participant roles is appropriate to the task of explaining the differing contributions of the shaman, the patient, who remains largely inert, and the legions of spirits who are brought into play in the performance space?

At its most general, *participation* can be defined, at least heuristically, as the engagement, and therefore *coengagement*, of social actors in an ongoing activity. An "actor" in this gloss can be either less than an individual (an agent acting in the limited capacity of a role incumbent), or greater than an individual (a collectivity). There are of course many different kinds of engagement, levels of intensity, and degrees of symmetry and asymmetry between interactants, just

---

1. The shaman's awareness is both the expert knowledge of the process in which he is engaged and his felt sense of the copresence of the spirits he lowers to the altar.

as there are various rhythms, durations and successions of social engagement. These differences entail differences in *participation status*, at least at a micro-analytic level. Similarly, there is an unavoidable relation between the units of activity called "acts" or "events," and the engagements they presuppose and entail, however one chooses to formulate them. In this paper, I will relate them principally by way of a third concept: discourse genre.

Discourse genres can be viewed formally as regular groupings of hierarchically defined structural units of text, for example the opening and closing sections, verse parallelisms, and sequential invocations of spirits characteristic of the Maya ritual genre *saántiguar* 'sanctification'. Alternatively, genres can be defined as principles of discourse production immanent in communicative practice, such as the modes of address typical of sixteenth-century Maya letters (Hanks 1987), and the performance styles diacritic of political oratory or academic lectures. In clear cases, genres are recognized and labeled by native actors, although this need not be so. One can readily imagine novel genres of action emerging in social life apart from any native recognition or categorization of them. Perhaps we should assume, in fact, that emergence is the basic mode of being of genres, and that category labels, like mnemonic devices, grow mainly out of retrospection. For the purposes of this paper, I will take genres to be defined by the interplay of formal linguistic features, native metalinguistic typifications and the actual practices in which actors engage.

Defined at the level of practice, genres mediate between event types and modes of participation: the totalization and segmentability that distinguish *events* as units from *action* as an ongoing process depend on the same genre types which govern the engagements of participants. To take a handy example, Maya shamanic performance is divided into a number of named genres, each of which defines a type of event with recognized consequences and specific, highly constrained types of participant engagement. These engagements, as I said, pose interesting problems for the notions of "speaker," "addressee," and other participant roles. There is the fact that while the shaman performs in the first person, saying, "I request the blessing" and so forth, he invokes all of the most actively engaged spirits by way of third-person reference. Are they direct addressees therefore, or somehow displaced "targets" of the ceremony? Further-more, all ritual speech in Maya could be construed as a sort of semiquote, insofar as shamans claim to have learned its forms either from other shamans, from dreams, or in charismatic dialogues with the very spirits they invoke in the third person. Shamans are not merely relayers of divine speech, however, since they consciously change their prayer forms over time, in order to beautify them. What kind of speaker is this? The patient is copresent in a curing event, and enjoined to concentrate his or her faith on the process, yet the same patient is presented in speech as an anonymous human, a gift of God in need of repair. How do we fit this partial engagement into the participant roles without creating new, ad hoc categories for each event type? The icons adorning shamanic altars are participants also, in that they provide the material face for the spirits they stand for, yet surely we would hestitate before according an active role to an item of paraphernalia.

Such questions have led me to rethink the categories of participation, at least as they apply to ritual events, and more generally to puzzle over the criteria by which we assign role incumbencies in the social description of language use. As Goffman (1981 [1979]) observed with subversive eloquence, and conversational analysts have further demonstrated, participant formations in talk are complex and dynamic structures that shift with the flick of an eyebrow and inevitably involve much more than the familiar labels "speaker" and "addressee" would lead us to suspect. Linguists have begun to recognize the consequences of these issues for pragmatic description, and Levinson in particular has made stimulating proposals regarding the decomposition of participant roles. In a recent paper (1987: 163), he lumps together issues of participation with the phenomenon of "deixis," whereby he means the overall situatedness of language, claiming this to be of "fundamental and multistranded" importance to linguistics. I agree with this assessment, and would add to it the complementary one that the same issues are of key significance to an anthropology of language. It is from the latter perspective that I will address participant roles in this paper, in an attempt to clarify what seem to me to be misrenderings in the linguistic approach.

A central dimension of Maya shamanism is the *production and transformation of lived space*. More than any other single aspect of ritual performance in this culture, space making is the point of contact for issues of participation, genre, and power, that is, the capacity to define and change human experience. *Space* in this context denotes not simply a set of geometrically defined relations, but rather a socially constructed medium, encompassing actors' bodies, perceptual fields, movements, engagements, and orientations. *Lived space* is the object and the vehicle of experience, as well as a feature of the setting in which experience takes shape. It is an unavoidable part of social action, and hence of participant relations (cf. Goodwin 1984; Kendon 1985). This is particularly so in the ritual field, where the connections between placement and agency, orientation and moral disposition, residence and role are epitomized. These considerations lead me to view participant roles as an integral part of the larger social framework of action, rather than as isolable nodes that can be cut off from social processes and decomposed in the manner of linguistic categories. Two salient consequences of this view are the interpenetration of roles with spatial arrangements, and the unavoidable diachronicity of role formations. For if speaker-addressee relations are really the precipitate of social processes, then they develop and must be defined relative to a historical context.

PARTICIPATION FRAMES AND GENRES

Linguists and anthropologists have become increasingly aware of the complexity of participation frameworks in talk, as well as of the relevance of participant organization to language structure and use.[2] This has been due in large measure to the pioneering work of Goffman (1981 [1979]), C. Goodwin (1981, 1984), M. Goodwin (1985, 1987), and sociologists of the microanalysis of routine conversation (Atkinson and Heritage 1984). Goffman developed the concept of participation frameworks from the related one of "footing." An interactant's *footing* is his "alignment, set, projected self" relative to his ongoing speech. For instance, a speaker who asserts a proposition as a matter of vouched-for fact takes up a different footing than one who utters the same proposition as a hypothetical statement based on hearsay, or as quotation attributed to some other speaker. The shifts involved in such cases are ubiquitous in talk, and Goffman saw them as evidence of the need for some set of roles more finely distinguished than the traditional Speaker and Hearer. After all, different footings may imply different actualizations of the Speaker role, and an adequate description of conversation must draw out these distinctions and relate them one to another.

Without attempting to recapitulate Goffman's discussion, we can summarize his conclusions.[3] Under the rubric of "participation framework," he decomposed the Hearer role into "ratified participants," who are party to the interaction proper, versus "overhearers" who are on the periphery. Apart from the participation framework, he developed a "production format" in which the Speaker role was analyzed into the "animator" who actually phonates the utterance, the "author" who is responsible for the choice of words and senti-

2. The following summary of participation frameworks draws heavily on Hanks (1990: chapters 4–5).

3. Further discussed in Hanks (1990: chapters 4–5) and Levinson (1987).

ments, and the "principal" who is the ultimate source and the one responsible for the position expressed by the utterance.[4] Some of the most obvious examples of these distinctions come from institutional settings in which a spokesman animates text scripted by a writer-author in the employ of a principal, such as an elected official. Given this beefed-up inventory of roles, Goffman went on to classify interactions according to the participant configurations on which they rest: *Dominating* communication is the primary engagement among ratified participants, as opposed to *subordinate* communication, which is subsidiary. "By play" is subordinate exchange between ratified participants, "cross play" is subordinate communication between a ratified participant and at least one bystander, and "side play" is subordinate communication among bystanders. Notice that this classification breaks out of the Speaker-Hearer dyad as the privileged unit of interaction, by including bystanders, at the same time that it unsticks the relation between utterer and Speaker, Hearer and ratified addressee. For what the production and participation frameworks allow one to describe are the *multiple embeddings* that occur in talk, when discourse attributable to one actor is layered into the speech produced by another. As is typical of Goffman's writings, we arrive at an unsettling vision of interaction in which the parties are disengaged from the masks they wear, everyone shifting and playing peek-a-boo, as it were, behind the empty personae of the social stage.

From a linguistic perspective, one is troubled less by the possibilities for bad faith and deniability that Goffman thrusts before us, than by the prospect of increased complexity in the description of utterance interpretation. How can interactants keep it all straight? If the context is constantly being revised and its interactants are (or at least might be) all playing multiple roles, then how can one ever understand pronouns, demonstratives, expressive elements, and other linguistic forms whose interpretation depends upon utterance context? Levinson (1987) examined Goffman's framework and determined that, although it goes in the right direction, it is still underdifferentiated relative to the distinct nuances of participation status that interactants use and recognize. Based on a wide range of comparative evidence, he proposed to decompose the roles further into component features, including (but not limited to) *participant, transmitter (cf. animator), motive, address, recipient,* and *channel-link,*

---

4. Goffman treated the participation and production aspects of talk separately, as is clear from his terminology. The motivation for this move is unclear to me, as is the justification. If one assumes that interactions really are *interactively* negotiated, then it would appear unjustified to propose an analysis of the Speaker role that treats it apart from the modes of reception. In this paper, no such schism will be assumed.

from which internally complex categories could be defined by Boolean operations (1987: 172ff.). Like feature matrices in universal grammar, this one is elaborated on the basis of evidence that, for any feature, there exists some language (and in this case, some variety of interaction in some language) in which the distinction is maintained. It would follow from this that the feature must be present in a universal inventory, even though in any given language it may not be distinctive.

C. Goodwin (1987) has shown that the mapping between actors and roles in talk is potentially, indeed often, many to many, with a single individual occupying several roles at the same time, and a single role occupied by more than one individual. The attaching of participant roles to actors is subject to negotiation and dispute, forcing us to distinguish carefully between role configurations as such and the incumbencies of actors relative to them. In combination with the more finely subdivided roles, this fact results in a very considerable increase in the complexity of participation frameworks. When we add to this the additional fact that interactants deploy gaze, gesture, posture, and phonation in various ways (some reinforcing, some not), the problem becomes all the more acute.

There is nothing necessarily wrong with positing such complex interactive work that must be accomplished in communication; on the contrary, there is every reason to believe that at least this level of complexity is involved. Still, one wonders by what mechanisms interactants in everyday talk manage the flow of information in so many dimensions simultaneously and with such apparent ease. If the traditional roles of Speaker and Addressee are so patently oversimplified, why is it that natural languages develop correspondingly simple pronominal systems, instead of more "accurate" ones in which *I* and *you* would be split apart into a dozen or so distinct forms for the distinct role relations they may signal?[5] If, as Irvine (this volume) shows, interactions may variously implicate other interactions past or merely possible, does it then follow that for all such examples additional role features must be mustered?

For answers to these questions, I think we should look to the study of society and not to the study of grammar. The phonological model of feature

5. Levinson (1987) asks the same question in different terms. I am aware that many systems are much more complex than English, as attested in a huge literature, but it is noteworthy that the complexity comes usually from number, gender, and deference codings rather than from the kinds of distinctions under discussion. Also, languages clearly do provide syntactic means for signaling these things, rather than lexical ones, but the question remains why the lexicalizations do not occur.

bundles is a powerful heuristic and can help significantly in systematizing distinctions and laying out a space of logical possibilities. Levinson (1987) uses it profitably and with an awareness of some of its limitations. Still, the approach underplays several crucial problems from an anthropological perspective. For one, it leaves up for grabs the criteria by which one justifies a given opposition. In grammatical systems, it is in relation to judgments of meaning difference that oppositions are identified, usually in terms of truth-functional sameness or difference. This is clearly not possible when what is being distinguished are nuances of social relations, such as degrees of responsibility for a statement or the outer limits of a participation framework. When does a formal distinction make a functional difference, and when should a putative functional distinction be formalized in the categories of sociolinguistic description? It is doubtful in my view that juxtapositions of exemplary interactions extracted from different societies will provide the proper grounding for a theory of participation, the way juxtaposed sentence examples in different languages *do* justify certain kinds of linguistic distinctions.

It goes without saying that the inventory of participant relations with which we undertake description should be no more elaborate than is needed, but how does one choose? Insofar as what is at stake are the varieties of interactive relations, the question comes down to how one constructs the social present in which speech takes place.[6] If we assume that ghost writers, unmentioned but implicitly targeted third parties, prior exchanges and fantasies are all really *present* in an interaction, since speakers obviously attend to them, then the roles needed to describe them will be correspondingly more elaborate than the ones needed under the opposite assumption. The self-evident inadequacy of basing participation frameworks on the merely physical copresence of interactants, what Goffman might have called animator-receiver relations, throws open the question of boundaries. It is not just the Speaker-Addressee dyad that is breached, but the familiar aura of concreteness that common sense imputes to "I-here-now." In undermining the view of participant roles as indi-

6. It is one of the hallmarks of conversation analysis that it takes a pointedly local view of interaction, recognizing, as Atkinson and Heritage (1984: 5) put it, "that, in a variety of ways, the production of some current conversational action proposes a here-and-now definition of the situation to which subsequent talk will be oriented." It seems to me that this view assumes that the boundaries between "here-and-now" and "then-and-there" (so to speak) can be assumed without further question. Detailed research on deictic space has convinced me of the opposite: the presumed locality of the indexical present is extremely variable in actual interaction, and cannot be defined without reference to the sociocultural background of the interactants and the space in which their interaction takes place. Much of what defines the here-and-now is neither local in the operative sense, nor is it accessible to audiovisual recording or transcription.

visible, one inevitably calls into question the limits of the phenomenal field in which they operate.

We can unravel three main strands in this knot of problems. The first has to do with the linkage between participant frameworks and other simultaneous components of speech events, in particular what I have called the social present. The second bears on the historicity of participant structures, that is, the emergence of role configurations and incumbencies through social time, as well as the diachronic relations between any given state of an interaction (viewed synchronously) and what precedes and follows it. Just as it is crucial, in my opinion, not to isolate participant structures from events, so too, it is crucial not to flatten sociohistorical processes into a synchronous structure. Finally, I will suggest that by giving more weight to the concept of *embedding*, we can account for at least some relatively complex frameworks without any increase in the number of basic categories.

From an anthropological perspective, it is obvious that participant roles must be viewed in relation to social contexts. It makes no sense to isolate a distinction, say between a performing shaman and the spirit agents from whom he learned his prayer, without spelling out the ethnographic significance of the relation. Similarly, it is distorting to describe a shaman in performance as acting alone simply because his spirit others are nowhere visible to the untrained observer. The spatiotemporal analog would be to describe a rain ceremony as taking place at a table in the woods, without noting that the table is constituted as an altar, the altar endowed with a directional orientation, the woods located in a specific relation to the productive lands of the benefactors of the ceremony, the timing of the event governed by the growth cycle of the crops in combination with the seasonal variations in rainfall, and so on. By taking participant roles in their social contexts, they can be simplified rather than multiplied. The descriptive burden forced on the participant features can be carried in part by the relations between the roles and other elements of context, as well as by the socially governed ways in which the roles combine.

If we shift focus from individual participant roles like Speaker and Hearer to whole configurations of roles taken in relation to other simultaneous components of events, it becomes clear immediately that not all *logically* possible combinations are *socially* possible. Actors with real social identities virtually never confront the range of choices implied by a logical space of role possibilities. They are massively constrained by their sense of propriety, by power and status asymmetries, by their habitual ways of interacting, by their engaged interests and calculations of likely outcomes, by their aesthetic evaluations of speech, and by setting and event context. The view of creativity and free choice underlying the linguistic model of categories, combinations, and infinite generativity is powerful and productive when applied to language as a system of thought. It becomes distorting if carried over into the description of language as a medium of social relations. And participation frameworks emerge in the course of social relations.

The thrust of these remarks is that participation frameworks may be more clearly analyzable if viewed from the perspective of some superordinate units such as *events* (roughly in the ethnography of speaking sense) or *genres* of practice. This will allow us to incorporate native understandings and habitual orientations toward speech, along with a less abstract view of utterance production. Utterances are part of social projects, not merely vehicles for expressing thoughts.

Another aspect of the cross-linkage of participant categories in events involves the default assumptions that interactants routinely make about face-to-face contexts.[7]

1. Barring special provisions or indications to the contrary, it is assumed that the speaker bodily given is the source of the words, propositions, and sentiments expressed. Hence, animator, author, and principal coincide until further notice.

2. Gaze, posture, gesture, and speech typically figure in communicative acts, and when so, it is assumed that they are deployed in a mutually reinforcing fashion, or at least in such a way as to modulate complementary aspects of a single coherent act (such as the Speaker-Addressee contact with gaze or body posture, manual gesture indicating a referent, and verbal description characterizing the referent).

3. Pending counterindications, the actor(s) bodily present to whom an utterance is directed is (are) the target.

4. As philosophers (e.g., Searle 1976) and psychologists (e.g., Clark and Wilkes-Gibbs 1986) have observed, participants must be able to identify the same referential objects (more or less) in order for canonical acts of verbal reference to be successful and fully consummated. This dependency further links coparticipants, and implies that if an animator is speaking for himself in an act of reference, then it is his copresent receiver who must be able to interpret the utterance, and not some ultimate target.

7. This paragraph is paraphrased from Hanks (1990: chapter 4 section 1).

These default assumptions are routinely circumvented in everyday interaction, but the point is that they serve to overdetermine certain correspondences until further notice.

A second thread in my argument is the *diachrony of participation frameworks*. On the one hand, social relations are always embodied in historical processes in the sense that they are played out through time. In conversation, there is always an earlier and a later, if only the microhistory of a single utterance. Linguistic relations of anaphora and cataphora are obvious reflexes of this fact, as are the exquisitely detailed sequential structures that conversational analysts have disclosed in everyday talk. On the other hand, participant relations can be seen to emerge out of prior conditions and to prepare the way for subsequent ones. The fact that an animator delivers speech scripted earlier for the purpose of subsequent quotation is a historical fact. One can treat the animation as a case of synchronous complexity by positing the ghost writer and ghost quoter in the shadow of the immediate present of an utterance. To do so, however, is to telescope the historical process into the act itself. Such a move may appear justified if one starts from the utterance as given object, and asks who is responsible for it. If on the other hand, one takes discourse practice as point of departure and asks how an utterance is produced, distributed, and received, and what consequences it has, then the historical dimension becomes central. Thus, while we may want to say that animator, author, and principal are all somehow present in the utterance, they are not present in the same way.

The third component is the issue of *embedding*. Goffman saw his new typology of roles as a way of displaying the layering of multiple actors, or *figures* of actors, in a single utterance (Goffman 1981 [1979]: 3, 147ff., 153).[8] This raises the interesting possibility that one could derive at least some of the complexity of participation frameworks not by multiplying the inventory of roles, but by embedding the roles. Instead of positing the distinct categories of animator, author, and principal for cases of reported speech and quotation, we might posit speaker 3, speaker 2, speaker 1, where the numbers indicate degree of remove from the originary source (cf. Hanks 1990: chapter 5). In the present context, the interdependency of roles and the diachronicity of participant frameworks are most relevant.

The interdependency between roles, the emergence of participation frameworks over time, and the phenomenon of embedding are necessary parts of an overall account, but they still give no basis for describing the social constraints on frame production. This is because they account only for what is

8. This phenomenon of embedding is discussed in more detail in Hanks (1990: chapter 5).

actually said, not for the background range of possibilities from which moves are selected. Goffman recognized the need to look beyond actual utterances and footings taken up, as evidenced in his notion of a "frame space": "When an individual speaks, he avails himself of certain options and foregoes others, operating within a frame space, but with any moment's footing, uses only some of this space" (1981: 230). This unit that Goffman calls a frame space encompasses both the actual and the virtual. Frame spaces may be subject to dispute, and are typically accessible only to actors of certain qualifications. They embody a perimeter of propriety beyond which a speaker is in violation: a public lecturer who drifts off into a private joke, a clergyman who engages in sexual banter with members of the congregation, a Maya man who willfully misquotes his father to his mother for the purpose of mocking him, a shaman who presents a rain ceremony in jest—all have breached the frame spaces of their genres. Rather than complicate the picture of participant roles, the idea of a space of possibilities is a way of bringing the weight of social organization to bear on issues of utterance production. We need to get away from the ultimately formalist view of speech according to which social context is relevant only insofar as it is explicitly signaled (see Hanks 1995).

It is not accidental that in talking about frame spaces one comes back to the notion of discourse genres. Goffman articulated the concept in describing the highly structured genre of radio talk, and it seems clear that some mid-level unit such as the genre is needed in order to ground a frame space. Genres also provide an appropriate vehicle to unify the elements of participant frameworks described above: the interdependency of roles and other aspects of event context, the diachrony of role configurations, and the embedding of participant frameworks.[9] Rather than discuss these in the abstract, let us turn to some details of Maya shamanic performance.

9. Conversation analysts have argued appropriately that linguistic and philosophical approaches to "pragmatics" have relied too heavily on native metalinguistic categories and "speech acts" viewed as individual productions. They propose instead to "deal with the systematically organized workings of interaction sequences" (Atkinson and Heritage 1984: 7). While I am sympathetic to this critique, and draw heavily on insights into participation structures deriving from this literature, it is worth pointing out that favorite terms like *assessments, proposals, invitations* and *topic initiations* are not entirely unlike genre labels. Like genre types, these terms summarize a variety of information regarding utterance form (whether viewed grammatically or in terms of sequence), preconditions, and likely outcomes. The claim that participants understand talk primarily by reference to its placement in interactive sequences has force and consequence for analysis, but can also obscure the equally significant fact that local sequences are played out by speakers against a background of social knowledge and habitual activities that goes far beyond the local conditions of utterances, which is in no way empirically observable in a transcript. The sociologi-

THE POLYCENTRIC SPACE OF SHAMANIC PERFORMANCE

Shamanic performance in Maya communities involves the use of highly specialized knowledge, not unlike the expert practices of clergy, psychoanalysts, and medical doctors in our own society.[10] It provides for that reason some of the most obvious examples of the social distribution of frame spaces, that is, the controlled access of recognized authorities to participation frameworks distinct from (though obviously related to) those of everyday interaction among nonspecialists. These expert frameworks incorporate role possibilities marked by vast asymmetries in knowledge, responsibility, rights of inquiry, and the consequences of categorization.[11] While the system I shall describe here appears decidedly exotic from a certain vantage point, I should make clear that the underlying dynamics involved are, in my opinion, anything but exotic. The details are different, but the problems are virtually the same in our own society. Furthermore, while I have selected a shamanic ritual as locus of observation, it is also my contention that analogous, if less dramatic, issues in role projection and occupancy arise in everyday Maya conversation.

Regardless of genre, Maya prayer, called *reésar* (< Spanish) or *payalči?* *t'àan* (lit. 'summon-mouth speech') is aimed at creating an encounter between the spirit agencies mentioned and a human beneficiary.[12] The latter may be

---

cal literature on conversation typically expresses recognition of this fact, yet the analyses themselves too often suffer from a lack of sociocultural context. This tendency is foreseen, perhaps, in Sacks's problematic claim that "sociology can be a natural observational science" (Atkinson and Heritage 1984: 21; cf. Hanks 1995 for a constrasting viewpoint).

10. My description of shamanic practices is derived primarily from intensive study with a single shaman, whom I will call DC. Between August 1980 and March 1981, I spent about twenty-five hours per week recording his performances and exegesis, and learning as much as I could about his practice in the Mani-Oxkutzcab region of Yucatán. Since then, I have returned to the field seven times, for a total of twenty-four weeks, during which I lived in his home and continued to study with him. I have observed and recorded other shamans in action, but have not succeeded in discussing their practices with them in any detail. My generalizations about the principles of shamanic knowledge and action should therefore be read as the product mainly of intensive work with a single man. There is no doubt in my mind that important variation would be uncovered, were one able to gather appropriate comparative data. Most of the knowledge is esoteric, however, and guarded in secrecy.

11. See Cicourel (1985, 1986) for discussion of interactions involving expert frameworks in medical settings.

12. Hanks (1984) sketches this background and concentrates on the *saántiguar* performance. Hanks (1990: chapters 3, 5, 7, 8) works through the system of spatial and temporal schemata mobilized in major ceremonies of the agricultural cycle as well as the purification of domestic space. Chapter 5 presents a brief analysis of the participant frameworks in divination.

an individual, as in the main curing ceremonies focused on a sick person, or a collectivity, as in the communal agricultural and household ceremonies. There is in Maya culture a fundamental connection between humans and the spaces they inhabit. This emerges in pervasive homologies between social and natural space and body parts, as well as in the shared technologies of cleansing space for the purpose of effecting well-being in those who inhabit it. Richly developed in shamanic knowledge, but present too in the common sense of nonspecialists, is a division between horizontal spaces split into five cardinal sectors (cardinal directions plus center) and vertical spaces graded from lower to higher. Both axes have moral corollaries linking eastern and higher with goodness, western and lower with evil, or at least ambivalence.

In all shamanic practice to my knowledge, space making and transformation is the core focus of therapeutic intervention: persons and places are encompassed through ritual performance by a *perimeter* of spiritual agencies. Within this protective enclosure, an encounter is brought about, a kind of visitation in which the elemental earth of body or land is cooled, swept off, and cleaned by spirit forces. The ability of a shaman to get results is contingent on his ability to bring about such an encounter while protecting himself and any bystanders from the potential danger of being struck by the forces he sets in motion. This aspect is of utmost importance according to shamans and nonspecialists alike: in order to make anything happen, the shaman must know how to *peksik* 'move' spirits from their points of origin, but also how to *sutlaántik* 'return them all' after the fact. In spatial terms, he erects a boundary around the altar during performance, which is then dismantled at the close.

There are several peculiarities of *reésar* that must be pointed out even in such a cursory overview as this one. The first is the use of signs of the cross to key the onset, major internal transitions, and the end of performance. This is clearly a precipitate of the fused Catholic-Mayan sources of ritual speech, and functions to signal the special footing of performance. Ritual speech is also delivered in a distinctive performance style consisting of canted breath groups, a great deal of phonological and syntactic parallelism, disproportionate frequency of certain pragmatic particles and explicit performative formulae (equivalent to the Austinian, I beg, I request, I address and so forth). There are precise conventions governing the order in which spirits are invoked. Invocation takes place through *reference* to spirits by proper name, not second-person address, which is restricted to *Diós Padre* 'God the Father' and *Jesu Cristo* 'Jesus Christ'. Consequently, while scores of spirits are lowered to the altar of performance during a ceremony in which they coparticipate, virtually none of them is a canonical second-person Addressee. Therefore, we cannot distinguish Addressees from others merely by scanning the linguistic forms.

Part of the identity of any spirit is its placement in the cosmos, which is organized along vertical and horizontal dimensions. Position so defined is the main conditioning factor in the sequential order of invocation in prayer. The standard conventions stipulate that for any set of spirits, depending on the genre of prayer and the phase of performance, low precedes high or high precedes low. For spirits located at the same vertical level, principles of cyclic order take over, assigning clockwise (E > S > W > N > C) or counterclockwise (E > N > W > S > C) sequence, once again depending on genre and phase of performance. These norms are overridden for various reasons, and they do not govern all spirit reference, but they illustrate nicely the transposition of a spatial array into the temporal order of ritual address.

The participant structures in curing performances involve mainly three categories of actors, the shaman acting as specialist who executes the performance, the patient or beneficiary who undergoes treatment, and the spirit agencies who are summoned and actually cure. The ideal engagement of shaman and beneficiary is intensely focused on the event and the desired outcome. This is embodied in the frequent statements of purpose throughout the prayer, in the shaman's exhortations to the patient to help him with proper thoughts during it, and in the bodily postures of both individuals. Standing in front of the shaman's altar and facing it, the patient is enjoined to gaze upon the icons while concentrating on well-being. He remains otherwise inert. Although coded in the third person only, the patient is indexically present in the prayer in a number of features, including the choice of spirits invoked and the intensity of delivery style (both of which depend upon the illness being treated, and hence presuppose a prior diagnosis). Despite this de facto presence of the beneficiary, most nonspecialists are unaware of the intricacies of shamanic practice and only vaguely cognizant of what is taking place.[13] The shaman stands behind and slightly off to the side, facing the altar, but usually gazing away from it, or upon the patient.

---

13. This is undoubtedly an overgeneralization to the extent that (1) many men dabble in shamanic learning during their lifetime and so get a little knowledge; (2) many women are ritual experts in their own right, mainly in Catholic prayer. This gives them entrée to a portion of what goes on in shamanic practice; (3) shamans discuss aspects of their practice with patients for the purpose of teaching and healing. The fact remains however that compared with the systematicity and ideological depth of shamanic knowledge, these inklings are fragmentary and full of blank spots.

Unlike calendar experts and "daykeepers" in the Mayan highlands (Ted-lock 1982), Yucatec shamans do not undergo standardized training, and I have observed significant variation in performances by four shamans from the area of this research. While common knowledge has it that shamans canonically apprentice themselves to a master, with whom they must engage in sorcerous combat to establish their ultimate independence, there are in fact various modes of learning. These include apprenticeship, which may be relatively brief or extended, as well as dreams in which the individual travels to sacred places and has instructive encounters. DC recounts that in the early stages of his learning (about forty years ago) he was frequently called out of his home during the night by guardian spirits perched in tall trees. These spirits, the very Jaguar Lords whom he invokes today, spoke to him and told him the forms of ritual address by which he could call on them. He would then take pains to write down what he had learned as accurately as possible (no small feat given that he is illiterate) and commit it to memory. Since prayer is a living speech, constantly beautified by the shaman as his knowledge grows, it does not remain fixed.

The significance of these facts for present purposes is that they imply a particular role status for the praying shaman. He is not merely a Speaker in the standard sense, since he is using words taught him by his Addressees and gleaned from charismatic experiences over a lifetime. Nor is he a canonical "animator" of quotation, since he has steadfastly reworked the message to embody his own experiences, and customizes it to fit the immediate circumstances (Hanks 1984). If we take the position that his participant role is a function of his relation to the words he utters, then the role is a funny mixture of things, and it differs, moreover, according to which portion of a prayer one examines. (Some of it would be virtually quoted speech, some relatively individualized turns of phrase, some standard expressions common to most shamans, etc.). Furthermore, since the spirits he invokes are among the ones from whom he learned the prayer, these would-be Addressees are simultaneously the authors, principals, and targets of the address. Rather than force all of this description into the participant roles, we do better to recognize that this is a historical problem, in the sense that the shaman's prayer is the sedimentation of language acquired over a lifetime, and the special status of divine Addressees is the product of a long tradition. The shaman in prayer is a "Speaker," and the genre of speech is reésar. It is a characteristic feature of this genre that any instantiation implicates other dialogues (to borrow Irvine's phrase) in which spirits engage, as well as sessions of contemplation and refinement in which the language is haȼ'uȼkináʔan 'beautified'. By attempting to analyze participant roles from a purely synchronous perspective and using only the methods developed by Goffman and Levinson, we risk producing a description that is involuted in terms of categories and empty in terms of sociohistorical content.

Spirits are coded in the third person, like the patient, but they are made present in a specific formula never applied to the patient: the shaman in prayer requests the 'blessing' (*b'eéyntisyòon*) of God "at the altar of *x*" where *x* is a spirit name. In being portrayed as possessing the place of performance, spirits are made present. In the course of a single performance, scores of spirits become the possessors of the altar in standard sequence, and this possession is in force *only during the performance*. Outside the ritual frame, the shaman's altar is a table like any other, and it is in no way the privileged place of the spirits. While both patient and spirits are third-person nonparticipants in grammatical terms, in cultural terms, the former is a silent recipient and the latter are agentive participants summoned to the altar by the shaman, and capable of consequential action. One of the descriptive problems with ritual participation is indeed how to characterize the transposed mode of shaman-to-spirit address.

To Banish the Wind: Participation in the Pa? ʔìik'

With these introductory remarks, we shift attention to the genre of Maya *reésar* which is called the *pa? ʔìik'* 'banish, chase away, smash wind'. This is the Mayan equivalent of exorcism, and it involves, literally, introducing a class of earth spirits into the body of a human patient for the purpose of forcing out nocent winds that have lodged there. The ceremony is dangerous for all involved, and potentially for the well-being of the shaman's domestic space, as well as for any visitors who come there. Performed only in cases of extreme illness, it is full of fire and intensity, as the shaman calls on Michael the Archangel to thunder down cracking lightning and flame from his swift sword, chase out the evil, and crush it beneath his foot. A sort of high-voltage Manichean electroshock treatment, the prayer is delivered in maximally intense performance style, with tense jaw and rapid articulation punctuated by periodic stamping of the shaman's foot. Whereas other ritual treatments may be repeated in sets of five and nine over a period of days or weeks, this one is performed only once. The patient may be instructed to change his clothing afterwards, as a precaution against subsequent contamination.[14]

---

14. These remarks are based on a recorded performance with follow-up discussion with DC, a practicing shaman.

Cross

Statement of purpose

kanan kàahó?ob'

Statement of purpose

dyòosil le sùuhuy lú?um o?

Cross of purpose

yunçiló?ob'

Statement of purpose

archangels

Statement of purpose

Cross

FIGURE 6.1 Schematic structure of *pa? ?ìik'*

The *pa? ?ìik'* ceremony unfolds sequentially according to a recognizable schematic structure, summarized in Figure 6.1.

The three signs of the cross, at beginning, middle, and end key the discourse as being produced in the specialized frame of the genre. The lines that I have labelled "statement of purpose" literally are "in order to" statements that make the goal of the prayer explicit, as in, "In order that the force of all the Lord Jaguar spirits come down, I ask their blessing that they might clean the earth of the body given by Jesus Christ" (breath group 3). Such statements occur saliently at five intervals, the middle one combined with a sign of the cross. In between these statements and bracketed by the crosses, four major classes of spirits are invoked by proper name: the *kanan kàahó?ob* 'town guardians' are spirits that reside in population centers, of which eight are mentioned. These were once living humans who became enchanted at different historical periods, and now oversee affairs in Yucatán. The *dyòosil le sùuhuy lú?um o?* 'gods of the sacred earth' are morally ambiguous earth spirits that reside beneath the surface of the earth and are summoned actually to sweep through the patient's body. The *yunçiló?ob'* 'revered lords' are widely known jaguar spirits and directional spirits that reside in the space above the surface of the earth but below the heavens. They oversee the affairs of men and are frequently enlisted helpers of shamans. The archangels are derived from the Catholic pantheon, headed by Michael the Archangel, but accompanied by several others of obviously Maya descent. The sequential order of the prayer is the one shown in the figure, which is to be read top-to-bottom.

The *pa? ?iik'* performance forces us to consider the limits on participant status. What does it take to be a participant? If Goffman's work breached the boundaries of dyadic models of talk while also splitting apart interactive roles from the actors occupying them, ritual performance breaches the boundaries of bodily copresence, as well as the familiar assumption that participants must, after all, be humans.

Without attempting a programmatic statement of the requisites for participanthood, there seem to me to be several basic features. A participant must be capable of *engaging* in interaction, at whatever level. This implies the capacity for oriented focus of attention, and usually implies the ability to reciprocate address with a communicative gesture of some kind. Obviously, this gesture need not be speech, and it may be difficult to produce or may be variously defective (as in an interlocutor who is drunk or injured). In the clearest cases, a participant is the unmediated object of attention of at least one other participant, at least intermittently. That is, while interactants need not pay constant attention to one another, it is probably best to restrict participant roles to actors of whom at least one participant is aware. A tangible sign of this attention is produced when a speaker directs an utterance or other gesture at the participant, making of him or her an Addressee. On this point, Goffman and Levinson opened up an important line of questions in distinguishing the recipients from ultimate targets. Actors who receive or communicate a gesture only through the mediation of some other actor will not be considered participants in this paper. Rather, they may be participants in what Irvine has called "implicated dialogues" distinct from the current one, but in some historical relation to it.

Local norms and understandings of speech also have a crucial role in defining the minimum conditions on participation status. If, as I have argued, participant frameworks are part of social practices, then they cannot be defined without reference to native metalanguage and broader ideologies of discourse. Who can speak under what conditions, in what forms, and to what effects are all issues about which native actors have ideas. These ideas may be formulated in explicit canons or even rules. They may be subject to debate or expert definition. Or they may be relatively inchoate assumptions that people share, to a greater or lesser degree, as a matter of common sense. But in each case, they have to do with local standards for producing, distributing and receiving utterances, and for defining what counts as present and real. Similarly, these standards are what define the relative importance of phonation, gesture, proximity, and other aspects of the actional setting of speech. Thus, according to the cosmological premises underlying the *paʔ ʔìik'* or other shamanic performances, spirits who never speak and never appear in visible form must be included nevertheless as participants. Similarly, a shaman, like the one under discussion, is neither the unique principal of his utterances, nor is he merely the relayer of speech whose principals are spirits. Rather, from his own perspective, he is something in between the two, a sort of virtuoso actor improvising on the basis of a divine script. From the perspective of the nonspecialist patient, the shaman might be viewed as a master in sole control of his power, or he might be seen as an intermediary whose power is occasional and whose utterances are only sometimes effective. He may even be seen as a charlatan to be consulted only as a last resort. The point is that local understandings of what is going on have a material bearing on how we define the participation framework. Moreover, such ideas are not all universally shared, but depend upon the perspective of the agent in question, be it an individual or group.

Centered Subspaces

We can say, then, that the generic category of *reésar* called *paʔ ʔìik'* corresponds to a relatively specialized space of possible participant footings. These include the shaman-beneficiary-spirit relations typical of all therapeutic ritual performance, along with some more specific ones. The spirit agencies involved in this genre are unique in that they include classes of earth spirits not invoked in other types of ritual. The engagement of these spirits in acts of entering and coursing through the body of the patient are also without analogue in the other curing genres.[15] One corollary of this actual occupation of the body is the acute danger described above. The frame space includes the possibility of uncontained and hence potentially destructive movement on the part of the spirit participants.

In speaking of possible participant relations that constitute a space, only

---

15. There is a fairly close analog to this process in the major ceremony called *heǧ lúʔum* 'fix earth', which cleanses domestic space in the same way that the *paʔ ʔìik'* cleanses the human body. The key difference is that while the latter is focused on a human individual, the former is focused on the space inhabited by a collectivity. The two ceremonies differ radically in superficial detail, the collective one involving food offerings, a pit oven to bake breads and several hours of prayer, whereas the *paʔ ʔìik'* lasts only minutes and involves no food offerings.

part of which is actually occupied at any point, we focus on the *bodily actualizations of participant relations*. This is especially appropriate to ritual, where the physical proximity of shaman and beneficiary, the oriented gaze of both, the proximity of the altar, and the directional orientation of icons are all part of the necessary stage for performance. It is also pertinent to the global significance with which lived space is invested in Maya culture. If participant engagements entail certain orientations of attention, then body space is always implicated, at least to the extent that it is the perceptual, postural, and kinetic orientations of the body that habitually express attention focus. One way to view participant relations, then, is through their spatial embodiments (see Kendon 1985).

A space of participation possibilities is divisible into subspaces corresponding to roles and sectors occupied by interactants. The roles of Speaker, Animator and Principal for instance constitute subspaces within a larger frame, just as do those of Addressee and Receiver. Given the interdependency of roles, no subspace can be isolated a priori and defined without reference to the states and occupancies of the others. The term *sector* is intended to designate portions of a space that may not be definable as roles, but that are nonetheless integral to the space as a whole. For instance, the altar at which the *pa? ?iik'* is performed is a very significant sector of the space, and yet it is neither a role nor a participant as such. If we define the space in such a way that it includes both roles and sectors, both of which may be occupied by actors, then we may be able to describe more clearly the interdependency between categories of participant and places of participation.

The central roles in a *pa? ?iik'* performance are the shaman-speaker, the beneficiary-object, and the spirit agencies put in motion. The sectors most significant to successful performance are the altar, the icons, specific places in the local geography, the micro-spaces internal to and around the human body, and the vertical organization of spirit sites beneath and above the surface of the earth. Each of these is reflected in exacting detail in the prayer, and any mismatch between roles and sectors can result in breakdown or worse. In the metadiscursive understandings of experts, these linkages are specified precisely, although they are also the subject of more broadly distributed common sense. The bond between roles and sectors is immediately evident when one considers easily imaginable mappings that are in fact absolutely excluded in Maya culture: the shaman cannot sit while the patient stands, nor can either face away from the altar, nor can the shaman speak as if earth spirits were sky spirits, or evil were above good in space, nor could spirits be introduced into the beneficiary's body from top-to-bottom rather than bottom-to-top, nor is it conceivable that an icon be placed beneath the altar or off to the side, or facing away from the performers, and so on.

What I am proposing is that by examining roles and spatial arrangements *as parts of an integral framework*, we can treat their interdependence in a simple, straightforward way. This may also bring to light underlying continuities between role incumbency and spatial position, both of which fall under the rubric of *occupancy*. It is an ethnographic truism that spatial arrangements often express social relations such as hierarchy or reciprocity. Taking this fact at face value and working towards a more encompassing notion of participation, we get a better account of participant roles than can be achieved otherwise.

There is an important difference between subspaces that are what I will call *centered* and ones that are not. A centered subspace is one organized relative to a zero-point from which vectors radiate in any direction and to any distance of remove. Body space and deictic space are centered in this sense, because objects are located in them *relative to* actors, activities, and utterance events. In contrast to centered spaces, *grid* systems are defined by dimensions and axes which intersect without necessarily presupposing any privileged center point. The coordinates of longitude and latitude and the cardinal directions are in principle grid works in which any object can be located without reference to terms such as *near, far, right, left, front, back, above* and *below*, all of which are centered. It should be emphasized at this point that the notion of centered space is *not* tied to the location of a midpoint between two extremes, or in the interior of a circle or sphere. Rather, it is a relational concept tied to the specific relativity of an orientational zero-point from which other locations are defined by vectors proceeding outward. In fact, while grid systems do define a perimeter beyond which a location is "outside," centered spaces provide no basis on which to distinguish inside and outside, focusing instead on directionality and distance from a zero-point.

Participant structures are centered in at least two senses: (1) A participant formation, such as a conversational dyad, serves as a perspectival center, an actional origin point relative to which objects of reference and description are identified. Thus, for instance, demonstrative terms like Maya *téʔel aʔ* 'right here' and *b'ehéʔel aʔ eʔ* 'nowadays' are always interpreted relative to the speech event contexts in which they are used, and therefore relative to the interactional center of an exchange. (2) Participant structures are centered in a second crucial respect, which is that the structure itself contains at least two differentially oriented subspaces, corresponding to the interactants. The

Speaker's and the Addressee's perspectives may coincide to a large degree, but they are never truly identical. Rather than identity, it is relations of reciprocity and relative (a)symmetry that mediate between coparticipants.[16]

Like all forms of orientation, the performance of *pa? ?iik'*, rests on a combination of the two kinds of space, which interact with one another continually. The centered subspaces with which we shall be concerned are the human bodies, the altar, the icons, and the canonical addressee, while the main non-centered spaces are the places in the local geography, the body parts visited, and the sites at which spirits are distributed in vertical and horizontal space. We will take these up in the order cited.

Body

It is the body of the patient-beneficiary that has suffered the intrusion of noxious wind, and the same body that will be swept clean by earth spirits and by the swift sword of Michael the Archangel. It is the body that stands in front of the altar facing the icons in expression of devotion, and the body that will perish if the therapy fails. It would be difficult to overestimate the significance of the corporeal presence of the patient in the performance of the *pa? ?iik'*. Similarly, the shaman stands just behind the patient and off to his right side throughout the event. The two are sufficiently close together so that the shaman can brush and lightly strike the patient's body from head to foot with fresh flowers while praying. The flowers are held in his right hand, as is the case in all forms of *saántiguar* 'sanctification,' and the ostensible purpose of the gesture is to enact the striking of the body by the spirits that will cleanse it.[17]

While the patient and shaman are close enough for physical contact, there are major asymmetries between their respective spaces, and these embody the greater asymmetry between their roles in the event. The patient cannot see

16. There is a further point that must be borne in mind when distinguishing centered from grid systems of orientation, namely, whether we define them at the type level or at the level of actual processes involving real agents. At the type level, both centered and grid systems can be defined abstractly as contrasting forms, the one with an origin and the other without. At the token level, where agents occupy positions and orient themselves relative to them, centering has to do with the actor's perspective and momentary engagements. The origin is not merely a point from which others are defined, but a complex, rapidly changing, process.

17. My notes (F.52.A) indicate that this ceremony is actually a specialized type of *saántiguar*, although significantly different from it. The striking action is described as *haçik* 'strike', which is the same term used to describe the action of spirits and winds on the body. Where we would say that a breeze blew on a person, in Maya one says that it "struck" him or her. Like a blow from a hand or weapon, a strike by wind is almost always capable of harming the recipient, even when administered carefully for therapeutic purpose.

the shaman, being focused on the altar before him, whereas the shaman, from behind and alongside, looks upon the patient while brushing him. The patient is immobile and silent, whereas the shaman is moving and praying, surrounding him with his sound and touch. In addition to the effleurage and light blows to the patient's body, the shaman punctuates his prayer with periodic sharp stamping gestures by which he enacts the driving out of the evil wind and the embedding of it in the earth from which it came (see just below).[18] The combination of the visual image of the altar with the tactual and auditory image of the shaman's performance sets up the conditions for a synthesis between the altar space and the bodily sensations being produced. Activities and subspaces are steadfastly interwoven.

In most shamanic performances in my experience, there is an audience, consisting of other patients waiting their turn, friends or family members who accompanied the patient on the visit, or household members passing in and out of the altar area. In the case under discussion, a young woman arrived with her infant for treatment during the performance. In the scores of *saántiguar* events that I have witnessed and recorded, there is frequently a group of spectators, who observe at their own leisure, alternating between focused attention on the shaman, silent waiting, and sometimes animated interaction among themselves. They are in a sense canonical bystanders who engage in a range of side play activities. I have never seen a spectator attempt to engage a patient under treatment, although I have witnessed one attempt to engage the shaman while performing. (The bid was brushed aside with a perfunctory response.) Otherwise, cross play appears to be extremely rare. Whereas shaman and patient are highly focused, the spectators are peripheral and have correspondingly more freedom to shift their focus and engagements.

Altar

The altar is a key sector in the performance space, although it is not a participant as such. It is the locus of the enactment, but more crucially, it is the point at which spirits are convened and their cleansing action is effected. Recall that the invocation of spirits takes place by way of reference and description, not direct second-person address, and that one of the main forms of description predicates a possessive relation between the spirit and the altar. This is illustrated in Example 1, which is the fourth breath group of the prayer.

18. My notes are inadequate to tell precisely when these stamping gestures are performed, but the slapping sound is occasionally audible on the tape recording, and the semantic content of the prayer suggests that it takes place mostly in the last third, when the actual exorcism is realized.

Example 1

ʔinyuúŋ́ tíal ink'aáti bakan šan
    ubeéyntisyòono bakan
tučùun umèesa šan uyùuŋ kanán k'àaši bakan šan
    učuúmuk ukàahi bin ʔoòšk'u¢kàaʔ bin šan
kubin ink'aáti bakan šan
    usàanto podere bakan
tučùun umèesa bakáan señor načoʔ bakan
kubin int'aŋko bakan šan ʔinyuúŋ́ ##   [F.52.A.6:13–6:28][19]

My lord! In order that I request evidently too
    the blessing evidently
at the base of the altar too of the lord of the forest guardians evidently too
    of the center of the town they say of Oxkutzcab they say too
it goes along I request evidently too
    the blessed power evidently
at the base of the altar of Señor Nacho evidently
it goes along I address them evidently too, my lord! ##

This breath group is the first in a section of the prayer devoted to gathering the spirits distributed in population centers around the local region (see below). The formulation "at the base of the altar of *x*" is a standard one that is used with great frequency in all forms of *reésar*. By being portrayed as the owners of the altar, the spirits are made present, which is the precondition of visitation in the body of the patient. The implication of successive descriptions in this form is that the altar "changes hands" throughout the performance, as each spirit and spirit class is made temporary owner.

The spatial setting of prayer is different in character from that of everyday activities, particularly from the perspective of the shaman. In prayer, there is an almost total absence of spatial deictic terms corresponding to English *here*, a point of sharp contrast between ritual and nonritual genres.[20] In contrast to nonritual interactions, ritual space is inherently decentered, or perhaps more accurately, empty-centered. The altar serves as a geometric zero-point relative to which relations are defined, insofar as it is the ground to which spirits are brought. But the center is not really embodied, in the sense that the shaman presents himself as an anonymous "elemental man" (*ʔah k'eban* lit. 'sinner') rather than as "so-and-so," and the location of the altar is never described more

19. Square bracket numbers indicate [Field tape. Number. side. (interval of) minute:seconds]. The symbol ## indicates the intake of breath. Final arrows indicate intonation contour, up for rising, level for level, and down for falling.

20. I use the term *ritual* here in the narrow sense of those genres Maya people define as belonging to shamanic practices.

precisely than *té? tulú?umi k'eban* 'there on the earth of sin'. This locates it relative to the heavens in a cosmological matrix, instead of relative to the actors in an everyday one. Furthermore, the directional orientation of the altar derives entirely from the cosmological organization of spirit sites, just as it is occupied by the spirits who come to it one by one over the course of the prayer. It has a *front* fixed by the East to which it faces, because this is the axiomatic locus of Jesus Christ. The extensional values of left and right, and of other centered relations in everyday discourse shift as the center-point rotates; but the value of East for a Maya shaman never changes, regardless of his own orientation or that of the altar. This all implies that the altar is a locus of interaction between centered and noncentered spaces, in which the former are subordinated to the latter.

The significance of the front side of a Maya altar is attested in a number of facts. Not only is it oriented so as to face East (or Southeast in some cases), but no one is permitted to pass in front of it during the performance. The spatial arrangement of participants is invariable: the beneficiary faces the altar in front of him, from behind the altar. The shaman stands or sits behind and to the side of the beneficiary, and any spectators remain behind the shaman. In the larger ceremonies in which a pit oven is prepared and breads baked for offering, the pit oven is always placed to the West of the altar, that is behind it, and the only actor permitted to pass in front is the *b'ó?ol*, or shaman's assistant, who circulates periodically with a brazier of incense to perfume the road of the spirits. These relations are diagrammed in Figure 6.2.

The altar is an icon of humanity. It shares the space and directional orientation of the participants, and it is the locus to which the spirits are lowered. Located "on the earth of sin," it shares with mankind the stain of imperfection. When the performance is over, it serves as a table, a receptacle for a random assortment of objects from papers to tools, food, dirty clothing and so forth. In the performance, the transformation is complete, and it is swept clean of these shreds of everyday life, in just the same way that the body of the beneficiary is swept clean of the winds and deleterious forces accumulated in daily life.

Icon

Above the surface of the altar are the shaman's icons and paraphernalia. These include at least one crucifix, fresh flowers, a candle lit during performance, and any number of sacred images accumulated over the shaman's lifetime. The orientation of the icons is the inverse of that of the altar as a whole, since they face the participants directly. The icons are called *sàantos* 'saints', whether

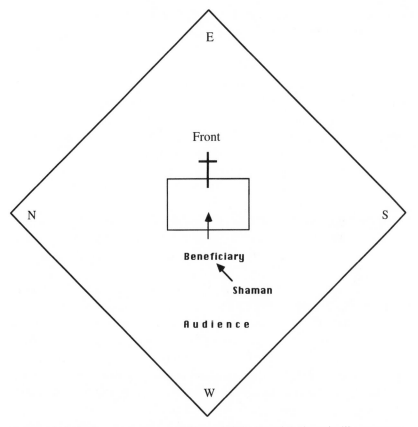

FIGURE 6.2 Performance space of the *pa? ʔìik'* "banish the wind" ceremony.

images or cruciforms, and they are the iconic embodiment of the spirits. Just as Jesus Christ is axiomatically located in the East facing his enemies (the source of evil) in the West, so the *sàantos* are located on or above the Eastern extremity (the front side) of the altar and face the participants to the West. The vertical dimension is significant: East is inherently higher than West, and the *sàantos* are always atop the altar. It would be heretical to put a *sàanto* on the ground beneath an altar, probably sufficient to precipitate accusations of witchcraft, just as it would be to perform with one's back to the *sàanto*. The positional arrangement is explicitly regimented in the metadiscourse of the shaman, and recapitulated faithfully in all the altars I have seen. In this icon-ography, the altar is the earth of man, and the icons are the face of God. Hence the subspace of altar-with-icons amounts to an instrument of mediation between the human and divine coparticipants.

Addressee

As I noted earlier, the canonical addressee of *reésar* is God, being *Diós Padre* 'God the Father' or *Diós Mehenb'il* 'God the Son', also known as *Jesu Cristo*. These two spirits are located at the uppermost portion of the cosmos, in the heavens, and they are the ultimate source of all power radiated through the legions of lesser spirits who act as their "soldiers." Whereas good spirits are located throughout the cosmos in the five cardinal sectors, it is East, the locus of God the Father and Son, that is axiomatically highest and the ultimate source of goodness. All other spirits are invoked in third-person descriptions like the one illustrated above, but these two are addressed in the second-person *you*, and in the many vocative phrases *ʔin yuúŋ* 'My lord' that occur throughout the prayer. Hence, stated in terms of categorical features, [+ Adr] presupposes [+ East].

In addition to being located in the East, the canonical addressee faces man in the West. In the *saántiguar* and in other genres of prayer, God is explicitly requested to turn His attention to the participants in the performance, stated as *sutik awič apaktikóʔon téʔ tulúʔumi k'eb'aŋ* 'turn your eye to look upon us there on the earth of sin'. This directional orientation of gaze is a metonym for the intervention of the divine addressee in the affairs of men. It is another embodiment of the principle that spatial orientation is a form of role incumbency, even when the actor is God and the role is Savior.

Noncentered Subspaces

The foregoing subspaces and roles are inherently centered and display their directional orientations by their physical dispositions. In addition to them, there are three crucial subspaces that are put in play in the *paʔ ʔiik'* that are not centered in the same sense. These are the local places at which guardian spirits reside, the vertically defined sectors inside the patient's body, which will be occupied by the cleansing spirits, and the cosmological sites from which the spirits are raised and lowered to the altar. The fact that spirits are moved and places mentioned in determinate sequence introduces directionality into them, putting them on trajectories towards the altar. This effectively incorporates them into centered relations relative to the space and time of performance. However, this does not alter the fact that these places are defined independently in a quasi-absolute fashion, quite apart from their being mobilized in any performance. The organization of the cosmos is therefore gridlike in our terms, but undergoes a process of phenomenal centering as it is actualized in prayer.[21]

Local Geography

The "town guardians" are spirits who formerly walked the earth as men, but were transformed through enchantment into immortal representatives of Maya spirituality. To my knowledge, all of these transformations are held to have occurred just before, during, or just after the Spanish conquest, which therefore serves as a kind of fixed temporal center. This event is considered by DC and some other Maya men with whom I have discussed it to be the dawn of a new age, comparable to the periodic annihilations and recreations of humanity recounted in Maya creation myths. The places mentioned in the prayer under study are, in order of citation: Oxkutzcab (the place of performance), Mani, Tipikal, Teabo, Chumayel, Chichen Itza, Izamal, and Uxmal. The movement described by this path is (very roughly) counterclockwise starting towards East-Northeast. It is also noteworthy that these are all places that DC has visited, in some cases many times, and from which patients come to him. These places are therefore bridges between the macrohistory of Maya Yucatán and to the biography of the performer.

Body Parts and Spirit Sites

Depending upon the purpose, the human body is variously divisible into parts and sections. For instance, traditional measures of length use the arms and hands, while emotions are discussed in terms of the heart and the ?oól 'core, will; capacity for sensate experience'. The digestive process involves the gut and the organs therein, and fever often involves the circulation of blood through named regions. In the pa? ?ìik' ceremony, seven sectors of the body are cited by name, and these names provide the basis for named participants who become agents in the participation framework of the ritual. They are cited

---

21. Maya cosmology *could* be considered a centered system. The identification of God the Father with the sun (yùuŋ k'ìin) as the ultimate source of life and power could be viewed as a relation of force radiating from a center-point. As spirit sites get progressively more distant from this center, their inherent power and beneficence decreases, until one arrives at the underworld spirits, who are malevolent and whose power is highly restricted. This theocentric view, however, fails to take into account that from an earthly perspective, cardinal sectors present themselves as an absolute grid pattern in which objects can be localized without reference to the divine center. In any case, the divine zero-point is not an *actional* center used in computing the relative locations of other points.

in the following order: the *táan ʔòok* 'sole', *pàač ʔòok* 'instep', *k'al ʔòok* 'ankle', *toʔòok* 'calf', *muk' ʔòok* 'thigh', *héʔe ʔòok* 'groin', *čiʔ hóʔol* 'head'. I do not at present know the exact motivation for these body zones as opposed to the scores of other possible ones. It is clear however that these seven spots are ordered from low to high, and that to each one corresponds a class of spirits whose name derives from that of the body part. Thus to the sole corresponds the "sole spirit," to the calf the "calf spirit," and so on. These spirits have several distinctive features: (1) They reside beneath the surface of the earth, and therefore they are capable of harming men as well as helping them. (2) Each one is a class, not an individual, and there are no named individuals in the class. Earth spirits are generic in this sense, whereas higher ones receive individuating names. (3) The spirits occasionally come up above ground, whether by having been invoked in shamanic performance or by fiat, and when they do they move about only at a specific height above the earth. This height is reflected in the name of the class: sole spirits course along the very surface of the earth, calf spirits at the height of the calf, thigh spirits at the height of the thigh and so forth.

Lacking proper names and circulating only within vertically defined planes, the earth spirits embody a purely spatial logic in which location *is* identity. The fact that they reside inside the earth (below its surface), and that when above ground, they are defined by human body parts, effectively links the body to the earth on which it stands. This connection is reflected in a number of other elements in shamanic practice. The physical aspect of the human body is described as its *lúʔum* 'earth.' The veins through which blood circulates in the body correspond to the 'veins' through which water circulates in the earth.[22] Heat, water, and wind are elements common to both body and earth. Terrestrial space is therefore of a piece with corporeal space, and the spirit forces that inhabit the earth are life forces not unlike the animacy of the body (both are called *yiík'al* 'momentum, movement, life force').

Above the surface of the earth are the layers of the heavens, beginning with the *yoók'ol kàab* 'above earth' and reaching through successive layers to the highest portion of heaven, called *glòoria*, the site of God the Father. As shown in Figure 6.1 above, the *paʔ ʔìik'* prayer projects a movement from the terrestrial space up to the jaguar guardians and then to the higher archangels (located just beneath the top of the heavens; see Hanks 1984). This lower to

---

22. This analogy is more accurate than might appear at first, since Yucatán is geologically a limestone formation with underground rivers.

higher trajectory is the same at a more global level as the one we saw in the order of earth-spirit invocation. It is the standard order of participant invocation observed in other genres of performance as well.

Along with the jaguar spirits are cited four classes of earthly wind spirits, called *šmaya? tuún ?ìik'* 'purify stone wind', *šmisi? tuún ?ìik'* 'sweep stone wind', *šmoson ?ìik'* 'whirlwind', and *škí?ičpam kó?olebi čočola? ?ìik'* 'beautiful lady salty wind'. Like the earth spirits, these bear their functions in their class names. With the exception of the female spirit in final position, these are all associated with the agricultural practice of burning a dried milpa plot, in preparation for planting. The whirlwinds fan the flames to assure complete burn, the sweeping and purifying winds follow up to sweep the ashes resulting from the burn. They are thus axiomatically very hot winds that cause fever in the human body. The whirlwind in particular is only a source of illness, never enlisted as a helper in curing rituals. In one case, as DC told me after the event, the whirlwind was the intrusive spirit that was threatening the patient's life and that had to be driven from the body. Mentioned in the midst of helping spirits, then, is the one source of illness that is the focus of the entire performance. The archangels fight fire with fire, to put it bluntly, and in the final sections of the prayer Michael the Archangel is loosed on the whirlwind spirit with his swift sword, to banish it from the body and drive it back into the bowels of the earth from which it came.

It bears reiterating that this entire process is one of spatial transformation: higher triumphs over lower; an ill wind has risen up into the human body, only to be driven back into the earth. The places of origin of spirits are predictive of their capacities and roles in the illness and curing process. The bodily positions of the participants play out the same spatial logic in which placement and orientation are part of the definition of roles, and to take up positions is to be incumbent in the roles to which they correspond. In the specialist understanding of a Maya shaman, these spirits, whose identity derives from the earthly and corporeal locations, are not only participants, but among the most effective participants in the event.

DIACHRONY IN PERFORMANCE

No description of the space of possibilities in which the *pa? ?ìik'* performance takes place can explain the dynamic of the process unless joined to an account of its diachrony. The performance itself unfolds over time, inscribing the positional arrangements and orientations of interactants in the local history of an enactment. This temporalization is subject to explicit norms, such constraints as that lower spirits are canonically invoked before higher ones, and that for any horizontal plane, either clockwise (E > S > W > N > C) or counterclockwise (E > N > W > S > C), orders are observed. That is, viewed as text, the prayer is structured in accordance with certain principles of cohesiveness and thematic development. When we look to the relation between the performance as a whole and the social context in which it takes place, another order of historicity becomes evident: the decision to perform this ceremony in the first place presupposes a prior event of diagnosis, as well as the use of medicines on the part of the patient. The patient was an old man, perceived by the shaman to be on the edge of death, and the ritual has certain intended consequences for his subsequent well being. In this section, we will briefly explore these two diachronies, the first internal to the performance and the second external to it. This inside-outside division is of course preliminary in the sense that the performance joins the two, at least insofar as it is successful.

The schematic structure of the *pa? ?iik'* prayer as portrayed in Figure 6.1 shows a clear and inexorable progression. Starting with direct address to the divine Addressee, the shaman invokes in controlled sequence town guardians, earth spirits, jaguar spirits, agricultural spirits involved in the burning process and, finally, the archangels. There is a recognizable vertical dimension in this order, placing low before high, but there are other less obvious ordering relations, as well. One of these is the alternation between guardian-helper spirits and what might be called active-combat spirits. The town guardians and the jaguars do not *do* anything in this ritual beyond standing watch over the process, to assure that none of the dangerous winds breaks free. Any time an evil force is dislodged, such as the whirlwind spirit in the patient's body, there is a real risk of assault on the shaman or any innocent bystanders (in this case, myself and the woman with her child who was sitting behind the altar, waiting for treatment). The basic participatory function of the guardian spirits, as well as the Lord Jaguars, is to establish a protective perimeter around the altar at which the process takes place, a role requiring their copresence and oriented attention.

In contrast to these two classes of spirit participants, the earth gods corresponding to body parts, the burning winds, and the archangels engage in violent combat with the whirlwind; they literally enter the patient's body and drive it out. What is noteworthy is that it is only after the town guardians have all been invoked (breath groups 4 through 16) that the earth gods are set in motion (breath groups 21 through 29). Immediately thereafter, the purpose of the event is reaffirmed and a sign of the cross erected. While I have not had the opportunity to discuss this detail with DC, it is my opinion based on other performances and discussions that the sign of the cross functions as an additional boundary marker, containing the earth spirits to this sequential phase in the overall procedure. Immediately after the medial sign of the cross, the jaguar spirits are posted around the altar (breath groups 32–33), and the burning spirits are bought in (34–38). In the agricultural cycle, as we saw above, these agencies help to clean the land by sweeping and sifting after the whirlwind spirits have fanned the flames to an intensity sufficient for complete burning. In this setting, the jaguar lords watch over the field at its five cardinal points, and protect it from venomous snakes and other malevolent forces that may injure the farmer. The contiguity of these classes of spirits in agriculture is recapitulated in the prayer, and once again, the guardian spirits are put in place *before* the potentially dangerous burning spirits. This enactment within the patient's body of a process derived from the agricultural cycle is a further instance of the fundamental continuity between the human body and the earth.

In the last fifteen breath groups of the prayer, after the intrusive whirlwind spirit has been identified and encompassed, the archangels make their appearance. The nature of their participation in the event is expectably quite different from that of the others, in accordance with their lofty origins and correspondingly greater power. The archangels are engaged in all of the major agricultural ceremonies. They contribute to the process of rain making and distribution, and are considered in general to be the most powerful spirit class in the cosmos (below God the omnipotent). While they are thoroughly benevolent to man, the very power they wield makes them potentially dangerous. In the *pa? ?ik'* performance, only two archangels (out of a set of at least five) are mentioned by name. These are *ht'uúp arkanhel* 'Youngest Brother Archangel' and *migel arkanhel* 'Michael the Archangel' (breath groups 51–54). What is distinctive about the way that Michael the Archangel is invoked is that he is mentioned six times. Whereas spirit classes, such as *le yum baálanó?ob* 'the Lord Jaguars' may be mentioned more than once, it is very rare for a named individual spirit to be cited more than once. The conventions governing the sequence of citation normally assure that individuals appear just once in their proper turn. In this prayer, the six citations of Michael the Archangel can be broken down into three couplets. In each one, the spirit is first mentioned, and then portrayed as crashing down upon the evil in combat. This is illustrated in the following excerpt (the second couplet in the sequence; breath groups 45–46).

Example 2

Ɂinyuúŋ
  tíal ink'aátik upodere bakan
    ti tulaákal asàanto bin šan
  Ɂuúč ink'aátk ub'èeyntisyòono bakan
    ti migel Ɂarkanhel → ##

léemb'anak utàal b'ey šan
  uk'aák'il usàanto Ɂespàada bakan
migel Ɂarkanhel
  tukantíiȼi le kwèerpoa
Ɂinyuúŋ↑ ## [F.52.A.13:26]

My lord!
In order that I request the power evidently
  of all your saints it is said too,
it has arrived (that) I request their blessings evidently
  to Michael Archangel ##

With lightning bolts it comes thus too
  the fire of his blessed sword evidently
of Michael Archangel
  to the four corners of this body
My lord! ##

The first breath group in Example 2 is a near-canonical couplet in which the shaman presents his request "for the power, for the blessings," "to your saints, to Michael Archangel." This phrasing puts the archangel in the position of culminating the verse block, just as, being highest in the cosmos, he culminates the power refracted throughout all the other saints. In this context, the archangel is a metonym for the legions of helper spirits, and the pairing of him with "all your saints" is the image of good that will triumph over the evil of illness. In the second breath group, the verse structure is attenuated, and sustained only weakly by the end rhyme, but the imagery is more striking. *leémbanak* is an auxiliary element derived from the root *lem*, meaning variously 'excessive, strong, hard, vigorous' (Barrera Vasquez et al. 1980: 445). In the reduplicated form, *lelem*, it is the noun meaning lightning, the action of which is *lemb'al* 'to crack, illuminate [of lightning]'. In the present context, the reference is clearly to the power of lightning as it descends upon the earth from the sky. The subject of this action is the biblical swift sword of Michael the Archangel, which complements the light, heat, and destructive power of lightning with that of fire. This image at once recalls the burning of the corn field in the previous sections of the prayer, the ascendancy of the heavens over the nether forces of the earth, and the violent combat between the forces of good and evil. Furthermore, the introduction of such heavenly combat into the body of the patient complements the equation of flesh with earth, by the opposite equation of body space with the heavens. The reference to the four corners reinforces this, since all cosmic spaces, heaven and earth alike, are conceived of as having four corners plus a center (hence the ubiquity of the cardinal points in ritual). This point goes beyond the niceties of symbolic structure in the prayer. One of the basic premises of shamanic practice in contemporary Maya culture is that good and evil are always and everywhere in tension one with another—from the limited confines of a single organ in the body to the expanses of the cosmos. This constant interplay is part of the ultimate "glue" that holds the world together according this system.

After each of the three invocations of the swift sword of Michael the Archangel, the jaguars are invoked again, as a class. They are accompanied in this context by a female deity named *škíʔičpam kóʔolebil sarakotén* 'Beautiful Lady Sarakoten' whose identity is unknown to me. The participant role of this deity consists in her aiding the archangel to drive the evil wind down into the earth, and the Lord Jaguars help also in stamping it (literally) into the earth. At this point in the performance, the shaman stamps his own foot sharply on the ground while praying. Example 3 illustrates the textual component of the performance (breath groups 47–48; follows immediately the text in Example 2).

Example 3
> yàa bin yakaʔhastáa
>> tulaákal uyiík'al e hmèentah k'àaso inyuúŋ →
> tíal inmaánsih šan
>> tunoh yòok bey šan
>> škíʔičpam kóʔolebil sarakotén bey šan
> uyakčaʔtáa šan
>> tumèen yum balan ʔìik' → ##
>
> ʔinyuún → ʔusàanto podere bakan
>> kutàal ink'aátmatik šan
> ti udyòos yoók'o kàab' šan
>> tink'ubi šan
> tunoh uk'aʔ → ## [F.52.A.13:39]
>
> It'll also be chased out it is said
>> all the force of the evil doer, My Lord!
> in order that I pass it too
>> by the great foot so too
>> of Beautiful Lady Sarakoten so too
> that it be stamped out too
>> by the Lord Jaguar spirits ##

My Lord! The sacred power evidently
  my request comes (for it) too
to the gods of the above earth too
  I deliver it too
to the great hand (of the Jaguar Lords) ##

What is going on in this portion of the prayer is that the archangels, in the person of Michael the Archangel, drive the evil spirit down from the heavens, at which point it is picked up by the female deity who stamps it further down, delivering it into the spatial domain of the Lord Jaguars (the "above earth"), who then escort it back down into the earth. This type of cooperative coparticipation between different classes of spirits is typical in shamanic practice, and used to move evil out of the realm of human experience.

In summary, the prayer text is a delicately structured instrument for the creation of a participation frame in which major spirit classes are made present in controlled sequence, and engaged in a concerted assault on the evil in the patient's body. The process synthesizes the body with heaven and earth, and reenacts on a local scale the cosmic struggle between good and evil. This basic interplay between local and global, between principles governing ritual participation itself and ones governing the cosmos in which it is enacted is also the key to the larger diachrony of the event.

The timing of the *pa? ?iik'* performance is controlled by a variety of factors. The most obvious is the prior interpretation of the patient's condition, which establishes the conditional relevance of the event. In the case under study, the old man's condition had been described to DC by his younger brothers, who had come seeking advice and medicines in the weeks prior to the performance. When the man arrived, DC did not recognize him, and the first three and one half minutes of interaction were spent trying to establish his identity [F.52.A. 1:33ff]. He had come alone, and was nearly deaf, making conversation all but impossible. Evidently sizing up his present condition at the same time as he established his identity, DC instructed him to come over to the altar and stand in front of it (assuming the proper bodily position for a patient).

At this point, DC remarked to me that the man's condition had become grave, and that I was about to hear a performance unlike any I had heard in the past. This strip of interaction was marked by long pauses (10–16 seconds) in between utterances as DC prepared to perform and talked with me. The man was essentially an unengaged bystander relative to our talk, poised silently before the altar as DC and I related his case to our own ongoing dialogue. Immediately prior to his arrival, we had been discussing body parts, in particular the function of the groin and the head. In the talk just prior to the start of the performance, we continued our dialogue, discussing the man as if he were not there. Although his apparent obliviousness to our conversation and near deafness encouraged this form of interaction, it is also my opinion that it was a mode of domination. Talking about the man in his presence, without inviting his participation, DC relegated him to the status of a nonparticipant. Like a patient in a modern hospital, examined and discussed by physicians making their rounds, the man was present as a case of such and such a kind rather than as a coparticipant.

In this preliminary interactive phase then, there were actually two frames simultaneously in play: DC and I were coparticipants in the last phases of our dialog, whereas the patient, soon to be beneficiary of treatment, was already assigned his positional orientation in the performance frame. Once the man was properly installed in front of the altar and DC was prepared to begin, there was a radical transformation of the participation framework. My role changed from coparticipant to audience, and I sat behind and off to the side of the altar. During the prayer, the participation frame was as described in the foregoing, with the man serving primarily as a corporeal locus for the battle between good and evil. The shaman remained a first person addressing the omnipotent God and setting in motion the spirits who would actually carry out the exorcism.

After a pause of seven seconds upon completing the final sign of the cross, DC addressed the old man, picking up their conversation where it had left off before the performance. The theme was the medicine DC had sent to the man through his younger brothers, and he asked him at this point whether he had finished it. This is a standard part of the clinical episode for DC, the preparation of medicine in the form of powders always following immediately upon the prayer performance. Having established that the man had in fact not yet finished the medicine already given him, DC informed him that the cost of treatment was "just ten pesos" and that he would give him more medicine when he finished what he had already. He instructed him to use the medicine given him, and to be sure to change his clothes upon arriving home. The man's responses were short and uninformative, "ahah, good, ok." Once again DC had to ask him whether he could even hear him. "Tell them to give you a change of clothes, you hear me? Make sure you change these clothes you've put on, because I performed a *pa? ?iik'* on you. Do you hear me?" The man grunted and took his leave. In this last exchange, DC summarizes the entire event in the genre label; the fact that he feels the need to tell him what has just taken place is a fair indicator of the asymmetry on which the genre is based.

Turning back to me, he remarked that the man was smiling because he did not even know that he had less than five minutes to live when he arrived. "Grinning death," he called it. This remark summarizes nicely the vast asymmetry in the knowledge base of the patient and the shaman, as well as the authority of the shaman's role. The entire architecture of participation that the prayer erects is beyond the awareness of most patients (including this one, by all indications). Yet it must connect with the lived experiences of the patient in order to be effective. Despite the judgment of gravity on the part of the shaman, the closing interaction is prospective, foreseeing the return of the man for more medicine, and the change of his clothing. At this point, not only is there a major shift in the participant framework, coincident with the end of the performance, but the patient is returned to a world of habitual engagements; he will change his clothes, take his medicine, and go about his business as in the past. He will have sought and returned from a "banish the wind" treatment. The reference to his family members also projects him back into the familiarity of the domestic group with which he lives. This return to the habitual ground of routine experience is crucial, in my opinion. It is the point at which the patient regains the historicity of his own biography, once again becoming an active participant.

THE UNIVERSALIZATION OF SPACE

It would be counterproductive to attempt a description of participation structures in the *pa? ?ìik'* performance without incorporating culturally defined discourse genres, without relating the roles one to another and to the spatial transformations in which they are embedded, and without calling on the historical relations between the event and the past experiences of its participants. Such an approach would amount to an excessively local view of participant roles, in which local sequences of utterances take precedence over events, individual roles over embodied configurations, and in which a commitment to the synoptic present obscures the social foundation of that present. Context cannot be treated as the scenery to which language and interactive structures are related once they have been "objectively" defined on other grounds, linguistic or sociological. In ritual performances, as in everyday language use, context interpenetrates language from production through reception. To borrow Goffman's turn of phrase, participant roles cannot be treated as "merely contextualized"; they are "inherently contextual."

I have tried to show the ways in which the roles of shaman, patient, and spirits are interrelated in the curing ceremony called "banish wind" in contemporary Maya culture. The first step is to recognize that this genre of ritual performance regiments a participation framework in accordance with the goals for which it is performed. The concept of discourse genres allows us to unify in a single framework the projected ends of performances, features of the spatial and temporal setting, aspects of the reconstructible past of shaman and patient, along with the roles and footings sustained during the event. In effect, rather than deflecting attention from the problem of participant roles, genres provide a way of limiting the descriptive load placed on them. Roles like Speaker and Addressee can be formulated in straightforward, abstract terms, which are then subject to added specification when joined to genre categories. (The same strategy is applied to abstract semantic representations, which are subject to sometimes complex pragmatic interpretations.)

Part of the social function of discourse genres is to regiment what I have called a space of possibilities. This space encompasses both interactive roles and the positional arrays in which they are realized. To split the roles apart from the subspaces with which they are joined in the event is to destroy a crucial part of their cultural logic. We can see this in the execution and reception of gestures in everyday speech, which depend upon bodily access between interactants. It is patent in the case of ritual performances, and subject to explicit conventions: the locations and directional orientations of shaman, patient, and spectators relative to the altar and its icons are only the visible embodiments of a spatial dynamic on which the effectiveness of the entire event depends. Lowered and raised to the altar from their axiomatic resting points in the cosmos, spirits become first the possessors of the altar, and then agents who enter and cleanse the body of the patient. Already posted at the perimeter of performance space, guardian spirits watch over and contain this process. This bounding function is described by DC as "raising a wall of fire around the altar," an image that makes clear that encompassment is containment. Our ability to understand this process depends upon our treating participant roles and subspaces as interwoven dimensions of a single construct. As a generic space of possibilities, this construct regiments the footings available to interactants, both as resource and as constraint.

The diachronic dimensions of performance are in evidence at the relatively local level of event structure, that is, the sequence of phases through which the performance must pass in order to be properly executed. Like speech acts, ritual performances also have various preparatory conditions, things which must already be in place at the onset of the event. For the *pa? ʔik'* these include prior diagnosis of the patient's illness, the arrival and proper positioning of the patient, and the appropriate commitments of attention and good will. Furthermore, the shaman relies on an indefinitely large stock of knowledge and experience with spirits, which is the ultimate source of his words. It does not follow from this that we need to posit a special category of "shamanic speaker," but rather that we recognize that ritual genres come prepackaged with implied historical foundations. In most cases, no one but the shaman knows of these prior and ongoing experiences in any detail, just as no one else knows precisely what he is doing at any point in performance. In fact, it is not even necessary that we assume that *he knows*. The point is that the whole dimension of past and future experiences radiating out of the performance is imputable and reconstructible, at least in fragments. The same holds, *mutatis mutandis*, for the patient-beneficiary, who is enjoined to conduct himself in certain ways following the event. My discussions with DC lead me to doubt that he knows which parts of his speech derive from which sources, and to doubt even more whether this apparent lacuna has any significance to him or anyone else. It is his habitual indwelling in prayer, his daily contact with spirits, and his lifetime commitments that determine the character of his engagement. If we make the mistake of attempting to capture this in an inventory of participant roles, we risk reducing to a set of categories matters that belong more properly to a habitus.

The effect of the *pa? ?iik'* ritual is to alleviate the suffering of the patient. The cultural logic of the performance is to create an actual space (not just a virtual one) in which the polycentric orientations of human interactants, spirit forces, inhabited space, biographies, and shared histories are synthesized. In summoning spirits to the altar, the shaman converts a coordinate cosmological space into an action-centered one, at once particularizing the former and universalizing the latter. Whereas a political leader may claim dominion by identifying himself with the state and the state with himself, a Maya shaman asserts control by identifying the space of his performance with absolute space. His ability to exercise this power rests at least partly on his capacity to mediate the participant engagements of which the space is constituted. In order to take effect, this mediation requires not the shared understanding of role functions, which is virtually never secured, but rather the shared occupation of the performance frame. As co-occupants in the spatiotemporal manifold of the ritual event, human and spirit participants actually encompass one another. Models of communication as information exchanged between discrete role incumbents provide little basis for understanding this process. Rather than focusing only on the fragmentation of interactive roles and the accomplishment of local orderliness in talk, we should also seek models that permit us to explain the integration of events and their embeddedness in a wider sociocultural order.

REFERENCES

Atkinson, J. Maxwell, and John Heritage (eds.)
1984   *Structures of Social Action: Studies in Conversation Analysis.* Cambridge: Cambridge University Press.

Barrera Vasques, Alfredo et al.
1980   *Diccionario Maya Cordemex.* Merida, Yucatan: Ediciones Cordemex.

Cicourel, Aaron
1985   Texts and discourse. *Annual Review of Anthropology* 14: 159–85.
1986   The production of objective knowledge: Common sense reasoning in medical decision making. In G. Böhme and N. Stehr, eds., *The Knowledge Society.* Dordrecht: Reidel. 87–122.

Clark, Herbert H., and Diana Wilkes-Gibbs
1986   Referring as a collaborative process. *Cognition* 22(1): 1–39.

Goffman, Erving
1974   *Frame Analysis.* New York: Harper and Row.
1981 [1979]   *Forms of Talk.* Philadelphia: University of Pennsylvania Press.

Goodwin, Charles
1981   *Conversational Organization: Interaction between Speakers and Hearers.* New York: Academic Press.
1984   Notes on story structure and the organization of participation. In *Structures of Social Action: Studies in Conversation Analysis*, J. M. Atkinson and J. Heritage (eds.), 225–46. Cambridge: Cambridge University Press.
1987   Interstitial participation. Paper presented at the 86th Annual Meeting of the American Anthropological Association, Chicago.

Goodwin, Marjorie Harness
1985   Byplay: The framing of collaborative collusion. Paper presented at the 84th Annual Meeting of the American Anthropological Association, Washington, DC.
1987   The interplay between dyadic and multiparty formats within argument. Paper presented at the 86th Annual Meeting of the American Anthropological Association, Chicago.

Hanks, William F.
1984   Sanctification, structure and experience in a Yucatec Maya ritual event. *Journal of American Folklore* 97: 131–66.
1987   Discourse genres in a theory of practice. *American Ethnologist* 14: 64–88.
1990   *Referential Practice: Language and Lived Space among the Maya.* Chicago: University of Chicago Press.
1995   *Language and Communicative Practices.* In Critical Essays in Anthropology. Boulder, CO: Westview Press.

Kendon, Adam
1985   Behavioral foundations for the process of frame attunement in face-to-face

interaction. In *Discovery Strategies in the Psychology of Action*, G. P. Ginsburg, Marylin Brenner, and M. von Cranach (eds.). London: Academic Press.

Levinson, Stephen
    1987   Putting linguistics on a proper footing: Explorations in Goffman's concepts of participation. In *Goffman: An Interdisciplinary Appreciation*, P. Drew and A. Wootton (eds.), 161–227. Oxford: Polity Press.

Searle, John
    1976   *Speech Acts: An Essay in the Philosophy of Language*. Cambridge: Cambridge University Press.

Tedlock, Barbara
    1982   *Time and the Highland Maya*. Albuquerque: University of New Mexico Press.

The Texture of Institutions

7 Socialization to Text: Structure and Contradiction in Schooled Literacy

James Collins

INTRODUCTION

A commonplace of current social theory is that society is like a text—a set of relations and significant forms and practices which participants and analysts "read" in making sense of their past experience and current circumstances. Another commonplace is that actual texts—whether written, spoken, or multi-modal—are always significantly shaped by the social and historical conditions of their production and reception. The difficulty lies in grasping the complex reciprocal relatedness of the social and textual.

The discussion which follows explores this issue by examining three aspects of textuality: (1) actual written texts and verbal practices tied closely thereto; (2) ideologies of text; and (3) institutional discursive practices. Examining these differing aspects of textuality requires that we think about relationship. What interplay can we expect to find between the "levels" of physical text, textual ideology, and institutional practice? What "links" connect the local pragmatics of text and larger ideological and institutional shapings of authoritative language? In exploring these questions, we will present an argument that moves back and forth between a general analysis of literacy, viewed as a complex of authoritative ideas about and practices with language in contemporary (American) society, and a specific case study of early reading instruction, viewed as a common route to identity-formation through encounters with text.

First, thanks must go to the children, teachers, administrators, and families in urban communities in Chicago and the Bay Area who allowed and bore the scrutiny of the original field research upon which this chapter is based. The initial context for this chapter was a paper entitled "The Regimented Pragmatics of Text," copresented with Elizabeth Mertz at the American Anthropological Annual Meetings, Chicago, November, 1987. Although we subsequently separated our chapters, the process of co-writing joint analysis was a valuable challenge. Support for writing came in part from a National Academy of Education Spencer Fellowship, which I held in 1989.

LOCATING TEXT AND "SUBTEXT"

The case study presented below concerns learning to read in primary school, and the specific analyses focus on texts and interactions oriented to those texts. In order to understand those interactions, however, it is necessary to be clear about their context, about the institutional and ideological matrix in which they receive their full import as conflictual, contradictory, interactional socialization to distinct "images" of text. Before turning to the specific interactional analyses, let us therefore consider the wider institutional-ideological context of the ethnographic case. In particular, let us examine some of the general ideas about texts that inform much basic literacy education, the particular institutional literacy which these ideas underpin, and the general expectations about pedagogical interaction in terms of which that institutional literacy is organized. Having established a plausible "subtext," we will then turn to the analysis of interactional particulars in their immediate ethnographic context.

TEXTUALISM

Underlying the ideological and institutional shaping of basic literacy in our society is a general complex of ideas about written language that might be called *textualism*, the central features of which are beliefs in the fixity of text, the transparency of language, and the universality of shared, available meaning (see Olson 1977, for a classic statement of textualist credo). Such assumptions about fixity, transparency, and universality have been contested for some time now by anthropological, philosophical, and literary studies of meaning. For example, the transparency of literal, referential language-in-text has become more questionable as anthropologists have shifted attention to myriad functions performed by language other than reference (Hymes 1974), as philosophers have shown the dependence of reference itself on complex contextual preconditions (Searle 1969), as literary scholars have shown the intricate play of metaphor, projection, and contextual precondition that enters into the most "neutral" descriptive language (Barthes 1977). Nonetheless, textualist assumptions are quite strong in our general intellectual culture and quite common in educational institutions and practices (see de Castelle and Luke 1983).[1]

Giving specific institutional form to textualism in our (North American) school systems is a technical conception of literacy, which focuses upon public

---

1. Olson (1977) argues that historically specific assumptions about text are basic to ideas about objective knowledge and the nature of subjectivity. His arguments about connections between *conceptions of* text, science, and mind are of considerable interest, even if we reject his progressivism and preliterate/literate dichotomies.

display of selected skills (for example, reading aloud) and context-independent assessment of error. Technical conceptions of literacy define reading and writing as skills, as precise, decomposable, quantifiable things; typically such conceptions focus on the surface of language (that is, the sounds and apparent referential content [O'Neal 1972; Graff 1979; Rose 1985, 1989; Street 1985]). Adherence to or departure from standard language is treated as one measure of error, and thus textualism feeds into linguistic prescriptivism, some particular consequences of which we will see below.

Schooled Literacy

The technical conception of literacy is part of what Cook-Gumperz (1986) has called schooled literacy: the universalistic literacy, context-independent and evaluated by tests under prior assumptions of differential achievement, which figures centrally in formal education and has slowly become the official norm for all literacies. Central to schooled literacy is the assumption that literacy comprises a uniform field or set of capabilities, rather than diverse, historically specific scriptal practices, and that these capabilities are assessable by context-independent and functionally general criteria. In short, schooled literacy presumes (and enacts) *a* literacy rather than multiple literacies. Such a view—and institutional implementation of such literacy—arose with the modern school, the systems of "universal" education which have spread throughout the world since the nineteenth century. Like the larger educational apparatus of which it is a part, schooled literacy assumes differential achievement. It is a stratified literacy, with achievement calibrated by technical (standardized) measures of skill, and with hierarchy and segregation as basic principles.

The "Normal Order" of Schooling

Let us now consider the "normal" interaction order of pedagogy. Briefly, this order is one in which teachers assign and assess turns at talk (with the sequential exchanges organized into higher-level, curriculum-shaped units such as lessons). Such conversational asymmetry reflects differences in the social power of actors: teachers are expected to know more than students and to control student activities (Mehan 1979). It reflects what might be called a larger symbolic logic of the school, one in which officially sanctioned knowledge is exchanged for respect and obedience. The teacher instructs and directs, the children defer and learn (Willis 1977). It carries out ubiquitously and persistently a discursive form—the question or examination—essential to the practice and recognition of knowledge in formal educational settings (Foucault 1975).

This normal order is maintained, or violated, in particular educational settings, in particular pragmatic contexts. A key aspect of the structuring of such contexts involves the relational distinctions between "good" and "bad" performance, "high" and "low" achievement. These distinctions are structural, though they do not derive from but rather intersect the basic symbolic logic of the normal order. They result from the stratifying imperative of modern education, in which there is a finely differentiated system of interlocking educational institutions (e.g., "tracked" primary, secondary, and tertiary schools), with differentiation and stratification based on putatively universal criteria of skills (esp. literacy and numeracy) and justified by arguments about the efficient adjustment of instruction to skill and of educational attainment to appropriate type of work.[2] There are, of course, many contradictions within such a hierarchical, differentiating process, which become quite tangible when we look at particular classroom settings.[3] More generally, as we will attempt to illustrate below, the assumptions of textualism, the expected order of classroom discourse, and the stratifying logic of educational grouping do not operate as a tightly integrated structural-functional system. The stratifying procedures which intersect the normal classroom order are both cause and effect of schooled literacy; and schooled literacy both relies upon and reinforces the assumptions of textualism. However, the relations between these different dimensions of textuality are often in conflict as well as correspondence, and effects produced in one domain often pose unexpected problems in another.

CASE STUDY

Textualism, schooled literacy, and the expected order can be seen as important elements of a complex ideological and institutional substratum that underlies early literacy training in our society. As noted earlier, the case study which follows examines interaction in early reading lessons. It is thus most directly concerned with the more tangible of the levels discussed earlier—written texts and the verbal interaction tied closely thereto. However, the interaction analyses comprising this case study continuously explore links between the immediate discursive complexities of socialization to text in early reading lessons and the larger ideological and institutional matrix of such lessons.

2. The "stratifying imperatives" of schooling can be seen as a particular institutional response to diversity—segregate and rank—in a larger social system in which educational credentialing serves as a device for rationing class privilege.

3. Such contradictions also become quite tangible, though in a very different fashion, more "macro" than "micro," when we examine the social history of modern public education. Nasaw (1979) provides a thorough and suggestive example of such history.

The material is taken from an ethnographic study of a primary school serving a working-class Black community on the south side of Chicago. In the larger study, several classrooms of an economically- and "skill"-stratified population of students were observed for an entire term (late January through June), with a focus on the relation between conversational and narrative processes and literacy practices. In addition, incoming and outgoing achievement data were collected, interviews with families and long-term community residents conducted, and basic socioeconomic data for families and the community compiled in order to construct socioeconomic and achievement profiles for individual students, classrooms, and the school and community. The larger project and various analyses have been reported elsewhere (Collins 1983, 1985, 1987a, b).

The study which follows is of a third-grade classroom in the school, a classroom which was relatively heterogeneous compared to others, in terms of students' entering test scores and their socioeconomic backgrounds. The study contrasts high- and low-ranked reading groups. These are activity groups, differentiated by apparent ability, as assessed by test scores and teachers' impressions. Such rankings are set up in kindergarten or first grade and tend to endure, or perpetuate themselves, as a massive literature attests (see Oakes 1985 for a discussion). Reading lessons occur in such subgroups, rather than in the larger classroom. That is, for the activity of reading, classrooms would be divided into three or four groups (four groups in the classroom being discussed), and reading would occur in such groups on a regular basis, with each group working with the classroom teacher, at a separate table at the back of the classroom, while the rest of the class members would be occupied with individual work at their desks. Keep this "ecology" of the classroom in mind—a subgroup working with the teacher while the remainder of the class works as individuals on assigned tasks (e.g., a fill-in-the-blank exercise sheet)—as we discuss subsequent interactional processes that involve group-internal or group-and-larger-classroom dynamics.

There is a "radial" organization of the activity of reading within groups. Students and teacher are organized in a circle, and reading typically consists of one student reading aloud from the assigned text, with the entire group then answering questions. The teacher is at the center of the process, as the assigner of turns at reading and turns at answering questions.

Four analyses were conducted on a total of six reading lessons from the classroom, one each from the beginning, middle, and end of the study period for the highest-ranked and the lowest-ranked groups. The analyses focus on dialect correction during reading; internal and external disruptions of group reading; spontaneous peer-correction during reading; and, finally, the uses of questions and answers.[4] The first and last analyses reveal diverging orientations to text; the second and third examine the unstable dynamics of the normal discourse order during reading.

The analysis of dialect correction assesses the extent to which non-adherence to the standard language affects the practices of reading, that is, the extent to which the text is treated as an object for faithful utterance. The analysis of the uses of questions and answers explores a converse orientation: to what extent the text being read is treated as an object of interpretation. The analysis of external and internal disruption of group reading examines whether violations of the "normal order" result from larger classroom or group-internal dynamics; the analysis of spontaneous peer correction explores how the problem of differential competence at the official task—reading aloud—is collectively handled by students and teacher. As we will see below, peer correction is often treated as a form of internal interruption, as a sanctionable violation of the normal order. Both peer correction and "interruption," in turn, contribute to differing instructional climates in which differing orientations to text "make sense" as provisional solutions to the dilemmas of group dynamics and textual ideology. Taken together, the various analyses provide distinct perspectives on the ways in which children orient to and enact cultural models of text. Reading lessons are performances—text-oriented performances—by individuals and collectivities, in which durable relations to self and others are constructed through engagement with text—text as conceived by self and others and as physically present in the hands of the group.

DIALECT SUPPRESSION

The practice of correcting nonstandard pronunciation (as opposed to actual errors of word-recognition) during reading is one manifestation of linguistic prescriptivism, a basic and long-standing cultural orientation to language in the United States, with various connections to textualism.[5] The ideological core of

4. Some of the analyses were new, for example, the tabulation of dialect corrections. Others separated interactional measures which had been aggregated in the earlier studies, in order more fully to understand the dynamics of "violation" of expected turn-taking procedures.

5. The connections between textualism and prescriptivism are indirect, but discernible. In his formulation of the textualist position, Olson (1977) draws an explicit connection between belief in an "autonomous" text and a reading instruction program which begins with phonological decoding, that is, "phonics." Baugh (1988), among others, has shown how this pedagogical program interacts with prescriptivism. In an early, insightful analysis, Bloomfield (1927, 1933) described how prescriptivism was driven by various confusions about the relation between spoken and writ-

prescriptivism is simple—that "correcting language" leads to social better-ment—but the practice is quite complex. In school settings, dialect correction often actually distracts from the pedagogic task it supposedly advances, as vari-ous critics have pointed out (Sledd 1972; Newmeyer 1978; Baugh 1988). It is a complex practice because it typically focuses on pronunciation, especially in early reading, but pronunciation is a dimension of linguistic difference about which speakers have unreliable intuitions.[6]

In the following analysis, the number of dialect corrections unrelated to word-recognition errors were tabulated for the high and low group lessons. As we might expect on semiotic principles, dialect correction was inconsistent: there were always many more "instances of dialect," for both groups, than were corrected. There were, however, consistently more corrections of dialect in low-ranked lessons.

Although members of both groups were strong vernacular speakers, there were twice as many corrections for low-ranked readers, as shown in Table 7.1. That is, enforced similarity between standardlike pronunciation and orthography was differentially imposed.

In addition, correction focused on stereotyped features of vernacular speech rather than on equally pervasive, but less salient, nonstandard usage. This can be seen if we look at actual transcript examples:

Example 1: Dialect correction during reading

        Text: . . . as she landed with a thud

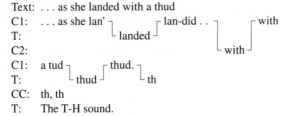

        CC: th, th
        T: The T-H sound.

Note: C1, C2, C3 denote different individual children. CC denotes a chorus.

The corrections in Example 1 are relatively straightforward. Like many

ten language, powerful but little-understood tensions between a centralizing literate code and an increasingly plurilingual society. Williams (1961) provides a similar argument, with more atten-tion to the historical, class-based institutions that underpin prescriptivism and the development of standard English.

    6. Empirical studies of the relative inconsistency of speakers' (and hearers') awareness of phonological variation can be found in numerous sociolinguistic studies (e.g., Labov 1972; Trudgill 1984). Proposals about the semiotic bases of this differential awareness are too complex to be discussed here but can be found in Silverstein (1976, 1981) and Errington (1985).

Table 7.1: Dialect Correction by Ability Group

	High Group	Low Group
Number of corrections	5	11
Number of lessons	3	3
Number of minutes	85	78

speakers of Black Vernacular English, this young reader deletes final /-d/ in consonant clusters (landed becomes lan') and uses /t/ where Standard English has /θ/ (written *th*). In neither case has he necessarily misrecognized a word; rather it is his nonstandard pronunciation that is at issue. The θ/t alternation and final /-d/ deletion are both stereotyped features of vernacular speech. In this classroom, they attracted attention frequently, accounting for eight of the sixteen corrections of Table 7.1. As we see from the other students' response (their chanting "th . . . th"), the correction is familiar.

Often corrections involved more complex relations between print and pronunciation, as the next example illustrates:

Example 2: Dialect correction during reading
    Text: Mike saw Dad's shaving cream.
    C: . . . Mike saw Dad [dêd] ⌐   ⌐ . . Dad [dæd] shaving cream
    T: └ Dad's ┘ [dædz]

In this example there are actually two ways in which the student's pronunciation differs from Standard English phonological norms: (1) the vowel of "Dad" is a midfront with central offglide [ê] rather than low front [æ], as in standard; and (2) the noun-final -*s* is deleted, rather than pronounced, as in standard. The *s*-deletion is a typical target of prescriptive correction (and hypercorrection), and the teacher's correction focuses on it.[7] Assuming Standard English phonology, the omission of final -*s* could be taken as evidence of an unfolding ambiguity in syntactic constituency (Dad's shaving cream (the shaving cream of Dad) or Dad shaving cream (Dad engaged in the odd act of shaving cream)). But whether the teacher's motivation was simple prescriptivism or an estimate of syntactic ambiguity, the student responds to the other

7. In the transcripts used for this analysis, the deletion of word-final -*s* was otherwise likely to be corrected. It accounts for four of the sixteen total corrections, indeed, for two others during the lesson from which this excerpt is taken. -*S* deletion is a salient feature of African-American street speech, and it is a form about which there is overt awareness, and prejudice, among non-speakers. As a stigmatized form, it is often the occasion for hypercorrection by speakers, as Baugh (1983) among others has documented.

difference, adjusting his vowel pronunciation and changing to a more standard low front [æ]. This misunderstanding of a dialect correction occurred in other lessons and highlights the fact that dialect difference is complex. Simply juxtaposing standard to vernacular, the form of correction in this and other examples requires that students rapidly infer just what aspect of their reading-aloud speech is in error.

There are a number of questions raised both by the corrections and their patterning. The issue of representativeness of findings is difficult, for the size of our sample is small. We are talking about six lessons, taken at simple intervals, from one classroom in one school, showing a total of sixteen overt dialect corrections (that is, pronunciation corrections showing no obvious relation to word-recognition difficulties in reading). Based on this sample, we cannot say whether such a pattern would occur in a multiracial school and classroom, in a school and classroom with a different social class mix, or in schools and classrooms which had eliminated ability grouping. A change in racial or social class composition, or in institutional procedures for handling diversity, would affect the context of early literacy activities and the prescriptive practice that often accompanies those activities. There are reasons, however, for viewing this patterning of prescriptive corrections as more than coincidence. For one, the tendency to correct bears out what the teacher in this classroom said about language: she firmly asserted the need to correct her students' speech, to teach them to "speak properly." It also agrees with the general prescriptivist assumptions and practices found in our schools for at least the past century, which always work most strongly against the working- or lower-class student, the child of immigrant or minority background. That the low-ranked readers in this study were also from lower-income backgrounds and were also more frequently corrected for their speech fits into the general historical pattern (see Bloomfield 1933: 496–506; Graff 1979; Newmeyer 1978; and Wright 1980, for historical accounts, and Baugh 1988; O'Neal 1972; Silverstein 1987; and Sledd 1972 for contemporary analyses and accounts; see Collins 1988, for an analysis of prescriptivism in mixed-race classrooms).

What to make of the general historical pattern in relation to the particular interactional practice is a different matter. Despite its historical durability, we must avoid viewing prescriptivism simply as some abstract cultural-linguistic authoritarianism, immanent in American culture. It is authoritarianism, but viewing it abstractly obscures its nature and dynamic. We must instead ask how dialect correction, or, more generally, the desire to contain or eliminate linguistic difference, emerges in specific situations. In the case at hand, the interesting question is how group differences become relevant. Since members of both groups were strong speakers of Black Vernacular English, why was the low-ranked group corrected more frequently? Why would reading be more oriented towards the surface aspects of pronunciation (and away from the depths of meaning) for one group? The beginnings of an answer may lie in other inter-actional dynamics of the reading lessons.

THE PRIVILEGES OF GROUP

Our second analysis focused on attempts by the teacher to maintain order during classroom lessons. We use *order* to refer to the expected sequence of one performer at a time, reading or talking, with teacher control of turn-taking. This is the dominant form of instructional discourse. It is both a powerful social rule and, as with all interactive processes, a collective achievement. We were interested in the oft-reported differences in how ability groups adhere to such a conversational regimen and in the sources of such differential adherence.

The maintenance of a normal order can be perspicuously assessed by analyzing sanctions directed at external and internal disruptions. External disruptions are behaviors occurring in the larger classroom, outside of the reading group, which nonetheless disrupt group reading, typically by distracting the teacher's attention from the lesson at hand, and attracting a teacher sanction. Internal disruptions are behaviors within the group that depart from the norm of teacher-controlled sequential participation (for example, when a group member talks to a peer or looks away during someone else's turn at reading) and that also attract a teacher sanction. Studying the former tells us something about the practical status of groups vis-à-vis the rest of the class; studying the latter tells us something about the differing groups' abilities or dispositions to conform to the expected interactional etiquette.

Table 7.2 compares the frequency with which high- and low-ability lessons were interrupted by some external distraction, that is, by some class member outside of the group behaving in such a way as to provoke a sanction from the teacher.

As the table indicates, such external interruptions occur roughly twice as frequently during low-ranked lessons.

Table 7.2: External Interruptions during Reading Lesson

	High Group	Low Group
Number	18	43
Number of lessons	3	3
Number of minutes	85	78

External interruptions typically disrupt the process of reading, as shown in Example 3, from a low-ranked lesson:

Example 3: Sanction of external interruption

Text: "Hello, Little Ant," said a grasshopper.

T: Kevin, start reading.

C: "Hello . . Little Ant" . . said . . to- . . a Grasshopper-

T: Wait a minute, wait a minute. Ethan! Quiet, please! . . . Start again.

In this passage, the reader has begun slowly, self-correcting on one word ("to- . ."), and then nearly finishing the first sentence. As he is completing that sentence, there is noise from other class members, distracting the teacher and causing her to halt the reading. (The teacher's "Wait a minute" begins as he is still finishing the final word.) She then has Kevin begin anew, presumably because she and perhaps other group members were distracted during his initial effort.

Our finding is that lowest-ability reading lessons are twice as likely to be disrupted by nongroup members than are highest-ability reading lessons. This finding, which agrees with other studies (McDermott 1976; Eder 1981), goes against the common assumption that low-ranked students are simply less disciplined, for the greater disruption comes from the non-low-ranked classmates. A plausible reason for the higher incidence of external disruptions during low-ranked lessons is that these lessons are the activities of low-status students and, as such, they merit less respect in the competitive classroom economy.[8] This is certainly part of the story, but we must try to situate notions like status in the actual classroom conditions being studied. There is more at issue than a simple correlation between group status rank and external disruption, for this correlation cannot account for the pattern of internal interruptions, to which we now turn.

Table 7.3 presents a comparison of the groups on internal interruptions, group-internal behaviors that attract a teacher sanction.

As we see from the table, there is a higher incidence of internal disruption in low-ranked lessons, that is, low-ranked readers are more likely to depart

8. Academic achievement confers rank, and students are quick to see through euphemistic labels for hierarchy (such as Robins for low groups and Bluebirds for high groups), and they know the relative level of particular reading books which they and other groups are using. My fieldnotes contain numerous instances of students putting each other "in their place," often within a group, as when low-group members formulaically taunted one another, "Dummy, you can't read." Other ethnographic studies report similar incidents of status assertion and rivalry (Rist 1970; McDermott 1976); on the general issue of grouping and status, see Rosenbaum (1980) and Oakes (1985).

Table 7.3: Internal Interruptions during Reading Lessons

	High Group	Low Group
Number	17	30
Number of lessons	3	3
Number of minutes	85	78

from the expected order than their high-ranked counterparts. We should note that the magnitude of difference (1 : 2::high:low) is similar to that for external interruptions. In other words, low-ranked lessons are carried out with more internal and external disruption.

As with external sanctions, internal disruptions and sanctions can interrupt the flow of reading, as in example 4:

Example 4: Sanction of internal interruption
    Text: "Don't work," said the grasshopper.
    T: All right, the next page Tremaine.
    C: "Don't . . work," . . ⌐ said . . said the grasshopper.   ⌐
    C2:   ⌐ "Don't work," said the grasshopper. ⌐
    T: Shh! Donita!

In example 4 the assigned reader has begun slowly, and a fellow group member begins to read also, perhaps as a prompt and model, perhaps merely in *sotto voce* accompaniment. This coreading is sanctioned, briefly interrupting Tremaine's turn at reading aloud.

Why should there be a higher incidence of teacher sanctions in low-ranked lessons? It must be excruciating for young readers when a story simply fails to unfold, as in the preceding example. However, we have argued against a view that low-ranked readers are simply "less disciplined," less willing or able to attend to the official task. Could it be that the similar magnitude of difference for internal and external interruption in high vs. low lessons (1 : 2) is due to a covarying of kinds of interruptions?

Table 7.4 presents a cross-tabulation of the incidence of internal and external disruption by lesson and group.

While the relationship between kinds of interruption is not rigid, the pattern is clear: Lessons with more external distractions also have more internal distractions. Thus in lessons 1 and 3, there are high internal and external rates for low-group sessions, while in lesson 2 there are low rates for both types of interruption. In lesson 2 there are high rates of internal and external disruption for high-group sessions, and low rates in lesson 3. This patterning suggests a reciprocal cause and effect: External distractions upset the complex internal

Table 7.4: Internal and External Sanctions by Lesson and Group

	High Internal (External)	Low Internal (External)
Lesson 1	8 (5)	17 (18)
Lesson 2	8 (12)	3 (6)
Lesson 3	1 (1)	10 (19)

dynamics of collectively attending to sequential group reading; the disrupted internal dynamics in turn affect the larger classroom environments, leading to and allowing for additional external interruptions. This argument suggests that what we call "lack of discipline" or even "attending to task" are as much a product of interactional circumstances as of context-independent dispositional states.[9] Otherwise put, the ability to attend depends on the conditions of attending.

THE PERILS OF MUTUAL SUPPORT

Let us try to tease apart additional aspects of this reciprocal dynamic by turning from teacher sanctions to student practice, the calling out of answers. Calling out occurs when group members who are not assigned the current turn at reading nonetheless read along with or "call out" the correct (or incorrect) words or phrases to the assigned reader as he or she reads aloud. The calling out of answers by the nonassigned reader can impede the reading process, depriving the assigned reader of that moment for evaluation and error-correction which is part of any complex cognitive task. However, as any student of classroom organization knows, calling out is also a common form of mutual support from peers involved in the same task. After examining the overall incidence of calling out, we will further analyze this interactional category, trying to distinguish peer rivalry and interruption from timely support. But first let us look at the overall incidence of calling out.

Table 7.5 presents a tabulation of calling out by ability-group lessons: all instances of peers coreading or otherwise providing current readers with "answers" (whether correct or not); and all instances of teacher sanctions of calling out.

As we can see, low-ranked readers call out more than twice as much as their high-ranked counterparts, a finding which should not surprise. Low-

---

9. McDermott's early work (1976) argued in this vein. He found that low-group lessons were subjected to greater external disruption and also showed group-internal avoidance of the reading task.

Table 7.5: Student Calling Out of Answers by Ability Group

	High	Low
Calling out	43	98
C.O. sanctioned	2	10
Rate of sanction	5%	10%
Number of lessons	3	3
Number of minutes	85	78

ranked readers are typically less proficient at reading aloud, and hence appear more in need of assistance from teachers and peers. We should note, however, that as with dialect corrections, only a fraction of calling out attracts a teacher sanction, and, again, the low group is sanctioned more frequently than their high-ranked counterparts (10% vs. 5%).

Why should low-group members be sanctioned at a higher rate? One possible reason is that they call out answers in an interruptive fashion, while high-group members call out in a more supportive fashion. In order to explore this possibility, we divided calling out subcategories—"timely support" and "untimely rivalry"—and calculated the frequency of each. "Timely support" was defined as calling out which occurred after a pause or at the end of a phrase or sentence. "Untimely rivalry" was defined as calling out which occurred without any pause, that is, which occurred either simultaneously with, or as abruptly latched onto, the assigned reader's performance.[10]

Table 7.6 presents the incidence of types of calling out by ability group, based on one lesson each (occurring on the same day and showing a high frequency of calling out), with a calculation of percentage of untimely calling out.

The results shown in Table 7.6 do not indicate that low-group members are simply more likely to interrupt. Although the total number of untimely "callings" is higher for the low group, the rate of such callings is actually lower (about 40% vs. 50%). In other words, the low-group lessons show a higher incidence of timely peer support.

If teacher sanctions were strictly a response to rate of interruptive calling out, we would expect an equal sanction rate for the two groups. How do we explain the unequal sanction rate shown Table 7.5, especially given the results

---

10. The microsynchrony of group interaction is always intricate, and it is notoriously difficult to categorize interactional behavior reliably. In the case at hand, the two types of calling out were at times quite similar, fractions of a second distinguishing one from the other. We were interested, however, in whether a group inclined toward one or the other type of peer participation, and so felt that even relatively crude temporal categories would capture the general pattern.

Table 7.6: Types of Calling Out

	High Group	Low Group
Timely support	18	31
Untimely rivalry	17	24
Percent untimely	50%	40%
Number of lessons	1	1
Number of minutes	28	23

of Table 7.6? In addressing this question, we need to remember that sanctions do not appear to be determined by any particular type of departure from the normative order. Instead, departures from the expected order cluster, and so do sanctions against those departures.

To get a more tangible sense of this clustering, let us now examine a long transcript example, taken from a low-group lesson, in which internal and external sanctions are a prevalent aspect of the interaction order, and in which we see timely peer support sanctioned.

Example 6: Clustering of calling out and internal and external sanctions

```
     Text:   "Can I have some food?" asked City Mouse
             "I did not find a thing to eat
             on the way."
             Country Mouse said, "Follow me
             and you will get some food."
             Then away went Country Mouse.
             And away went City Mouse.
 1   T:      All right, the next page Tremaine.
 2   C1:     "Can I . . ┐        ┌ have some food," aksd City
 3   C2:               └ have ┘
 4   C1:     Mouse ┐
 5   C2:          └ Country Mouse
 6   T:      No, he's right, that's right . . . City Mouse
 7   C1:     "I . . didn't ┐        ┌ did not fu- find
 8   T:                   └ did not ┘
 9   C1:     a . . . ┐        ┌ thing to eat . . . On the way . .
10   T:             └ thing ┘
11   C1:     Country Mou- ┐
12   T:                  └ Wait wait wait "I did not find" . .
13           read that sentence again
14   C1:     ┌ "I did not—. . ┐
15   T:      └ Corliss!        ┘ Bring that up here [T walks away]
16   C1:     find . . . food . ┐
17   C2:                      └ on the way"
```

18   C1:   "... I did not find food—⌉
19   C3:   ⌊ on the way"
20   C1:   "On the way?"
21   T: Have you finished with all of your work? [T addressing student outside
              reading group]
22   C2:   "On the way." ⌉
23   T: ⌊ Shh! [T sanctioning group member]
24   C1:   "I did not find food-⌉
25   T: ⌊ The blue one! [sanction outside group] ...
              [several seconds pass]
26   C2:   Tremaine ... Tremaine [several seconds pass]
27   C1:   ... On the way" .. Coun- Country Mouse said,
28   ..   ⌐ "Follow me ..
29   C2:   follow— ⌉   ⌡
30   T: ⌊ Shh! ⌡
31   C1:   and— ⌉   ⌐ —and you will get some-
32   T: ⌊ Shanona! Sit down! ⌡
33   C1:   something to eat" ... They was—⌉   ⌐ —They was- They
34   T: ⌊ away ⌡
35   C1:   They away went ... Country Mouse wi- And away went
36   City Mouse—⌉
37   T: ⌊ Sherman! Have you finished copying the
38   story? ... Yes? Then Mitchell go back to your seat so
39   Sherman can sit at his own desk [external sanction]
40   [five-second pause before questions begin about the passage just read]

In this excerpt the assigned reader has various assists from peers and the
teacher. The peer exchanges between Tremaine (C1) and Kevin (C2), a close
friend, are usually timely support, as in lines 4–5, 16–17, 20, and 22, and
28–29, and sometimes the support provides incorrect information, as in the
"Country Mouse" called out on line 5. An early problem for the teacher is that
Tremaine fails to treat the phrase "on the way" as part of the preceding line
(part of the sentence on the preceding text line). Just as the teacher begins to
correct this faulty parsing of the sentence, by demanding a rereading, a distraction occurs which takes her away from the group (line 15). Tremaine has begun
rereading in line 14 and finishes in line 16 with the teacher repetition ("I did
not find ..."). Then he does something interesting: He substitutes semantically
plausible "food" for "a thing to eat," as if his error had been word-recognition
after "find ...", rather than reading intonation and phrasing. Kevin tries to
help Tremaine during the teacher's absence (lines 17–19), but a reading strictly
following the text is never achieved. (We should note that despite the distractions and errors, these youngsters are getting it right. They are reading in a way

that captures basic text meaning: participants, objects, and actions are maintained as in the text.)

Upon the teacher's return, she sanctions one of those attempts at timely peer support (line 23). Tremaine begins anew (line 24), but another external distraction occurs, and the teacher is again drawn away. Kevin calls to Tremaine, apparently trying to get him to start (line 26), which he does (line 27). Kevin assists in line 29 and is sanctioned immediately (line 30); quickly thereafter another external disturbance occurs (line 32). Tremaine struggles with several challenges: (1) a substitution of "food" for "thing to eat" that goes unnoticed; and (2) difficulty with the literary phrasing, "Then away went . . ." (lines 33–36). As he finishes there is a final distraction of the teacher's attention.

There are several lessons we can draw from this classroom excerpt. One is that calling out may be a laudable form of peer support, and perhaps also a resource for teaching, if reading were redefined as a more collective activity, and the supporters' errors (e.g., line 5) became a source for discussion as well as sanction. As with most social interaction, however, joint activities such as reading aloud are complex achievements, and this brings us to our second lesson: Disruptions cluster. External interruptions disrupt the harmony of group reading, including the ways in which students provide assistance and the teacher's likelihood of seeing assistance itself as an interruption. The external classroom environment affects the internal environment of reading groups, and timely support can then veer toward interruption, attracting sanctions and causing further interruptions as readers individually and collectively strive to make sense of a text.

Viewed from the standpoint of our general argument, the interactional analyses discussed thus far exemplify a series of contradictory relations and effects. Grouping by perceived ability creates status hierarchies, one result of which is greater disruption of low-group reading; grouping also concentrates those who are least competent at the official task—reading aloud. Although calling out is an understandable, often laudable, form of mutual support among those students who need it most, it is also a violation of the norm of teacher control, a violation which becomes more salient as other incidents of disruption increase. So external sanctions feed internal sanctions and both together fragment the reading process, leading to an increased focus on reading as words-in-isolation, fertile ground for phonologically-focused prescriptivist impulses.

As noted earlier, dialect corrections are likely to occur during moments of interactional and task difficulties—when reading slows and attention is likely to fix upon the segmentable surface of language, on "how it sounds," rather than on the flow of encoded and construable meaning. Dialect correction and interactional difficulties do not simply correlate, however. Lesson 1, which had the highest number of internal and external disruptions for the low-ranked readers, had a low number of corrections (two); and lesson 2, which had the lowest number of disruptions, had a higher number of corrections (three). However, the highest number of corrections in a low-ranked lesson (six) did occur in lesson 3, which also had a high number of internal disruptions and the highest number of external disruptions (see Table 7.4). The general point is that dialect correction tends to occur when words are relatively isolated. This can happen when there has been a series of distractions and reading is proceeding slowly and haltingly or when some aspect of the task causes a word or sentence to stand out. As an example of the latter, one of the dialect corrections occurring in lesson 2, otherwise interactionally "smooth" for a low-ranked lesson, was when students were reading a text title (they read This and That as [dIs æn dæt] and the ð alternation was corrected (similar to example 1 above). Interactional difficulties and prescriptive practices reinforce an orientation to text as template for authorized pronunciation. Another orientation, linked in inverse fashion to the interactional dynamics sketched above, emerges when we look at our fourth and final analysis: the use and sequential structure of questions during reading lessons.

QUESTIONS AND ANSWERS: DIALOGUE OR INTERROGATION?

This final analysis focused on teacher-uptake of student answers during the question periods that typically followed a turn at reading aloud. Such question periods were led by the teacher and involved all the students in the group (who were supposed to bid for the right to answer a given question by raising their hands), although some questions might be addressed to particular students. Uptake occurs when a teacher's question incorporates a prior response from a student, that is, the criterion for local uptake was whether questions incorporated any part of an immediately preceding answer. Uptake thus indicated whether there was at least referential continuity between a response and subsequent question.[11] As defined, uptake simply focuses upon question-answer-

11. More technically, uptake was defined in terms of overt, zero-anaphoric, or paraphrastic incorporation of a student's answers into a subsequent question. There were two preconditions for uptake. First, the student's answer had to make an original contribution, rather than simply paraphrase what the teacher had said. Second, that original contribution had to be incorporated into the subsequent *question*, not merely acknowledged (see Collins 1987b for further discussion).

Table 7.7: Incidence of Uptake in Q-A Sequences

	High Group	Low Group
Uptake/Total Q	120/249	66/177
Percent uptake	48%	37%
Minutes	67	49
Q per minute	3.7	3.6

Note: Based on a sample of four lessons (two high; two low).

question sequences, but it provides a measure of whether questioning is used simply to check factual text knowledge or whether there is an unfolding dialogic exchange about the text.

Table 7.7 shows the frequency of uptake in questions (versus nonuptake) for matched sets of high- and low-group lessons.

As the table indicates, there were ability-group differences in rate of uptake, that is, in the tendency for a student's answer to be incorporated into a subsequent question. There were not, however, differences in the rate of questioning (3.7 versus 3.6 questions per minute), only in the rate of uptake. Before discussing possible reasons for the difference, let us first examine more closely what uptake and nonuptake involve.

Contrastive examples can be seen in Examples 7 and 8. Example 7 is taken from a high-ranked lesson, and uptake of a subsequent answer is indicated with a (+) in parentheses; example 8 is taken from a low-ranked lesson, and nonuptake is indicated with a (−) in parentheses. In the question-answer exchanges in example 7 there are sets of embedded questions, one identifying what a Crane is, the others locating the character Katy Crane in the story.

Example 7: Incorporation of answers into questions (+)
    T: All right, so who's the next person to come along?
    CC: Katy-Katy ⌈ Crane ⌉
    T: ⌊ Katy ⌋ Crane. And what's a crane? (+)
    C: Another kind of bird.
    T: Another kind of bird.
          And what do they tell Katy Crane (−)
    CC: To hide too . . to hide
    T: All right, that she's gotta hide too. She tells them about the hole in the
          sky and everything else and she better hide too. What are all these birds
          doing . . . to hide? (+)

The students' response to the first question (Q: "Who's the next person . . . ?" A: "Katy Crane.") leads a related question incorporating that answer (Q: "What's a Crane?"). The third question "What do they tell Katy

Crane" is ambiguous. It clearly incorporates the referent "Katy Crane" from the penultimate answer, but it is analyzed as nonuptake ($-$) because it does not incorporate material from the immediately preceding answer (uptake is defined on strictly adjacent answer-question sequences). The final question also shows incorporation (previous A: ". . . to hide"; subsequent Q: "What are these birds doing . . . to hide?"), and so is analyzed as uptake ($+$).

Such linked questioning, in which students' answers are drawn into subsequent questions, can be contrasted with a more fragmentary pattern found in the low-ranked lessons. In these latter lessons, questions were often cast in a yes/no format, and nonuptake of answers was more common, as shown in Example 8.

Example 8: Nonincorporation of answers into questions ($-$)
    T: Does the Ant wanna play with the Grasshopper?
    CC: No!
    T: No. What does the Ant wanna do? ($-$)
    CC: Work . . . uh, help work.
    T: All right, he has work to do, he has work to do.
          What does the Grasshopper wanna play with him, how do they wanna
          play? ($-$)
    CC: Hiding . . hiding . . hide 'n go seek.
    T: All right, he wants to hide in the grass and he wants the Ant to come and
          look for him.
    C: Ain't this the Ant?
    T: Yes, that's the Ant.
          Ramone! (external distraction) . . .
          All right, the next page . . .

In this exchange the students provide correct answers to the teacher's queries, but subsequent questions do not incorporate those answers. What occurs instead are a series of questions which assess comprehension without building upon students' responses. Thus neither the students' "No!" in line 2 nor "Work" in line 4 are drawn into subsequent questions. The overall result is a sequence of queries more akin to interrogation than dialogue, in that the assessment of comprehension through questioning does not seem to respond to student replies beyond noting whether they are acceptable or not. Often this response takes the form of a simple repetition of the answer with sentence-final, declarative intonation, followed by a new question, as in the first exchange (T: "Does the Ant wanna play?" CC: "No!" T: "No. What does the Ant wanna do?" [$-$]).

Given that strings of nonuptake questions often occur in portions of lessons where there has been some internal or external distraction (as in the external distraction at the end of Example 8), it seems plausible that here we have questions used to maintain order as much as to engage understanding. Asking questions in such a fixed manner provides a minimal compliance with the official task of reading in a situation made disorderly by a set of contradictory arrangements and demands. It provides a public assessment of comprehension which evaluates responses but does not build upon them. The relative disorderliness of low-ranked lessons seems to encourage such interactional rigidity; conversely, the relative orderliness of high-ranked lessons seems to enable and encourage the conversational flexibility and engagement more typical of those lessons.

CONCLUSION

We are dealing with a complex synergism in the preceding analyses, and I have argued that the interactional dynamics of the second and third analyses lead to the differing orientations to text shown in the first and fourth analyses. In the first analysis we examined variations in what might be called a "pragmatic" orientation to text as template for authorized pronunciation; in the fourth analysis we examined variations in a converse, "semantic" orientation to text as object of interpretation.[12] The pragmatic, prescriptivist orientation seems to result in part from the relative fragmentation of the reading process, and it contributes to that fragmentation. The semantic, interpretivist orientation seems to result in part from the relative stability of the reading process, and it contributes to the referential and illocutionary coherence of that activity.

The differing orientations emerging in this classroom are not anomalous. As I have discussed elsewhere (Collins 1986), there is a large if eclectic literature suggesting that "poor readers" acquire early and maintain consistently a view of reading as fluent pronunciation of text. Conversely, "good readers" acquire early and maintain consistently a view of reading as an interpretive process, a learning from text.

At first glance, the semantic orientation seems clearly better: it emerges from orderly classroom activities with high-achieving students; it matches our (literate, academic) notions about "learning from text" by extracting referential content and applying it to the circumstances at hand; and it fits with the

---

12. See Silverstein (1976) on this distinction between pragmatic and semantic aspects of language. Very crudely put, the pragmatic aspect concerns language use, in this case that phonological differences are indices of esteemed and stigmatized social background, and that utterance of text is corrected towards the esteemed variant. The semantic aspect concerns the denotational meaning encoded in language, in this case that reading a text is oriented toward interpretation and meaning extraction.

text-interpretivist orientations that have characterized our elite intellectual culture since the medieval period. The pragmatic orientation, on the other hand, seems clearly worse: it emerges from disorderly classroom activities with low-achieving students; it does not match our assumptions about learning from text; and it fits the text-authoritarian orientations that have characterized our mass education systems since the nineteenth century (see Resnick and Resnick 1977, 1989 on the elite and mass textual traditions).

Perhaps, however, things are not quite so straightforward. The low-ranked readers, acquiring a pragmatic orientation, may be learning something rather fundamental about literacy: that it is a matter of scriptal practices embedded in social relations, often relations of domination. This is a view supported by the rapidly accumulating literatures in the history and anthropology of literacy (de Castelle and Luke 1983; Heath 1983; Marvin 1984, 1988; Ohmann 1987; Street 1985), as well as by many studies in this volume. In this knowledge they are ahead of the high-ranked readers, acquiring a semantic orientation, for whom literacy is about decoding autonomous (fixed, transparent, universally available) text. The important point, however, is not merely to reverse the pole of valuation, so that "bad" becomes "good," but rather to see that both orientations are effects and constituents of a system of stratified literacy.

Consider also the group dynamics which contribute to the diverging orientations. Against the argument that low groups were merely less disciplined, we presented detailed information about the interactional matrix out of which different patterns of disruption emerge. It is also clear, however, that greater departure from the pedagogic norm is a persistent structural effect, whether we are concerned with intraclassroom ability groups, extraclassroom curriculum tracks, or tiers within a stratified tertiary education system. As Willis (1977) argued in his classic ethnography of a working-class high school, those who reject (and are rejected) by the school are less orderly, less disciplined. Students in low-ranked groups, tracks, and tiers are less socially mobile and, collectively, less accepting of institutional arrangements.[13] But in their undisciplined ways they achieve a practical insight into the profoundly inegalitarian aspects of schooling, an insight their high-ranked and achieving counterparts may lack. Again, the point is not that the rejecting, resisting students are right and their more docile, achieving counterparts deluded. It is rather that failure and suc-

13. Drawing a relation between class struggles, pedagogic etiquette, and educational achievement, Bourdieu and Passeron (1977) have phrased the opposite orientation with nice irony: "Mobility is the reward for docility."

cess, resistance and accommodating mobility, are linked fates, constitutive dichotomies in a system that attempts to hierarchize and segregate the profound divisions of class, race, and gender that characterize our societies.

In the preceding we attempted to explore relations between particular text-oriented interactions and large-scale ideological formations and institutional practices. After presenting general arguments about textual ideologies and their particular, historical, and institutional form, we turned to the examination of an ethnographic case and sociolinguistic data. In the sociolinguistic analyses we examined the distribution of particular features of interaction in order to discern regular, recurring aspects of diverging interactional orders and the resulting orientations to text. We also conducted interpretive analyses of transcript examples, in order to gain a better sense of the discursive complexities that underlay particular distributions. It is only by confronting the complexity of interaction, as recurring pattern and emergent particularity, and the complex relations that hold between ideology and action, institution and setting, that we can begin to appreciate the intricate reciprocity of the social and the textual.

REFERENCES

Barthes, R.
  1977   *Image, Music, Text*. New York: Hill and Wang.

Baugh, J.
  1983   *Black Street Speech: Its history, structure, and survival*. Austin: University of Texas Press.
  1988   Why what works hasn't worked for nontraditional students. *Journal of Negro Education* 57: 417–31.

Bloomfield, L.
  1927   Literate and illiterate speech. *American Speech* 2: 432–39.
  1933   *Language*. New York: Henry Holt.

Bourdieu, P., and J.-C. Passeron
  1977   *Reproduction in Education, Culture and Society*. Beverly Hills: Sage.

Cook-Gumperz, J.
  1986   Literacy and schooling: An unchanging equation? In *The Social Construction of Literacy*, J. Cook-Gumperz (ed.), 16–44. Cambridge: Cambridge University Press.

Collins, J.
  1983   Discourse analysis and early literacy: A linguistic perspective on minority education. Ph.D. dissertation, University of California, Berkeley.
  1985   Some problems and purposes of narrative analysis in educational research. *Journal of Education* 167: 57–71.

1986   Differential treatment and reading instruction. In *The Social Construction of Literacy*, J. Cook-Gumperz (ed.), 117–37. Cambridge: Cambridge University Press.

1987a   Conversation and knowledge in bureaucratic settings. *Discourse processes* 10: 303–19.

1987b   Using cohesion analysis to understand access to knowledge. In *Literacy and Schooling*, D. Bloome (ed.), 67–97. Norwood, NJ: Ablex.

1988   Language and class in minority education. *Anthropology and Education Quarterly* 14: 299–326.

de Castelle, S., and A. Luke

1983   Defining "literacy" in North American schools. *Journal of Curriculum Studies* 15: 373–89.

Eder, D.

1981   Ability grouping as a self-fulfilling prophecy: a micro-analysis of teacher-student interaction. *Sociology of Education* 54: 151–62.

Errington, J.

1985   On the nature of the sociolinguistic sign: Describing the Javanese speech levels. In *Semiotic Mediation: Sociocultural and Psychological*, E. Mertz and R. Parmentier (eds.), 287–310. Orlando: Academic Press.

Foucault, M.

1975   *Discipline and Punish*. New York: Random House.

Graff, H.

1979   *The Literacy Myth*. New York: Academic Press.

Heath, S.

1983   *Ways with Words*. Cambridge: Cambridge University Press.

Hymes, D.

1974   *Foundations in Sociolinguistics: An Ethnographic Approach*. Philadelphia: University of Pennsylvania Press.

Labov, W.

1972   *Sociolinguistic Patterns*. Philadelphia: University of Pennsylvania Press.

McDermott, R.

1976   Kids make sense: An interactional account of success and failure in a first-grade classroom. Ph.D. dissertation, Stanford University.

Marvin, C.

1984   Constructed and reconstructed discourse: Inscription and talk in the history of literacy. *Communication Research* 11: 563–94.

1988   Attributes of authority: Literacy tests and the logic of strategic conduct. *Communication* 11: 63–82.

Mehan, H.

1979   *Learning Lessons*. Cambridge, Mass.: Harvard University Press.

Nasaw, D.

1979   *Schooled to Order: A Social History of Public Schooling in America*. New York: Oxford University Press.

Newmeyer, F.
1978   Prescriptive grammar: A reappraisal. In *Approaches to Language: Anthropological Issues*, W. McCormack and S. Wurm (eds.). The Hague: Mouton.

Oakes, J.
1985   *Keeping Track*. New Haven: Yale University Press.

Ohmann, R.
1987   *The Politics of Letters*. Westbury, CT: Wesleyan University Press.

Olson, D.
1977   From utterance to text: The bias of language in speech and writing. *Harvard Education Review* 43: 257–81.

O'Neil, W.
1972   The politics of bidialectalism. *College English* 33: 433–38.

Resnick, D., and L. Resnick
1977   The nature of literacy: A historical exploration. *Harvard Education Review* 47: 370–85.
1989   The varieties of literacy. In *Social History and Issues in Human Consciousness*, A. Barnes and N. Stearns (eds.), 171–96. New York: New York University Press.

Rist, R.
1970   Student social class and teachers' expectations: the self-fulfilling prophecy in ghetto education. *Harvard Education Review* 40: 411–51.

Rose, M.
1985   The language of exclusion: Writing instruction at the university. *College English* 47: 341–59.
1989   *Lives on the Boundary*. New York: Penguin.

Rosenbaum, J.
1980   The social implications of educational grouping. In *Review of Research in Education*, vol. 8, D. Berliner (ed.), 361–401. Washington, DC: American Educational Research Association.

Searle, J.
1969   *Speech Acts: An Essary in the Philosophy of Language*. Cambridge: Cambridge University Press.

Silverstein, M.
1976   Shifters, linguistic categories, and cultural description. In *Meaning in Anthropology*, K. Basso and H. Selby (eds.), 11–55. Albuquerque: University of New Mexico Press.
1981   The limits of awareness. *Working Papers in Sociolinguistics*, no. 84. Austin: Southwest Educational Development Laboratory.
1987   Monoglot "standard" in America: Standardization and metaphors of linguistic hegemony. *Working Papers and Proceedings of the Center for Psychosocial Studies*, no. 13, Chicago.

Sledd, J.
    1972   Doublespeak: Dialectology in the service of Big Brother. *College English* 32: 439–56.

Street, B.
    1985   *Literacy in Theory and Practice*. Cambridge: Cambridge University Press.

Trudgill, P.
    1984   *Sociolinguistics: An Introduction*. 2d ed. Harmondsworth: Penguin.

Williams, R.
    1961   *The Long Revolution*. New York: Columbia University Press.

Willis, P.
    1977   *Learning to Labor*. London: Routledge and Kegan Paul.

Wright, E.
    1980   'School English' and public policy. *College English* 42: 327–42.

8 Recontextualization as Socialization: Text and Pragmatics in the Law School Classroom

Elizabeth Mertz

SULLIVAN v. O'CONNOR

Supreme Judicial Court of Massachusetts, 1973.
363 Mass. 579, 296 N.E.2d 183.

KAPLAN, J. The plaintiff patient secured a jury verdict of $13,500 against the defendant surgeon for breach of contract in respect to an operation upon the plaintiff's nose. The substituted consolidated bill of exceptions presents questions about the correctness of the judge's instructions on the issue of damages.

The declaration was in two counts. In the first count, the plaintiff alleged that she, as patient, entered into a contract with the defendant, a surgeon, wherein the defendant promised to perform plastic surgery on her nose and thereby to enhance her beauty and improve her appearance; that he performed the surgery but failed to achieve the promised result; rather the result of the surgery was to disfigure and deform her nose, to cause her pain in body and mind, and to subject her to other damage and expense. The second count, based on the same transaction, was in the conventional form for malpractice, charging that the defendant had been guilty of negligence in performing the surgery.

. . .

As background to the instructions and the parties' exceptions, we mention certain facts as the jury could find them. The plaintiff was a professional entertainer, and this was known to the defendant. The agreement was as alleged in the declaration. More particularly, judging from exhibits, the plaintiff's nose had been straight, but long and prominent; the defendant undertook by two

I would like to acknowledge the financial support of the Northwestern University Law and Social Sciences program for the pilot study described in this article. I would also like to thank Jim Collins, Bob Nelson and David Van Zandt for their very helpful comments on earlier renditions of this article.

operations to reduce its prominence and somewhat to shorten it, thus making it more pleasing in relation to plaintiff's other features. Actually the plaintiff was obliged to undergo three operations, and her appearance was worsened . . .

* * *

P: What errors were alleged in the appeal of Sullivan v. O'Connor. . . . Ms. [A]? ( ) What errors were alleged in the appeal of Sullivan v. O'Connor?

A: Um the defense claimed that um the judge failed in allowing the jury to take into account for damages anything but a claim for out-of-pocket expenses.

P: Well that's a rather general statement. How did this get to the appellate court?

A: Well the um the the patient was a woman who wanted a—

P: How did this case get to the appellate court?

A: The defendant disagreed with the way the damages were awarded in the trial court.

P: How did this case get to the appellate court? The Supreme Court once a—I think this is true—they asked some guy who'd never argued a case before the Supreme Court before—they said to him—he was a Southerner—and they said to him—ah—(*)Counsel how did you get here? (Laughter) Well, he said, I came on the Chesapeake and Ohio River (*)(Louder laughter). How did this case get to the supreme judicial court?

A: It was appealed.

P: It was appealed, you say. Did you find that word anywhere except in my problem?

* * *

INTRODUCTION

The vital role of entextualization and recontextualization[1] in struggles over social power in modern American society is perhaps nowhere more evident than in the U.S. legal system. An important part of attorneys' work, whether at trial or in appellate briefs, is the struggle to succeed in imposing a particular recontextualization of precedent, statute, and rule so that their clients can "win." And in the opinions of courts—particularly those of appellate courts—there are authoritative recontextualizations that translate fairly directly into

1. See Bauman, 1987; Bauman and Briggs 1990.

social results, results that are not necessarily limited to the particular cases at issue.[2] Attorneys and judges first learn the art of recontextualizing legal texts in law school, in another institutional setting in which the unfixing and re-centering of discourse performs a pivotal role as the semiotic mediation of social transformation.

The social transformation that is accomplished in the law school is a change in social identity of the sort that is immediately familiar to students of initiation rites and processes (see Van Gennep 1960, Turner 1974). During the first year of law school, according to widely accepted folk theory, law students undergo a transformation referred to as "learning to think like a lawyer." Although many aspects of the social setting within which law students are immersed are thought to contribute to this transformation, a critical common denominator in otherwise somewhat diverse experiences is the law school classroom. If a major goal of law school socialization is to change students' "way of thinking," then a crucial medium through which this goal is to be accomplished is the spoken and written language of the law school classroom.

This chapter analyzes the recontextualization of legal texts in law school classroom discourse, discovering in the institutional discursive practice an ideology of text to which law students are socialized. The structure of classroom discourse mirrors the ideology it seeks to impart at the same time as it directs attention to aspects of text that are ideologically significant (in Peircean terms, classroom discourse is an "indexical icon" of the epistemology it attempts to convey; see Silverstein 1981; Parmentier 1993).[3] As we unpack the powerful

2. This is in part because of the role opinions play as "precedent," to be discussed below. Note that there are several kinds of appellate courts in the United States; one notable distinction is that between intermediate appellate courts and supreme courts, whether at the state or federal level. In the federal system there is a single Supreme Court, and that Court has higher authority to interpret federal texts (i.e., the U.S. Constitution) than the intermediate federal appellate courts, which are bound by the rulings of the Supreme Court. A similar hierarchy exists at the state level. This hierarchy of interpretive authority has implications for the authority of the texts produced by different courts. Below the intermediate appellate courts on the status hierarchy are the trial courts, which are bound by the opinions of their intermediate appellate courts as well as by those of the relevant supreme court. (The intermediate courts are for these purposes the authoritative interpreters of supreme court opinions.) Judges in trial courts also issue opinions, although these tend more to be limited in their authoritative scope to the conflict at hand.

3. Silverstein (1981) and Parmentier (1993) have demonstrated the way in which political oratory can operate as an indexical icon of the social structure it reinforces. One interesting implication of this sort of analysis is that, in certain crucial institutionalized situations, the pragmatic structure of language may work at a level of which speakers are unaware to render certain social outcomes "natural" or inevitable. This subliminal aspect of the pragmatic structure of major cul-

linguistic practice through which law students are socialized, we can perceive not only the role of recontextualization in their socialization to this form of professional life, but also the shape of a particular ideology of entextualization and recontextualization that is central to wider legal praxis. Here the recontextualization process has multiple social implications, both as a crucial part of the social transformation in professional school, and also as an indexical icon of a linguistic praxis and ideology central to the formal legal structure of modern U.S. society. Legal recontextualization, to a significant extent, performs the semiotic mediation of social praxis.

LOCATING THE TEXT:
LEGAL DE- AND RE-CONTEXTUALIZATIONS

We have seen that an ideology of "textualism" underlies the orientation to text imparted during the initial years of socialization in U.S. educational institutions (see Collins: this volume). The view of texts as fixed and transparent, conveying universally available meaning, is combined with a technical conception of literacy, under which interpretation of texts is a skill to be publicly displayed and evaluated in a context-independent, quantifiable fashion (see also Cook-Gumperz 1986). Not only the texts that are read, then, but even the performances of those texts in class come with their own entextualization preordained, for the institutional context puts a premium on the extractability of text and performance from context. The goal of the recontextualization of written texts in reading-class performances is precisely the decontextualization of the performance in an individual-focused assessment of ability or skill; the key "official" function of the recontextualizing performance is to serve as index (and, interestingly, icon) of this underlying skill. As Collins demonstrates, this institutional framing of students' recontextualizing performances is an exercise of social power with profound consequences (cf. Bauman and Briggs 1990: 34–38). Within the broader institutional frame, Collins discerns two different approaches to text: a relatively more fragmented approach focused upon the pragmatics of pronunciation, and a more "orderly" approach stressing the extraction of referential content through a focus on semantic interpretation (Collins: this volume). The referentialist orientation, of course, maps the institutional theory of text more closely.

The theory of text that emerges in first-year law school pedagogy differs from both of the approaches found by Collins, although of course both pronun-

---

tural discursive forms would seem to be of particular interest in situations where language is used for socialization and the creation of new social identities.

ciation and semantic comprehension of text are presupposed skills in a law school classroom. However, the discursive practice of the first-year class can in large measure be conceptualized as a structured attempt to undermine the semantic-interpretive orientation which students bring with them from earlier schooling. Instead, students' attention is focused upon the way in which legal texts index their contexts of production and use. The oral exchange between professor and student points students' attention to a particular aspect of text pragmatics, in a structured dialogue often referred to as the "Socratic method" of teaching.[4] The structure of this dialogue reinforces a linguistic ideology under which language transforms mental processes at the same time as it imparts a theory of text—a theory that is generally not made explicit through semantic description, but is continually demonstrated in the pragmatics of classroom speech.

The classroom dialogue is a socialization to legal texts and to the distinctive facets of a legal "reading" of those texts. Although there are of course many interesting variations and differences within the legal tradition regarding how to approach particular kinds of legal texts, there are points of commonality discernible in the analysis of legal genres. The focus of much of the first year in American law schools is reading cases; the textbooks are called "casebooks," and consist for the most part of a series of edited appellate court opinions (or cases). Learning to decipher these cases in many instances calls for an understanding of constitutional provisions, statutes, or regulations that are at issue, so that an adequate understanding of the "case" genre often requires proficiency in other genres as well. If we analyze the opinions reproduced in law school casebooks as instances of a genre, we can begin to trace the outlines

4. The Socratic method emerged as part of a larger theory of the law that was introduced at the Harvard Law School in 1870 by Christopher Columbus Langdell. (The story is replete with symbols significant in the American cultural tradition.) Modeled upon an ideal type of the question-and-answer style of Socratic dialogue, and based upon casebook readings from appellate cases, this teaching method soon became the dominant mode of teaching in American law schools (Stevens 1983: 59–64). Langdell sought to instate the study of law as a true science:

> Law, considered as a science, consists of certain principles or doctrines. To have such a mastery of these as to be able to apply them with constant facility and certainty to the ever-tangled skein of human affairs, is what constitutes a true lawyer; and hence to acquire that mastery should be the business of every earnest student of law. (Langdell 1871)

The data of legal science were to be found, for the most part, in legal opinions, which were to be studied in the way that zoologists or botanists studied animals and plants, so that the data could be properly classified. The Socratic method was thought to be a superior way of teaching students this classification process.

of an ideology of text and language that is quite different from the "textualism" and "schooled literacy" found in other arenas of U.S. culture.[5]

Here I can only sketch in provisional fashion the outlines of this ideology, with the caveat that much more work will be required in order to fill in the sketch—particularly as regards historical change and variations across legal settings and genres (see also Brigham 1978; Levi 1949; Mertz 1987, 1988, 1990; White 1973, 1984, 1986b).[6] The cases that are reproduced in law school casebooks are generally appellate court opinions, written to resolve issues which parties have appealed following initial resolution of the dispute in the trial court. The opinions are discrete texts whose entextualization is also in a sense prefigured, as we shall see. Appellate court judges, whether in the state or federal system, frequently rely upon prior cases as "precedent," following an interpretive doctrine known as *stare decisis*:

> To abide by, or adhere to, decided cases. Policy of courts to stand by precedent and not to disturb settled point. . . . Under doctrine a deliberate or solemn decision of court made after argument on question of law fairly arising in the case, and necessary to its determination, is an authority, or binding precedent in the same court, or in other courts of equal or lower rank in subsequent cases where the very point is again in controversy. (Black 1983: 731)

The precedential authority of a case text depends upon the hierarchical position of the court from which it issues as well as upon the topic in question, so that on matters of federal constitutional law, U.S. Supreme Court opinions are deemed "binding" upon lower federal courts and all state courts. Conversely, on matters of state law, opinions issued by the supreme courts of the individual states are viewed as authoritative. Appellate courts at times explicitly overrule their own precedents, or they may "limit" prior decisions by imposing narrow interpretations upon precedential texts. A case only operates as "precedent," of course, when it is drawn upon in subsequent opinions. The interpretive act by which one case becomes viewed as precedent for another depends upon a creative simile in which aspects of both cases that have been defined as being in some sense crucial are analogized.

Where a "textualist" ideology regards the text as fixed, then, the U.S.

---

5. I will here focus upon cases, because case analysis is traditionally the primary emphasis of first-year law school classes. (Indeed, full analysis of just the case law genre is beyond the scope of a single article.)

6. In particular, the semiotic structure of a precedential text in relation to a key interpreting "successor" text is analyzed in Mertz (1990).

"case law" tradition depends upon a conception of texts as subject to changing interpretation, as fundamentally reconstitutable through the process of recontextualization in subsequent cases. This is not to say that cases are not also given authoritative, determinist readings. But the cultural constitution of cases as "precedent" has a double-edged quality; subsequent interpretation at once "creates" the authoritative meaning of a precedential case, and yet is constrained by the framing discourse of the language used in that precedential case. What a case "means" only emerges as it is interpreted as precedent in subsequent cases; at the same time, because subsequent discourse is constrained and framed by the terms of argument set up in precedential cases, any subsequent authoritative interpretation relies in a fundamental way upon the authority of the prior text. In terms of meaning and authority, these legal texts are mutually constitutive.

Thus it is the very capability of a text to be reconstituted when it is recontextualized as precedent that makes it powerful within the textual tradition; case texts are "fixed" and "refixed" in the continual process of ongoing legal opinion writing and reading. As Edward Levi noted in his astute analysis of this sort of legal discourse, "the kind of reasoning involved in the legal process is one in which the classification changes as the classification is made" ; it is at once "certain" and "uncertain" (1949: 3–4).[7] An often-invoked adage emerging from the ideology of law school teaching is that there are "no right answers" to questions asked about case law in class (see, for example, Delaney 1982: 74). This is somewhat puzzling, for observation of law school classroom exchanges makes clear that at one level there are, if not "right," then certainly "wrong" answers. But the "no right answers" ideology is a response to the essentially contestable character of case law texts; meanings may be "refixed," new interpretations may be forged, and attorney adversaries in practice will argue vastly different interpretations of the same cases in efforts to harness powerful case law precedent for their purposes. Students may give "wrong" answers when they fail to observe the canons for reading legal texts, or fail to discern the limits to contestability. But to accept the notion that a legal text is sufficiently "fixed" that it contains "right answers" is precisely to miss a key canon for reading legal texts.

The textualist credo also views language as transparent, so that texts are to be read for literal, referential meaning which is universally available (see Collins: this volume). Here again there is a sharp contrast with the case law

---

7. Similarly, James Boyd White defines legal reasoning as "an organized and systematic process of conversation by which our words get and change their meaning" (1984: 268).

tradition. It is perhaps not surprising to find that legal writing is characterized by the inaccessible "expert" language found in many professions (see Cicourel 1981; O'Barr 1981). But there is a more profound inaccessibility, for even were all the technical vocabulary to be transformed somehow into more accessible language, the "meaning" for which lawyers read the text would remain elusive to those reading for referential content. A legal reading of case law focuses rather on the metapragmatic structure of the text, in which lies the key to its authority. This metapragmatic structure is (at least) twofold, indexing both the context of prior cases in the textual tradition now reanimated as precedent for this particular case, and the interactional context of this particular case in its prior transformations (on interactional text see Silverstein and Urban: this volume). We have discussed the first aspect, that of precedential textual context; let us now examine the peculiarly legal interactional text provided by the procedural history of a case.[8]

Just as the authority of a case as precedent is in part a function of the position (in a clearly demarcated status hierarchy) of the court from which it issued, the authority of a case as decision on the immediate conflict at issue depends upon its "procedural history." By the time a case has reached an appellate court, it has been shaped by the procedures of the trial court[9] below and by the procedures invoked during the appeal, so that there is a strong semiotic framing of the issues to which an appellate court may speak. Issues not raised at trial or on appeal may generally not be addressed by an appellate court, and the appellate court may not rule on issues that would be raised by a different factual situation. When the text of an appellate court opinion addresses such out-of-bounds issues, that part of the opinion is called *dictum* and is deemed not to be authoritative or binding. Only that part of the opinion that speaks to issues "properly before the court" is thought to be authoritative; this part is called the *holding* of the case. Of course, the distinction between holding and dictum opens a great deal of room for semiotic maneuvering of various kinds. A critical part of reading legal opinions, then, if one wishes to understand them

8. Note that procedural history is only one variety of the interactional texts that can be found in legal opinions. Insiders can read certain appellate opinions as expressions of power struggles among competing judges or justices, as the products of negotiations among judges and their clerks (who write substantial portions of many decisions), as attempts to mediate political or social struggles of various sorts, and so forth.

9. Alternatively, the case may have been shaped by the procedures of the administrative agency whose decision is under review, or, in *habeas corpus* cases, by the earlier trial and appeal(s) from whose result the petitioner seeks relief. For ease of reference I use the trial court as a model here.

as socially powerful texts, is discerning the frame that is imposed by prior oral and written contextualizations of the same conflict in courts below—and by the semiotic frame imposed by the litigants as they choose particular issues to appeal. This is perhaps best illustrated through an analysis of the way in which law school classroom discourse undermines a standard referentialist approach to text.

THE CASE STUDY: THE LAW SCHOOL CLASSROOM

This paper draws upon work done in several law school classrooms as part of a pilot study of the language of law school education. Because the pilot study was narrow in scope, my conclusions here should be read as heavily circumscribed; a fuller study is currently underway to assess the generalizability of these conclusions.[10]

THE "NORMAL ORDER" OF LEGAL TEACHING

As in the elementary school classrooms of Collins' study, the professors in law school classrooms control and evaluate students' turns at talk. Indeed, the classrooms of this study were still more rigidly controlled, with virtually no verbal exchanges between students unmediated by the professor. Even the rare arguments between students were channeled through professorial questioning of the two parties.

From the ideology of law school pedagogy there emerges a stereotypic image of the highly stylized teaching genre that is sometimes referred to as the "Socratic method." The degree to which the cultural stereotype mirrors—or ought to mirror—actual practice is to date largely unstudied and somewhat controversial (see Cole 1984; Cramton 1982; re controversy see, e.g., Condlin 1981; Heffernan 1980; Kennedy 1983; White 1986a). Some aspects of the broader structure of the classes I observed are aptly captured by the stereotype of law school teaching that is described by legal academics as well as in popular accounts (see, e.g., Teich 1986; Strong 1973; see also Turow 1977 and *The Paper Chase* [film]).[11] Professors begin class by calling on a student, who may

10. I am also constrained from commenting upon the gender implications of my findings at this point; that, too, will have to await the larger study involving eight law school classrooms.

11. There were some differences in approach in the classrooms of the pilot study; I focus here upon shared aspects conforming to the canonical Socratic discipline. In the broader study we are finding some variation from the classic Socratic style, with two classes in particular (interestingly, both taught by women) lapsing regularly into periods of what we call "unfocused" dialogue, in which the structure of turns remains an alternation between professor and student, but with multiple students chiming in rather than just one designated student interlocutor.

then be expected to participate in dialogue with the professor for as long as an entire class period. Although the answers that a student gives may lead the conversation in unexpected directions, this can only happen if the professor chooses to incorporate students' answers in his or her subsequent questioning. Thus even potentially creative aspects of the exchange are carefully channeled and controlled.

In their work on graduate school education in France, Bourdieu and Passeron noted a number of ways in which the formal European lecture method enforced professorial authority:

> The lecturer finds in the particularities of the space which the traditional institution arranges for him (the platform, the professorial chair at the focal point on which all gazes converge) material and symbolic conditions which enable him to keep the students at a respectful distance. . . . Elevated and enclosed in the space which crowns him orator, . . . the professor . . . is condemned to a theatrical monologue and virtuoso exhibition by a necessity of position far more coercive than the most imperious regulations. (1977: 109)

The discipline of the law school classroom, with regulations that require more than respectful distance and silence, can in a sense be seen as still more authoritarian. Kennedy (1983: 3) describes this discipline as a loss of autonomy, for while students in lecture have freedom to drift away from the professor's message if they so choose, law students must always be ready to be called on, and to perform in front of the large audience that is their law school cohort. This emphasis on performance—on discipline to perform rather than just listen— contributes to professorial authority in a new way. For if, as Bourdieu and Passeron (1977: 109) would have it, the college professor in lecturing imparts "the Word" much as a religious figure would, the law school professor requires students to divine and repeat back "the Word" as revealed to students through submission to the flow of professorial questioning.

This method requires students to remain in conversation with the professor, while never modifying the demand that they conform to certain stylistic requirements. This is one important way in which the imposition of discourse style in a law school classroom setting imparts quite a different message about power than is discernible in "lower-class" classrooms studied by scholars like Collins (this volume) and Gee (1985). For here students are often forced to assume the new style; they are not generally permitted to "give up," as the African-American child of the Gee study was (Gee 1985: 24). In one sense, the power imposed in the law school classroom is more authoritarian; and yet, it is empowering also, in the sense that students are not allowed to disengage. Students are not permitted to go off and "practice"; they must remain in and master the dialogue. The law school professor is thus at once giving students no choice and telling them that they are capable of performing this genre.

THE LOCAL PRAGMATIC SURROUND

The class that will be the focus of this analysis conformed fairly closely to the stereotypic, highly regimented, "traditional" law school classroom. The students in this classroom received their initial reading assignment before their first class. It was posted on a student bulletin board in the student area of the law school, and there was an expectation that they would arrive in class the first day with their book bought and first assignment read. Subsequent assignments were posted on the board throughout the semester. There was no formal notification given students about these expectations; knowledge was imparted through informal student networks.

Like many first-year students in other law schools, students in this classroom were assigned to a cohort that would take almost all of their first-year classes together. After the initial class, the professor circulated a seating chart, and the students filled their names in. The professor then had a larger chart constructed, with a picture of each student's face and corresponding name in the appropriate slot. This he used when calling on students in class each day. The physical setting was a large classroom, seating around one hundred students. The seats rose in height from front to back along three sides of the center of the classroom. In the center was a small platform upon which the podium rested, with a desk beside it. Behind the podium were blackboards.

Class began when the professor called it to order and delivered a brief exposition of a problem or question derived from the readings. The professor then posed a question, looked down at his seating chart, and called out a name. Address was formal, using surnames prefaced by "Mr." or "Ms." This professor typically asked a student a series of questions—and occasionally continued speaking with the same student for the entire class hour. More often, however, he called on two or more students for extended exchanges through the course of one class hour. When dissatisfied with an answer, he often asked for volunteers and called on students who raised their hands, returning then to the designated student after other students had answered that particular question.

At no time during the study did a student who was called upon respond by saying that he or she had not done the reading for the class. The professor in this class had a daily sign-up sheet for students who were unable to do the reading; each student was permitted a limited number of "unprepared days" each semester. On other days, the students were expected to be prepared.

The marked, almost ritual structuring of student language characteristic of the law school classroom can be analogized to other kinds of rituals designed to socialize members of society to new statuses (see Turner 1974; Van Gennep 1960). The linguistic discipline of the first-year law school classroom, transcending a variety of pedagogic styles and political philosophies, can be viewed as part of an initial process through which previously learned linguistic conventions and conversational expectations are broken down.

LEGAL PRAGMATICS: RECONTEXTUALIZING LEGAL TEXTS IN CLASSROOM DISCOURSE

A closer examination of classroom exchanges sheds light on the way in which law school classroom discourse breaks down expectations associated with the textualist approach to reading as it recontextualizes legal texts. This recontextualization occurs within the highly structured bounds of the professor-student exchange, and focuses students' attention upon (that is, indexes) particular aspects of the indexical structure of the legal texts. The structure of classroom discourse frames the reading of legal texts in terms of the texts' social power, so that students are trained to filter what they are reading in terms of the way the text indexes its own authority; given a certain procedural stance or doctrinal requirement, certain parts of the "story" told in a legal opinion are important, while others are not. The key to the reading is not the semantics of the story told but the pragmatics of the legal text.

Let us take as an example the case with which this article began, *Sullivan v. O'Connor*, and its recontextualization in a classroom exchange. The "story" of this case is that of a woman, a professional entertainer, whose nose was deformed during the course of plastic surgery by a physician who had promised to "enhance her beauty and improve her appearance." In her first response to the professor's question, "How did this get to the appellate court?" Ms. A. attempts to tell this story: "Well the um the the patient was a woman who wanted a—"; the professor, however, is after a different reading, and immediately interrupts to repeat his question, "How did this case get to the appellate court?"

This second question, with its repetitive poetic quality, is also a quintessential example of nonuptake. Uptake in a question-and-answer sequence, as Collins (this volume) notes, is measured by whether subsequent questions incorporate any referential material from an immediately preceding answer.

Repeating the original question is perhaps the "purest" form of nonuptake possible, as it contains no referential acknowledgment of any intervening answer. (Of course, in pragmatic terms, the repeat itself indexes an unsuccessful answer, and this structural pragmatic message is often reinforced through pitch and intonation.) From studies comparing high- and low-status elementary classrooms (Anyon 1981; Collins: this volume; Leacock 1976), we know that "lower-ability" classes, and working-class or other nonelite classrooms, are more likely to involve more authoritarian control on the part of teachers, as characterized by, for example, more frequent interruption of children's narratives, more frequent correction of perceived mispronunciations, more emphasis on the text as something to be pronounced rather than read for meaning, and finally, less uptake. Uptake could be viewed as one measure of control, for even in very structured exchanges, a student whose answer is acknowledged in subsequent questions is having some impact upon the direction of the conversation. However, a comparison of these studies with the law school example demonstrates that the significance of uptake is highly contextual, so that a straightforward reading of linguistic structure as an index of relative social power is highly problematic. Understanding the social significance of discourse structure, predictably, requires contextual analysis.

If we examine carefully several excerpts from law school classroom exchanges, we see that, as in the lower-status classroom, the discourse is predominantly characterized by nonuptake. (An asterisk indicates added emphasis; parentheses indicate a barely audible utterance.)

Example 1
> P: . . . on March 1. (pause) B promises to pay Seller ten thousand dollars for Whiteacre March 1. March 1 comes and goes. . . . B now sues Seller for breach . . . of Seller's promise to deliver the title to Whiteacre on March 1. Seller defends saying it is true that I did not deliver title on March 1 but B did not tender ten thousand dollars on March 1. That is a good defense. Would you explain how the law goes about saying that it is a good defense . . . Ms. A.?
> A: Well the . . . it's a concurrent condition that in order for the Seller to tender title Buyer must pay ten thousand dollars and that the Buyer pay ten thousand dollars—
> P: Well all right now you y—I just wanted to talk about this one (thought) all right for the moment . . . it's correct, what you said, but let's just talk about this—this is—B is entitled—now I asked you in this assignment to describe e-exactly how—what the condition is that will make this defense good. (−)
> A: That Seller could say—he could have transferred title to a Buyer (for) ten thousand dollars.

P: Well now there are two parts (inaudible) It doesn't make any sense to talk about one half of it without the other half—what are the two parts? (−)

A: Seller would have to tender title if Buyer tendered the ten thousan—

P: Well, n—name the two parts, would you, because people have a lot of trouble with this. (−)
(pause)
When you describe a condition what two things do you have to talk about? (−)

A: Oh(*) (that one) the duty it's conditioned on and the event constituting the condition

P: Okay. The duty and an event. And the event is the condition. You can describe that event without talking about the duty but there's no sense in doing it because uh—it's going to sound (inaudible) (it's not going to mean anything). All right. Now the duty in this case that we're talking about is . . . (pause) in this case . . . (+)

A: Um—the Buyer's duty to tender the ten thousand—

P: No.
(−)

***

Although there was one instance of uptake in this excerpt, the exchange is overwhelmingly characterized by nonuptake, and thus resembles more closely discourse in the lower- , rather than higher-status classrooms of the elementary school studies. And this particular exchange is taken from a Socratic dialogue with a "virtuoso" student who was able to sustain the dialogue with only minimal interruption for the entire class hour. Although there was some variation between professors in this study, professorial interruption was far more common than uninterrupted student speech in all classes, and professors maintained tight control of the discourse. Indeed, professors who differed widely in philosophy and style of teaching still controlled classroom discourse to the point that students were never permitted a verbal exchange among themselves that was not mediated by the professor (i.e., "Mr. X, what is your response to Ms. Y?"); similarly, nonuptake predominated.

If we stopped our analysis at this point, we might conclude that the uptake structure of law school classroom exchanges resembled that of low-ranked reading classes rather than high-ranked ones. However, a more detailed look at the pragmatic structure reveals some key differences. Although law school exchanges are largely characterized by nonuptake, there is uptake, and it does not come at random points. In Example 1 uptake occurs when the student produces a pair of technical terms. Nonuptake occurs when the student attempts to produce a narrative that tells us a "story" with the two actors, Buyer and Seller. We saw a similar pattern in the exchange centered on *Sullivan v.*

O'Connor, in which the professor interrupted an attempt to give us the "story" of the woman and the surgeon. Let us examine that exchange, part of which is repeated as Example 2, from the point of view of uptake structure.

Example 2

P: What errors were alleged in the appeal of Sullivan v. O'Connor . . . Ms. A? (pause) What errors were alleged in the appeal of Sullivan v. O'Connor?

A: Um the defense claimed that um the judge failed in allowing the jury to take into account for damages anything but a claim for out-of-pocket expenses.

P: Well that's a rather general statement. How did this get to the appellate court? (−)

A: Well the um the the patient was a woman who wanted a—

P: How did this case get to the appellate court? (−)

A: The defendant disagreed with the way the damages were awarded in the trial court.

P: How did this case get to the appellate court? The Supreme Court once a— I think this is true—they asked some guy who'd never argued a case before the Supreme Court before—they said to him—he was a Southerner—and they said to him—ah—(*)Counsel how did you get here? (Laughter) Well, he said, I came on the Chesapeake and Ohio River (*)(Louder laughter). How did this case get to the supreme judicial court? (−)

A: It was appealed.

P: It was appealed, you say. Did you find that word anywhere except in my problem? (+)

***

Example 2 gives us an uptake structure quite similar to that in the first example, with only one uptake for every four exchanges between professor and student. As in the first case, the professor employs nonuptake in stopping the student from telling the story of the case. And as with the first example, uptake occurs when the student produces a technical term.

What model of text, then, is being conveyed by this tightly controlled turn-taking? In both of the examples above, uptake, pointing to (or indexing) a successful response, occurs when students produce technical terms. And these are not just any technical terms. In Example 2, the professor sought a procedural term, *appealed*, that told the history of the case as it is presented in the opinion the students read. As noted previously, this procedural history frames and delimits the current text's authority; the words in the opinion only have force because the case was formulated and reformulated in a particular way through successive procedural stages, and they only have the force that is prescribed by the procedural stance of the opinion. Thus the technical term that the professor is training the student to notice here links the text to previous linguistic contexts, to courts and opinions that were part of the procedural development. The uptake structure of classroom discourse is pragmatic in the sense that it conveys meaning by virtue of its contextual grounding, referring both to the written text assignment and to the unfolding linguistic context provided by the teacher-student exchange. This contrasts, for example, with a lecture, which can be characterized as conveying much more heavily semantic meaning, independent of any particular context or set of listeners. And if the uptake sequence is a pragmatic structuring of classroom discourse, the technical term it highlights in Example 2 is a key to the pragmatic structure of the written text—a structure by which the legal opinion takes on authority in the current context, a contextual connection that provides social power. In other words, by virtue of its having reached this court in a certain procedural stance, this court is empowered to decide on some things but not on others, and the words of the court only have effect within that framework. Thus the pragmatic structure of law classroom discourse is used to train students to read legal texts in their pragmatic structures.

Example 1 provides a slightly more complex case. Here, the technical words are not procedural; rather, they are doctrinal categories, derived from past cases, that structure the authority of the text in a different way. These doctrinal categories provide conceptual presuppositions that allow the text to speak authoritatively, for example, regarding the question, "On what authority can the judge say this is a good defense?" The judge's authority in this case rests on proper deployment of the doctrinal categories, which themselves derive their authority from their genealogy through previous cases perceived to be in some way similar. Once again, the technical vocabulary involves reference to previous legal language—to cases distilled into doctrinal categories. Again, there is a pragmatic reflexivity—language referring to previous linguistic contexts to achieve authority. And again, this aspect of the text is conveyed to students using a similar reflexivity—the language of the classroom referring to the language of the case, which provides the context which gives it meaning.

Toulmin has used the term "warrant" to talk about the background information that allows us to make assertions (Toulmin 1958: 98–99). In this case, the professor is focusing students' attention on the pragmatic warrants that give legal texts their authority—and is doing so using the pragmatic structure, rather than the semantic content, of classroom speech. This isometry may account for the pervasive sense that the Socratic method is "better suited" to law school teaching than lecturing, despite studies that show no appreciable difference in results (see Kimball and Farmer 1979; Lorenson 1968; see also Teich 1986).

The approach to text inculcated in the law school classroom, then, differs considerably from that conveyed in lower-status reading classes. There non-uptake blocks students from narrative control so that the text remains language to be repeated, or pronounced. In the law school classroom negative uptake is part of a structure designed to break down a straight semantic reading of texts, as it undermines the norms of normal conversation. Instead of approaching texts as semantic "stories," and classroom exchange as a chance to tell these stories, students are trained to focus upon texts as socially created and authoritative (as indexed through the successful deployment of technical terms), at the same time as they must themselves successfully deploy technical terms in a disciplined discourse.

CONCLUSION

To understand the intersection of language and power in law school education, then, it is not enough to look broadly at the "kind" of language used. Instead, examination of linguistic detail and textual structure as they contribute to new entextualizations is necessary if we are to understand the way in which language shapes students' educational experience. Here we have seen how a highly regimented discourse style contributes to an authoritative approach to language, as law students are trained to read and speak about the texts that they will call upon for authority in the practice of their profession.[12]

What does it mean to talk about cases as "recontextualized" in classroom discourse or subsequent case law? Although occasionally stretches of discourse are repeated—read by professor or student, or quoted in subsequent cases— more often recontextualization does not involve iconic repetition of the language of the case. Bauman and Briggs note that "a rigorously entextualized stretch of discourse may be reported, or translated, or rendered in a frame other than performance" (1990: 74); we seem to be dealing here with just such an instance. Professors and students, and authors of subsequent cases, are not performing the opinions upon which they draw. Authors of subsequent opinions recontextualize precedential cases as pragmatic frames providing a distinctive legal context for the decision at hand; that context is a semiotic creation constituted through the application of language from prior cases to the case at issue (interpreted always through the pragmatic warrants inherent in the status of the issuing court and the framework of procedural history). Classroom discourse

12. I do not imply here any transparent continuity between the discourse style of the classroom and the discourses used in legal practice of various sorts. Rather, the classroom discourse is a semiotic disciplining to a new form of *reading* and *discursively organizing* texts, and this reading can of course be multiply recontextualized in the various speech settings of legal practice.

recontextualizes the texts of legal opinions as pragmatic structure, and that structure connects each opinion with (minimally) two kinds of previous linguistic contexts: the "doctrinal" setting distilled through a peculiarly legal reading of prior precedential cases, and the "procedural history" constituted by a semiotic structuring of previous enactments of this particular conflict in "lower" courts. The individual case as pragmatic structure is recontextualized in law school classes through a discourse form that itself conveys an approach to text through pragmatic structure rather than semantic content.

The contrast between this kind of recontextualization of text and that found in the elementary school classrooms of Collins' study (this volume) provides some suggestive insights for further exploration of the relation between recontextualization and social power. Together, our studies describe three different approaches to text: the "low-ability" reading class focus on the text as something to be pronounced correctly; the "high-ability" reading class emphasis on the text as a carrier of semantic meaning; and the law school class orientation to text as a creative index of its contexts of production and use. An interesting commonality emerges between the lowest and highest status classrooms; in both, there is a break with the "liberal" notion that semantic "meaning" is what a text is all about. Instead, the meaning of texts lies in the pragmatic orientation which teachers impart through regimenting classroom speech. At the same time, there is an obvious difference between highest and lowest status classrooms. The "low-ability" students are taught to submit to the text—pronounce it and nothing else, whereas the law student's pragmatic discipline is aimed at mastery and manipulation.[13] In exploring contrasts among such differing social settings and approaches to text, we can begin to see the relation between social power and the regimentation of text, enacted in the critical process of socialization to text through the decentering and recentering of written texts in classroom speech.

13. It is of course possible that the same approach to text could be conveyed using other means; the point is not that there is a determinate connection between semiotic form and meta-discursive message. Indeed, in controlled experiments in which first-year law school classes were divided into groups, some taught Socratically and others not, students performed at generally comparable levels on exams (see Kimball and Farmer 1979; Lorenson 1968). From this vantage the mystery is actually why Socratic teaching has endured, given its multiple and vociferous critics. Although a standard response is that the method is more "efficient" for large classes, studies have shown comparable results with lecture methods that similarly require only one professor for large groups of students. The suggestion of this article is that the discourse form is particularly semiotically congenial because it mirrors a process of recontextualization that lies at the heart of legal "readings."

REFERENCES

Anyon, Jean
1981   Social class and school knowledge. *Curriculum Inquiry* 11: 3–42.

Bauman, Richard
1987   The decentering of discourse. Paper presented at the 86th Annual Meeting of the American Anthropological Association, Chicago.

Bauman, Richard, and Charles Briggs
1990   Poetics and performance as critical perspectives on language and social life. *Annual Review of Anthropology* 19: 59–88.

Black, Henry Campbell
1983   *Black's Law Dictionary*. St. Paul, MN: West Publishing Co.

Bourdieu, Pierre, and Jean-Claude Passeron
1977   *Reproduction in Education, Society and Culture*. London: Sage Publications.

Brigham, John
1978   *Constitutional Language*. Westport, CT: Greenwood Press.

Cicourel, Aaron
1981   Language and medicine. In *Language in the USA*, C. Ferguson and S. Heath (eds.), 407–29. Cambridge: Cambridge University Press.

Cole, John O.
1984   The Socratic method in legal education: Moral discourse and accommodation. *Mercer Law Review* 35: 867–90.

Condlin, Robert J.
1981   Socrates' new clothes: Substituting persuasion for learning in clinical practice instruction. *University of Maryland Law Review* 40: 223–83.

Cook-Gumperz, Jenny
1986   Literacy and schooling: An unchanging equation? In *The Social Construction of Literacy*, J. Cook-Gumperz (ed.), 16–44. Cambridge: Cambridge University Press.

Cramton, Roger C.
1982   The current state of the law curriculum. *Journal of Legal Education* 32: 321–35.

Delaney, John
1982   *How to Do Your Best on Law School Exams*. Bogota, NJ: Delaney Publications.

Gee, James
1985   The narrativization of experience in the oral style. *Journal of Education* 167: 9–35.

Heffernan, William C.
1980   Not Socrates, but Protagoras: The Sophistic basis of legal education. *Buffalo Law Review* 29: 399–423.

248   Elizabeth Mertz

Kimball, Edward, and Larry Farmer
   1979   Comparative results of teaching evidence three ways. *Journal of Legal Education* 30: 196–212.

Kennedy, Duncan
   1983   *Legal Education and the Reproduction of Hierarchy.* Cambridge, MA: AFAR.

Langdell, Christopher C.
   1871   *Selection of Cases on the Law of Contracts.* Boston: Little, Brown.

Leacock, Eleanor
   1976   Education in Africa: Myths of "modernization." In *The Anthropological Study of Education*, C. J. Calhoun and F. A. J. Ianni (eds.), 239–50. The Hague: Mouton.

Levi, Edward H.
   1949   *An Introduction to Legal Reasoning.* Chicago: University of Chicago Press.

Lorenson, Willard D.
   1968   Concentrating on a single jurisdiction to teach criminal law—an experiment. *Journal of Legal Education* 20: 361–65.

Mertz, Elizabeth
   1987   "Realist" models of judicial decision-making. *Working Papers and Proceedings of the Center for Psychosocial Studies*, no. 15, Chicago.
   1988   The uses of history: Language, ideology and law in the United States and South Africa. *Law & Society Review* 22: 661–85.
   1990   Consensus and dissent in U.S. legal opinions: Narrative structure and social voices. *Anthropological Linguistics* 30: 369–94.

O'Barr, William M.
   1981   The language of the law. In *Language in the USA*, C. Ferguson and S. Heath (eds.), 386–406. Cambridge: Cambridge University Press.

Parmentier, Richard J.
   1993   The political function of reported speech. In *Reflexive Language: Reported speech and metapragmatics*, J. A. Lucy (ed.), 261–86. Cambridge: Cambridge University Press.

Silverstein, Michael
   1981   Metaforces of power in traditional oratory. Unpublished manuscript.

Stevens, Robert
   1983   *Law School: Legal Education in America from the 1850s to the 1980s.* Chapel Hill: University of North Carolina Press.

Strong, Frank R.
   1973   The pedagogic training of a law faculty. *Journal of Legal Education* 25: 226–38.

Teich, Paul F.
   1986   Research on American law teaching: Is there a case against the case system? *Journal of Legal Education* 36: 167–88.

Toulmin, Stephen
  1958   *The Uses of Argument.* Cambridge: Cambridge University Press.

Turow, Scott
  1977   *One L.* Harmondsworth, UK: Penguin Books.

Turner, Victor
  1974   *Dramas, Fields and Metaphors.* Ithaca: Cornell University Press.

Van Gennep, Arnold
  1960   *The Rites of Passage.* Chicago: University of Chicago Press.

White, James Boyd
  1973   *The Legal Imagination.* Chicago: University of Chicago Press.
  1984   *When Words Lose Their Meaning.* Chicago: University of Chicago Press.
  1986a   Doctrine in a vaccuum. *Journal of Legal Education* 36: 155–66.
  1986b   *Heracles' Bow.* Chicago: University of Chicago Press.

Strategic Entextualization

9 The Construction of an LD Student:

A Case Study in the Politics of Representation

Hugh Mehan

CONSTRUCTING SOCIAL FACTS: CLARITY FROM AMBIGUITY

Proponents of various positions in conflicts waged in and through discourse attempt to capture or dominate modes of representation. They do so in a variety of ways, including inviting or persuading others to join their side, or silencing opponents by attacking their positions. If they are successful, a hierarchy is formed in which one mode of representing the world (its objects, events, people, etc.) gains primacy over others, transforming modes of representation from an array on a horizontal plane to a ranking on a vertical plane. This competition over the meaning of ambiguous events, people, and objects in the world has been called the "politics of representation" (Holquist 1983; Shapiro 1987; Mehan and Wills 1988). The concerns in this chapter are continuous with those in the rest of this volume because, as we shall see, one kind of politically contested representation is the lexical label, and lexical labels are "texts," minimal ones, to be sure, but texts all the same. Indeed, the process of lexical labeling is itself an entextualization process. Complex, contextually nuanced discussions get summed up in (and, hence, are entextualized through) a single word.

There are many ways in which a certain group of people can be designated by lexical formulation: "guest workers," "potential citizens," "illegal

A version of this chapter appeared as "Beneath the Skin and Between the Ears: A Case Study in the Politics of Representation," Chapter 9, in Seth Chaiklin and Jean Lave (eds.), *Understanding Practice: Perspectives on Activity and Context*, pp. 241–68, Cambridge: Cambridge University Press, 1993.

A number of conventions have been used in the transcripts reproduced in this paper:
Key to Transcript Conventions:
1. Speakers: CLT = Classroom Teacher; Prn = Principal; SET = Special Education Teacher; Psy = School Psychologist; Mot = Mother.
2. Syntactic organization markers: ( ) = unclear talk; **every**body = emphasis; (hhh) = laughter; rea:ad = stretched talk; // = overlapping utterances; (3) = pause measured in seconds.

aliens," "undocumented workers." Each formulation or way of representing this group of people does not simply reflect unique or exhaustive characteristics given in advance. Each mode of representation relationally defines the person making the representation and constitutes the group of people, and each does so in a distinctive way. To be a *guest worker* is to be an invited person, someone who is welcome and in a positive relationship to the employer; to be a *guest worker* is to be someone who is contributing to the economy, productively, by laboring. The formulation *potential citizen* invokes similar positive connotations. It does so within the realm of citizenship and politics, however, rather than in the realm of market economics, as the guest worker formulation does. The potential citizen is not yet a complete citizen, but is on the path of full participation in the society. The *illegal alien* designation invokes many opposite ways of thinking. *Illegal* is simple and clear: a person outside of society, an idea reinforced by the *alien* designation—foreign, repulsive, threatening. Finally, representing this group as *undocumented workers* implies that it comprises people who contribute economically, but do so in an extralegal capacity.

So, too, a recent surrogate-mother case illustrates that a newborn baby is subject to multiple and competing interpretations. The case turned on the issue of whether the baby's mother had the right to retain her after she had agreed to give her over to the (artificially inseminating) father. Those who favored her right to do so resisted the use of the term *surrogate mother* in favor of a designation *natural mother*. They drew the analogy between the surrogate-mother case and disputes over adoption or custody after divorce. This language portrays custody as an issue involving interpersonal relationships and commitments involving parents and children. Those who favored the (artificially inseminating) father's claim to the child (and therefore opposed the "surrogate" mother) invoked language associated with contracts and legally binding arguments. This mode of representation led one commentator to say it made the Baby M case "bear an uncanny resemblance to the all-sales-final style of a used-car lot" (Pollitt 1987: 667).

A similar competition over the meaning of ambiguous events in the world is played out in schools every day when educators try to decide whether a certain child is "normal" or "deviant," belongs in a "regular educational program" or in a "special education program." Deciding whether students are "normal" or "special" is a practical project that occurs routinely in U.S. schools. Although this activity is as old as schools themselves, in response to recently enacted state and federal legislation, this classification and sorting activity has become more formalized. There are now procedures mandated by law, especially PL 94–142, the "Education for All Handicapped Students Act," concerning the referral of students to special education. This law, established to provide an equitable education to handicapped youngsters in the least restrictive environment possible, imposes time limits for the assessment of students and specifies the participants involved in decision making. For example, final placement decisions are to be made by a committee composed of the student's teacher, a school psychologist, a representative from the district office, the child's parents, and, in some cases, a medical official.

In general, I am interested in how the clarity of labeled social facts such as "intelligence," "deviance," "health," or "illness" are produced from the ambiguity of everyday life. In the work described in this chapter, I concentrate on a particular instantiation of that general interest—the production of student identities. In short, I am asking: How are student identities produced? How does a student become a "special education" or a "regular education" student?

The construction of handicapped students operates on at least two semiotic planes simultaneously. One is the plane on which the categories such as "educational handicap" and "learning disability" (LD) are established in the first place. Relevant here is the social history of the category of disability, its relationship to previously important notions like mental retardation and feeblemindedness, the continuing importance of medical discourse, the semiotic processes involved in the establishment of the law, including the role of politicians and various pressure groups, such as the Council of Exceptional Children. In this social history, learning disabilities have been understood to be intrinsic to the individual and are presumed to be caused by central nervous system dysfunction or a hereditary condition. Coles (1987) traces this thinking to diagnoses conducted by a Glasgow medical officer in 1907. Difficulties in learning to read were diagnosed as "congenital word-blindness" by Hinshelwood, who concluded that the root of this "disease" lay in children's brains because he had observed that dysfunctional reading symptoms found in adults with brain lesions were analogous to those of certain children with reading problems. This thinking started what has become a medicalization of children's difficulties in schools. In this medical model, the child is the focus of diagnosis; he or she has a pathology which is subject to treatment. The medical model is explicit in the Education for All Handicapped Students law which has specific provisions for correcting the physical state of students. Moreover, the underlying assumptions of the medical model have been extended beyond the physical condition of students to the mental condition of children considered for special education. Attributes such as intelligence, aptitude, potential, or mental ability are considered to be internal states or traits of students which are subject to diagnosis and treatment.

The indexical plane of practical application of such attributes is the second semiotic plane on which LD students are constructed. On the indexical plane, the historically constructed and legally prescribed categories are articulated with potential instances in actual educational practice at the school site. Relevant in these situations are the decisions that educators make about children in the context of the legal and fiscal constraints imposed by the law, competing programs, and other practical matters at the local level. Ideally, consideration should be given to both planes and the linkage between them. However, I will not say more about the historical plane in this chapter because of space limitations.

Language plays a powerful, constitutive role in transforming the ambiguity of student behavior to the clarity of "regular" or "special" student on both the historical and the indexical plane. Multifocal discourse generated in face-to-face encounters becomes devoiced and decentered and emerges in the form of frozen, artifactualized texts such as student records as the decision making process unfolds from classroom to final committee meeting.

A Social Fact of the School System: Handicapped Students

In order to understand the process by which students are considered for placement in one of a number of special education programs or are retained in regular classrooms, we followed the progress of students' cases through the special education referral process mandated by PL 94-142. During the 1978–79 school year in which my colleagues and I (Mehan et al. 1986) observed this sorting and classification process in a midsize school district in Southern California, 141 students out of a total school population of 2,700 students were referred for "special education"; 53 of these cases were considered by the committee with responsibility for final placement decisions. The disposition of these cases is shown in Table 9.1.

Most (36) of the students considered by the Eligibility and Placement (E&P) Committees were placed into the Learning Disabilities (LD) group, and some (7) were placed in the Educationally Handicapped (EH) program.[1]

1. The LD group is a "pullout" educational program in which students spend a part of their school day in their regular classroom and the other part of the day in a special education classroom. The EH program is a special education program in which students spend all of their school day in a special education classroom.

Table 9.1: The Disposition of Fifty-three Cases Considered by Placement Committees

Placement	Number
Educationally Handicapped (EH)	7
Learning Disabled (LD)	36
Severe Language Handicapped (SLH)	3
Multiple Handicap	2
Speech Therapy	3
Off-Campus Placement ("Private Schooling")	0
Counseling	0
Reading	0
Adaptive Physical Education	0
Bilingual Education	0
No Placement (Returned to Classroom)	1
Placement Process Interrupted	1
Total	53

Notably, no students were placed in special programs outside the district, and only one student considered by the committee was retained in his regular classroom.

These figures, which represent the aggregate number of students placed into educational programs, would conventionally be accepted as an example of a "social fact." Furthermore, each number in the table represents a point in a student's educational career, that is, his or her identity as a special education or a regular education student. Hence, we have two senses of social structure here: one represented as aggregate data, the other represented as social identities.

Given this statistical distribution, I am asking, What practices produce this array, these careers, these identities? In answering this question, I propose to show that these "social facts" of the school system are constructed in the practical work of educators in their person-to-person and person-to-text interaction. In the analysis that follows, I explore a way of showing how the routine practices of educators as they carry out their daily work construct a "handicapped" student by tracing one student's case through the special education referral process. The major steps in this process are "referral," "educational testing," and "placement."

In order to uncover the discursive and organizational arrangements which provide for an array such as the one in Table 9.1, my colleagues and I employed an interconnected set of research methods. In addition to observing in classrooms, teachers' lounges, testing rooms, and committee meetings, we interviewed educators and parents, reviewed students' records, and videotaped events which were crucial in the construction of students' identities. Students' records provided such baseline data as the age, sex, and grade of students, the official reason for referral, the name of the person making the referral, the date of referral, psychological assessment information, and final disposition of cases. Information available from school records was checked against information that became available to us through observation, videotaping, informal discussions, and more formal interviews with educators in the district.

Observations in classrooms and analysis of lessons videotaped there gave us insight into the reasons teachers referred students and the relationship between teachers' accounts of student behavior and students' classroom behavior. Videotape gathered from educational testing sessions and Eligibility and Placement Committee meetings served as the behavioral record we examined for the educators' sorting and classifying practices. It also served as a multipurpose document for interviews with participants in these key events in the referral process.

Constructing an LD Student: The Case of Shane

We discovered, upon the analysis of the materials gathered by these diverse research techniques, that the student classification process in the Coast District had a number of components. The school's work of sorting students most frequently started in the classroom, continued through psychological assessment, and culminated in evaluation by the E&P committee. Thus, as Collins (1981) suggested, a "social structure"—the aggregate number of students in various educational programs or their identity as special or regular students—is generated in a sequence of organizationally predictable interactional events (classroom, testing session, meetings).

An important feature of this process is the transposition of entextualizations from context to context. Discourse from one setting in the sequence of events in the referral process generates the given text used for discussion in the next session. So, for example, after a teacher and students interact in the classroom (discourse), the teacher fills out a form (a text-artifact). Its text is introduced into the discourse of the School Appraisal Team (SAT) meeting. From the discourse of the participants in that meeting, another artifact, another piece of text, is generated, this time a "summary of recommendation," which instructs the school psychologist to begin educational testing. The administration of the educational test transpires as face-to-face interaction between tester and student. Based on that discourse, the tester writes a report. That text-artifact is sent to the placement committee, where it becomes part of the file, which, representing the child, becomes the basis of the final placement decision. Such artifactual texts, generated from a particular event in the sequential process (e.g., a testing encounter), become the basis of the discursive interaction in the next step in the sequence (e.g., a placement committee meeting). These texts are decentered and indeed de-"voiced" in that as they move through the system, they become institutionally isolated from the interactional practices that generated them in the preceding events.

STEP 1: CALLING FOR HELP

The process by which a child becomes "educationally handicapped" usually begins in the classroom when, for whatever reasons, a teacher refers a child by completing a referral form. Completing the form and making the referral do not automatically make the child LD or educationally handicapped; but unless that bureaucratic step is taken, the child cannot be eligible to achieve that status.

On October 10, approximately one month after the start of school, the fourth-grade teacher at the Desert Vista School referred "Shane" for possible placement in special education for his "low academic performance" and his "difficulty in applying himself to his daily class work." [2]

In order to gain more insight into the teachers' reasons for referring students than was available on official referral forms, we videotaped classroom lessons and viewed them with the teachers. Following guidelines concerning these "viewing sessions" that proved productive in the past (e.g., Cicourel et al. 1974; Erickson and Shultz 1982), teachers were asked to "stop the tape any time they found anything interesting happening." While watching a videotape of a math lesson in which Shane and others were participating, the teacher stopped the tape just after Shane said, "No way" while assembling a pattern with geometric shapes called tangrams:

130 **Teacher:** Yeah, he, he starts out like that on a lot of things. It's like, "I can't do it." He's just glancing at it. . . . He's very apprehensive about approaching anything. But once he gets into it, and finishes something he's just so pleased with himself. And I'll say, "Hey I thought you said, 'No way.' Well?"

Later in the interview, the teacher stopped the tape again and commented:

406 **Teacher:** I mentioned before, yeah, that whenever he's given some new task to do it's always like, too hard, "No way I can do

2. Source: Referral form in student's school record.

it," until we, "Oh, come on, you just get into it and try it!" When he finishes, I mean it's like fantastic, you know that he did it.[3]

These comments reinforced the teacher's representation of the child as one who has trouble applying himself to his school work. It is interesting to note, however, that all the other students in the lesson expressed similar consternation with the difficulty of the task. Nevertheless, the teacher did not treat the comments by the other students as instances of the concern over work difficulty; she did, however, treat the comments by Shane as exemplifying this reason for referring him. This gap between referral reason and students' behavior was a general pattern in our study (Mehan et al. 1986: 69–97), which implicates the problematic nature of the behavioral record beneath special education referrals and the important role that teachers' expectations and conceptions play in forming judgments about students' behavior.

STEP 2: REFINING THE DEFINITION

The referral was forwarded to the next step in the referral system, the School Appraisal Team (SAT), a committee composed of educators at the Desert Vista School. At its first meeting in October, the school psychologist was instructed to assess Shane. For a variety of practical reasons which plague bureaucratic processes such as this referral system, including a large backlog of cases, and difficulty in obtaining parental permission and necessary records from another school district, the recommended assessment did not take place until December and January—two months after the original referral.

The school psychologist administered a battery of tests to Shane on December 6, including an informal assessment called the "Three Wishes," the Goodenough Draw-A-Man Test, and portions of the WISC-R. The SAT met again on January 4. After hearing the results of the first round of assessment, the committee recommended that the psychologist complete testing. After the Christmas break, the school psychologist completed the WISC-R and administered the CAT and the Bender Gestalt. On February 2, the committee heard the full report of testing. The psychologist reported that Shane had a verbal I.Q. of 115. He was reading at a fourth-grade level. His arithmetic and spelling tested at 3.0 and 3.5, which "put him below grade level." His test age on the Bender Gestalt was 7.0–7.5, while his actual age (at the time) was 9.0, which put him "considerably below his age level." Based on this assessment, the SAT recommended that Shane be considered by the Eligibility and Placement

3. Source: Interview of teacher conducted by Alma Hertweck.

(E&P) Committee for possible placement into a program for the Learning Disabled.[4]

We see illustrated here the process by which general calls for help from a classroom teacher become refined and specified in official language. The teacher had said Shane "has difficulty in applying himself to classwork." That vague appeal is now transformed into a technical assessment: Shane's academic skill is expressed in numerical terms (I.Q. of 115, test age of 7.5). He is compared to a normative standard: he is "behind grade level." No longer is he a child "who needs help"; now he is possibly a "learning disabled child."

The consequence of this refining is fundamental to the way in which the diagnostic process creates handicapped students and handicapped students' careers. Students' identities are sharpened as they move from regular education classrooms to testing rooms and finally to meeting rooms.

Step 3: Resolving Competing Representations of the Student

When the E&P Committee met on February 16 to discuss Shane's case, the following dialog took place:

EDM #33

92	**Psy:**	does the uh, committee agree that the, uh learning disability placement is one that might benefit him?
93	**Prn:**	I think we agree.
94	**Psy:**	We're not considering then a special day class at all for him?
95	**SET:**	I wouldn't at this point //
96	**Many:**	=No.

The committee decided to place Shane into an LD group, a pullout educational program in which students spend a part of the school day in the regular classroom and the other part of the day in a special program. The "special day class" indexed by the psychologist (line 94) is the EH program in which students spend the entire school day in a special classroom.

When we observed these E&P meetings, we were struck by an interesting feature about the interaction among the committee members. Although committee members came to meetings with a variety of opinions about the appropriate placement of students, by meeting's end one view of the children,

---

4. Source: School Psychologist's Assessment Summary. This report was also read to the E&P Committee on February 16 (see below for my discussion of this report in the context of the E&P meeting).

that one recommended by the district, prevailed. Furthermore, this agreement was reached without debate or disagreement. For example, before the E&P meeting reviewed in this chapter, the classroom teacher, reflecting on the changes in the student she referred in October, was no longer convinced that Shane needed special education. The mother, worried about the stigmatizing effect of even a mild placement such as the LD group, didn't want any special education for her child. Although definite and vocal before the meeting, they were silent during the meeting. In trying to understand how committee members (including parents) lost their voices while routinely coming to agreement with the school's recommendation, we turned our attention to the discourse of the placement committee meetings prior to the occurrence of the "decision to place" students.

During the course of the meeting, four reports were made to the committee, one by the school psychologist, one by the child's teacher, one by the school nurse, and one by the child's mother. These reports varied along three dimensions: (1) the manner in which they presented information, (2) the manner in which they grounded their assertions, and (3) the manner in which they represented the child. By arraying the reports along these dimensions, we find three registers being spoken in the meeting, three ways of denoting: a psychological register, a sociological register, and a historical register. Competing versions of the child are presented in these registers, but one, the version of the child presented in the psychological language, prevails.

Mode of Presentation

The information that the committee obtained from the classroom teacher and the mother appeared in a form different from the information made available by the school psychologist. The information that the psychologist had about the student was presented to the committee in a single uninterrupted report, whereas information was dialogically elicited from both the classroom teacher and the mother. Here is the psychologist's opening statement to the committee:

1 **Psy:** Um. What we're going to do is, I'm going to have a brief, an overview of the testing because the rest of, of the, the committee has not, uh, has not an, uh, been aware of that yet. And uh, then each of us will share whatever, whatever we feel we need to share.
2 **Prn:** Right.
3 **Psy:** And then we will make a decision on what we feel is a good, oh (3) placement (2) for an, Shane.

The school psychologist then provided the committee members with the information she had about the student:

3   **Psy:** Shane is ah nine years old, and he's in fourth grade. Uh, he, uh, was referred because of low academic performance and he has difficulty applying himself to his daily class work. Um, Shane attended the Montessori School in kindergarten and first grade, and then he entered Carlsberg–bad in, um, September of 1976 and, uh, entered our district in, uh, '78. He seems to have very good peer relationships but, uh, the teachers, uh, continually say that he has difficulty with handwriting. 'Kay. He enjoys music and sports. I gave him a complete battery and, um, I found that, uh, he had a verbal I.Q. of 115, performance of 111, and a full scale of 115, so he's a bright child. Uh, he had very high scores in, uh, information which is his long-term memory. Ah, vocabulary, was, ah, also, ah, considerably over average, good detail awareness and his, um, picture arrangement scores, he had a seventeen which is very high //

4   **SET:**   =Mmmm //

5   **Psy:** =very superior rating, so he, his visual sequencing seems to be good and also he has a good grasp of anticipation and awareness of social situations. Um, he (5) (she is scanning her notes) scored in reading at 4.1, spelling 3.5, and arithmetic 3.0, which gave him a standard score of 100 in, uh, reading, 95 in spelling, and 90 in arithmetic. When compared with his [overall] score, it does put him somewhat ah below his, you know, his capabilities. I gave him the Bender Gestalt (clears throat) and he had six errors. And his test age was 7–0 to 7–5 and his actual age is nine, so it, uh, he was considerably beneath his, uh, his uh, age level. (2) His—I gave him the, uh VADS and his, um (5 or 6) (looking through notes) both the oral-aural and the visual-written modes of communication were high but the visual oral and the oral written are lo::ow, so he, uh, cannot switch channels. His expressive vocabulary was in the superior range (6). Uh, visual perception falls above age level, so he's fine in that area (6). And fine motor skills appear to be slightly lower than, uh, average, (voice trails off slightly), I saw them. (3) He read words very quickly when he was doing the academics but I didn't see any reversals in his written work. Uh, I gave him several projective tests and, um, the things that I picked up there is [*sic*] that, um he [does] possibly have some fears and anxieties, uh, (5). So I had felt ah, that per-

haps he might, uh, uh, benefit, um, (3) from special help. He also was tested, um, in 1976 and at that time he was given the WISC-R and his I.Q. was slightly lower, full scale of a 93 (3 or 4). His, um, summary of that evaluation, uh, was, uh, he was given the ITPA and he had high auditory reception, auditory association, auditory memory. (2) So his auditory skills are good. (3) He was given another psychol–psychological evaluation in 1977. He was given the Leiter and he had an I.Q. of 96 (6). And, um (3 or 4) they concluded that he had a poor mediate recall (2) but they felt that was due to an emotional overlay and they felt that some emotional conflicts were, uh, interfering with his ability to concentrate.

At the end of this presentation, the psychologist asked the student's teacher to provide information:

5   **Psy:** Kate, would you like to share with u:s?
6   **CLT:** What, the problems I see ( ) Um . . .
7   **Psy:** Yes.
8   **CLT:** Um. Probably basically the fine motor types of things are difficult for him. He's got a very creative mi:ind and expresses himself well ( ) orally and verbally and he's pretty alert to what's going on. (2) Maybe a little bit [too] much, watching **every**thing that's (hh) going (hh) on, and finds it hard to stick to one task. And [mostly] I've been noticing that it's just his writing and things that he has a, a block with. And he can rea:ad and comprehend some things when I talk to him, [but] doing independent type work is hard for him.
9   **Prn:** Mhmmm, putting it down on paper . . .
10 **CLT:** Yeah::, and sticking to a task //
11 **Prn:**   =mmhmmm //
12 **CLT:**   =and getting it done, without being distracted by (hehhehheh)
13 **SET:** How does he relate with what the other kids do?
14 **CLT:** Uh, very well. He's got a lot of frie:ends, and, uh, especially, even out on the playground he's, um (3), wants to get in on the games, get on things and is well accepted. So:o, I don't see too many problems there.

In this sequence, we have the classroom teacher beginning to present some of the characteristics of the student (8), being interrupted by the principal (9), before the special education teacher took the floor (13). From that point on, the special education teacher asked the classroom teacher a series of questions about Shane's peer relations, reading level, and performance in spelling and math.

After the school psychologist asked how Shane handled failure, the questioning shifted to the mother, who was asked about her son's fine motor control at home:

46   **SET:** How do you find him at [home] in terms of using his fingers and fine motor kinds of things? Does he do//

47   **Mot:**   =He will—as a small child, he didn't at all. He was never interested in it, he wasn't interested in sitting in my lap and having a book read to him, any things like that//

48   **SET:**   =Mhmmm//

49   **Mot:**   =which I think is part of it you know. His, his older brother was just the opposite, and learned to write real early. [Now] Shane, at night, lots of times he comes home and he'll write or draw. He's really doing a lot//

50   **SET:** ( )

51   **Mot:** =he sits down and is writing love notes to his girl friend (heh-heh). He went in our bedroom last night and turned on the TV and got out some colored pencils and started writing. So he, really likes to, and of course he brings it all into us to see//

52   **SET:**   =Mhmmm//

53   **Mot:**   =and comment on, so I think, you know, he's not [**negative**] about//

54   **SET:**   =no//

55   **Mot:** =that any more//

56   **SET:**   =uh huh

57   **Mot:** He was before, but I think his attitude's changed a lot.

These transcript excerpts show that the information that the psychologist had about the student was presented to the committee in a single, uninterrupted report, while the mother's and classroom teacher's information was elicited by other members of the committee. The school psychologist's presentation of the case to the committee was augmented by officially sanctioned props, including the case file itself (a bulky manila folder on display in front of the psychologist), test results, and carefully prepared notes. When she spoke, she read from notes. By contrast, neither the mother nor the teacher had such props. They spoke from memory, not from notes.

Grounds of Assertions

The members of the committee supported their claims about the child in different ways. The psychologist provided a summary of the results of a given test or subtest in a standard format. She named the subtest, reported the student's score, and gave her interpretations of the results. For example:

> I gave him a complete battery, and I found that, uh, he had a verbal I.Q. of 115, performance of 111, and a full scale of 115, so he's a bright child.
>
> He had very high scores in, uh, information, which is his long-term memory.
>
> His, um, picture arrangement scores—he had a seventeen, which is very high, very superior rating.

While the psychologist reported information about the student based on quasi-scientific tools, the classroom teacher and mother based their reports on firsthand observations. For example, the teacher provided general statements, "He's got a very creative mind and expresses himself well" (8), as well as some more specific assertions: "He can read and comprehend some things when I talk to him, but doing independent type work is hard for him" (8). While the psychologist's observations were confined to a relatively short period of time (hours of testing) and a circumscribed setting, the classroom teacher's and mother's observations were based on a longer period of time and a less circumscribed spatial and social arrangement. For the teacher, this period was a school year and the space was the classroom, while the mother's observations concerned the child's actions in a wide variety of situations spanning a lifetime.

Thus, information gathered by systematic, albeit indirect, observations (i.e., that from specialized tests) *was presented to* the committee, while information gathered by direct, albeit unguided or unstructured, observation (which included information about classroom experiences and home life) *was elicited from* informed participants. Furthermore, the mode in which information was presented to the committee varied according to the status and official expertise of the participants in the meeting. The most highly technical information (that from tests) was made available by the most highly trained and highest ranking people in attendance at the meeting, whereas the personal observations were made available by the participants with the least technical expertise and lowest ranking. Speakers of officially higher rank and who spoke with their authority grounded in technical expertise presented their information, while speakers of lower rank, who spoke with authority based on first hand observations, had information elicited from them.

Mode of Representation

Shane's mother, his teacher, the school psychologist and the school nurse discussed the student and his academic performance differently. The student was characterized by the psychologist as having "troubles" and "problems": "He has difficulty applying himself to his daily work" (3); "He cannot switch channels" (5); "He has some fears and anxieties" (5). The classroom teacher characterizes the problem in a similar way: "The fine motor types of things are difficult for him" (8); "Doing independent type work is hard for him" (8).

While the student's problem is the focus of attention for the entire committee, the mother and teacher discuss the student in a register different from that of the psychologist and the nurse. Notable in this regard are comments about the student's motivation: "He enjoys math" (28); "He enjoys handwriting and wants to learn it" (30); "He seems to enjoy handwriting and wants to learn it" (30); "He really tries at it hard and seems to wanna learn it better" (34). The teacher also introduced a number of contingencies that influence the student's performance: (1) His performance varies as a function of preparation: "If he studies his spelling and concentrates on it he can do pretty well" (22). His performance varies according to the kinds of materials and tasks: "It's hard for him to copy down [math] problems . . . if he's given a sheet where he can fill in answers and work them out he does much better" (28); he does better on group tasks, "but doing independent type work is hard for him" (8). If the tasks at hand are a means to some other end desired by the student, then his performance improves: "If there's something else he wants to do and knows he needs to do and knows he needs to get through that before he can get on to something else, he'll work a little more diligently at it" (45).

The mother's representation contrasts even more sharply with the psychologist's than does the teacher's. She spoke about changes through time, continually contrasting her son as he was at an earlier age with how he is now. In each of these contrasts, she emphasized improvements and changes for the better. Although she seems to acknowledge the official committee position about Shane's problem, she provided an alternative explanation about the source of the problem. For her, the locus of difficulty was not within him ("it's not physical," "it's not functional"), but it was to be found in his past experience and the situations he has been in.

In short, the teacher, like the psychologist, characterized the issue before the committee as "Shane's problem." The teacher's characterization, unlike the psychologist's however, had a contingent quality. She spoke sociologically, providing contextual information of a locally situated sort. The mother's representation, by contrast, has a historical dimension; she spoke in terms that implied changes through time.

STRATIFYING REGISTERS OF REPRESENTATION

Committee members often came to E&P meetings with differing views of the student's case and attitudes about the student's placement. During this meeting, the various members of this committee perceived Shane differently. The psychologist located the child's problem beneath his skin and between his ears, whereas the classroom teacher saw the student's problem varying from one classroom situation to another, and the mother saw the child's problem changing through time. That is, the teacher and the mother provided accounts about the student's performance in conceptual discourses that were different than the psychologist's version of the student's academic difficulties.

This discussion, if left here, would be at best an interesting example of perspectival differences in representation that occur in face-to-face interaction. That is, psychologists, teachers, and parents have different discourses for talking about even the same children because of their different experiences and backgrounds. While the perspectival dimension of representation is certainly an important aspect of the social construction of this child's identity, closing the discussion at this point would leave out a crucial ingredient: these modes of representation are not equal. By meeting's end, one mode of representation, that voiced in a psychological register, prevailed. The psychological representation of the student supplanted both the sociological and historical representations of the student.

So, the question that must be asked is, How did the psychologist control the discourse, dominating the other voices in the conversation? Or, asking this question in another way: How is the stratification of these modes of representation accomplished discursively?

In order to answer these questions, it is instructive to look at the manner in which the committee treated the descriptions of the child offered by the committee members. The reports by the psychologist and the nurse were accepted without question or challenge, while those of the mother and the teacher were interrupted continuously by questions. This differential treatment is at first surprising, especially in light of the differences in the manifest content of the three descriptions. The psychologist's description is replete with technical terms ("VADS," "Bender," "detail awareness," "ITPA," "WISC-R") and numerical scales ("I.Q. of 96," "full scale of 93," "test age was 7–0 to 7–5"), while both the mother and the teacher describe the student in lay terms ("He has a creative mind," "Doing independent work is hard for him," "He wasn't interested in sitting in my lap and having a book read to him").

Thus, the speaker who includes technical terms in her discourse *is not asked* to clarify terms, while the speakers of a vernacular *are asked* to clarify their terms. No one in the meeting asked the psychologist for more details or further information. In fact, the mother only requested clarification once during the course of the entire meeting and that was just as the formal business was being concluded. Her question was about "P.E." :

422 **SET:** check over ((( ))) (5–6) I don't think I addressed P.E.
423 **Psy:** I don't think we uh, [oh], ok, we do not need that, okay, he does not need physical edu //
424 **Mot:**   =(I want to ask something about that while you mentioned P.E. You mean physical education)
425 **???:** Mmhmmm
426 **Mot:** Does the school have a soccer program or is that just totally separate from um, you know, part of the boys' club o::r//
427 **Prn:**   =Right. It's a parent organized, um, association //
428 **Mot:** =Is there something(one?) at the school that would have information on it if it comes up in the season, because Shane really has expressed an interest in that.

The differences in the way in which the three reports were treated, especially the requests for clarification of technical terms during the committee meeting, helps us understand why the psychologist's representation was accorded privileged status by the committee. The psychologist's report gains its authority by the very nature of its construction. The psychologist's discourse obtains its privileged status *because* it is ambiguous, because it is shot full of technical terms, *because* it is difficult to understand. The parents and the other committee members do not challenge the ambiguity of the psychologist's report because the grounds to do so are removed by the manner in which the psychologist presents information, grounds assertions, and represents the child in discourse.

Meaning is said to be negotiated in everyday discourse. Speakers and Hearers work collaboratively to achieve understanding. According to observers from a wide variety of perspectives, a first maxim of conversation is that Speakers will speak clearly; they intend to make sense and be understood (Merleau-Ponty 1964; Sacks, Schegloff and Jefferson 1974; Grice 1975; Searle

1969; Gumperz 1982). Hearers contribute to meaning in discourse by making inferences from the conversational string of utterances. They display their understanding actively through "back channel work" (Duncan, 1972), which includes eye contact, head nods, syllables such as "uh huhs," and phrases like "I see" or "I understand." Under such assumptions, when the Hearer does not understand, "a request for clarification" is in order. The manifest purpose of such requests is to obtain more information. The request for clarification is generated by Hearers when they do not think that the Speaker is speaking clearly.

The grounds for this kind of negotiation of meaning are removed from the committee by the way in which language is used by the psychologist. When the psychologist speaks, it is from an institutionally designated position of authority. Furthermore, the psychologist's representation of the child is based on her professional expertise. The privileged status of the psychologist's expertise, in turn, is displayed in the technical language (register) of her report.

There is a certain mystique in the use of technical vocabulary, as evidenced by the high status that the specialized lexicon of doctors, lawyers, and scientists is given in our society (West 1984; Philips 1977; Shuy and Larkin 1978; Latour and Woolgar 1985; Wertsch 1986; Cohn 1987). The use of technical register indicates a superior status and a special knowledge based on long training and specialized qualifications.

A certain amount of this mystique is evident in the psychologist's language and is apparent in the committee's treatment of it. When technical register is used and embedded in the institutional trappings of the formal proceedings of a meeting, the grounds for negotiating meaning are removed from under the conversation. Because the Speaker and Hearers do not share the conventions of a common register, Hearers do not have the expertise to question, or even to interrupt the Speaker. To request a clarification of the psychologist, then, is to challenge the authority of a clinically certified expert. The other members of the committee are placed in the position of assuming that the psychologist is speaking knowledgeably and, in the instance, disinterestedly, and the Hearer does not have the competence to understand.

When technical register is used, even though the possibility for active negotiation of meaning is removed, the guise of understanding remains. To be sure, the understanding is a passively achieved one, not the active one associated with everyday discourse. Instead of signaling a lack of understanding via such implicit devices as back channel work and explicit ones like requests for clarification, the committee members (including the parents) remain silent, thereby tacitly contributing to the guise that common understanding has been achieved.

CONCLUSIONS

In conclusion, I'd like to make some specific points about the research I have been conducting on the institutional construction of identities and some more general points about the constitutive model of discourse which is implied by this work.

THE INSTITUTIONAL CONSTRUCTION OF IDENTITIES

By looking at the language of groups of educators as they engage in the work of sorting students, I have tried to demonstrate the situated relevance of social structures in the practical work activities performed by people in social interaction. Educators carry out the routine work of conducting lessons, assigning students to ability groups or special programs, administering tests, and attending meetings. The notion of *work* stresses the constructive aspect of institutional practice. Educators' work is repetitive and routine. Its mundane character should not overshadow the drama of its importance, however, because steps on students' career ladders are assembled from such practice. The enactment of routine bureaucratic practices structures students' educational careers by opening or closing their access to particular educational opportunities.

Essentially, the teacher is calling for help. Her call is cast in general, not specific, terms. This call starts the process that constructs students' institutional identities. These often undifferentiated appeals become refined and specified in official language as they move from regular education classrooms to testing rooms and finally to meeting rooms. Through this process, the child becomes an object. The members of the committee do not have access to the teacher-student interaction; only the residue of that interaction is represented in a file, a decontextualized text-artifact. At the outset, the child was a participant in discourse with his teacher and his classmates. But, from that point on, the child's contribution to his own career status drops out. The child is only represented in text. The only way we gain access to the child is through textual representations of his interactions. The child becomes objectified as the case moves from the classroom to testing to committee meeting.

I found three registers spoken in the committee meeting, which is the last step in this identity-construction process: a psychological, a sociological, and a historical one. The psychological discourse included absolute and categorical statements about the student's abilities. On the basis of information from systematic, albeit indirect, techniques of observation, the locus of the problem was placed within Shane. The result was a "context-free" view of the child as one who had a general disability which, therefore, cut across situations. The classroom teacher spoke in a sociological idiom; she tempered her report with contingent factors of a situational sort. On the basis of information from unsystematic, albeit direct, observation, she said that the student's performance was influenced by his state of motivation, kinds of classroom tasks, and types of materials. The result was a "context-bound" view of the child as someone who had specific problems which appeared in certain academic situations, but who operated more than adequately in other situations. The mother's discourse, lastly, was historical. Based on years of direct observation, she provided particulars about the biography and history of her son and noted changes and improvements across time as well as situational circumstances as the source of his difficulties.

The psychologist's recommendations were accepted without challenge or question, while the sociological and historical recommendations were routinely interrupted with requests for clarification and further information. I propose that the resolution of competing versions of the child can be understood in terms of the authority that reports gain by their manner of presentation, their method of grounding truth claims, and their modes of representation.

The psychological representation gained its authority from the mastery and control of a technical vocabulary, grounded in a quasi-scientific idiom. Because of the fact that for the other participants here the psychologist's report was obscure, difficult to understand, and ambiguous—not in spite of it—the grounds for questioning or challenging were removed from the conversation. It is this technical, quasi-scientific authority that contributes to the stratification of languages of representation and thereby the construction of children's identities.

When people have competing versions of ambiguous events that transpire in the world, they often try to negotiate a commonly agreed upon definition of the situation. Often, consensus is achieved when one or another of the protagonists relinquishes his or her representation of the world as the preferred version, after having heard superior information or having been convinced of the efficacy of an argument. In the case considered here, the resolution of competing modes of representation was not negotiated. The members of the committee resolved the disjuncture between sociological, historical, and psychological versions by credentialing the psychological version as the official version of this student. Thus, an institutionally sanctioned version of experience is superimposed upon multiple and competing versions of experience.

DISCOURSE AS CONSTITUTIVE ACTIVITY

The constructivist view of social life poses mutually constitutive relations between modes of thought, modes of discourse and modes of action. Discourse does not passively reflect or merely describe the world. Because discourse, use of language, is action, different discourses constitute the world differently. Events in the world do not exist for people independently of the representations people use to make sense of them. Instead, objects are defined through elaborate enactments of cultural conventions which lead to the establishment of such well documented "institutional facts" (Searle 1969) as "touchdowns," "marriages," "insults," "banishments," "property rights" (D'Andrade 1984), and, as I have proposed, "learning disabilities" and "educational handicaps." When the constitutive rules of discourse are in effect, behavior becomes action, and actions become "touchdowns," "marriages," "illness," "schizophrenia," "deviance," "intelligence" and "educational handicaps."

Modes of Representation

When discourse is viewed as activity that culturally constructs clarity out of ambiguity, then we should not be surprised to find multiple modes of representation. Marriage, schizophrenia, and learning disabilities are constructed by cultural conventions in much the same way that touchdowns are constructed by the constitutive rules of football. Just as crossing the goal line counts as a touchdown only if the appropriate players are present and its facticity has been duly constituted by the referees, so a student's behavior counts as a learning disability only if the appropriate institutional officials apply the appropriate institutional machinery (educational testing, parent conferences, placement meetings, etc.). Without the orderly application of that institutional machinery, educational handicaps do not exist as a category of situations to be authoritatively represented.

In the case we have considered, there were many ways in which Shane could have been formulated: "normal student," "educationally handicapped student," "gifted student," "learning disabled student." Each formulation or way of representing Shane does not simply reflect or merely describe his characteristics; each mode of representation constitutes him, and does so in a different way. To be a "normal student" is to fit within the parameters or norms of intelligence; to be a "gifted student" is to have exceptional talents. To be "educationally handicapped" or "learning disabled" is to have an inherent disorder. Importantly, each of these formulations characterizes intelligence or talent in terms that place it inside the student. Intelligence, whether normal, exceptional or lacking, is treated as a personal and private possession. This way of characterizing people exemplifies the use of dispositional properties in the explanation of people's behavior. Each of these modes of representation naturalizes the child, thereby masking the social construction work which generated the designation in the first place. In short, we know the world through the representations we make of it (Bakhtin 1981). A particular way of representing events in discursive language influences, first of all, the way we *think about* the events represented, and, second, the way we *act toward* the events.

The Politics of Representation

Modes of representing events vary according to the perspective from which a representation is constructed. *Perspective* here refers to the standpoint from which a person is participating in discourse. One dimension of perspective is the person's physical location in the here-and-now of face-to-face situations (Gurwitsch 1966). Another is the person's location in social institutions, cultural arrangements, and sociohistorical space-time (Bakhtin 1981).

We have found that professional educators (i.e., school psychologists), for a variety of biographical, historical, and cultural reasons, describe students in dispositional terms, whereas parents and, to a lesser extent, classroom teachers, formulate students in more contextual terms. Although there are many possible modes of representing the world and communicating them to others starting from particular biographical, historical, and social-cultural perspectives, the course of history can be envisioned as successive attempts to impose one mode of representation upon another.

It is not accidental in this "politics of representation" (Holquist 1983; Shapiro 1987; Mehan and Wills 1988; Mehan et al. 1990) that institutionally grounded representations predominate. For example, psychiatrists' representations prevail over those of patients, professional educators' representations override parents' formulations. Institutional officials speak with a technical vocabulary grounded in professional expertise. Ordinary people speak in a common vernacular grounded in personal experience. More and more often in our increasingly technological society, when a voice speaking in formalized, rationalistic, and positivistic terms confronts a voice grounded in personal, common sense or localized particulars, the technical prevails over the vernacular.

When categorizing this student, these educators reproduced the status relations among the different discourses that exist in society. A universalizing discourse that is given higher status in the meeting and whose designated variables are read into the child, thereby decontextualizing the child, is the same discourse we see gaining power and authority in recent times. Thus, the concrete, face-to-face encounters which generate an instance of a category are also creative moments that reproduce the relations among categories that we see gaining ascendancy historically. The next chapter by Michael Herzfeld deals with a related issue in the politics of representation, but in his case the issue is not struggles over the lexical label attached to a child. Rather, it is the broader (but still entextualizing) attempt to define a nation through a "reading"—on the part of scholars/political actors—of its folklore.

REFERENCES

Bahktin, M. M.
  1981   *The Dialogic Imagination: Four essays*. Michael Holquist (ed.), Caryl Em-
            erson and Michael Holquist (trans.). Austin: University of Texas Press.

Cicourel, A.V. et al.
  1974   *Language Use and School Performance*. New York: Academic Press.

Cohn, C.
  1987   Sex and death in the rational world of defense intellectuals. *Signs* 12:
            687–718.

Coles, G.
  1987   *The Learning Mystique: A Critical Look at Learning Disabilities*. New York:
            Pantheon.

Collins, R.
  1981   Micro-translation as a theory building strategy. In *Advances in Social Theory
            and Methodology*, K. Knorr-Cetina and A.V. Cicourel (eds.), 81–108. New
            York: Routledge & Kegan Paul.

D'Andrade, R. G.
  1984   Cultural meaning systems. In *Culture Theory: Social Origins of Mind*,
            R. Shweder and R. A. Levine (eds.), 88–119. Chicago: University of Chicago
            Press.

Duncan, S.
  1972   Some signals and rules for taking speaking turns in conversation. *Journal of
            Personality and Social Psychology* 23: 283–292.

Erickson, F., and J. Schultz
  1982   *The Counselor as Gatekeeper*. New York: Academic Press.

Gumperz, J.
  1982   *Discourse Strategies*. Cambridge: Cambridge University Press.

Gurwitsch, A.
  1966   *Studies in Phenomenology and Psychology*. Evanston: Northwestern Univer-
            sity Press.

Grice, H. P.
  1975   Logic and conversation. In *Syntax and Semantics*, vol. 3, *Speech Acts*, P. Cole
            and J. Morgan (eds.), 41–58. New York: Academic Press.

Holquist, M.
   1983   The politics of representation. *The Quarterly Newsletter of the Laboratory of Comparative Human Cognition* 5(1): 2–9.

Latour, B., and S. Woolgar
   1985   *Laboratory Life*. Princeton: Princeton University Press.

Mehan, H., A. Hertweck, and J. L. Meihls
   1986   *Handicapping the Handicapped: Decision Making in Students' Careers.* Stanford: Stanford University Press.

Mehan, H., and J. Wills
   1988   MEND: A Nurturing Voice in the Nuclear Arms Debate. *Social Problems* 35(4): 363–383.

Mehan, H., C. E. Nathanson, and J. M. Skelly
   1990   Nuclear Discourse in the 1980s: The Unravelling Conventions of the Cold War. *Discourse and Society* 1(2): 133–65.

Merleau-Ponty, M.
   1964   *Signs*. Evanston: Northwestern University Press.

Pollit, K.
   1987   The strange case of Baby M. *The Nation* May 23: 667, 682–88.

Philips, S.
   1977   The role of spatial positioning and alignment in defining interactional units: The American courtroom as a case in point. Paper presented at the American Anthropological Association meetings, Houston, Texas.

Sacks, H., E. A. Schegloff, and G. Jefferson
   1974   A simplest systematics for the organization of turn-taking in conversation. *Language* 50: 696–735.

Searle, J.
   1969   *Speech Acts: An Essay in the Philosophy of Language*. Cambridge: Cambridge University Press.

Shuy, R., and D. L. Larkin
   1978   Linguistic considerations in the simplification/clarification of insurance policy language. *Discourse Processes* 1: 305–21.

Shapiro, M.
   1987   *The Politics of Representation*. Madison: University of Wisconsin Press.

Wertsch, J.
   1986   Modes of discourse in the nuclear arms debate. *Current Research on Peace and Violence* 10: 102–12.

West, C.
   1984   *Routine Complications: Troubles in Talk Between Doctors and Patients*. Bloomington: Indiana University Press.

10 National Spirit or the Breath of Nature?

The Expropriation of Folk Positivism

in the Discourse of Greek Nationalism

Michael Herzfeld

COMPETING VISIONS

The clash of diametrically opposed ideological readings of a collective self—especially a national one—allows little quarter on either side. The common ground that permits such contestation in the first place is rarely visible. In this regard, the case of modern Greece is especially instructive. The Greek nation-state was brought into existence in 1821–34, and its difficult gestation depended upon its accepting a humiliating dual role: it was expected to serve, at one and the same time, as the revered ancestor of Europe and as Europe's cultural borderland contaminated by the proximity of the Orient.

A similarly paradoxical logic allowed European elites to treat their own local peasantries as at once romantically pure and actually crude, an attitude that the local Greek elite at first—and to some extent thereafter—faithfully reproduced in its relations with its own peasant compatriots. In time, however, this condescending stance generated a nativist reaction even among members of the elite, a reaction that, while itself largely inspired by West European models, nevertheless ostensibly both rejected the terms of Greek identity set by the West and refused to claim inherent cultural superiority over the peasantry for itself. The two distinct discourses of national identity that thenceforward developed in strong mutual opposition shared important elements of their imagery and rhetorical tactics. Without such common ground, there could have been no debate; but the debate entailed a denial, on both sides, that any common ground existed.

I shall focus here on a particular segment of the debate that exhibits these ironic predicaments at both the national and the academic levels simultaneously, and that also by extension suggests a similar problematic at the level of anthropological discourse itself. The commonality subsists, I suggest, in the tendency of all discourse about culture to embrace some form of essentialism. In nationalistic discourse, this is often realized as an assumption that national culture is carried by genetic descent. I shall further suggest that this innatist aspect of nationalism, while elaborated in the course of a long European intellectual tradition, may have originated, and certainly today derives much of its persistence, from a widespread set of ideas that we might provisionally call "folk positivism." By looking at nationalism in these terms, we shall constantly remind ourselves that scholars and politicians do not have a monopoly on particular ways of conceptualizing the world.

Throughout the entire history of Greek statehood, texts about the definition and character of Greek culture purport to reject each other's fundamental premises as they vie for supremacy. Their struggle—which basically revolved around the essentialist question, "Do we belong to Europe or to the Orient?"—reproduces within Greek cultural debates the larger problem of the global status of Greek culture today, much as the West's mixture of romantic ancestor-worship and cultural disdain for the modern Greeks in general reappears internally within Greece as an elite dismissal of vernacular culture as the "Turkish" delusions of a fundamentally pure and Hellenic peasantry. Just as the West would lead the Greeks to a greater awareness of their cultural heritage, moreover, the Greek elite would provide the same service for its illiterate followers within the Greek nation. Such attitudes were common in the romantic nationalisms of nineteenth-century Europe, of course, but in the Greek case were sharply highlighted by the twin circumstances of geographical proximity to Turkey, the alleged quintessence of all things Oriental, and of the siting of Europe's spiritual origins on Greek soil.

Modern Greek studies have been sadly neglected in academic circles, although the situation has changed somewhat in recent years (see Herzfeld 1987; Jusdanis 1988). This marginality has pinpointed a critical issue for the various contributing disciplines: certain political and ideological assumptions have permitted, or even condemned, the modern successors of Hellas to lie at the outer edges of the modern humanistic canon. Here, then, academic practice faithfully follows political realities. The political and academic marginalization of Greece thus lends a particularly sharp interest to the complex relationship between an encompassing nationalistic discourse and the specific texts of the opposing ideologies within that discourse—ideologies that directly concern the relationship between Greece and a Europe so defined as to exclude and enfold Greece by turns. It is, moreover, precisely because modern Greece has been allotted such a minor role in the academic canon—so pitiful, as conventional humanists would have it, before "the glory that was Greece"—that the history of academic interest in Greece demands critical epistemological attention.

In epistemological wars and nationalistic debates alike, the argument is between canonical explanations and revolutionary zeal. Here, it pits the self-consciously literate "Western humanistic tradition" against the subversive marginality of a Greece aggressively bereft of its articulate glories. What I hope to show in this paper is that the exclusive propensities of both sides reproduce a problem that underlies them both: both start from a basis of what I shall call "folk positivism"—the conceptual reification called "common sense" that aims at clarity but in the process produces reductionism and essentialism. On the one side lies the authority of letters (and literalism, another version of the essentialist position), on the other an attitude of commonsensical contempt for the learned and the literate. This intellectual disemia[1] is not, of course, uniquely Greek; it appears in the English-speaking world, for example, as a contest between Latinate elegance and Anglo-Saxon bluntness. Like the latter, it pits one kind of reification against another. The success of such discourses in informing collective wisdom about national identity often depends on the ability of the official or elite rhetoric to match the terms and logic of folk positivism. While the latter, at other times, can also generate critical reaction and resistance, I would argue that it is in part through the successful evocation of this common ground that disenfranchised populations may also be led, as Gramsci saw, to acquiesce in their own humiliation (see Cowan 1990; Femia 1981; cf. Herzfeld 1992).

The decentering of discourse as I am considering it here is not simply the single-stage ideological expropriation of a text or corpus of texts. We must be careful not to reify the dynamics of discourse in a politically contested situation, and thereby to blur the distinction made in these essays between text and discourse. The very idea of a text is, at one level, a piece of folk positivism, for it implies the essentialist assumption of a bounded semantic universe located outside the passage of time: the idea of a folksong *Urtext* is a good example of this way of thinking, for it shows clearly the underlying assumption that there must be a "correct version" rather than a series of realizations of an otherwise fluid discursive practice. The idea of a text in this sense is a *denial* of discourse; but that denial is itself, inevitably, a strategy rather than a structure, a discursive practice rather than a textual entity, a grab for conceptual control rather than something that must be taken at face value. Discourse constitutes the *a priori* common ground of a set of texts, yet it is also what makes possible the denial

1. *Disemia* subsumes, but does not privilege, *diglossia*; it is the principle of opposition between an extroverted ideology of formalism and idealized self-presentation on the one side, and an introspective cultural account based on an often quite self-critical view of the society and culture on the other (see Herzfeld 1987: 101–22).

of that common ground: such is the paradox of simultaneous existence and suppression already mentioned. It thus becomes easier to see, in the modern Greek context, how various discourses became the ideal vehicle for the equally paradoxical, but more concrete, coexistence of respect for the Greeks'/peasants' basic Hellenism and contempt for their Turkishness. The ontology of folklore texts is invested with a rigidity that effectively disguises the negotiability of their significance.

If the isolated textual artifacts (or variants) do display overtly common features, these lie less in the formulae, the recognizable bits and pieces of highly conventional language, than they do in the *processes* of intertextuality that ultimately constitute the life of the discourse. Initial expropriation may be succeeded by something that looks very like a counterhegemony and that uses tactics similar to those entailed in the initial expropriation. These tactics belong, not to the texts in which they appear, but to the discourse in which they are entailed. A generalized example will help to make the point clear. The reaction to colonial historiographies of Africa has not infrequently been the reversal of equivalences within an otherwise unchanging hegemonic *symbolism* (see Houtondji 1983; Mudimbe 1988); yet how many present-day anticolonialists will acknowledge the parentage of their discourse? For the liberation of a discourse may subject it to new abuse, to the routinization of popular sentiment (e.g., fascist forms of "populism"). The word *liberation* is itself liable to such abuses of habituation. To revert once again to modern Greece, Socialist party rule since 1981 has produced two characteristic reactions: expropriation by the conservative opposition of the socialists' hugely libertarian rhetoric, and the day-to-day bureaucratic routinization of that rhetoric under the Socialists.

The context for the present discussion is nineteenth- and early twentieth-century Greece, a period of intense language politics centering around the problem of diglossia. In Greece, diglossia took the form of a contrast between the neo-Classical register (*katharevousa*, 'purist [language]') used until 1975 for most official purposes, and the ordinary spoken language (*dhimotiki*, 'demotic/popular [language]') in all its dialectal variety.[2] This polarization of language, however, is but one realization of a deep ideological split which often took its symbolic form from the play of two opposed historiographies. The first of these, the "Hellenic," is neo-Classical, Western-oriented, formalistic, and aggressively referential. It is opposed to the "Romeic" theme—a nativistic

---

2. I have capitalized Classical to remind readers that this means specifically Classical Greece—that is, a temporally specific cultural identity, rather than the more abstract sense usually indicated by the use of a lowercase initial letter.

reaction historically predicated on the Byzantine and later roots of modern Greek culture, and stereotypically associated with informality and spontaneity and with disdain for the legalistic precision of "pen-pushers" (*kalamaradhes*).[3] Represented by Kazantzakis's insubordinate antihero Alexis Zorbas (whose bluntly stereotypical character perhaps comes across better in his film incarnation as "Zorba *the* Greek"!) and the shadow-theater trickster Karagiozis in opposition to the Hellenists' Plato and Pericles, it entails as much intellectual idealizing as the latter. As we shall see, moreover, it absorbed a good deal of the Hellenists' formalism (see Tziovas 1985). The two poles of this polarity are subtly manipulated in practice, and tend to color each other. For this reason, it is important not to reify the two historical images of the Greeks as *Ellines* or *Romii*, and to realize that each term—as well as others of more restricted currency—may sometimes be associated with features more usually attributed to the other. Nowadays, especially, *Ellines* has through official usage become so clearly the dominant term for "Greeks" that it often carries the self-deprecatory implications formerly found almost exclusively as an aspect of *Romii*. Critics who complain that this form of binarism oversimplifies the "actual" situation have thus missed the point: the binarism, which is unimpeachably "emic," *does*—"emically"—oversimplify the play of rhetorical strategies, but it does so precisely because rigid readings (e.g., declarations that "we Greeks are like this or that") are part and parcel of the various players' respective strategies.

By placing a particular debate under the microscope of discursive and ethnographic critique, I hope here to demonstrate by example why attacks on the "reality" of binary oppositions fall squarely into the essentialist error that almost invariably characterizes nationalistic ideologies.

I shall focus almost exclusively on a trio of studies, each written from a distinctive ideological perspective, and all intended as contributions to the establishment of a true, reified national identity. These studies are concerned with Greek folksongs, an important element in early attempts to define and refine the culture of the modern Greek nation-state. Folksong studies in Greece followed rather than preceded independence: they were intended to ratify and reinforce a *fait accompli* rather than to provide the justification for an intended revolution in the future. In the early decades of independence, as the country expanded through a series of territorial acquisitions, this seemed a fairly straightforward task. But in 1822, a century after the initial fight for indepen-

---

3. *Kalamaradhes* is still the contemptuous label applied by Cretans and Cypriots to the mainlanders, whom they regard as irredeemably effete and corrupt.

dence, the collapse of the Greek armies in Asia Minor wrecked irredentist dreams of ultimately restoring Alexander's and Constantine's empires to Greek control, and set the process of expansion back considerably.

Aggressive nationalism of the neo-Classical variety, which had traded on expectations of sympathy from the Classically educated West, now found itself exposed to unaccustomed ridicule from some educated insiders. In 1929, there appeared a sustained attack on the nationalist tradition in Greek folklore studies. That work, Yanis Apostolakis's *Folk Songs, Part I: The Collections*, painstakingly took apart the texts that the major early collections had attributed to "the folk," and attempted to show that they were learned compounds of fragments at best, forgeries at worst. Apostolakis's main targets were Spyridon Zambelios and Nikolaos Politis, whose collections (published in 1852 and 1914, respectively) represent high-water marks in the history of nationalist Greek folklore studies.

Apostolakis castigated these scholars for what he claimed was a series of wholly unwarranted, aesthetically unpalatable, and culturally unnatural textual emendations. I say "culturally unnatural" by intention, since a major theme of the book is its association of the foreign or externally derived models of the Hellenic cause with a learned perversion of "nature" that impugned the traditions of the "true" Greeks. Clearly, the "restored" nature of Apostolakis's textual housecleaning was no less cultural than what it tried to replace: it was an act of populist nationalization-as-naturalization.[4] His attempt was sometimes well supported by documentary evidence, but more frequently relied on an implicit, innatist theory of aesthetic judgment, according to which—like Zambelios before him—he could claim that, as an educated native, he had a double advantage: he not only knew instinctively what was genuine, but had the sophistication to render his understanding explicit.

The result, however, is a double layer of obfuscation: a second stratum of judgmental essentialism now overlays the first. But, while it may be impossible to get back to the originals, whatever we may understand by that subtly denaturing term, we can at least follow the process whereby the second phase entails an ironic replay of the hegemonic tactics of the first. Indeed, we should be well prepared for such a state of affairs, because Apostolakis (1929: 7) tells

4. Nineteenth-century nationalism made much of the etymological connection between "nature" (Latin *natura*) and "nation" (*natio* 'birth'). A segmentary hierarchy of commonalities of birth was thus converted into mass "nationality." The naturalization of the quintessentially cultural phenomenon of national statehood is still with us; see Anderson 1983; Handler 1988; Herzfeld 1987, 1992; Kapferer 1988.

us early on that his target is the profession of the "philologists" and the "learned," while his argument deploys precisely the classic scholastic techniques of a detailed *apparatus criticus*—a program of textual intervention that relies on the author's "commonsense" reading of textual minutiae. It is ostensibly an attack on what Mouzelis (1978) has called the "formalism" of official Greek culture; but—its language apart[5]—it employs the same techniques as what it attacks. It is, in this sense, directly analogous to Bourdieu's (1977: 37) "officializing strategies."

Apostolakis's critique focused on what he saw as the usurpation of the oral word by the written—a common demoticist criticism. But the written-oral pair has other implications as well. It is a surrogate binarism for the clash of ideologies unequally pitting the literate West, heir to Hellas, against the "illiterate" and "innate" purity of the Greek folk. Rural attitudes to literacy today are certainly not all complimentary (see Meraklis 1984: 73), and literacy has come to stand in the eyes of many for the bureaucratic exercise of power. If for the one camp the "Western" ability to write affirms those intellectual skills that are considered "natural" to a Greek, for the other the orality of folksong offers the only hope of return to an unmediated national essence. The argument about folksong texts is thus also an argument about the "nature" of discourse itself. It is an argument, above all, about the relative status of written and oral forms, and their respective ability to carry forward the essence of national culture. Because it thus poses a challenge to the dominance of the philological canon whose techniques it nonetheless also uses, it concerns not just modern Greece, but the Western humanistic tradition as a whole.

In the subsequent illustrations, then, we shall follow a demoticist attack on Hellenist models of Greekness, phrased in stridently innatist terms that somewhat surprisingly reproduce the methods and even some of the claims of the Hellenists themselves. We shall see that the Romeic concern with "nature" requires its own formalism, and that it asks us to make assumptions that are no less denatured and ahistorical than those of the Hellenists. The textual dictates of Apostolakis will help us discover something about the principles behind the demoticist classification of folkloric materials, and especially about the link that the linguistic demoticists hoped to make between nature and Greekness.

5. Language is an important part of Mouzelis' understanding of Greek formalism, as it indeed is for many Greeks to this day. It is a major arena in which the clash of ideologies is played out. Its centrality, however, should not blind us—as it has blinded many commentators—to the fact that each diglossic register can serve as a disguise for the *opposing* ideology. See also note 1, above.

Theirs was an attack on the learned world, the printed word, and the foreign straitjacket into which the Hellenist "pen-pushers" had forced the free Greek spirit; but their weapons were scholarship, publication, and models of national essence given particular prominence by German writers like Herder and Hegel.

Indeed, their rhetoric was that of *Geist*, the German romantic concept of "spirit." Its own local terminology drew further authority from authentically Classical resonances, thereby cementing the conflation of Hellas with Europe. This was a feature of both sides to the debate. Thus, in the demoticists' argument, the Hellenists' intellectualist concept of *pneuma* ('spirit' ; cf. Latin *spiritus*; English *pneumatic*) had forced the nature (*fisi*: cf. Greek *fisao*; English *blow; physical*) of the people into a formality that was inappropriate to it. While there was considerable disagreement about what kind of nature was to be invoked, neither side had any doubts that nature was the key, nor was there any dispute about its ultimate Greekness. The issue was not merely the now epistemologically familiar one of naturalization, but concerned *whose* and *which* naturalization should be recognized.

It is worth noting that Apostolakis, for whom Zambelios was a violator of the Greek folk *fisi*, took considerable trouble to demonstrate a link between that "nature" and Politis's spiritual goal (1929: 139–42). Arguing that "[t]he true scholar never lets life (*zoi*) out of his sight," he suggested that for Politis— who is here implicitly contrasted with Zambelios—the editing and classification of folksong texts were "natural (*fisika*) and self-evident matters" and represented an attempt to "protect from the destruction of time and people one of the strong foundations of our intellectual life (*pneumatiki zoi*), the folksongs." Here he adopts the Hellenists' rhetoric of national spirit, *pneuma*, and connects it with a notion of "life" that has today become the intellectualist justification of folk forms ("drawn from life") to which villagers often appeal against the anticipated snobbery of formally educated outsiders. Apostolakis is willing to credit Politis with some appreciation of *fisi*: this, he says, is what a real scholar should be examining at all times. But there is still an element of irony in Apostolakis' treatment of Politis, who is generally acknowledged as the key figure in the annals of Greek nationalist folklore scholarship. While Apostolakis does note that Politis attempted to extract "[t]he logical (*loyiko*) and actual meaning of the pieces from the various variants" (1929: 141), he soon (1929: 145) concludes that the method does not work: "[just a]s the collections of Zambelios and Khristovasilis [a turn-of-the-century compiler] do not give us pleasure, so too Politis's *Selections* do not refresh (*anapavoun*) us." Ultimately, this is a contest between subjectivities: despite Apostolakis's tactfully conciliatory stance towards the great Politis, he is anxious to show that his innate understanding surpasses that of the scholar most widely credited with having given form and order to folklore studies in Greece.

The ideological distance between Apostolakis and his targets certainly seems illusory at times. For example, Apostolakis expropriated the national/ "natural" name of the Hellenes; he does not undercut his position by attempting to restore the popular self-designator *Romios* for the national name, as others had done,[6] but projects an alliance of "all Greeks" under their official name of "Hellenes," rescued from the alleged misuse of that name by the sophistry of academic formalism (Apostolakis 1929: 7). The tactic, which accepts the growing routinization of the official self-designation of all Greeks, exemplifies the point I made above about the importance of recognizing binarism in processual rather than purely formalist terms:

> There are many causes for people's estrangement from folk song, not only here but elsewhere as well, and there is no reason for me to mention them. About one alone shall I speak, and this because it is only found here, and nowhere else in the world: it is that strange decision made by our intellectual guides to change the natural language and put in its place some poor concoction they got out of their heads, something that makes you laugh and cry at the same time. Again and again, when you chance to forget that you are Greek (*Ellinas*) and you observe as a foreigner (*ksenos*) would, a cold laugh takes hold of you at the serious labor of the learned: they resemble the person who goes right ahead and cuts off two healthy legs in order to replace them with wooden ones.

Here is all the language of ideological naturalism, drawn up against the artificiality of the purist *katharevousa* in a demotic so aggressive that it represents almost as great a distortion of everyday speech (*endiposes* for *endiposis*, p. 6), and adumbrating the *special* experience of the Greeks who must suffer from the imposition of learned mentors to the *universal* tragedy of the disappearance of the folk song as an idiom—both in themselves highly stereotypical assumptions that serve Apostolakis's specific ideological concerns. Apostolakis's was an almost literal attempt to inflate national character—the national spirit—with the breath of nature. But this was a nature no less cultural than the elevated culture that it charged with being unnatural.

6. In the early years of this century, there was considerable debate amongst intellectuals— possibly the only people to whom it mattered—about the rival merits of the two "national names" (*Ellines* vs. *Romii*). The folklorist Nikolaos Politis himself delivered the irredentists' *coup de grâce* to the latter option when he declared that, since the Romanians already had this name, they would be obliged to change it if the Greeks exercised their right to it (1901: 18; Herzfeld 1982: 128)!

In addressing Apostolakis's tactics here, I shall mostly concern myself with his attack on Zambelios. There are a number of reasons for this. First, Politis was a more meticulous scholar and gave detailed sources for his emendations, so that Apostolakis's task was both easier and in some sense less critical than it was with his attack on Zambelios; moreover, respect for the founding father of Greek folklore studies appears to have restrained him from the more active restructuring that we meet in his treatment of Zambelios. Second, given that Zambelios's collection was published more than seventy years earlier, it provides a more dramatic—and thus also more heuristic—contrast with the presuppositions underlying Apostolakis's self-appointed mission. Third, Zambelios was working at a time when few educated Greeks had much knowledge of the country's folk traditions, and so chose to operate in a manner which sought more actively to proselytize both those learned in the cause of folklore and the folk—through the eventual effects of education, in which his work was destined to play a minor but influential role—to the cause of Hellenism. (Politis, by contrast, evidently took for granted as a respectable academic goal the instruction of the elite in folklore, and treated the Hellenism of the folk as given.) Finally, Zambelios's more florid (and perhaps self-consciously Hegelian) appeals to the continuity of the national "spirit" seem to play a more explicit ideological role, and also exclude any serious interest in possible foreign parallels or even derivations; they thus exemplify the strong nationalism that Politis shared in a subtler form, allowing us to perceive all the more clearly what Apostolakis's goals were in reversing the textual emendations. Politis's interest in cross-cultural comparison, which allowed him to see Greek folklore as historically interconnected with that of many other cultures and epochs, complicates the contrast between his own views and those of Apostolakis: in some ways, it made him a less uncompromising nationalist than his nativist critic.

For there should be no doubt about one aspect of this literature: all three writers, the Hellenist nationalists Zambelios and Politis and the revisionist Apostolakis, were engaged in an ongoing debate that did not merely rely on factual description but actually constituted significant aspects of the histories they respectively espoused. Their evocations of national consciousness were attempts to create, define, and propagate versions of it. The battle that Apostolakis waged with the Hellenist writers was encoded in the disemic registers of language ("diglossia"), definition-vs.-use, *pneuma*-vs.-*fisi*, neo-Classicist *Urtext* and continuity vs. either Near Eastern or entirely introspective cultural models that implied freedom both from Western tutelage and from excessive formality—a celebration of strategies over rules, of indeterminacy over formalism. Apostolakis even carries this commitment back into his own epistemology, arguing (1929: 7) that *method itself* is inimical to an understanding of the textual "flow" of the texts themselves, since it entails focusing on artificially isolated textual segments: never was the link between populist nationalism and an almost Feyerabendian rejectionism more clearly suggested.

Apostolakis employed the rhetoric of freedom and contingency, which were hallmarks of the Hellenists' liberal hero pitted against oppression by the necessities of an inescapably cultural nature, and yet his methods were the familiar ones of philology. For these reasons, his work offers a highly suggestive commentary on today's forms of epistemological and political rejectionism and on their embarrassing relationship to the canons that they claim to have dismantled.

THE PREMISE OF THE WORD:
LOGIC AND NATURAL LANGUAGE

Apostolakis opens fire on Zambelios in a characteristic way. He takes a four-line song text composed, he alleges, of a pair of distinguishable distichs (1929: 12–18):

> tu andriomenu t'armata dhen prepi na puliunde,
> mon' prepi tus stin ekklisia ke eki na liturghunde.
> prepi na kremonde psila s'arakhniasmeno pirgho,
> i skuria na troi t' armata k' i yi ton adriomeno.

> The brave man's weapons should not be sold,
> But they should [be put in] the church and services held over them.
> They should be hung up high on a cobwebbed tower,
> For rust to eat the weapons and the earth [to eat] the brave man.

Apostolakis begins with a formal *explication de texte* of more or less traditional type, arguing that the first two lines are given unity by the pivotal *prepi* (should), and he produces several "variants" in order to demonstrate the traditionality of this form. The second distich, on the other hand, is differently structured, and has a formal autonomy—note the emphasis here on *form*. Apostolakis then reinforces the contrast on semantic grounds, pointing out that "[t]he first [distich] is an expression of the highest respect, the second of sorrow and revulsion" (1929: 17). They do not belong together:

> If [the scholar] pays a little attention, his puzzlement begins to give
> birth to suspicions about the song, that it is not a genuine folk song,

because the way in which the two distichs are combined, aside from not existing in the folk variants, is not the least bit poetic, not to say logical (*loyikos*). (1929: 17)

Note the appeal to authenticity ("it is not a genuine folk song") validated by philological method ("existing in the folk variants" recorded by earlier scholars and observers), as well as to "logic." As for the criteria of "poetic" quality, Apostolakis probably felt sure of his grounds; later in the book, he appeals quite explicitly to the innatist thesis that any Greek could expect to understand *inside himself* the truth or falsity of a song text by virtue of inherited and natural instinct. His view is thus remarkably similar to that of Zambelios, who seems to have felt that as both a native and an intellectual he had a double claim, innate on the first grounds and disciplined on the second, to the only true knowledge of Greek folk culture. This ideological shadowing of his philological foes appears also in Apostolakis's canny adoption of their methods. At the end, with a flourish of citations, he produces an archival source to show that Zambelios derived the two distichs from separate sources, each of them respectably "folk" on its own grounds; he thus conscripts the earlier textual material in the service of an argument that proves ultimately to be no less philological than its target.

It may well be that, in his own terms, Apostolakis was quite right: the two distichs may never have been sung together. But such probabilistic conclusions hardly justify sweeping charges of intent to falsify. Apostolakis appealed to his own sense of folk style in conjunction with standard philological methods in order to challenge Zambelios's textual emendations. Zambelios, on the other hand, had also justified his emendations on innatist grounds. The differences between their respective positions lay in the audiences they sought to convince rather than in the methods that they employed. Zambelios's assumptions rested on an *external* (i.e., Western-derived) conception of the national culture, an equation of Classical learning with the revival of an innate spirit. Apostolakis's innatism, by contrast, appealed to a powerfully anti-intellectual streak within Greece itself, where it was especially strong among those who felt that they had been dispossessed by the educated elite. Ironically, Zambelios had castigated the learned clerics of *past* eras—specifically, the Byzantine—for their foreign-inspired, small-minded suppression of the Hellenes' native wisdom: he, too, thought oral tradition was the repository of the enduring Greek spirit. But for Apostolakis, as for the demoticists generally, it was the learned of the present rather than the past who were especially guilty of encrusting this true nature of the Greeks:

> The combination [of the two distichs] is thus unnecessary, so let
> the two songs be read as the people speaks them. (1929: 18)

But note: let the two songs be *read* in this way. The dead hand of literacy is
never far away.

Apostolakis then proceeds systematically on his skeptical way through
a long list of songs from Zambelios's collection that he considers to be false in
some way. In the next example, he charges Zambelios with having attributed
to a speaking bird a "trivial" order to the hero to confess:

> The motif would have its reason (*loghos*) if, instead of the bird's
> calling on Lambros to make his confession, we heard Lambros
> himself telling of his sins and giving instructions to the bird.
> (1929: 19)

Perhaps so; but it is clear that here Apostolakis's opinion of what is fitting
belongs to an antiacademic aesthetic that is as rigid as his corresponding brand
of antipurist purism in regard to language. It is not insignificant in this context
that "reason" and "discourse" correspond to the same term (*loghos*) in Greek,
or that this is in turn cognate (in both Greek and English) with the "logic"
which Apostolakis would like to invest with "necessity." The arguments, ostensibly "natural," actually appeal to that culturally determined common sense
that requires reification as its only defense against the corrosive realization of
contingency: folk positivism.

This is a view of the cultural universe as governed by rules, by the deter-
minism of the canon. Revealingly, Apostolakis praises the demotic language of
his third example (1929: 20–22) as having "not a single slip-up." It is also
interesting, however, that Apostolakis here nonetheless wants to distinguish
himself from the turn-of-the-century demoticists who, having (as he remarks
rather acidly) just discovered the joys of folk song, "fainted as soon as they
heard" certain lexemes that could be accounted uncompromisingly demotic:
manula (*mana* 'mother', + dimin. ending, in place of the Classically-derived
mitera); *pedhi mu* 'my lad', a common colloquialism; *ksenitia*, the condition
of being abroad gloomily celebrated in many a dirgelike song; *filakhto* 'amulet', a demotic form associated with folk practice. Apostolakis has a sterner
cast. Yes, he says, these early demoticists—his ideological antecedents—
were quite right to praise such language, but their enthusiasm blinded them to
fatal semantic inconsistencies. What are these inconsistencies, and why did
Apostolakis consider them to be so significant?

Here is the text, followed by a summary of Apostolakis's objections to it.

s' afino ya, manula mu, s' afino ya, patera,
ekhete ya, adherfakia mu ke sis ksadherfopules.
tha figho, tha ksenitefto, tha pao makria sta ksena.
tha figho, mana, ke tha 'rto ke mi polilipiese.
apo ta ksena, opu vretho, minimata su stelno
me ti dhrosia tis aniksis, tin pakhni tu khimona
ke me t' asteria t' uranu, ta rodha tu maiu.
tha na su stelno malama, tha na su stelno asimi
tha na su stelno pramata, pu dhen ta siloyese.
—pedhi mu, paene sto kalo, ki oli i ayii konda su
na mi se piani vaskama ke to kako to mati.
thimisu me, pedhaki mu, k' eme ke ta pedhia mu
mi se planesi i ksenitia, ke mas alismonisis.
—kalia, manula mu ghlikia, kalia na skaso prota,
para na mi sas thimitho sta erima ta ksena.
dhodheka khroni aperasan ke dhekapende mines,
karavia dhen ton idhane, naftes dhen tone kserun.
proto fili, anastenakse, dheftero ton planai.
trito fili, farmakero, ti mana alismonai.

I am leaving you, little mother mine, I'm leaving you, father,
Be in good health, little siblings and girl cousins.
I'll leave, I'll go abroad, far away to foreign parts.
I'll leave, mother, and I'll come [back], so don't be full of sorrow.
From foreign parts, wherever I am, I'll send you messáges
With the dew of spring, the hoarfrost of winter,
And with the stars of Heaven, the roses of May.
I'll send you gold, I'll send you silver,
I'll send you goods that you can't imagine.
— 'My child, fare thee well, and may all the Saints be at your side,
And may you have your mother's wish as your amulet
So that the evil eye may not take you, the wicked eye.
Remember me, my little child, me, and my children,
Let the foreign life not lead you astray so you forget us.'
— 'Better, little mother mine, better rather that I should burst,
Than that I should not remember you while I'm in the desert-like
    parts out there abroad.'
Twelve years went by and fifteen months,
No ships caught sight of him, sailors do not know him.
With the first kiss he sighed; the second leads him astray;
[with] The third kiss, the poisoned one, he forgets his mother.

Apostolakis objects to this song on several grounds. First, despite the enthusiastically received linguistic demoticisms already mentioned, there are other elements that seem either morphologically (*tu maiu*) or idiomatically (*mi polilipiese; karavia dhen ton idhane, naftes dhen tone kserun*) inappropriate. One could of course retort that purisms such as *tu maiu* do occur in respectably demotic usage, since *katharevousa* and demotic Greek do not exist in isolation from each other; indeed, even self-conscious and committed demoticists often use elements of the purist register contextually in order to establish a tone of authority, irony, or distance. Apostolakis, however, is, as it were, a purist in his demoticism. For him, this mingling of registers is not only unlikely but aesthetically displeasing. Nor is he alone: to this very day, ideological demoticism opposes folksong language to learned diction on an aesthetic, rather than a use-oriented and semantic, basis of comparison (e.g., Dizikirikis 1983). As for the phrase *mi polilipiese*, something very like it does occur in a well-attested Cretan folksong in which a son bids his mother not to allow her guests to grieve for his death (*na mi variokardhisoun*) (e.g., Romanias 1965: 79). Now it is beside the point (and anyway unprovable) that Apostolakis probably just got it wrong: the point is simply that his argument, which derives its authority from the canon whose style it adopts but whose logic it ostensibly attacks, would have seemed irrefutable—and was the only kind of argument that *could* in all probability have seemed irrefutable in an age when Classical philology was both politically and intellectually the ultimate touchstone of cultural truth.

The task of restoring the text lies, Apostolakis implies, in bringing back voices that are *not heard*:

> Whoever has an ear slightly trained in folk poetry cannot avoid noticing the *abnormal* language of the song. There are *unusual* words and phrases in there . . . while others are *not even demotic* . . . (1929: 21; my emphases)

This is the rhetoric of a rigid canonicity, one that rejects the possibility that folk singers might have introduced formalisms in full awareness of what they were doing and why they were doing it. Note, too, that Apostolakis reintroduces the role of the academic expert through the back door ("Whoever has an ear slightly trained in folk poetry cannot avoid noticing . . . "). Such professionalism sits better with his use of philological criteria than with his avowed, populist ideology.

His preemptive reading of the collective folk mind allows Apostolakis to save his choicest objections, not for linguistic clues, but for what he calls "the psychic content of the song" (1929: 22). He complains, to begin with, that the young man's words of farewell to his mother are more appropriate to a "green romantic youth taking leave of his heart's true love." Again, it is hard not to be seduced, not so much by the logic of this suggestion, as by the degree to which it offers a measure of distance from nationalistic rhetoric. And he may well be right. But—again—that is not really the point. What should instead attract our critical attention is the implicit claim, not significantly different in this regard from Zambelios's, to an instinctive understanding of what fits and what does not.

In the same vein, Apostolakis also complains that such a message would more appropriately be carried by something moving—a bird, for example— than by the sender himself:

> Their movement, their journey, are enough to hold the imagination
> to its endless flights, which it makes afire with the pain of separa-
> tion and the longing to return. (1929: 22)

Paradoxically, in support of this judgment, he cites a text from the *other* collection he will attack later in his own book, that of N. G. Politis! While it is true that he also praises Politis as the person with whom "the correct examination and study of folk song begins" (1929: 134), Politis's scholarship is a curious source of support for Apostolakis's particular concern to go back to some spiritual ancestry that transcends mere philologism. It seems that his use of Politis here, as well as his convoluted attempts to coopt Politis's intentions (if not his achievements) into the demoticist search for "life," represent strategies of self-legitimation in the face of the established academic elite's indubitable power. In order to attack Politis, he needed first to invoke him.

In his analysis of the Zambelios text just discussed, Apostolakis also objects to the mother's reply: Why does she not also mention her husband, the boy's father? "Such an omission," he grumbles, "is strange, if not *unnatural*. And we ourselves have heard on our own with how much respect and how much tender love a woman regarded her husband in the Greek house (*sto elliniko to spiti*)" (1929: 22–23; my emphasis). This thoroughly romantic statement hardly fits the commonly held perception of the house interior as the quintessentially Romeic place where quarreling and sin are sheltered from external view by its Hellenic façade (Iakovidis 1975; see also Herzfeld 1987: 118). It is, in fact, a view of the family that owes more to West European romantic models than to Greek social experience. Here, too, we notice an extraordinary reversal: the *house* (interior) has become *Hellenic*; the façade, so to speak, has taken over the intimacies of the interior. Thus the demoticist argument appeals to purist values and even key symbols for validation in a more dramatic way even than the citation of Politis that I have just mentioned. This prefigures such extraordinary but similar expropriations as the tendency that appeared in the aftermath of the 1981 Socialist parliamentary victory to conflate socialism with Hellenism—a startling implosion of the traditional opposition between Hellenic/European "individualism" and "Slavic communism" (see Herzfeld 1982: 57).

Finally, and most comprehensively of all, Apostolakis adds a critique of song structure, or what he calls "technique." This is a classic device of philological folklore and permits an especially normative critique of texts. The song in question, says Apostolakis, breaks "laws" of textual composition—a curious appeal to formal criteria, unless it be on the analogy (as it must) of "natural laws," in the hands of a committed demoticist, although it is one that was to have subsequent imitators. One of these is Kostas Romaios, who although a writer of the demotic language adheres closely to the neo-Classicist orthodoxy of unbroken continuity between ancient and modern Greek culture; he devised the simplistic "rule of three" (1963). This is a predictive model dealing with precisely the $"a{:}b{::}(a{+}b){:}c"$ structure that we see in the final line of the text under discussion ("With the first kiss . . . "). On the face of it, then, Apostolakis appealed to a surprisingly formalist view of folksong texts.

Ultimately, however, this critical attack on technique turns out to be another appeal to innatist criteria. Having accepted that repetition is common in folk texts, Apostolakis objects to its appearance here:

> With repetition, feeling has evaporated. The phrase, *ke sis ksadher-fopules*, next to the beginning of the song, *s'afino ya, manula mu*, ends up sounding watery and colorless. Nevertheless, the repetition enters in the interests of better expression, and a correct [*sic!*] folk song would achieve it; this, however, is the secret of its art. There, repetition does not say the same thing over and over, but brings it closer and closer in, so that in the end it reveals it; with the first word the phrase projects the meaning in a vague and general way, in the second it intensifies its color, and in the third it shines like lightning from brilliance and light. (1929: 23)

These are curious words from a self-professed critic of romantic self-delusion. (Perhaps the romanticism of his analysis of family life ought to have prepared us for something like this.) Note, too, how the final sentence of the passage reproduces the folk song technique itself—the "rule of three" again, with the intensified "doubling" of the third item. Apostolakis may have identified with what he regarded as the language of the folk poets in ways of which he was not

himself fully aware. Yet his adoption of a stylistic device from the folk repertoire, whether unconscious or not, does not necessarily support his claims to
an insider's understanding. It simply suggests that, for reasons of his own, he
found the folk rhetoric appealing, and was able to use it for his own manifestly
intellectual and scholastic ends.

Apostolakis is not always consistent in his mode of reasoning. He goes
on to argue as follows:

> And the meaning reaches its perfect expression, not through logic,
> but through its aesthetic expression, which then and only then suc-
> ceeds in folk song, when its symbols, the words, enclose within
> themselves as much as they can of the sensual world (color, sound,
> movement), or, if they are abstract, when its logical meaning is
> not first heard but becomes lost in a crowd of recognizable features
> of the experienced world. In this way, all the emphasis falls on
> the final word; the preceding ones continually prepare it, without,
> however, fading away and being forgotten. (1929: 22–23)

A reversal has occurred: logic has now become inappropriate to the task at
hand. The same criterion that guided instinct to a safe judgment of textual
accuracy does not serve *within* the text; the locus of "inside" has now shifted
from the culture as a whole (in which discourse *is* logic, both being *loghos*) to
the specific text (to which the rule-governed and logic-bound techniques of
philology are external).

Apostolakis's criticisms of Zambelios continue at great length and in the
same vein, and end abruptly (1929: 133). His discourse seems clearly designed
to deploy a deeply philological argument against philology, a covertly Hellenist
argument against neo-Classicism, and a puristic subversion of linguistic and
aesthetic purism. It seems probable, on the face of it, that many of Apostolakis's criticisms are justified at the level of saying that Zambelios emended
texts in a way that corresponded to no known folk recension. In this sense, too,
Apostolakis reverses Lévi-Strauss's (1955) argument that exegeses of texts
should be treated as variants of the underlying textual structure in their own
right: he says, instead, that only those variants that originated with the folk and
have resisted scholarly contamination are worthy of serious study. In the process, he also implicitly excludes his own analysis from critical scrutiny: on the
one hand he claims immunity by virtue of a privileged insiderhood, while, on
the other, the very idea of including his own renderings of the folk texts as
variants rather than as restored *originals* is, from his vantage point, preposter-

ous. In his work, the expropriation of folk discourse by ideological demoticism has led to a recasting of the permissible.

A Cautionary Tale

Here, then, is the rub. In recontextualizing the discourses that scholarly tactics have so frequently deracinated, we are confronted with a persistent strain of folk positivism. Indeed, we should probably expect no less from writers who claim, without irony, to derive their understanding from their membership in the folk consciousness. Apostolakis insisted that the folk never put a verbal (and especially a metrical) foot wrong. His call to reject logic, rules, and formal or learned devices is seductive indeed. But we have seen in the brief survey just attempted that, in practice, the argument depends on at least a covert deployment of highly objectivist rhetorical strategies. In the same manner, my own exposition follows—and how could it be otherwise?—a more or less standard philological tactic, that of textual exegesis. In linking the Apostolakis text to the "rule of three" in folk songs, especially, I am willy-nilly perpetuating an agenda that Zambelios and Politis began. The trick is to remain aware of this ironic predicament. The alternative is a humorless and repressive binarism. The call for theoretical sophistication in the study of "national" traditions (e.g., Lambropoulos 1988, 1989), while certainly of inestimable importance in resisting the totalizing effects of nationalist or ethnocentric modes of analysis, does not necessarily escape the latter. As Margaret Alexiou (1989: 43) has so cogently said, also in the modern Greek context, "to try to pre-determine future canons by strategies of exclusion or rejection is tantamount to the worst kind of totalitarianism." Canon may replace canon, new forms of innatism the older appeals to "nature."

The folklorists who were engaged in defining modern Greek culture faced political consequences of some magnitude in their work. On it depended, not only the internal self-recognition of an entire people, but the tenor of its political and cultural relations with Western Europe and eventually with the rest of the world. In this task, the demoticists—whose nativist "nationism" has been ably analyzed by Tziovas (1985, 1986)—fought with the tools they had been trained to use. These tools included assumptions about their participatory rights to exegetical insight into folk tradition, a bemusing echo of the anthropological oxymoron of "participant observation" (see Herzfeld 1987: 16–17, 73). Demoticists shared a commitment to innatism with the very intellectual traditions they thought they were resisting. This innatism included a strongly proprietary interest in language.

It also included a rejection of neo-Classical formalism that nonetheless rests on what, at first sight, must seem a surprising adherence to normativity. But this is what has been at issue in the present discussion: for, given a common discourse, rules will not just go away. The very existence of a dispute over some common entity, here a reified national essence, presupposes the acceptance by all parties of at least the semblance of a set of rules (see Appadurai 1981). As recent practice-based approaches in anthropology have emphasized, the bathwater of orthodox structuralism contains the very lively baby of the *disposition to create structure*. Here, I return to my original point: that the expropriation of discourse may expropriate the expropriator. To argue with a system presupposes that one thinks one knows the code and can use it. The deformations perpetrated by Zambelios resurface in the equally arbitrary reformulations of Apostolakis, and in part reflect the realization by both of an underlying tendency of folksong texts to reveal common structures both semantically and metrically. Apostolakis's view of compositional strategies must incorporate some concept of rule, since—given the nature of his argument—he has to establish what the "correct" form of a demotic verse could be.

Could any writer on the subject do otherwise? Recognition of rule-like properties in texts constitutes the historical consistency of a discourse *about* texts. This is the real strength of Lévi-Strauss's recognition that analyses of texts reproduce the texts' common structure in new variants (an argument that itself arguably derives from the *Urtext* model of nationalistic folklore analysis!). Claims to originality in an argument about texts must always be suspect, because any discourse that engenders and sustains those claims originates in some sense in the texts themselves. I could not have presented the argument of this paper without, in the true "spirit" of "folk positivism," adopting strategies of objectification. I have, however, tried to do so in a manner that keeps reader and author aware of what is happening. Intentionally hegemonic traditions, nationalistic and intellectual, do the opposite.

REFERENCES

Alexiou, Margaret
    1989   Commentary. *Journal of Modern Greek Studies* 7: 41–43.

Anderson, Benedict
    1983   *Imagined Communities: Reflections on the Origin and Spread of Nationalism.*
            London: Verso.

Apostolakis, Yanis
    1929   *Ta dhimotika traghoudhia, meros A': I silloyes.* [*Folk Songs, Part I: The Collections.*] Athens: Kondomaris.

Appadurai, Arjun
   1981   The past as a scarce resource. *Man* (n.s.) 16: 201–19.

Bourdieu, Pierre
   1977   *Outline of a Theory of Practice*, R. Nice (trans.). Cambridge: Cambridge University Press.

Cowan, Jane K.
   1990   *Dance and the Body Politic in Northern Greece*. Princeton: Princeton University Press.

Dizikirikis, Yorgos
   1983   *I esthitiki tis Romiosinis: To dhomotiko traghoudhi kato apo to fos tis palis ton sinkhronon idheon*. [*The Aesthetics of Greekness (Romiossini): Folk Song in the Light of the Struggle of Contemporary Ideas*.] Athens: Filippoti.

Femia, Joseph V.
   1981   *Gramsci's Political Thought: Hegemony, Consciousness and the Revolutonary Process*. Oxford: Clarendon.

Handler, Richard
   1988   *Nationalism and the Politics of Culture in Quebec*. Madison: University of Wisconsin Press.

Herzfeld, Michael
   1982   *Ours Once More: Folklore, Ideology, and the Making of Modern Greece*. Austin: University of Texas Press.
   1987   *Anthropology through the Looking-Glass: Critical Ethnography in the Margins of Europe*. Cambridge: Cambridge University Press.
   1992   *The Social Production of Indifference: Exploring the Symbolic Roots of Western Bureaucracy*. Oxford: Berg.

Houtondji, Paulin J.
   1983   *African Philosophy: Myth and Reality*, H. Evans (trans.). London: Hutchinson University Library for Africa.

Iakovidis, Khristos
   1975   [Introduction]. *Neoklassika spitia tis Athinas ke tou Pirea*. [*Neo-Classical Houses of Athens and Piraeus*.] Athens: Dhodhoni.

Jusdanis, Gregory
   1988   East is East—West is West: It's a matter of Greek literary history. *Journal of Modern Greek Studies* 5: 4–14.

Kapferer, Bruce
   1988   *Legends of People, Myths of State*. Washington, DC: Smithsonian Institution Press.

Lambropoulos, Vassilis
   1988   *Literature as National Institution: Studies in the Politics of Modern Greek Criticism*. Princeton: Princeton University Press.
   1989   Modern Greek studies at the crossroads: The paradigm shift from empiricism to skepticism. *Journal of Modern Greek Studies* 7: 1–39.

Lévi-Strauss, Claude
1955   The structural study of myth. *Journal of American Folklore* 68: 428–44.

Meraklis, Mikhalis G.
1984   *Elliniki laoghrafia: kinoniki singrotisi*. [*Greek Folklore: Social Organization*.] Athens: Odhisseas.

Mouzelis, Nicos
1978   *Modern Greece: Facets of Underdevelopment*. London: Macmillan.

Mudimbe, V.Y.
1988   *The Invention of Africa: Gnosis, Philosophy, and the Order of Knowledge*. Bloomington: Indiana University Press.

Politis, Nikolaos G.
1901   *Ellines i Romii?* [*Hellenes or Romii?*] Athens.
1914   *Ekloye apo ta traghoudhia tou Ellinikou laou*. [*Selections from the Songs of the Greek People*.] Athens: Estia.

Romaios, Kostas
1963   *O nomos ton trion*. [*The Rule of Three*.] Athens.

Romanias, Alekos
1965   *I Levendoyenna: Ithoghrafika Kritis*. [*The Lineage of Brave Young Men: Folk Portraits of Crete*.] Athens: Dhifros.

Tziovas, Dimitris
1985   The organic discourse of nationistic demoticism: A tropological approach. In *The Text and Its Margins: Post-Structuralist Approaches to Twentieth-Century Greek Literature*, M. Alexiou and V. Lambropoulos (eds.), 252–77. New York: Pella.
1986   *The Nationism of the Demoticists and Its Impact on their Literary Theory (1880–1930): An Analysis Based on Their Literary Criticism and Essays*. Amsterdam: A. M. Hakkert.

Zambelios, Spyridon
1852   *Dhimodhi Asmata Elladhos*. [*Folk Songs of Greece*.] Corfu: Ermis.

Institutional Reanimations of Texts

11 Transformations of the Word in the Production of Mexican Festival Drama

Richard Bauman

INTRODUCTION

The linked processes of decontextualizing and recontextualizing discourse—of extracting ready-made discourse from one context and fitting it to another—are ubiquitous in social life, essential mechanisms of social and cultural continuity. Clearly, however, these processes operate in different ways and with different degrees of salience across the various sectors of social life and the modes of discourse by which they are constituted. One measure of this variance, and a useful key to the nature and significance of the decontextualization and recontextualization of discourse in social life, is the mode of communication we call *performance*. The performance forms of a society tend to be among the most markedly entextualized, memorable, and repeatable forms of discourse in its communicative economy. Likewise, performance forms tend to

Earlier versions of this chapter were presented at the Conference on Transformations of the Word held at Vassar College, May 29–June 2, 1987, organized by Robert DeMaria, Rachel Kitzinger, and Jeffrey Opland, and at Haverford College and Princeton University. For helpful comments on those earlier drafts I would like to thank Roger D. Abrahams, James Boon, Charles Briggs, John McDowell, Américo Paredes, and Richard Schechner. William Hanks's invitation to participate in his Workshop in Linguistic Practice at the University of Chicago gave me the opportunity to develop some of my ideas beyond the initial formulation; I benefited greatly from the Workshop discussion, especially the comments of Hanks and Norman McQuown. Special thanks to Pamela Ritch, *compañera de trabajo*, for her great insight into *colloqio* performance and her partnership in the field, Beverly Stoeltje for illuminating discussions about festival clowning, Ramón Godínez de Estrada for invaluable assistance in the field, Sterling Dickinson for keeping us informed about where the *coloqios* are, and Pedro Muñoz and Refugio Ramírez for their great patience, knowledge, and devotion to the *coloquio*. Thank too to Léonice Santamaría, Luis Davila, and especially Américo Paraedes for help with transcription and translation. The field research on which this paper is based was funded by the University of Texas, Indiana University, and the National Endowment for the Humanities; work on the final draft was carried out during my tenure as a Guggenheim Fellow and as a Fellow at the Center for Advanced Study in the Behavioral Sciences, with the support of funds from the Andrew W. Mellon Foundation. I am grateful to all these sources of support.

be among the most consciously traditionalized in a community's communicative repertoire, which is to say that they are understood and constructed as part of an extended succession of recontextualizations (Bauman and Briggs 1990). In one influential conception of performance, performance means "never for the first time" (Schechner 1985: 36), which locates its essence in the decontextualization and recontextualization of discourse, with special emphasis on the latter.

When performance is conceived in these terms, one of the key issues on which understanding of the process must rest is the dynamic tension between the ready-made, socially given element, that is, the persistent cultural entity that is available for recontextualization in performance, and the emergent element, the transformation of this entity in the performance process. This is a classic problem in the study of traditional symbolic forms, variously framed in terms of tradition versus creativity, folkloric variation, tradition and the individual artist, and the like. However it may be formulated, the problem raises a myriad of issues—as all classic problems must—including the ontology and epistemology of the socially given element, the function(s) of the performed form, the production process by which performance is accomplished, and structures of authority within the performance community. Of these, I want to foreground the issue of authority for special attention in this essay, though I will perforce deal with the others as well in varying degrees. More specifically, I will explore in a specific case study of festival drama in a Mexican community how orientations toward the authoritativeness of a socially given text—in this case, a play script—exercise a formative effect on the reanimation of that text in the production of performance. The organized production process by which festival drama is carried from script to performance constitutes a relatively circumscribed and accessible field of discursive practice in which a controlled investigation of recontextualizing transformations of the word may be carried out. This investigation traces the phase structure of the reanimation process, stage by stage, beginning with the text of the play script and proceeding through the copying of the actors' parts, the actors' learning of their lines, a series of ordinary rehearsals, the *ensayo real* (grand, or true, rehearsal), and the culminating performance. Close examination of each successive phase is the necessary basis for determining the overall dynamics of the reanimation process and the contrastive orientations to the text by which the process is shaped.

THE *COLOQUIO* IN TIERRA BLANCA

Central among the ritual events in festivals celebrated in the municipality of Allende, Guanajuato, are nightlong performances of the traditional Nativity play, or *coloquio, Tesoro Escondido* (*Hidden Treasure*), a folk drama that dates back to the sixteenth century in Mexico and has roots even earlier in medieval Spanish drama. The *coloquio* has been assumed by most literary scholars to have disappeared from active performance in Mexico at least a generation ago, but in fact the *coloquio* performance tradition is alive and reasonably well in parts of the state of Guanajuato. With Pamela Ritch, I am engaged in the ethnographic study of *coloquio* production in several rural communities, with special attention to Tierra Blanca de Abajo, a relatively isolated *ejido* community that lies northwest of San Miguel de Allende.

Tesoro Escondido is a traditional shepherds' play (called *pastorela* in other regions of Greater Mexico),[1] which centers on the journey of a group of shepherds to Bethlehem to adore the Christ child and the efforts of Luzbel (Lucifer), eventually vanquished by San Miguel, to keep them from doing so. The *coloquios* are widely associated with the Christmas season, but in the region around San Miguel de Allende at least, they have been detached from Christmas and are performed as the climactic event of community festivals, the greatest number of which occur in this region in mid-May in honor of San Isidro Labrador, the patron saint of the peasant villagers, or in early June in honor of the Santa Cruz.

Tierra Blanca's fiesta is also in honor of San Isidro, but is celebrated not on May 15th, but on January 15th, with the *coloquio* performance beginning on the night of the 15th and running through the morning of January 16. When asked why they honor San Isidro on this date, the people of Tierra Blanca give two answers: (1) they have a kind of sister-city relationship with another nearby community which holds its fiesta on May 15 and having theirs on a different date allows the members of both communities to enjoy each others' celebrations; and (2) January 15 is an advantageous date because the crops are all in, there is relatively less work to do, migrant workers from the community are home from their travels, and money for the fiesta is relatively more available than in mid-May.

1. The *pastorela* in Greater Mexico has been the focus of extensive research, dating back to the early investigations of Bourke (1893) in the Rio Grande Valley at the end of the nineteenth century. The most important works on the *pastorela* in the Republic of Mexico are Barker (1953), Litvak (1973), Mendoza and Mendoza (1952), Rael (1965), and Robe (1954). On the *pastorela/coloquio* in Guanajuato, see Castillo Robles and Alonso Tejeda (1977), Chamorro (1980), Litvak (1973), and Michel (1932). Few scholars have concerned themselves centrally with *pastorela* performance; Flores (1989, 1994) and Castillo Robles and Alonso Tejeda (1977) are the principal exceptions. The history of *pastorela* scholarship is reviewed in Cantú (1982) and Stowell (1970), the latter focused on work in the American Southwest. For a further account of the production and performance of the *coloquio* in Tierra Blanca, see Bauman and Ritch (1994).

Motivation of involvement in the production and performance of the *coloquio* varies among the participants. For many, it is primarily a devotional act, a means of paying honor to the patron saint of the community and securing his blessing in the form of sufficient rain for the crops, good health, and so on. Some individuals take part as an act of thanksgiving to San Isidro for a particular blessing, such as recovery from an illness, or the recovery of a lost animal; this may be framed as the fulfillment of a *promesa* to the saint, a promise to participate in the *coloquio* if he will bestow a particular favor. Another motivating factor, especially for those who organize the production, is the social prestige that accrues from taking responsibility for an observance that benefits the community. Within certain families, participation in the *coloquio* takes on the guise of a family tradition, a continuing responsibility that contributes to the definition of its members' place within the community. And finally, there is the attraction and joy of performance itself, the opportunity to take part in something that is beautiful, that heightens and enhances experience.

Coloquio performances in Tierra Blanca are lengthy and elaborate productions, twelve to fourteen hours in duration, involving forty-three actors, six hired musicians, and a corps of other functionaries (curtain pullers, special effects people, etc.). The play is produced each year by a shifting group of men, *los encargados* (persons in charge), who take on the task voluntarily as a communal and devotional responsibility. One man serves as the *primer encargado* (first *encargado*) and is primarily in charge of organizing the production. In addition to the six official *encargados*, there is an additional individual who directs the rehearsals and serves as prompter during the rehearsals and the performance.

The production process begins in early November, around All Saints' Day, proceeds through the selection of actors, the distribution and learning of the parts (*papeles*), a series of five to seven rehearsals (*ensayos*) ending with the *ensayo real* (grand, or true, rehearsal), and culminating in the performance on January 15. This process establishes a complex field of textual production and reproduction in which the text of the *coloquio* undergoes a series of transformations, and it is this transformational field that I will examine here as a process of reanimation. I take the text of the *coloquio* as the initial focus and point of departure because there is a sense in the community that there *is* a text—objectified, durable, and authoritative—represented by the *coloquio* script, called *el libro* (the book). Still, notwithstanding this framing of the text, there are different orientations on the part of participants toward the authoritativeness of the script which give shape to different modes of participation in the production process, and the tension between them has a powerful formative influence on the production and performance of the *coloquio*. These contrasting orientations will provide the central framework for this paper, identified, once again, by close examination of each successive stage in the reanimation process by which the script is brought to performance.

The first orientation accepts the text of the script as the authoritative reference point for the play. Participants and community members alike maintain when asked that the words are to be memorized, learned *"de pura memoria"* (completely by memory), exactly as they are in the script. As observed by the *primer encargado*, "Everything runs by exact phrases" (*"Todo corre por pura frase"*). The most strongly contrastive orientation shapes the participation of only a single character, the Hermitaño (Hermit), an aged holy man who accompanies the shepherds on their pilgrimage. His transformations of the text represent a markedly antiauthoritative counterstatement. Between the two lies a middle position of relatively limited scope, which manifests itself as an occasional playful breakthrough from the straight rendition of the text.

POR PURA FRASE
THE SCRIPT

In its first form, each speech is part of the script, which represents an authoritative textual frame of reference for the *coloquio*, the essential primary resource for the production of the play. Each community that wishes to produce a *coloquio* must have a script; Tierra Blanca has three, each a different version of the play. Of these, one is privately owned, and the other two are kept in the church when not in use. The scripts are prized, protected, and maintained with considerable respect.

The script from which the current version of *Tesoro Escondido* is produced in Tierra Blanca was purchased from a neighboring community around 1982. Some of its earlier history may be guessed at, but is not of concern to the people of Tierra Blanca or to our discussion. Prior to the purchase of the *libro*, Tierra Blanca had not done a *coloquio* for three years, but the stimulus of a new script revived the performances.

The script consists of seventy-four pages plus a title page, 8.5" × 14" in size, held together in a binder. In addition to the spoken or sung lines, the script gives the name of the character to whom each speech is assigned plus stage directions, such as "The Virgin appears and is seated," "Susana and Arminda dance and sing," or "The curtain is lowered."

The *coloquio* is composed in verse, and runs to more than 8,200 lines, arranged in double columns. The verse for the spoken dialogue of the *coloquio* is built on the classic octosyllabic line, for the most part with assonant endings on the even-numbered lines. There is some variation on this pattern: *versos pareados* (rhymed couplets), *redondillas* (quatrains rhymed *abba*), and *décimas* (a ten-line verse form with a variety of assonance patterns, most commonly *abbaaccddc*). Various forms of vowel elision and hiatus are employed to regularize the octosyllabic structure of the lines, though the poetic convention allows for seven- or nine-syllable lines, depending upon the position of the final stressed syllable.

Like other *coloquio* scripts documented in the literature, this one displays a range of irregularities and imperfections when measured by the standards of cultivated literary texts: deviations from the octosyllabic standard, spelling errors (including the omission of accent marks), grammatical errors, alterations of word boundaries (mostly involving prepositions or apparent prepositions, for example, line 8: *de dico* for *dedico, al canzar* for *alcanzar*), and garbled passages.

A significant feature of the text, and one which ramifies throughout the production process, is that its language is considered by the people of Tierra Blanca to be somewhat alien; they hear it as archaic, elevated, occasionally obscure. The *primer encargado* told us that "it is Otomi, the language of the old Mexico before the Spanish came." Identifying this elevated theatrical Spanish as an Indian language is an index of its strangeness. The script is far from incomprehensible, but some words, phrases, and passages are difficult to understand.

These problematic aspects of the text are recognized by the participants, most fully by the *encargado* and the prompter, who have the most extensive engagement with the full script. They speak of words being cut off (*palabras mochas*) or missing, of parts of the script not being well written, of the language being difficult, and so on. These flaws and difficulties in turn license a measure of practical flexibility in dealing with the script. Garbled lines may be fixed, actors may be forgiven for lapses in memory or delivery. I will deal with these matters in more detail below. The point I wish to make here is that the standard of strict fidelity to the scripted text is an ideal one, a construction that is able to sustain a certain degree of relaxation in practice without undermining or compromising the framing of the script as authoritative. There is no felt contradiction on the part of participants between insisting at one moment that the parts should be memorized exactly as written and allowing in the next moment that the script has some flaws that call for repair.

One final point about the script. In one way of thinking and speaking, the script *is* the play: the term *coloquio* can refer either to the script or the performance.

THE SIDES

From the script, the first transformation that the text undergoes toward performance occurs in the writing out of the parts (*papeles*) for the actors who have been recruited for the play. The cast members receive their parts in written form, copied out speech by speech by the *primer encargado*, sometimes with the help of the prompter. This is a formidable task, considering the length of the script, the limited education of the *encargado*, and the infrequency with which he employs the skill of writing for other purposes. Nevertheless, it needs to be done anew for each production because the copies never seem to survive the performance; they are roughly used (stuffed in pockets, studied while out herding cattle, etc.) and are not very substantial to begin with. One consequence of this worth noting is that changes introduced by the process of copying out the parts tend not to be cumulative though they may leave some residue in memory that carries over from year to year.

The copied parts take the form of a small booklet, for which we employ the theatrical term *sides*, sewn together out of separate leaves of paper by hand. Each page is approximately 5″ × 8.5″ of cheap, lined paper. Each set of sides consists of the speeches (*relaciones*) or entrances (*entradas*) of one character only, with each speech numbered consecutively. In effect, then, the copying out of the sides disassembles the play into sets consisting of the speeches of individual characters. The *encargado* produces them all, but the individual actors receive only their own. The individual sides, of course, are contextualized in the minds of the participants by their knowledge of the *libro*—they are metonyms of the script—and by memories of past viewings, past participation in the *coloquio* in this or another role, and indexical elements in the text that point to adjacent dialogue or other characters (as responses to earlier talk, for example, as in "All right, *Lindor*, don't get excited"). But the sides themselves decouple the words of each character from all others, so that each speech stands in relation to the preceding and subsequent ones of that character alone. Nevertheless, there is a time-line incorporated into the sides, each set of which bears a synecdochic, elliptical relation to the temporal structure of the *coloquio* plot. When the sides are actually distributed to the actors who will play the respective parts, bringing together a part and a player, the part becomes a role.

In addition to this transformation of the play into its constituent roles and each role into its constituent speeches, the sides introduce other changes, though these are relatively inconsequential for the actual speaking of the lines.

Like the script, the sides represent the writing of a person not fully practiced in the literate standards of written Spanish and exact textual fidelity. Accordingly, the script undergoes a range of scribal transformations in the process of copying out the parts. For example, while the script renders the text in octosyllabic lines, the sides are written with two lines of script compressed onto each line of the side, margin to margin, yielding sixteen-syllable lines, though the line breaks of the script are marked in the sides by a period in mid-line. Other alterations include spelling changes from the script to the sides, some of which represent corrections of spelling errors in the script, some of which introduce new misspellings. In the same manner, the sides correct certain flawed word boundaries in the script, but also improperly divide monomorphemic words into two (e.g., *donde* into *don de*). These spelling and word boundary alterations yield phonetically equivalent pronunciations when spoken aloud and thus do not affect performance. In addition, we may observe occasional grammatical changes from the script to the sides, such as "*Hermanos a donde me aprecian*" 'Brothers, wherever you esteem me' for "*Hermano a donde me aprecian*" 'Brother, wherever you [pl.] esteem me', the plural form *Hermanos* agreeing with the plural verb form *aprecian* and with the multiple addressees of the speech. Finally, the sides may introduce certain lexical substitutions, such as "*en esta nueva vida*" 'in this new life' for "*en esta nueva venida*" 'in this new coming [of Christ]'.

These are all relatively minor alterations, but they do have a formative effect on the performance because it is the sides, not the script, that are accessible to the actors. When the parts are learned, they are learned from the sides; the actors do not consult the script. We will track the further effect of these transformations in our examination of the rehearsals and the performance itself. For the moment, however, we may note that the standard of scribal fidelity that obtains in the rendering of the sides from the script, notwithstanding the insistence on the authoritativeness of the latter, allows for a variety of alterations from the original. Some of these are inadvertent or habitual, while others suggest conscious intervention aimed at producing better lines. This impulse must be partial, though, because the copyist is willing to allow some unintelligible lines to stand in the sides.

LEARNING THE PART

When the sides are distributed to the actors by the *encargado* during the month of November, the process of transforming the written word into the delivered word begins. Actors employ a variety of methods in learning their lines. Some individuals study the sides alone as time is available, in the evening, on Sunday, while out watching the livestock. The lines are read aloud, short speeches in their entirety, longer ones in sections (usually two lines at a time, which constitute an intonational and rhyming unit), until they can be recited from memory. Family members or friends may also be pressed into service at various points in the process, feeding lines to the actors from the sides to aid in the learning process and testing them in their recitations. In addition to these individual or cooperative efforts, the *encargado* offers his assistance to those actors who desire his help and otherwise assists in much the same manner as family members and friends.

It is at this learning point in the production process that certain characteristic features of *coloquio* performance style come into play. In particular, there is a highly conventionalized style of delivery that marks *coloquio* performance, keyed to the poetic structure of the text. The basic unit, as noted, is the end-stopped octosyllabic line. Each line characteristically receives three or four regular stresses, depending upon the syllabic and accentual structure of the given line, though the three-stress lines are marked by a breath pause at the end to allow for an empty beat which normalizes a four-stress pattern. Some actors maintain a regular line-by-line intonational pattern characterized by a slightly rising inflection on the final stressed syllable, usually the penultimate syllable in the line, followed by a return to the normal tone on the final unstressed syllable. Others group the lines into longer four-line units, with a rising intonation at the end of the second line and a falling intonation at the end of the fourth. While this delivery style is in part conditioned by the formal features of the line and verse structure in which the play is composed, there are additional factors that play a role as well, factors that do not reside in the written forms of the text.

First, virtually all the actors have seen other *coloquio* performances before they set foot on the stage. From earliest infancy, when mothers bring their babies to *coloquios*, through childhood, when boys and girls excitedly crowd the front margin of the stage, through adolescence and adulthood, members of the community attend the *coloquio* year after year; it is the culmination of an already heightened festival experience. Accordingly, every actor—even the youngest Virtue—has internalized the recitational style of delivery. This extends as well to those nonactors who are enlisted in the learning process, some of whom have taken part in earlier productions. Thus the recitational style is learned in effect before the lines, as part of the conventions by which a *coloquio* is done, and is brought into play from the very beginning of the process of learning a part.

There is, then, in learning the part, an interplay between the written text of the sides, community conventions, and personal experience as frames of reference. The play is still parceled out as a series of separate parts in the form of the sides, and within the sides into a sequence of speeches attached to a single character, but each actor's encounter with the sides is contextualized by exposure to and experience with the performance tradition.

REHEARSALS

Shortly after distributing the sides, usually at some point around mid-November, the *encargado* calls the first of a series of weekly rehearsals, or *ensayos*. Rehearsals are held on Saturday nights, beginning at around 9:00 P.M., and last through the night until 9:00 or 10:00 on Sunday morning. Summoned by the ringing of the church bell, participants gather in the church courtyard together with a group of local musicians (a special band from outside the community is hired for the performance itself) and approximately twenty to twenty-five onlookers, relatives and friends of some of the performers and devotees of the *coloquio*. From the very first, rehearsals are actually full run-throughs of the *coloquio* from beginning to end. Nothing is done more than once, even if it is done poorly; there is no repetition of parts or scenes until they are mastered. If an actor is late or absent, the rehearsal process proceeds without him (I use the masculine pronoun because the female participants were always present, in our observation), either skipping the missing part or with the prompter filling in the lines.

The rehearsals represent a significant transformation in the development of the *coloquio* toward performance, a phase in which the words of the script and sides are more richly contextualized and formally elaborated than heretofore. This is, most importantly, the first stage in which something approaching a full *coloquio* is enacted, though we cannot yet say it is performed. Performance rests on an assumption of accountability to an audience for an artistic display, subject to evaluation—performance counts (Bauman 1977). Rehearsals, however, represent a different framing of enactment; they are doings that explicitly do not count, even when, as here, they are done before an audience (Goffman 1974: 60–61).

If we look again at the text in terms of the transformations to which it is subjected in the rehearsals, we may observe that some of the changes have to do with dimensions of contextualization, while others are of a more formal internal nature. To begin with, in the transition from the learning of the parts to the rehearsal, the words of the play are transformed from the speeches of individual actors to cohesive dramatic dialogue, contextualized by the framing of the scenes in which they occur, the interactional structure of the dramatic action, and the adjacent speeches of other characters. One mechanism by which this cohesion is effected, for example, is formal parallelism between speeches. Another is the employment of terms of address, particles of assent and dissent, and so on, which tie speeches together interactionally.

A further transformation of the word introduced in the rehearsals centers on the presence of the prompter. The prompter is the functional center of the rehearsals, prominently and visibly placed and clearly in control of the event. He is the custodian of the script throughout the rehearsals and the performance. His role in the rehearsals includes summoning the actors for their entrances (recall that the sides contain no cue lines), cueing their recitations by reading the first line of a speech, and feeding the lines when memory fails (the actors do not refer to their sides in rehearsals). Anticipating for a moment the role of the prompter in the performance, where prompting is outside the performance frame in ways that will be noted below, it is especially significant as a dimension of the differential framing of the rehearsals and the performance that in the former the prompting is *in* the frame.

In actual practice, many of the actors do not have their scripted lines perfectly memorized, but if they proceed fluently through some semblance of their speeches, they are not interrupted or corrected by the prompter, even if they misspeak or skip a line or lines, as long as they conclude with the last one. If, however, an actor falters or stops in mid-speech, the prompter feeds him or her the next line. Even here, the actor may not repeat the offered line exactly, but if the prompt leads to a resumption of fluent recitation, that is sufficient. If not, a further prompt is offered at the next breakdown, and so on through to the end of the speech. In extreme cases, though this is not uncommon, especially for certain male actors who never bother to learn their parts, the prompter feeds an actor the whole speech line by line, setting up a kind of echoic doubling of the dialogue. It is especially noteworthy in this connection that notwithstanding the standard of full memorization, the prompter and *encargado* never take the actors to task for not knowing their lines. They may remark on it to each other, or they may observe to an actor that he has skipped a portion of his speech, but the run-through marches on.

There are, I should mention, certain breakdowns in the delivery of lines that are ultimately beyond the prompter's intervention. In one rehearsal we observed, for example, one of the actors was so drunk that he took off on a wild improvisation that was impervious to the prompter's attempts to feed the correct lines. The prompter simply sat back until the actor ran out of steam and then picked up with the entrance of the next actor.

As noted earlier, the rehearsals of the *coloquio* are framed in multiple ways that make them different from performance. One significant means of marking these enactments as not counting fully is the undercurrent of play that runs through the event. For the most part, this manifests itself in a stream of joking and horseplay that bubbles up on the margins of rehearsal activity but does not penetrate or tamper with the *coloquio* text. Occasionally, however, a bit of joking by-play does invade the text. In one rehearsal we observed, for instance, I myself became a joking resource. One scene in the play has the comic Indian offering to trade a dog to the shepherds, and at the point where he says, "Now let's make a trade," he turned to me—hanging around the edge of the rehearsal space with my tape recorder—and interjected, "my dog for your radio," paused for a moment, and then took up his scripted lines where he left off.

One dimension of transformation remains to be noted as coming into play at the rehearsal stage. Although numerous songs are interspersed within the more extensive spoken dialogue of the play, neither the script nor the sides include musical notation. At the rehearsals, however, the musicians enter the production process to accompany the songs and dances. Certain lines of the text are now transformed into song, regimented not only by the script but by the traditional, unwritten tunes of the *coloquio*.

ENSAYO REAL

Transitional between the regular rehearsals and the performance is the *ensayo real* (true, or grand, rehearsal), the last rehearsal before the performance. The *ensayo real* is definitely framed as a rehearsal, as a doing of the play that does not count as a performance but rather as practice. Nevertheless, this special rehearsal is keyed somewhat differently from the ordinary rehearsals in certain respects. For one thing, it is held on the outdoor stage newly erected each year for the *coloquio*, though without the curtains or backdrops used in the performance. In addition, several of the actors wear pieces of their costumes and use some of their props on this occasion, sufficient to mark it as out of the ordinary. Still further, the *ensayo real* draws more spectators (as many as 80–85), far short of the full audience that attends the performance but significantly greater than the small group of onlookers at earlier rehearsals. In all other respects, the *ensayo real* is conducted in the same manner as the earlier rehearsals. It does, however, evince at least one further dimension of textual transformation worthy of comment.

At the *ensayo real*, the cast is more nearly complete than at previous rehearsals, with at most only one or two members of the forty-three-person cast missing. Thus, the run-through is also more nearly complete, with essentially all the lines being delivered, by contrast with earlier rehearsals when the parts of absent actors are skipped.

Let us summarize the salient formal, functional, and contextual transformations that the text of the *coloquio* undergoes in rehearsal. We may note, first of all, that the prompter feeds lines to faltering actors from the original script. This means, in effect, that certain changes introduced in the copying out of the sides, namely, those that occur in prompted lines, are neutralized as the actors repeat the lines read to them from the script by the prompter. More significantly, there is clear room for textual slippage in the rehearsal process. When it comes to the actual declamation of their lines in rehearsal—and, to look ahead again, in performance—the actors have a degree of license with regard to the accuracy of their recitations. Notwithstanding the ideal standard of textual accuracy, what is truly required at a minimum is a relatively close approximation of the lines, fluently delivered. This applies, of course, only to the actors who are present and able to deliver their lines at all. The skipping of those parts assigned to actors who do not show up for rehearsal abbreviates the text significantly and the irremediable garbling of his part by our drunken actor wrenches it utterly out of shape, at least for the moment, though it can be brought back to an acceptable standard the following week when he is sober. While the skipping of parts diminishes the text, the echoic doubling of the dialogue represented by the pairing of prompted line and delivered line augments it, becoming at many points in the process a salient feature of *coloquio* presentation as the prompter's voice is audible not only to the actors but to the spectators as well. Joking interpolations, like those of the Indian, augment the text as well, using it in combination with situational circumstances to produce small, playful breakthroughs of recontextualization. And finally, the transformation of scripted words into song and the contextualization of each speech by adjacent dialogue add further semiotic density to the actualization of the text as reanimated in rehearsal. Thus the scripted text of the play is moved substantially closer to the culmination of the production process in performance.

PERFORMANCE

We arrive then at the performance itself. This climactic event takes place on the night of January 15 through the morning of the 16th as the culmination of Tierra Blanca's festival in honor of San Isidro. In formal terms, the performance of the text we have traced through the production process exhibits no further transformations of a kind we have not seen before.

The most powerful transformation attendant upon the performance lies in the invocation of the performance frame itself. This is the sole enactment of the play that counts publicly, the point at which the participants in the *coloquio* assume full responsibility to the audience for their display, now finally transformed into performance. The keyings of the performance frame (Bauman 1977) are multiple: the fiesta setting, the audience of 400–500 people, the fully dressed stage with curtains and backdrops, the electric lights strung for the occasion, the procession of the actors in full costume, and the removal of the prompter to backstage, out of the central frame of the action. This is the end point of the production process, an authoritative public performance of an authoritative text in the hope of bringing pleasure to the audience and doing honor to the patron saint of the community.

PARODIC COUNTERSTATEMENT

The process of textual reanimation that we have traced thus far through the production process represents the prevalent orientation toward the scripted text of the *coloquio* for the overwhelming majority of the cast. For all of them, the text is authoritative; the standard that guides their reanimation of the text from script to performance is textual fidelity, delivering the words as they are given in the script, *por pura frase*. As we have seen, there is some allowance for various kinds of deviation, but the ideal, professed standard, and orientation are clear and consistent.

There is, however, one notable exception to the pattern, namely, the Hermitaño who accompanies the shepherds on their pilgrimage, an aged holy man who is at the same time a blatantly burlesque character. A clear sign of the Hermitaño's special status within the play is that he is the only character who wears a mask throughout the performance, an indication of the ambiguity that surrounds his role. The comic qualities of the Hermitaño are manifested in a variety of ways, from his halting gait to his oversized rosary to his quavering voice, but his spoken words offer a special potential for burlesque that is centrally relevant to our analysis. For the Hermitaño in the production under examination, the verbal field represented by the production process is markedly different from that of the rest of the cast.

It is important to note that the actor playing the Hermitaño in this production is illiterate. He is a generation older than the rest of the cast and grew up in the period before compulsory primary education brought at least marginal literacy to the community. Accordingly, written sides are of less direct use to him. Moreover, he made no special effort to learn his part before rehearsals, unlike the rest of the cast. Thus, for this Hermitaño, the immediate process of reanimating the *coloquio* text toward this particular performance began with the rehearsals, though in a broader sense he had, like the other participants, a lifetime's experience of other performances to draw upon. In the rehearsals, and in the performance as well, he relied on the prompter to feed him his lines one by one from the script in the characteristic fashion. This gave him the opportunity, as we will see, to talk back to the script line by line.

As the rehearsals progressed, the Hermitaño learned some of his lines through practice. In his shorter speeches, when he did not require prompting, he tended to deliver the lines pretty nearly as they were given to him, in the manner of the other actors. In his longer speeches, however, he departed in a highly significant way from this standard practice, introducing a distinctive transformation of the text into his delivery. Let us examine his longest speech, in which his counterstatement reaches its fullest realization.

The speech in question, eighty-five lines in length, occurs in the ninth scene of the play and leads up to the point at which the Hermitaño meets the shepherds and joins them in their journey to Bethlehem. At the point of the speech, the Hermitaño is lost in a dangerous mountain wilderness and delivers a plea to God to lead him to safety, reaffirming his commitment to the devotional life he has chosen. As rendered in the text, the speech is earnest and heartfelt, a true expression of piety. As delivered by the Hermitaño, though, it is quite something else, a deeply and systematically parodic dialogue with the text, challenging and controverting its authority in a thoroughly carnivalesque way (cf. Flores 1989: 129–35). That is to say, there is a marked disjunction between the scripted role of the Hermitaño as a pious figure and the realization of the role as parodic burlesque. To anticipate a number of points developed in more detail below, the representation of the Hermitaño as a burlesque figure is a performance convention of the *coloquio* tradition. Accordingly, under the best of circumstances, the individual who is recruited to play the Hermitaño should be adept at the kind of parodic improvisation that the convention demands. In the production under analysis here, the actor who plays the Hermitaño is fully up to the demands of the convention, a man of quick wit, skilled at speech play, and a joker par excellence, who takes the scripted role and quite deliberately turns it upside down.

To comprehend what the Hermitaño is doing, it is important to bear in mind that he is fed his lines one by one by the prompter and that the prompted lines are audible to the onlookers at the rehearsals and to much of the audience at the performance, though subject to general constraints on audibility such as crowd noise. Having been fed a given line, the Hermitaño exercises one of two options. First, he may repeat it faithfully or with slight enough deviation to count as faithful, as with the other characters. The second alternative, and by far the most frequently chosen option, is to respond with a parodic transformation created by incorporating elements of the existing text in a manner that creates a conscious contrast arising from the juxtaposition of two unlike approaches (Gilman 1974: 3).

In the two rehearsals and the performance that serve as illustrative data for this analysis, only three lines are unaltered from the script across all three renditions, namely, the opening line and two others; all others are transformed at least once. Of those that are transformed, there is only one line that is parodied in the same way in two of the renditions (the *ensayo real* and the performance); no transformation is fully retained across all three. Clearly, the Hermitaño is improvising anew in each instance, though with some persistent elements as we shall see. Nevertheless, there are certain consistent patterns that characterize his parodic productions.

An effective vantage point on the Hermitaño's parodic counterstatement is offered by a consideration of his line-by-line dialogue with the text in terms of the twin concepts of cohesion and coherence. As employed here, cohesion has to do with the formal linguistic features that tie a discourse together. Coherence depends upon whether the interpretive effort yields comprehensible meanings. In these terms, then, cohesion is a formal relationship, coherence an interpretive, semantic one (cf. Enkvist 1978). The tension between the two endows the Hermitaño's speech with much of its comic efficacy.

The principal device employed by the Hermitaño in his transformation of the script is parallelism, constructing lines that retain certain features of the scripted (and prompted) lines while varying others. More specifically, his parallelistic rendering of the lines given him by the prompter rests on lexical and phonological ties. The following examples are illustrative of the most common patterns:

	Prompter	Hermitaño
1	y por otro lado un fuerte collado and on the other side a rough hill	y por aca está mi otro cuñado and over here is my other brother-in-law (rehearsal)
2	que sabe dar complacencia who knows how to give satisfaction	nos ha de dar a doña Crescencia he will surely give us doña Crescencia (*ensayo real*)
3	mi cuerpo ya sin aliento my body already out of breath	ya mi puerco no tiene aliento now my pig has no breath (rehearsal)
4	y aunque en selvas solitarias and although in solitary forests	aunque mis suegras son solitarias although my mothers-in-law are solitary (*ensayo real*) (note: *solitaria* here may also mean hermit or recluse)

5	así es que me conformo	yo me voy a conformar
	thus it is that I resign myself	I am going to resign myself
		(performance)

Looking first at lexical ties, we find words repeated in line-initial position (example 1), line-internal position (example 2), and line-final position (example 3); combinations of these may also be found (example 4). In some cases, the lexical ties consist of grammatical variants of the same word (example 5: *conformo/conformar*). The phonological parallelism likewise takes a number of forms: **assonance**, for example, /a/ in *aca esta* as tied to *lado* (example 1); **alliteration**, for example, /s/ in *suegras son solitarias* as tied to *selvas solitarias* (example 4); **rhyme**, for example, *Crescencia* as tied to *complacencia* (example 2); and **punning**, for example, *puerco* for *cuerpo* (example 3).

In addition to the lexical and phonological ties linking the Hermitaño's lines to those offered him by the prompter from the script, there are other formal correspondences as well. As a general tendency, the Hermitaño's lines are of relatively equal length to the scripted originals in terms of syllables, though there is frequent variance on both sides of the octosyllabic norm. Also, the intonation pattern that is characteristic of *coloquio* performance, as described above, marks both the prompter's offering and the Hermitaño's delivery.

Now all these formal ties between the Hermitaño's lines and the prompter's lines establish marked formal cohesion between the two (Sherzer 1978). Nevertheless, the Hermitaño's transformations at best require an interpretive struggle to make sense of, while at worst they make no apparent sense at all to members of the audience. There is ample cohesion but far less coherence.

Examination of the transcripts of the Hermitaño's speech reveals that in the great majority of cases the Hermitaño's lines represent a significant departure from the sense of the scripted lines fed to him by the prompter. Perhaps more importantly, they are semantically disjunctive with his own preceding lines, all the more so because his speech as delivered is a mix of lines from the text—those he repeats as prompted—and improvised transformations of the scripted lines of a very different style (more on this shortly). The puns, of course, are the most clearly subversive elements in his production, but the other devices of phonological parallelism (alliteration, assonance, rhyme) also exercise a paronomastic function that challenges coherence. As Roman Jakobson has argued persuasively, "Any conspicuous similarity in sound is evaluated in respect to similarity and/or dissimilarity in meaning" (1987: 87; cf. Redfern 1984: 99); as employed by the Hermitaño, the latter evaluation prevails, especially when the puns are compounded by additional disjunctive factors that he enlists in the service of his parodic counterstatement. Consider the following passage (rehearsal):

	Prompter	Hermitaño
1	Quién como Dios, solo Dios	Quién como Dios, solo Dios
	Who but God, only God	Who but God, only God
2	por su caridad infinita	y también con doña Josefinita
	by his infinite charity	and also with doña Josefinita
3	que al punto me facilita	también sí viene Susanita
	which readily makes it easy for me	also Susanita is certainly coming
4	salir de este bosque atroz.	y ya no tengo ni la hoz
	to get out of this atrocious forest	and now I don't even have the sickle
5	Aunque me falta la voz	ya me faltan las dos
	Although my voice fails me	now I lack both of them
6	siempre lo iré bendiciendo.	y ya me las van consiguiendo
	I will always be blessing that.	and now they are going to be procuring them for me
7	Parece que voy saliendo	ya me estoy imponiendo
	It appears that I am getting out	now I am getting used to it [2]
8	sin perder una pisada.	sin perder ni una pisada
	without losing a step.	without missing even a single fuck [3]

The lines that bracket the passage are rendered essentially as prompted, with one minor deviation in the last line (the addition of the negative particle, *ni*). Lexical ties between the Hermitaño's lines and the script appear only in line 5 (*me falta/me faltan*), but the passage is replete with phonological parallelism of the kinds discussed above, tying the Hermitaño's lines both to those of the script and to each other (2 to 3, 4 to 5, 6 to 7). Moreover, the Hermitaño's transformed lines make frequent use of other devices that commonly serve a cohesive function. One such device is conjunction. He uses *y, también*, and *y también* (and; also; and also) in lines 2, 3, 4, and 6, which also makes for lexical repetition. Another is ellipsis, the use of *las dos* (both) in line 5, apparently referring back to some nominal group with two members. Still another is pronominal deixis in lines 6 and 7. But whether the conjunctive forms are taken in relation to the prompted lines or the Hermitaño's own preceding lines, they do not seem to conjoin clearly related propositions, and the other anaphoric forms do not point to clear antecedents. Yet again, the initial suggestion of cohesion yields a measure of incoherence and what we are left with approaches disordered nonsense.

2. In Mexican popular usage, *imponerse* (to dominate, get control of) is synonymous with *acostumbrarse* (to get or become accustomed to). See Santamaría (1983).

3. In Mexican popular usage, *pisada* (step) is a vulgar term for sexual intercourse. See Santamaría (1983).

Notwithstanding the quotient of incoherence that I have just outlined, however, the Hermitaño's transformations of the *coloquio* text are not without a certain broader consistency that endows his production with a measure of subversive coherence. The basis of this dimension of coherence lies in the saturation of the Hermitaño's speech with inversive, carnivalesque images and themes that sustain a powerful symbolic dialogue with the scripted piety of the text. Parody itself, of course, is double-voiced and constitutes a core resource for carnivalesque counterstatement, and the terms of his parodic transformation of the text exploit the classic symbolic paradigms of festive folk humor as brilliantly explicated by Bakhtin (1968). Parodic sermons, akin in some respects to the Hermitaño's irreverent rendering of the pious speech that is scripted for him, have figured prominently for centuries in European festival and drama (Bakhtin 1968: 12–15, 84–86; Gilman 1974).

The most prominent of these carnivalesque elements employed by the Hermitaño is bawdy sex. The Hermitaño's delivery is replete with sexual symbolism (e.g., *hoz, pisada*) and references to his sexual liaisons—or ambitions—in irreverent opposition to normative expectations for an aged, supposedly celibate holy man whom the speech as scripted calls upon to be reaffirming his religious vocation. Many of his puns, rhymes, and other verbal harmonies turn on the names of women who are his implied or explicit sexual partners—Chencha, Crescencia, Rosalina, Susanita, Josefinita, Léonor, and others—and his lines are at their most coherent when they refer to sexual liaisons, as in the following example (performance):

	Prompter	*Hermitaño*
1	nuevo indicio y disciplina	por ahí también vive doña Carolina
	new evidence and discipline	around there also lives doña Carolina
2	por esta breñosa cuesta	también cuando me mira se acuesta
	by this craggy slope	also when she sees me she lies down
3	por un lado se presenta	porque si uno viene a convidarla
	presents itself on one side	because if someone comes to invite her
4	un risco muy elevado	que traiga su cobija lavada
	a very high cliff	let him bring his laundered blanket

These allusions are rendered all the more comically effective in that some of the names the Hermitaño employs are those of women in the community; Chencha, for example, is a nickname for Hortensia, the name of the girl who plays the shepherdess Gila in this production.

In addition to suggestions of sexual relations with named women, there are other forms of sexual innuendo in the Hermitaño's parodic transformation of his speech, such as a nicely inversive reference to "*todas las engañosas muchachas*" (all the deceitful girls; performance), who, it seems, have bested him at his own sexual game by leading him on and then scattering to the four winds, leaving him thwarted and unhappy. The most consistent secondary device employed by the Hermitaño to imply illicit sex is his frequent reference to in-laws, a form of sexual innuendo widely employed in Mexico and Latin America in general, as in the *albur*, a form of insulting badinage of which the Hermitaño's speech is suggestively reminiscent. First of all, it is inappropriate for a holy hermit to have parents- or children-in-law at all; to state that he has is to confess yet again that he has violated his vow of celibacy. More generally, though, to refer to someone as your mother-in-law or father-in-law is to imply that you have slept with her or his daughter; to refer to a man as your brother-in-law is to suggest that you have slept with his sister; and so on. The allusion to mothers-in-law in the plural (*suegras*, e.g., example 4, above) is especially blatant. Normally, a man has only one mother-in-law, and in Mexico, as in many other cultures, this relationship is stereotyped as problematic and is thus a source of humor in its own right. Reference to multiple mothers-in-law is a clear assertion that you have had multiple sexual partners.

Beyond the bawdy allusions and sexual innuendo, the Hermitaño employs a further range of carnivalesque resources (Bakhtin 1968):

1. Grotesque images:
   ya me quemo las jetas
   I almost burned my protruding lips (rehearsal)
2. Reference to bodily emissions:
   porque ya se me acabó la saliva
   because I am already out of saliva (performance)
3. Animalization:
   ya mi puerco no tiene ni aliento
   now my pig doesn't even have breath (*ensayo real*)
4. Beating: porque ya estoy bien batido
   because I am already well beaten (or defeated; performance)
   (note: *batido* may also have obscene connotations)
5. Incongruous rhetoric:
   en gran manera es todo de adobe
   for the most part everything is adobe
   (*ensayo real*)

This last is also a topical allusion: Tierra Blanca, the name of the community in which the play is performed, is a type of adobe plaster.

It is significant that this inventory of carnivalesque terms and images together with other effective puns tends to be retained more consistently across the three renditions we have recorded than any other elements of the Hermitaño's parodic transformations. The same names, the in-law references, the pig, the saliva, the beating, and so on all appear at corresponding points in more than one rendition, though the lines in which they are contained vary in their construction.

Thus, the Hermitaño's transformations of the word talk back to the authoritative text in a number of dimensions, challenging its authority by a complex set of interrelated subversive devices: paronomasia, parody, carnivalesque humor, and a significant coefficient of incoherence. All of these devices are powerfully reflexive, objectifying and foregrounding the pragmatics of the reanimation process, especially illuminating at this early stage of our explorations of this perspective on the discursive constitution of social life.

The first dimension of challenge we may identify is the speech style of the *coloquio* script, the *coloquio* register. As I have noted, the speech style of the *coloquio* has a certain alien, distanced quality to it, archaic, elevated, often magniloquent. As a ritual register, it claims sacred authority; the ritual integrity of the *coloquio* is seen to depend upon its use, and the stated ideology of the production is that it is not to be tampered with. Here, then, is the first target of the Hermitaño's subversion. Where the language of the *coloquio* is archaic, he renders it current; where it is elevated, he debases it; where it is magniloquent, he makes it coarse. The overall effect is the creation of a dramatic antilanguage (Halliday 1978: 164–182), a subversive counterregister.

In addition to subverting the authoritative language of the text, the Hermitaño's parodic transformations undermine the textuality of the script by rendering the discourse incoherent. Semantic coherence is only one foundation of textuality, but it is a powerful and primary one, considered the *sine qua non* of textuality by many commentators (e.g., Halliday and Hasan 1976). Coherence, of course, is an interpretive construction, and although the language of the *coloquio* is occasionally garbled and difficult to understand, the participants nevertheless attribute coherence to the script, the written text. At the same time, they recognize explicitly that the Hermitaño's transformations of the lines that are fed to him from the script introduce heavy semantic disjunction into the speech, transforming pious words into licentious discourse, line after line.

In refusing to submit to the style and textuality of his speech as scripted, in contesting their authority, the Hermitaño is at the broadest pragmatic level introducing a centrifugal, decentering counterforce to the centripetal force of the production process itself as a process of reanimating the *coloquio* text in performance. The contest is played out in plain hearing every time the Hermitaño renders the speech: the authoritative text maintains its presence in the voice of the prompter, and those lines that the Hermitaño does recite as prompted, and it echoes in the Hermitaño's parodic transformations, which are parasitic upon it. Moreover, the Hermitaño himself provides for the containment of his own challenge by uniformly rendering the lines at the boundaries of his speech either *por pura frase* or in a way semantically consistent with the scripted line. And in larger scope, after all, the Hermitaño's parody is surrounded and submerged—at least in quantitative terms—by recited speeches that submit to the authority of the scripted text. Nevertheless, a certain openness remains, revealed by the differential evaluations of the Hermitaño's transformations of the word offered by members of the community.

If the Hermitaño's parody is a metacommentary on the pragmatics of recentering, it is a metacommentary that can be interpreted in a number of ways. Some community members are critical, condemning the Hermitaño for willfully mangling the scripted lines, though it is conventional for him to do so. These people profess the fullest allegiance to the authority of the text and hold all members of the cast accountable for doing their best to adhere to this standard. They are the pious purists—what Bakhtin might call the grim ideologues—who would not have their religion compromised by the carnivalesque, traditional or not. Others are accepting. They attribute the Hermitaño's deviations from the script to his aging memory and illiteracy and the difficulties of the *coloquio* language. For them, the metamessage is that the reanimation process is difficult and the actors are fallible, some more than others. The Hermitaño misses more lines than anyone else and uses a different redressive strategy, covering his lapses by clowning, but breakdowns can happen to anyone. The rest of the community—the majority—goes beyond mere acceptance to approval. They consider both fidelity to the script and the Hermitaño's burlesque to be of value; both have expressive power, both enhance experience, both require a certain virtuosity. On balance, submission to the authority of the script is more effective in accomplishing the *coloquio*, but the Hermitaño's clowning is thoroughly enjoyable and enhances the play, all the more so as his burlesque, in various guises, is an unofficial and nearly universal *coloquio* convention in its own right. Those who would have him behave otherwise are themselves bucking tradition.

CONCLUSION

The close examination of the production process by which *Tesoro Escondido* is brought to performance reveals two strongly contrastive orientations toward the authoritativeness of the script that have a formative effect on the process itself and on the performance that is its goal. The majority of the participants, both actors and *encargados*, accept the authority of the written text and subscribe to a standard of textual fidelity, of rendering the scripted lines *por pura frase*. By its very nature, however, the production process demands a sequence of transformations of the word in the transition from written text to fully enacted performance as the lines are copied out, learned, rehearsed, and performed. These transformations involve intersemiotic translation from the written to the spoken (and sung) word, shifts in the contextualization of the constituent speeches, and differential framings of the enacted word from rehearsal to full performance. In the process, as we have seen, there is a certain degree of acceptable deviation from full textual fidelity and exact memorization, allowing for normalization of a linguistically difficult and sometimes garbled text. This margin of allowable deviation, however, is not seen as challenging or compromising the ideology of textual authority.

For the Hermitaño, by contrast, the process is guided by a very different orientation, a blatant challenge to the official standard. Because he is illiterate and has no use for the written sides from which the other actors learn their parts, the Hermitaño enters the production process at a later point, beginning with the rehearsals. But illiteracy alone does not preclude the memorization of lines; there is clear evidence in the literature on the *pastorela* of illiterate actors memorizing their parts by having them read out repeatedly by others (e.g., Bourke 1893: 190), and the Hermitaño in Tierra Blanca does in fact render some of his shorter speeches as scripted. The most marked transformations of the word in the Hermitaño's performance of his role stem rather from a different impulse, a carnivalesque subversion of the authoritative text, resting on parody, paronomasia, and the undermining of semantic coherence. The Hermitaño's participation represents a centrifugal counterforce within the reanimation process, not sufficient to break it down but certainly effective in maintaining an antiauthoritative dialogue with the voices of official order.

In recent years, there has been a growing sensitivity in anthropology and adjacent disciplines to such symbolic face-offs between order and disorder, in work on festival (e.g., Abrahams and Bauman 1978; Falassi 1987; Stoeltje 1989), symbolic inversion (Babcock 1978), the carnivalesque (Bakhtin 1968), and the like. Some of the best of this work has centered on discourse (e.g., Proschan 1981; Sherzer and Sherzer 1987; Stoeltje 1985), for which Bakhtin's rich and penetrating studies of Rabelais (1968), Dostoevsky (1984), and the emergence of novelistic discourse (1981: 41–83) have certainly provided a strong stimulus to the investigation of authoritative discourse and its dialogic counterstatements. My investigations of the production of *Tesoro Escondido* in Tierra Blanca draw centrally on these lines of scholarship, but I would maintain that the analysis of the dialogic tension between authoritative and antiauthoritative discourse in terms of the perspectives offered in this volume on the decontextualization and recontextualization of discourse (see also Bauman and Briggs 1990) enhances the study of this phenomenon in at least two other significant respects.

To begin with, past studies in the field have focused overwhelmingly on finished discourse, the textual products of full public performance, where I have concentrated my investigation on the discursive field represented by the production process, tracing the sequence of transformations of the word from the socially given text through the copying of the parts, learning of the lines, rehearsal, and performance. The end performance represents only one dimension of the engagement of *coloquio* participants with the authoritative text, whereas they are in fact differentially engaged with the text at each successive stage of the production process. Moreover, each stage of the reanimation process has a formative effect on those that follow, including of course the performance itself. If we are to comprehend the social life of discourse and the pragmatics of textuality in their fullest scope, investigation of the production process is essential (see Schechner 1985: 16–21).

In addition to extending the scope of analysis beyond end products to the full field of discursive production, I have also endeavored to fill what I perceive to be a second analytical gap in the literature by providing a degree of formal specificity missing from most studies of authoritative versus antiauthoritative discourse carried out in structural symbolic terms. To be sure, Bakhtin points to form-function interrelationships in his discussions of this dimension of dialogism (1981: 41–83), but he never goes on to show how they work in close formal terms. Once again, I submit that a full comprehension of discourse as socially constituted and social life as discursively constituted must rest on the elucidation of the interrelationships between form and function, an essential foundation of the perspective on the decontextualization and recontextualization of discourse developed here and throughout the volume. And performance, the functional efficacy of which rests so centrally on an intensification of formal reflexivity, memorability, and repeatability, offers an especially productive focus for investigations of this kind.

REFERENCES

Abrahams, Roger D., and Richard Bauman
1978   Ranges of festival behavior. In *The Reversible World: Symbolic Inversion in Art and Society*, B. Babcock (ed.), 193–208. Ithaca: Cornell University Press.

Babcock, Barbara (ed.)
1978   *The Reversible World: Symbolic Inversion in Art and Society*. Ithaca: Cornell University Press.

Bakhtin, Mikail M.
1968   *Rabelais and His World*, H. Iswolsky (trans.). Cambridge, Mass.: MIT Press.
1981   *The Dialogic Imagination: Four essays*, Michael Holquist (ed.), Michael Holquist and Caryl Emerson (trans.). Austin: University of Texas Press.
1984   *Problems of Dostoevsky's Poetics*. Caryl Emerson (ed. and trans.). Minneapolis: University of Minnesota Press.

Barker, George
1953   *The Shepherds' Play of the Prodigal Son*. Berkeley and Los Angeles: University of California Press.

Bauman, Richard
1977   *Verbal Art as Performance*. Prospect Heights, IL: Waveland Press.

Bauman, Richard, and Charles Briggs
1990   Poetics and performance as critical perspectives on language and social life. *Annual Review of Anthropology* 19: 59–88.

Bauman, Richard, and Pamela Ritch
1994   Informing performance: Producing the *coloquio* in Tierra Blanca. *Oral Tradition* 9(2): 255–80.

Bourke, John G.
1893   The miracle play of the Rio Grande. *Journal of American Folklore* 6: 89–95.

Cantú, Norma
1982   *The Offering and the Offerers*. Ph.D. dissertation in English, University of Nebraska.

Castillo Robles, Soledad, and Blanca Irma Alonso Tejeda
1977   El teatro folklórico en Cerritos, Guanajuato. *Boletín del Departamento de Investigación de las Tradiciónes Populares* 4: 41–46.

Chamorro, Maria del Carmen
1980   *"Los siete vicios": Una pastorela en Guanajuato*. Unpublished report, Dirección General de Culturas Populares, México.

Enkvist, Nils E.
1978   Coherence, pseudo-coherence, and non-coherence. In *Cohesion and Semantics*, J.-O. Ostman (ed.), 109–28. Åbo, Finland: Åbo Akademi Foundation.

Falassi, Alessandro
   1987   *Time Out of Time: Essays on the Festival.* Albuquerque: University of New Mexico Press.

Flores, Richard
   1989   *"Los Pastores": Performance, Poetics, and Politics in Folk Drama.* Ph.D. dissertation in Anthropology (Folklore), University of Texas at Austin.
   1994   "Los Pastores" and the gifting of performance. *American Ethnologist* 21(2): 270–85.

Gilman, Sander
   1974   *The Parodic Sermon in European Perspective.* Wiesbaden: Franz Steiner Verlag.

Goffman, Erving
   1974   *Frame Analysis.* New York: Harper & Row.

Halliday, M. A. K.
   1978   *Language as Social Semiotic.* London: Arnold.

Halliday, M. A. K., and Ruqaiya Hasan
   1978   *Cohesion in English.* London: Longman.

Jakobson, Roman
   1987   *Language in Literature.* Cambridge: Harvard Belknap.

Litvak, Lily
   1973   *El nacimiento del Niño Dios.* Austin: Center for Inter-cultural Studies in Folklore and Oral History.

Mendoza, Vicente, and Virginia R. R. de Mendoza
   1952   *Folklore de San Pedro Gorda, Zacatecas.* México, D.F.: Congreso Mexicano de Historia.

Michel, Concha
   1932   Pastorelas o coloquios. *Mexican Folkways* 7: 5–30.

Proschan, Frank
   1981   Puppet voices and interlocutors: Language in folk puppetry. *Journal of American Folklore* 94: 527–55.

Rael, Juan B.
   1965   *The Sources and Diffusion of the Mexican Shepherds' Plays.* Guadalajara: Librería La Joyita.

Redfern, Walter
   1984   *Puns.* Oxford: Basil Blackwell.

Robe, Stanley
   1954   *Los Pastores: Coloquios de Pastores from Jalisco, Mexico.* Berkeley and Los Angeles: University of California Press.

Santamaría, Francisco J.
   1983   *Diccionario de Mejicanismos.* 4th ed. Mexico, D.F.: Editorial Porrua.

Schechner, Richard
  1985   *Between Theater and Anthropology*. Philadelphia: University of Pennsylvania Press.

Sherzer, Dina, and Joel Sherzer (eds.)
  1987   *Humor and Comedy in Puppetry*. Bowling Green, OH: Bowling Green University Popular Press.

Sherzer, Joel
  1978   "Oh! That's a pun and I didn't mean it." *Semiotica* 22: 335–50.

Stoeltje, Beverly J.
  1985   The rodeo clown and the semiotics of metaphor. *Journal of Folklore Research* 22: 155–77.
  1989   Festival. In *International Encyclopedia of Communications*, vol. 2, E. Barnouw (ed.), 161–66. Oxford: Oxford University Press.

Stowell, Bonnie
  1970   Folk drama scholarship in the United States. *Folklore Annual of the University Folklore Association* (University of Texas) 2: 51–66.

Codafication [*sic*]

Greg Urban and Michael Silverstein

By way of conclusion, we wish to record here our own editorial sense of the ironic, some years after our actual project was undertaken and with much additional text under our belts. Observe that we have been engaging you in these natural histories of discourse through the medium of a curiously composite text artifact, of which we register the final alphanumerics.

So we wish to share with you some reflections from this particular (en)textual(ized) moment, and to issue an invitation. We do so in the hopeful spirit of that delicious trope suggested by Bauman's revelations about the manuscript appropriately enough entitled *Tesoro Escondido* 'Hidden Treasure'. We suggest that any such artifact as ours shares some of these same characteristics, for it is only one objectual mechanism semiotically inadequate to the dialectical work of textuality in which and by which culture lives— the work of entextualization/contextualization and reentextualization/recontextualization over micro- and macro-durational realtime. But just as the Hermitaño's spirited engagement with the (intendedly) faithful "performance of" the text finds/constructs poetic treasure far beyond any literal "reading" of the artifact seriously and straightfacedly rehearsed, we hope that your engagement with this artifact generates new en-/con-textualizations beyond our imagination.

As we said at the outset, this artifact has been formed through a process of disaggregation of a collective (en)text(ualization), as we each severally produced a piece of the emerging whole. Each paper produced was a given "take" on the themes we had been developing through a stimulated discussion of text artifacts on discourse and social action in the anthropological, sociological, and humanistic literatures. Each such disaggregated fraction regenerated, as it were, a whole text artifact of its own through the production of an empirical study, its oral presentation and discussion, and its artifactualization and further discussion. Each has undergone various editorial processes as an artifact, and the reassembly of the collectivity (with one or two exceptions) now represents an actual multiplicity of "voicings" of the common thematics of our original discussion. By themselves, some of the chapters are very transparently pieces of, icons of, (indexical) products of the collective discussion. Some take pre-existing personal, authorial themes and rework them with a shading that we, and perhaps you, can clearly recognize as proceeding from our discussion of en-/con-textualiztion. Some even pointedly attempt to encrypt the collective discussion through various prerogatives of authorial effacement, though of course they require of you a "reading" in precisely the terms of seemingly intended erasure of the collective text.

So our collective text, here capitalized (turned into chapters) and differ-entially authorized (recorded as the artifactual production of sociohistorical individuals), itself has a curious status as a moment in a complex and dialecti-cal process from-and-in which our relative roles, including yours, dear reader, are experienceable.

We intend, then, in this engagement with you, to capture the spirit of opening up at the same time as closing off, of supplementing by-and-in sum-marizing, of looking forward rather than backward, of giving an O.K. to dis-sensus as well as to consensus. No two authors in this book, we suppose, would read it in exactly the same way against their textual memory of our multiyear interaction. Yet we all—if we can speak for us—sense the generativity of the discourse encounter that produced it. We have all been, and some of us con-tinue to be, swept up in ideas that have emerged in the process of producing this artifact, however each entextualization of such ideas may differ.

Now "text" is, to be sure, a metadiscursive nominal (a denoting noun) that seeks to solidify what we have been arguing is fluid, to hold onto what slips ineluctibly away—like trying to stop time, to seize the past or present perfect and render it the present-future. The act of stopping (or at least of trying to stop) is a political act, and you can imagine that different readers will do it in different ways. In a culture whose ideology is the stable text, "out there" in the world, perhaps we have done our job if we have destabilized this notion further, in however small a manner.

At the same time, of course, what you have before you is a "text"—better yet, a "text artifact"—a physical thing seemingly recording fragments of our discourse. It is a fragment, moreover, that has been a long time in the making, like a palimpsest, erased and written over, erased and written over again and again, but with the traces of that history of composition showing through. (So where is the "composition," in the artifactual structure or in its history or, dialectically, in both?) The "moment" in writerly real time during which we are sedimenting this one text artifact, indeed, is distinct from the "moment" during which you are entextualizing it by your reading. Further, there is no single moment of sedimentation—as if sedimentation could occur in an instant. Instead, the originally sedimented text artifact is already long gone as such, superseded by a succession of such artifacts, each reflecting modifications, tinkering; some of that tinkering has been done by Michael Silverstein and Greg Urban, some suggested by the press reviewers and achieved by our coauthors, some introduced by copyeditors and compositors. You can only, at the time of your reading, imagine the threads that link the succession of artifacts preceding "this" one, "here," "now."

so there

We do not wish to belittle artifacts as opposed to texts. On the contrary, artifacts trigger entextualization processes and, as such, they make possible the circulation and transmission of culture in the first place. They are things in the world. Texts, so to speak, are "ideas in the mind" or aspects of interpreting minds in sociocultural contexts.

At the same time, we should not imagine that some specific "text" is simply contained in or carried along by the artifact. Indeed, our only evidence for the existence of texts is the production of subsequent artifacts. The text is not here on the page for you to see; it is a structured projection from what you see—dare we say like a cave-wall shadow? But unlike the Platonic cave, what casts the shadow here is not the "idea" but the "thing"—the artifact. Moreover, there may be different projections, different shadows, from the putatively same artifact.

No doubt you, O esteemed reader, have formed at least one such projection. And if you then speak or write about this book subsequently, that discourse and its attendant entextualizations will, of course, furnish evidence about this "text." Who knows but what a struggle may ensue over its correct reading, over its meaning! Yes, there is a text "here," but it is not something before you on the page. It is the one you will, in the best of all necessary worlds, tell us about subsequently.

Contributors

Richard Bauman is Director of the Research Center for Language and Semiotic Studies at Indiana University, where he is also Distinguished Professor of Anthropology and Folklore.

James Collins is Associate Professor of Anthropology and of Reading at the State University of New York at Albany.

Vincent Crapanzano is Distinguished Professor of Comparative Literature and of Anthropology at the City University of New York.

William F. Hanks is Professor of Anthropology and Linguistics at the University of Chicago.

John B. Haviland is Professor of Anthropology and Linguistics at Reed College.

Michael Herzfeld is Professor of Anthropology at Harvard University.

Judith T. Irvine is Professor of Anthropology at Brandeis University.

Hugh Mehan is Professor of Sociology and Education at the University of California, San Diego.

Elizabeth Mertz is Assistant Professor at the Northwestern University School of Law, and Research Fellow at the American Bar Foundation.

Michael Silverstein is Samuel N. Harper Professor of Anthropology, Linguistics, and Psychology at the University of Chicago.

Greg Urban is Professor of Anthropology at the University of Pennsylvania.

Index

Note: technical terms are identified parenthetically by content area, originator, or language of origin, where applicable.